STAIN
NEW ORLEANS

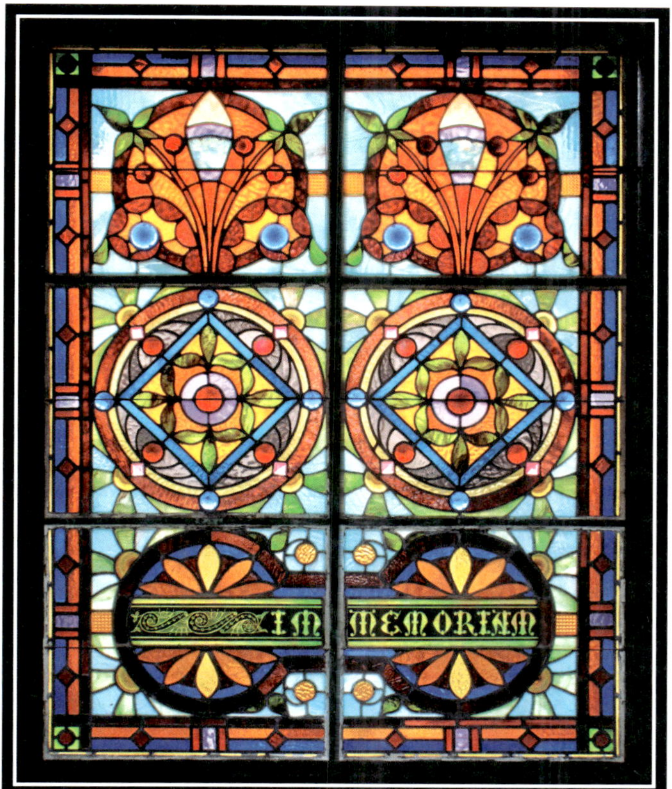

A FIELD GUIDE

Dale A. Carlson

Manufactured in the United States of America.

ISBN 978-1-7357935-2-8

Library of Congress Control Number: 2022900601

All photographs by Dale A. Carlson.

This book is dedicated to the memory of Carolin Venegas Jones.

ACKNOWLEDGEMENTS

I would like to thank the following people for their invaluable contributions to my two-year long mission to shoot every single pane of stained glass I could find in Metropolitan New Orleans, as well as those who assisted me in understanding more deeply the many complex histories of the subject matter presented in this book: Mat Grau, Jr., whose invitation to photograph the interior of the Chapel of the Holy Name of Jesus at Jesuit High School New Orleans inspired me to author this volume; Jeremy Reuther and Tom Bagwill, also of Jesuit High School New Orleans; Brian Morgan, organist at St. Stephen Catholic Church, New Orleans, who very kindly assisted me in gaining access to three church buildings; Samuel J. Corso of Dufour/Corso Studios, Baton Rouge; Milton Pounds of Pounds Stained Glass Studio, Covington; Patricia Andrews and Pame Tanner, whose research for many Preservation Resource Center sponsored stained glass tours over the years proved absolutely invaluable; Daniel J. Terrebonne of Christ Church Cathedral, New Orleans; Linda Harris of St. Augustine Catholic Church, New Orleans; Rev. Dr. Demetrese B. Phillips of Historic St. James A.M.E., New Orleans; Diane Stewart of St. Theresa of Avila Catholic Church, New Orleans; Harold Sears of St. Peter Claver Catholic Church, New Orleans; "Albinus", a parishioner at Trinity Episcopal Church, New Orleans; Dawn D. Dawson, Colleen Regan and Fr. Gill Enderle, all of the National Shrine of Blessed Francis Xavier Seelos, New Orleans; María A. Loyola of Blessed Francis Xavier Seelos Catholic Church, New Orleans; Rev. Duane Wiggin-Nettles and Dennis Whaley of Mt. Olivet Episcopal Church, New Orleans; Carol Thiele of Rayne United Methodist Church, New Orleans; Rebecca Lewis of Jackson Avenue Church, New Orleans; Michael Riemer of St. Paul Lutheran Church, New Orleans; Fr. Tom Stehlik of St. Joseph Catholic Church, New Orleans; Sam Mickal Solomon of Bancroft Property Investments, New Orleans; Rev. Dr. Charles J. Southall III of First Emanuel Baptist Church, New Orleans; Karri Maggio of Perez., New Orleans; Sierra Polisar and Tom Friel of the Newcomb Art Center of Tulane University; William R. "Billy" Pohlmann of Salem Church, New Orleans; Annahi Tapia and Adrien Genet of Touro Synagogue, New Orleans; Rev. Kelly Bedard and Julie Bedard of Trinity Lutheran Church, New Orleans; Pastor Daniel Lund III of Carrollton United Methodist Church, New Orleans; Hannah Jacuzzi of Southern Rep Theatre, New Orleans; Fr. Mark E. Thibodeaux of the Church of the Most Holy Name of Jesus at Loyola University, New Orleans; Jane Eustice, Fr. Michael Schneller and Teresa Miller of St. Francis of Assisi Catholic Church, New Orleans; Rev. Colleen Bookter of Algiers United Methodist Church, New Orleans; Rev. Phillip K. Brockett and Melissa Aguilar of Central St. Matthew United Church of Christ, New Orleans; Rev. John Dominic Sims of St. Anthony of Padua Catholic Church, New Orleans; PACE Catholic Charities of New Orleans; Sr. Donna Hyndman and Mary Lee Harris of the National Votive Shrine of Our Lady of Prompt Succor, New Orleans; Pastor Don Frampton and Bonnie Shoemaker of St. Charles Avenue Presbyterian Church, New Orleans; Fr. Jonathan P. Hemelt of Our Lady of the Rosary Catholic Church, New Orleans; Rev. Andrew Greenhaw of St. Paul's United Church of Christ, New Orleans; Msgr. John Cisewski of St. Katharine Drexel Catholic Church, New Orleans; Liz Yager of Temple Sinai, New Orleans; Pastor Lee Cormier of Canal Street Church, New Orleans; Fr. Eugene F. Jacques of the Church of the Holy Name of Mary, New Orleans; Rev. Anthony M. Bozeman of St. Raymond & St. Leo the Great Catholic Church, New Orleans; Fr. Oswald P. Pierre-Jules, Jr. of St. David Catholic Church, New Orleans; Luigi Mandile and Rev. William H. Terry of St. Anna's Episcopal Church, New Orleans; Rev. Michael M. Labre of St. James Major Catholic Church, New Orleans; Rev. Gregory T. Manning of Broadmoor Community Church, New Orleans; Rev. James Morrison of St. Andrew's Episcopal Church, New Orleans; Fr. Paul Desrosiers of St. Raphael the Archangel Catholic Church, New Orleans; Pastor Shawn Moses Anglim of First Grace United Methodist Church, New Orleans; Patsy Wilgus of Aurora United Methodist Church, New Orleans; Vickie Catsulis and Rev. Fr. George Wilson of Holy Trinity Greek Orthodox Cathedral, New Orleans; Tim Murphy of the Manresa House of Retreats, Convent; Susan Griffis of Christ Episcopal Church, Covington; Rev. Paul M. Bailey of Grace Memorial Episcopal Church, Hammond; Lea Smith of Holy Ghost Catholic Church, Hammond; Rev. Jeffrey L. Sims of Covington Presbyterian Church, Covington; Robert Fielding of Wharton's, Covington; John West of John West Glass Studio, Jarreau; Fr. Vincent Dufresne of St. Joseph Catholic Church, Paulina; Pastor Jeff Robinson of First Baptist Church, Hammond; Johnnie Alford, Mike Alford and Ruth Prats of St. Peter Catholic Church, Covington; Pastor Thomas Strong and Carol Wilken of Metairie Baptist Church, Metairie; Rev. Emile "Buddy" Noel, Phillip Anglin and Michelle Clements of Our Lady of Prompt Succor Catholic Church, Westwego; Marilyn Castle and Fr. Bac-Hai Viet Tran of St. Agnes Virgin and Martyr Catholic Church, Jefferson; Mary Johnson and Fr. Tim Hendrick of St. Catherine of Siena Catholic Church, Metairie; Adelaide Diaz and Fr. Fred Devall of St. Martin's Episcopal Church, Metairie; Jack H. Schulman of Congregation Gates of Prayer, Metairie; Fr. Andrew Rudmann of St. Clement of Rome Catholic Church, Metairie; Debi Petrolia of First United Methodist

Church, Hammond; Rev. S. Hunter Gray, Rev. Dylan Stinson and Rebecca Davis of New Covenant Evangelical Presbyterian Church, Mandeville; Lisa Dunk of Open Arms Ministries, Slidell; Diane Dalferes of Sacred Heart of Jesus Catholic Church, Lacombe; Lyn Gerhmann of Parkview Baptist Church, Metairie; Beth Bowles of Faith Presbyterian Church, Covington; Linda Biven and Fr. Walter Austin of Ascension of Our Lord Catholic Church, LaPlace; Dr. John Breaux of St. Genevieve Catholic Church, Bonfouca; Steve and Jane Maniscalco of Most Holy Trinity Catholic Church, Covington; Fr. Luke DeMeyer and Tim Moreau of Our Lady of Fatima Latin Mass Community, Lacombe; and finally, a huge thank you to whomever left wide open the back door of First Unitarian Universalist Church on S. Claiborne Ave on March 8th, 2020. I closed it and locked the place up after I was done.

Family and friends to whom I am endlessly indebted for their steadfast support and/or polite tolerance: my mother, Sherry McGinnis-Schmalenberg-Doerr, my father, A. Wayne Carlson, and my three brothers, Gregory, Jeffrey & Christopher Carlson; my step-parents, Stephen Doerr, Daniel Schmalenberg and Patricia Malinak-Carlson; Charlotte Haynes-Dively, Gabrial & Jennifer Szakal, Andy Johnston, Philip & Shakira Lieffers, Einar K. Kvaran, Jeffery Tong, Rob Kangas and the staff of the Oakland Community College Photography Department.

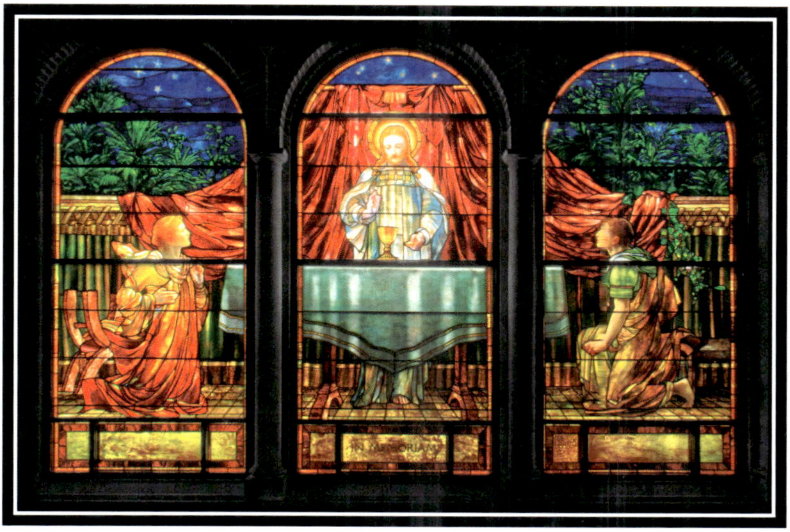

"Supper at Emmaus" by Tiffany Studios of New York City, installed at Woldenberg Art Center, Tulane University c.1995 (entry #84); originally installed at the chapel of Newcomb College, Garden District, c.1895.

FOREWORD

My late wife, Carolin Venegas Jones, introduced me to New Orleans over a four-day trip in October of 2009. It was love at first sight. When she was diagnosed with a terminal case of glioblastoma in 2014 we spent a few months in our home state of Michigan, doing what we had to do in terms of treatment, and then we moved to New Orleans, to squeeze all the joy we could out of the short time she had left. Oh, the new world we discovered in those five short months! My young love galvanized into true love by the time we left in May of 2015. In the years since her passing I have spent a minimum of one month out of every year in the Crescent City, often more, and somewhere along the line it got into my head that I wanted to somehow contribute to the preservation and continuation of the city's many dazzling cultural traditions.

I came to town for a multi-month trip again, in late December of 2019, determined to put this dream into motion, prepared to sell photography of New Orleans on the streets and at fairs and markets throughout the city. In between selling opportunities, I spent most of my time walking the neighborhoods, camera in hand, adding to my portfolio of New Orleans architecture and cityscapes. I took advantage of opportunities that presented themselves, and in early February of 2020 I enjoyed the great privilege of photographing the stained glass of the Chapel of the Holy Name of Jesus, also known as the Thomas J. Semmes Chapel, inside Jesuit High School of New Orleans. I was invited to do so by Jesuit High's recently retired, former Director of Alumni Affairs, Mat Grau, Jr., whom I had previously met while researching a prior book subject. It was while I was shooting this chapel that the idea of creating a guide to stained glass of the New Orleans metropolis first entered my mind, and soon it was my sole focus. Within a few short weeks, the advent of the Coronavirus pandemic would crush all future photography sales opportunities and keep me cooped up inside my 210 square foot Marigny apartment for over three months straight, doing little but shooting church windows by masked appointment and refining the photographic techniques showcased within this book.

Beyond satisfying my desire to contribute to the culture, the primary purpose of this book is to enumerate the many locations within the metropolis of New Orleans where one can see historically and aesthetically significant examples of stained glass artistry. Analyses of stained glass making techniques, flowery descriptions of the designs and subject matter depicted and biographies of prominent makers, while all worthy pursuits, are decidedly subordinate to my principal mission of exposing and celebrating through professional photography the superlative inventory of local stained glass available to anyone who cares to make the effort to see it. To this end, I have deliberately endeavored to minimize narrative and report only the most essential of historical facts regarding each commission.

While it is obvious how this book contributes to the preservation of New Orleans' singular stained glass legacy, how it continues the tradition is less so. To satisfy this goal in a modest way, and as an acknowledgement of the divinely inspired moment that led to this book's creation, I've made a commitment to the good people at Jesuit High School of New Orleans to donate 75 cents of every copy of this book that sells at the cover price to the maintenance and upkeep of live mass broadcast hardware used inside the Holy Name of Jesus Chapel. This commitment is made in perpetuity and I hope to be sending checks for years to come. I offer special thanks to Tom Bagwill, Mat Grau, Jr., Jeremy Reuther and the rest of Jesuit High School's staff for their willingness to be associated with my project and for their continuing endorsement of my publishing projects in which they've been included. I also gratefully acknowledge the influence of Rev. S. Hunter Gray of New Covenant Evangelical Presbyterian in Mandeville, whose gentle cajoling unknowingly led me to make this commitment to charitable giving.

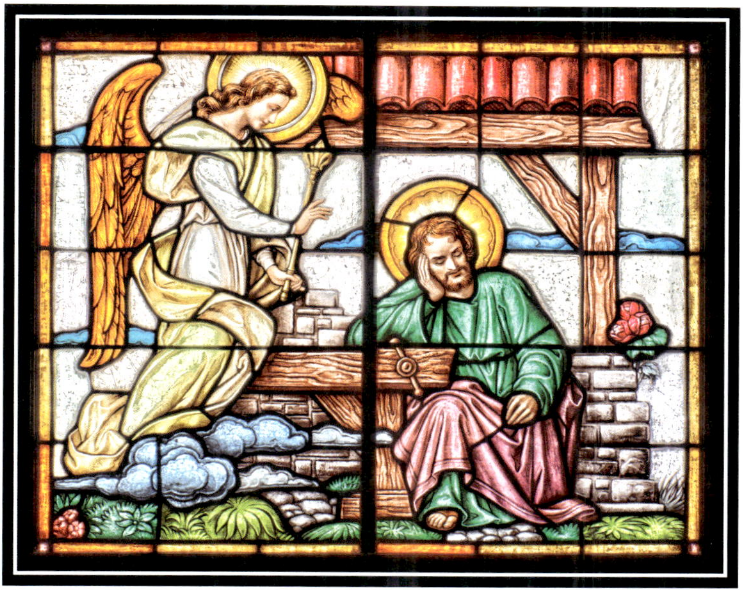

"Annunciation to Joseph" window at St. Joseph Catholic Church, New Orleans (entry #26). Maker and dates of installation undetermined.

RESEARCH

I have drawn upon a broad array of research resources in preparing this volume, the most informative being the New Orleans Public Library's archive of historic New Orleans newspapers, curated by NewsBank, Inc. and available to all online for the price of internet access and annual library membership dues. This massive collection spans the years of 1837 to 2017 and includes the vast majority of material published during that time under the banners of the Daily Picayune, the Times-Democrat, the Times-Picayune, the New Orleans Item, the New Orleans States, and the States-Item.

Second only to the NewsBank archive, and far more specific to my investigations, is the voluminous work of Patricia "Patty" Andrews and Pame Tanner, researching on behalf of New Orleans' Preservation Resource Center (PRC). From 1989 To 2019, as directors and developers of numerous PRC sponsored stained glass tours, Mrs. Andrews and Ms. Tanner authored an impressive library of local stained glass history that they were more than happy to share with me in its entirety. I thank them for enthusiastically and personally assisting me in developing a well-rounded understanding of the many complex histories of local stained glass installations.

Among the numerous books I have studied none became more essential to this project than the nine-volume series known simply as *New Orleans Architecture*, published almost exclusively by the Pelican Publishing Company of Gretna between 1971 and 2020, the ninth and most recent volume being the only exception. All nine contain facts that were reiterated in this book. Numerous site-specific tomes authored by local architectural historians Charles E. Nolan and Samuel Wilson, Jr. very helpfully presented what I consider to be the fullest accountings of the histories of St. Louis Cathedral, the Old Ursuline Convent, St. Alphonsus and Christ Church Cathedral. Henri A. Gandolfo's *Metairie Cemetery: An Historical Memoir* offered the deepest insights into the famed burial grounds of New Orleans' most affluent. Self-published church histories were also extremely helpful, most notably those of Mount Olivet Episcopal, Trinity Episcopal of New Orleans, St. Paul Lutheran in the Marigny, Jackson Avenue Evangelical in the Irish Channel, St. Joseph on Tulane Ave, St. Francis of Assisi in West Riverside, St. John the Baptist in Central City, St. Martin's Episcopal and Parkview Baptist, both in Metairie, and St. Peter Catholic in Covington. Various holdings of the vaunted Southeastern Architectural Archive (SEAA) at Tulane University further augmented my understandings of a long list of historic metro area structures that house significant stained glass installations.

Finally, in-person, telephone and email interviews with important contemporary glass makers Samuel J. Corso of Baton Rouge, Cynthia Courage of Metairie and Milton Pounds of Covington provided a litany of indispensable professional insights into the art, the culture and the community of stained glass making in New Orleans and outer Louisiana.

Full details of each source noted above, and many others, are included in the lengthy bibliography for any readers who care to examine the grittiest minutiae in my palette of research resources.

ATTRIBUTIONS

Ascertaining, separating and organizing into concise, easily digestible prose the many potential parties involved in the design, manufacture and installation of a single stained glass commission is a tedious task that frequently ends in dissatisfaction. The pertinent details are regularly, predictably lost to history or never recorded in the first place. In many cases a single individual or corporate entity executes all three tasks, but more frequently the tasks are divided between disparate parties. Sometimes one party completes two of the tasks and another executes one, installation most commonly being the odd man out. Sometimes only one party among the three is known while the others are not. Sometimes two are known while one is not. Sometimes not a single individual or corporation can be identified for any of the aforementioned tasks. It is very common for less than precise sources of historical data to erroneously report one contributing party as the executor of all three tasks. In some cases, the fabricator of a commission is reported upon the glass by corporate insignia while its designers go uncredited. Far too infrequently are both reported. Oftentimes secondary eras of installation at a given site comprise glass intended to mimic the appearance of the original, throwing yet another wrench into the works. Far too often, in New Orleans and elsewhere in the world, no maker's mark, corporate insignia or artist's signature of any kind can be located anywhere upon the many panes that make up a single commission.

So many conceivable combinations of these many varying circumstances were encountered in the course of my research. Sorting it all out is, well, excruciating. While every effort has been expended to report the pertinent facts in exacting fashion and to accurately discern and separate all involved parties, regrettably, too often, I cannot. I present herein as fact only that which I believe has been confirmed beyond reasonable doubt. For many of the remaining factual details of a given commissions, I frequently defer to the description of "undetermined", as it is likely, in my opinion, that the information exists out there, somewhere, but my best efforts to locate it have fallen short. Put simply, the complete story of many of the commissions enumerated herein remain unknown, the details of their design, fabrication and/or installation lost to the ages.

TYPES

For the purposes of this book, stained glass window installations are broken down into two primary types: *leaded* and *dalle de verre* (literally "slab of glass"). Very basically, while mindful of endless variations upon these generalities, "leaded" defines installations in which individual pieces of sheet glass, painted or unpainted, are held together as an organized design by a metal framework nearly always made of lead, referred to in the industry as "came" ("calme" in the U.K. and Australia), while *dalle de verre* designs are made up of thick slabs of glass bonded with a matrix of epoxy (cement in some older designs) to form the window panel. In both cases, the came and epoxy can be utilized as a design element. Very generally, glass varieties used in leaded windows are thin, usually around one-eighth of an inch, and *dalle* varieties are thick, usually around one inch. There are numerous exceptions. *Dalle de verre* windows, being significantly less common in this book than leaded, shall be identified as such within their individual entries. With the exception of two outliers, the remainder of the book features leaded installations that are identified as such here and now only.

Within the larger field of leaded window installations showcased in this book, there are three major divisions: painted, unpainted or a combination of the two. There are also widely disparate degrees of dominance within the spectrum of painted and unpainted combinations. Again, keeping in mind that this is a very limited division of stained glass window designing and fabricating styles, find below a short guide to numerous photographic examples within the entries of this book that cover most of the general descriptions given above:

1. Leaded, unpainted: #19, #31, #36, #98, #112. In these examples nearly every element of the design is created by the placement of uniquely shaped, unpainted, colored panes next to one another. Oftentimes late nineteenth and early twentieth century colored, leaded windows devoid of painted elements [#19, #31, #36] are referred to as "art glass".

2. Leaded, painted: #63, #132, #141. In these examples nearly every element of the design is affected by painting directly upon colored glass, even the non-narrative, patterned portions, rendering the shape of the individual panes far less important, but not insignificant. Technically speaking, *only* painted glass is "stained" in the literal sense implied by the word, but referring to all decorative colored glass window designs as "stained glass" has become the commonly accepted parlance. Typically, a re-firing of the glass is required

after paint has been applied, but again, there are many exceptions among widely varying techniques.

3. Leaded combination, unpainted dominant: #15, #90, #95. In these examples nearly every element of the design is created by the placement of uniquely shaped, unpainted panes of colored glass and their relation to adjacent panes, with the slightest exceptions of the angels in #15, the monk with child and the inscription in #90, and Christ as a shepherd and the inscription in #95.

4. Leaded combination, painted dominant: #46, #56, #99. In these examples nearly every element of the design is affected by painting directly upon colored glass panes, with the plainly evident exceptions of the outer trim of #46, the halo patterns and sky in #56, and a handful of fully unpainted panes in the lower-center portion of #99.

5. Leaded combination, balanced: #3, #17, #21. In these installations we see sections executed almost entirely of unpainted, uniquely shaped panes in one portion of the larger design and fully painted portions in others, establishing nearly equal balances of painted and unpainted elements.

6. *Dalle de verre*: #44, #65, #107, #110, #121. In these examples we clearly see a greater amount of space between uniquely shaped, thick panes of colored glass, facilitated by the epoxy compounds or cement into which the glass is permanently embedded. *Dalle de verre* glass is rarely painted upon, but it is not unheard of [*#106*]. Recognizable objects, anatomical detail and facial features are usually achieved purely through the shape and placement of unpainted slabs, as are patterns and non-narrative elements.

7. Outliers: Completely unique design and fabrication styles that defy categorization by this guide include the Belcher Mosaic Window Company design at Christ Church Chapel [*#24*] and the plexiglass tower at Second Zion Baptist Church No. 1 [*#74*]. A number of other less common design and fabrication styles are simply not represented in this book.

Glass varietals utilized in both leaded and *dalle de verre* window designs are too great in number and broadly disparate in their fabrication processes to be given their due within this book's limited scope and space.

SUBJECT MATTER

Again, for the purposes of this book, subject matter incorporated into stained glass windows breaks down into three mostly easy to comprehend categories: narrative, non-narrative and inscription. "Narrative" describes any element of the design that attempts to tell a story through images of real-life objects, be they realistic or abstracted, animate or inanimate [*#8, #13, #14*], while "non-narrative" describes the purely patterned elements, often devoid of recognizable objects, as well as recognizable, simple objects removed from any attempt to relate a fuller story [#*86*, #*137*, #*139*]. Many installations comprise both narrative and non-narrative elements.

Typically, narrative elements of windows within Christian churches incorporate stories and figures from the Bible [#*33*, #*76*, #*103*] or lives of saints [#*104*, #*110*], while in the Jewish stained glass tradition as it presents in Metropolitan New Orleans, the portrayal of narrative elements is nearly non-existent [#*36*, #*57*]. There is periodically some grey area bisecting narrative and non-narrative categorizations [#*75*]. In most cases, a lone saint or biblical figure removed from a larger story is regarded as narrative by virtue of the many identifying features incorporated into their image, through which the story of a life is told [#*16*, #*122*, #*126*], but the mere presence of a human figure does not always add up to narrative status [#*91*].

Outside of private residences, secular examples [#*30*, #*92*] are exceedingly rare in the metro area and are most commonly found at Metairie Cemetery [#*137-141*]. The subject matter incorporated is usually site-specific, be it narrative or non-narrative, but the pool of examples lacks any of the depth necessary to divine predictable trends.

The last element of subject matter to consider are inscriptions, usually reporting memorialized individuals [#*46*, #*133*], significant dates [#*1*, #*10*], the names of saints and biblical figures [#*122*, #*126*], corporate insignia [*back cover*] and less often sacred text and prayer excerpts [#*130*]. Inscriptions are most commonly painted [#*138*, #*140*], but they can also be etched and in some uncommon cases, designed in small glass panes [#*10*].

GEOGRAPHIC SCOPE

In my mind the area that makes up the New Orleans metropolis extends to all of the towns that abut Lake Pontchartrain, and those in close proximity to the north end of the Causeway and the intersection of I-10 and I-12. At fifteen miles from the Lake, the city of Hammond begs closer examination in this regard, as it is also encompassed by the Archdiocese of Baton Rouge rather than New Orleans. I felt compelled by the stained glass present there to include it herein, despite its distance. Also questionable is the great length down the River Road I chose to travel in search of significant examples. Given the number of tourists who visit this part of the country to explore plantation history, and the number of metro-Orleanian Catholics who make pilgrimages to Manresa, I felt comfortable in venturing all the way to Vacherie, the home of Oak Alley, on the West Bank and Convent on the east. What might, in my opinion, be considered the last outlier, Saints Peter & Paul in Pearl River, is included without corresponding photographs on account of Covid related access restrictions.

UNDERSTANDING THIS GUIDE

Each entry in this field guide to stained glass of the New Orleans Metropolis is ordered in a loosely chronological fashion and contains seven to ten parts: (1) a full color photograph of stained glass installed within the structure named by the entry, or in some cases, two photos; (2) the name of the structure at the time of its construction, or in some cases its most commonly known name; (3) the year or years of the structure's erection; (4) the structure's street address; (5) the New Orleans neighborhood or the suburban municipality in which the structure is located; (6) the structure's architect where known; (7) the structure's builder where known; (8) where necessary, concise notes regarding the histories of the structure, the congregation inhabiting it, and/or the stained glass found within; (9) where known, the designers, fabricator and installers of the stained glass; and (10) where known the years of stained glass installation.

"Architect undetermined" is entered for part (6) when the architect is unknown. Where the builder is unknown part (7) is stricken from the entry. In a few cases where a builder is reported but the architect is not, it is assumed to be likely but not certain that the builder also acted as the architect. Where the designers, fabricators and installers of the structure's stained glass are unknown the phrase "Stained glass makers and dates of installation undetermined" is entered for part (9). In many cases part (9) is incorporated into part (8).

Where no dates of installation are cited, it can be assumed that, to the best of my knowledge, the site's stained glass was installed during construction or very shortly thereafter.

At sites featuring multiple commissions by varying parties, the phrase "et al.", meaning "and others", acknowledges unidentified makers of the non-primary installations. At sites where no distinction between designer, fabricator and installer has been established for the primary windows, but a maker is known, the words "made by" or "by" are generically used to specify the designers and/or fabricators, while installers remain anonymous. The reader is asked to keep in mind the commonness of these distinctions being lost to history, and the high likelihood, in some cases, of other uncredited parties being involved.

In the vast majority of cases, I defer to historical information as it is engraved upon cornerstones or expressed upon the glass itself as the most authoritative recountings of the history that took place. Newspaper accounts are regarded as the penultimate word on these historical details.

The acronym "PRC" is used in place of the phrase "Preservation Resource Center" in nearly all instances. Also, in nearly all instances, the phrase "PRC researchers" is used in place of the full names of Mrs. Patricia Andrews and Ms. Pame Tanner.

PART ONE

THE CITY

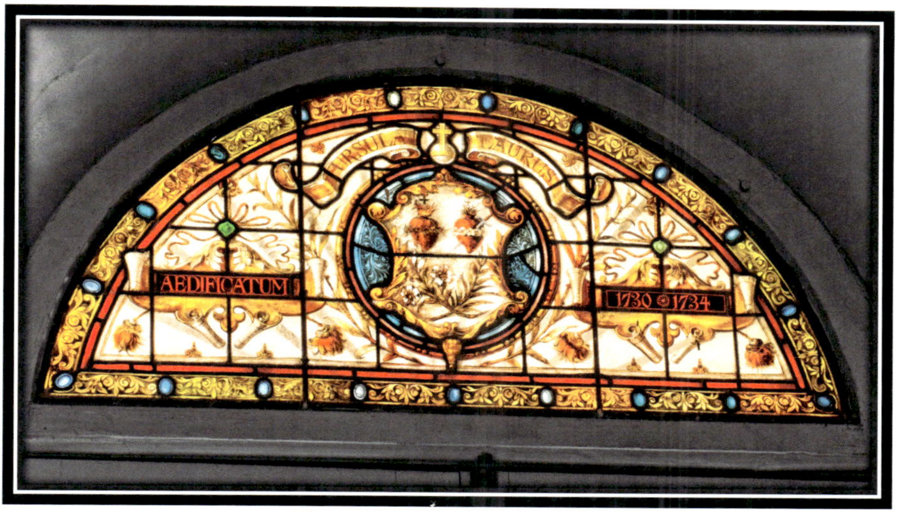

1. Old Ursuline Convent (1752-1753)

1116 Chartres St, French Quarter
Ignace François Broutin, architect; Claude Joseph Villars de Breuil, builder

This building served as the residence of New Orleans' bishops and archbishops from 1824 to 1899. Originally constructed as the third Ursuline Convent, it also incorporates a stairway salvaged from the second. The two stained glass panes found here, one on each floor, date to a renovation applied to this structure from 1889 to 1890. Their makers are undetermined. The erection date of 1730-1734 reported on the first-floor window refers to the second convent building's construction date. At the time of its 1889-1890 renovation this third convent building was incorrectly believed to be constructed at the time of the second, thus the misleading dates. According to an historical marker located at the entrance to the grounds the Old Ursuline Convent is the oldest extant building in the Mississippi Valley.

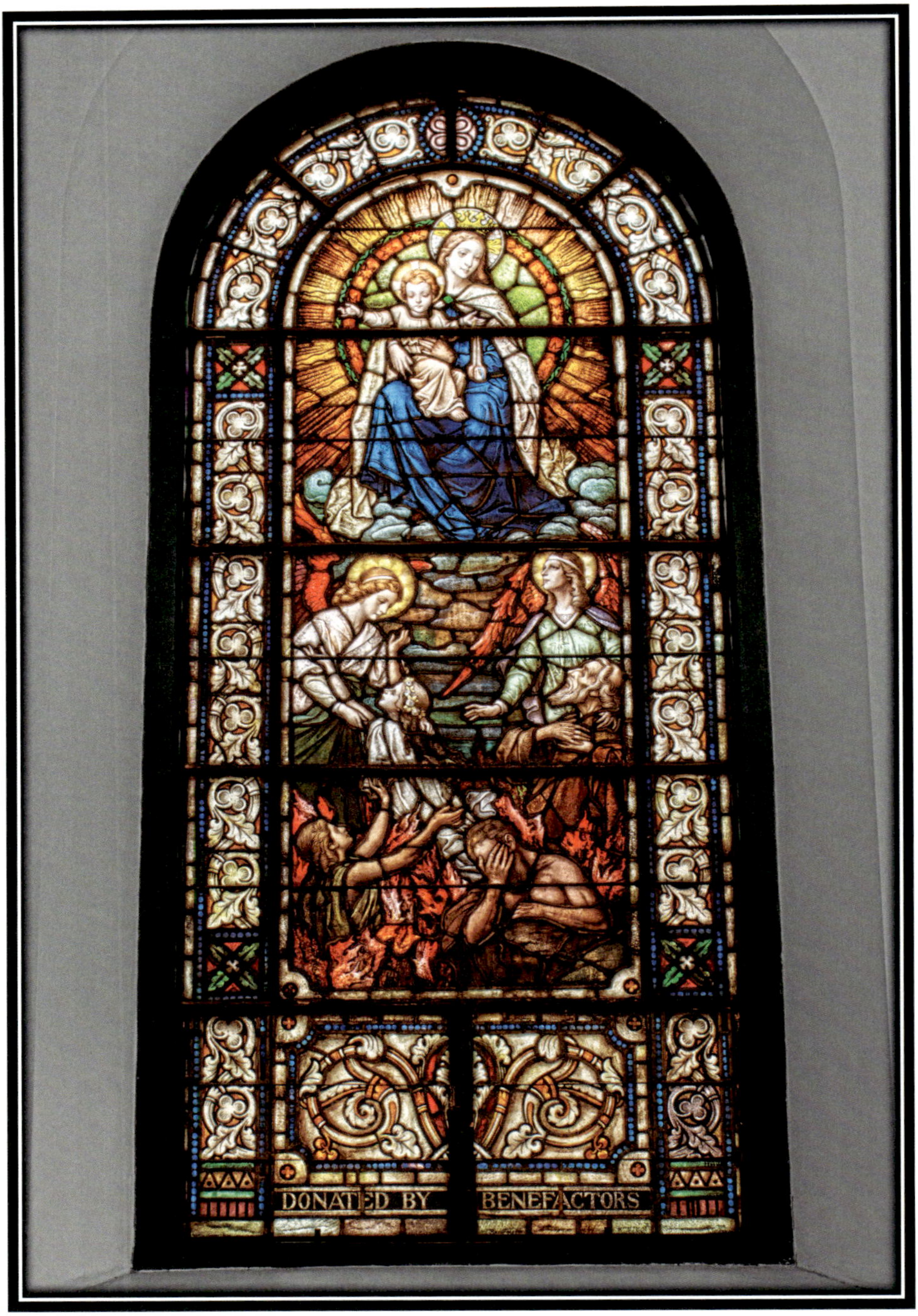
DONATED BY BENEFACTORS

◄2. Our Lady of Guadalupe Catholic Church (1826-1827)

411 N. Rampart St, French Quarter
Gurlie & Guillot, architect-builders

Formerly known as the Mortuary Chapel of St. Anthony of Padua; also known as French Mortuary Chapel. Origins of the primary nave windows, likely installed in the 1920s, are undetermined but Emil Frei Inc. of St. Louis is suggested by similarities to other local examples. Stylistically congruous transept windows, likely installed during a 1950s enlargement, were made by the studio of Professor Raffaele Albertella of Genoa, Italy.

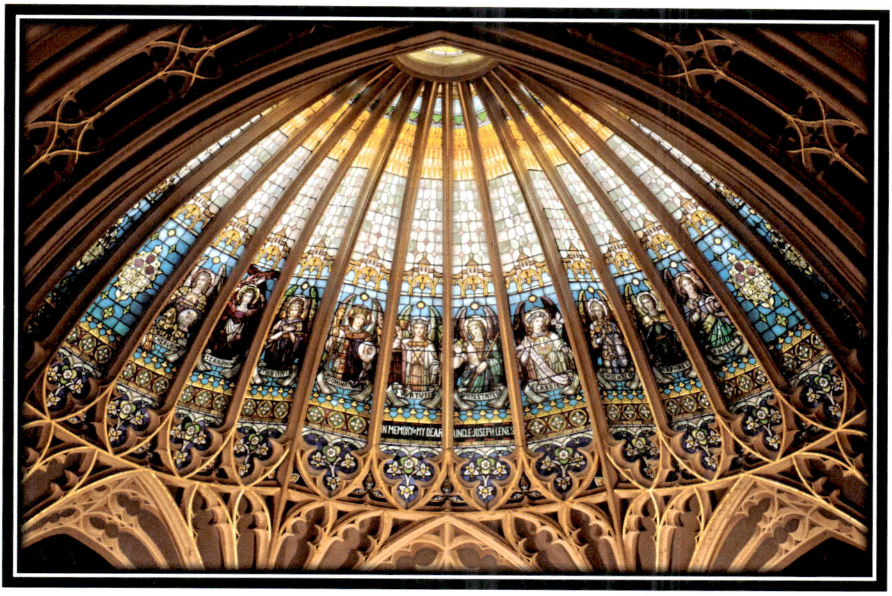

3. St. Patrick's Catholic Church (1838-1840)

724 Camp St, Central Business District
Charles & James Dakin + James Gallier, architects

PRC researchers attribute the skylight [pictured] and four other major windows at this site to Emil Frei Inc. of St. Louis; installed 1916 and after. A few more windows are attributed to Franz Mayer & Co. of Munich; installed c. 1922. A major window representing the 'Immaculate Conception of the Patroness of the United States' was designed by former rector Fr. Raymond A. Carra (1880-1940); also installed c.1922 and likely fabricated in Munich.

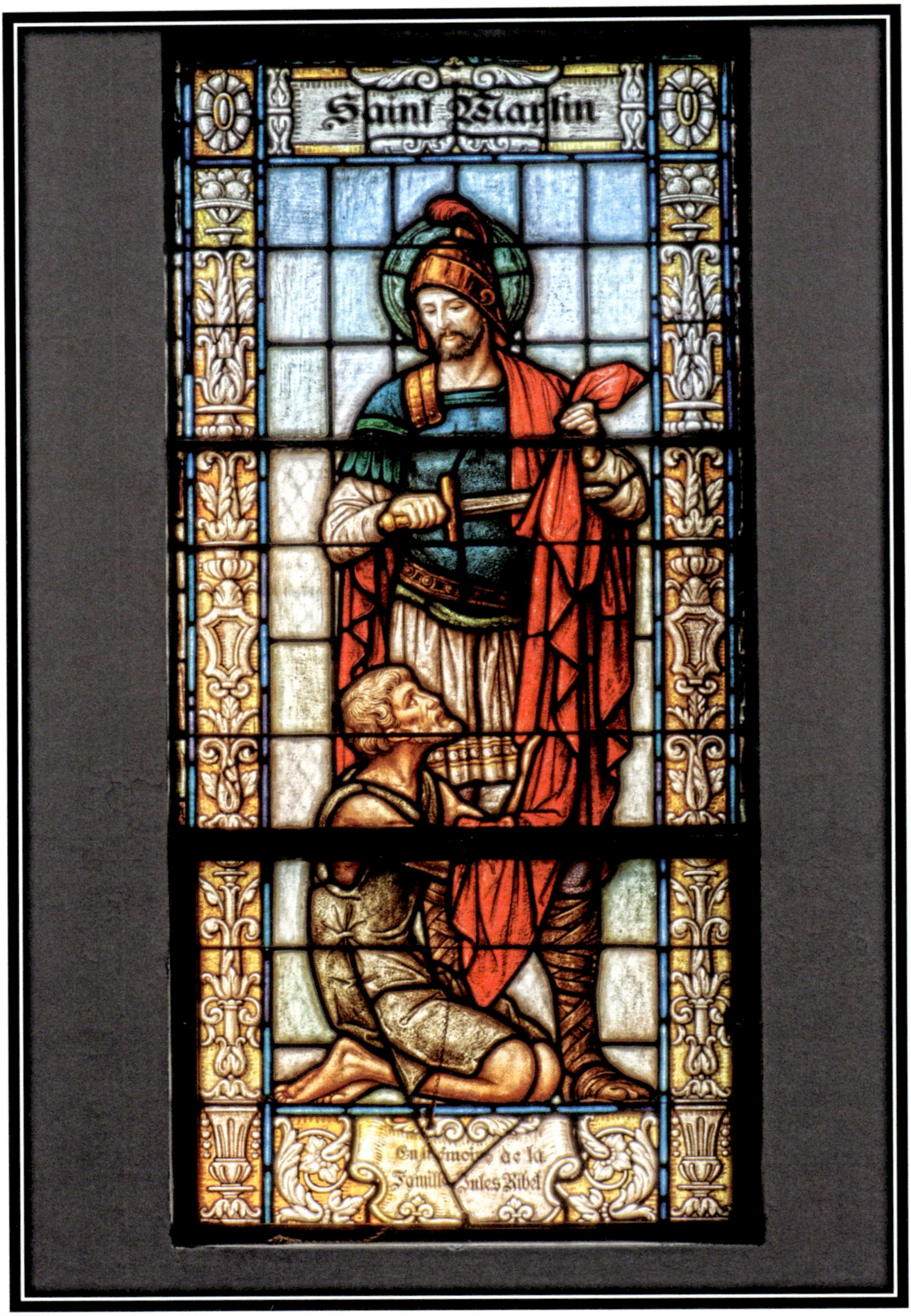
Saint Martin

◀4. St. Augustine Catholic Church (1841-1842)

1210 Governor Nicholls St, Tremé-Lafitte
J.N.B. de Pouilly, architect; Ernest Gocchaux, builder

Primary windows made by Emil Frei Studios of St. Louis; installed during a 1926 renovation managed by architects Emile Weil and Albert Bendernagel.

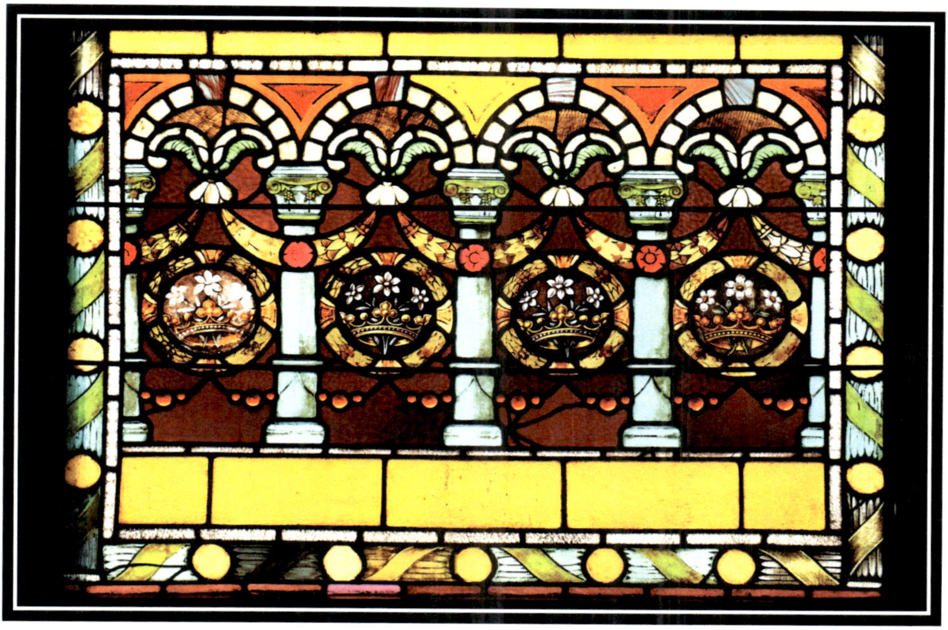

5. St. Mary's Catholic Church (1845)

1116 Chartres St, French Quarter
J.N.B. de Pouilly, architect

Stained glass makers and dates of installation undetermined.

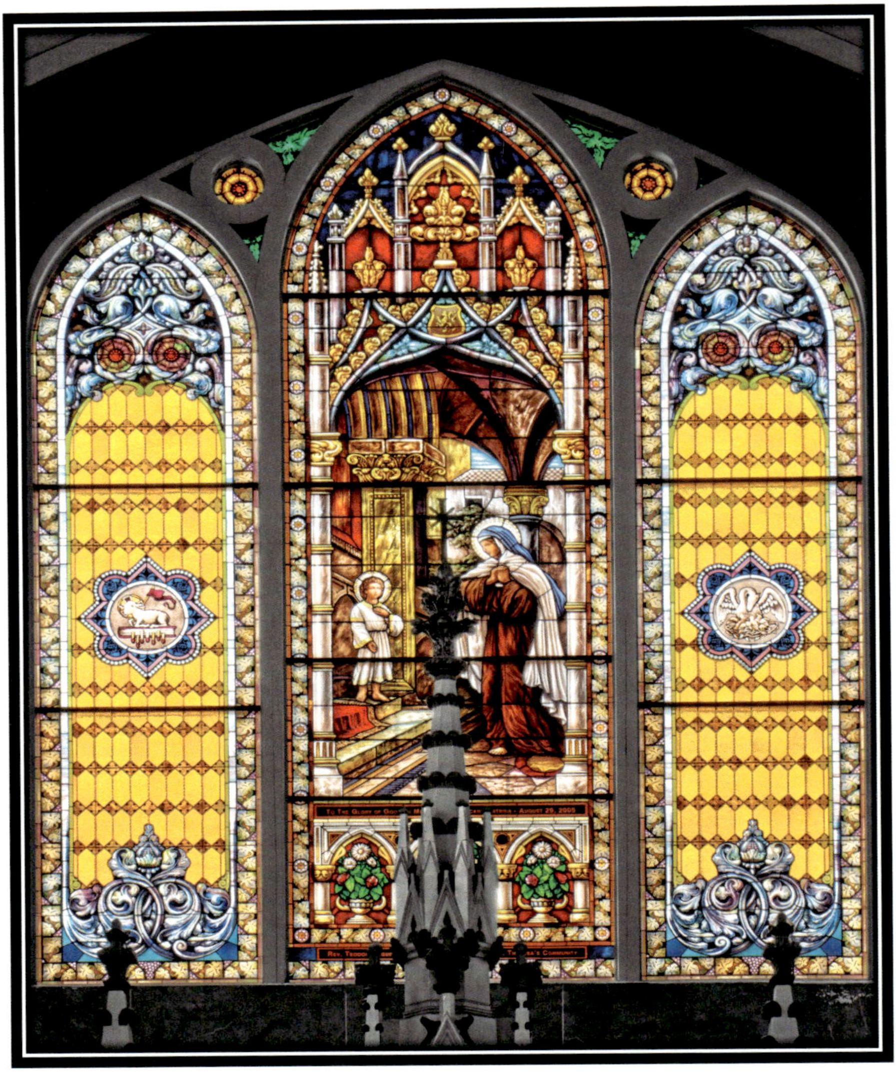

6. St. Theresa of Avila Catholic Church (1848-1849)

1401 Erato St, Lower Garden District
Theodore E. Giraud, architect

Primary windows fabricated by F.X. Zettler Co. of Munich, Germany; other contributors probable. Window shown is replica fabricated by Conrad Schmitt Studios of New Berlin, Wisconsin; original destroyed during Hurricane Katrina. Find one memorial window donated by the architectural firm of Diboll & Owen in narthex; maker undetermined.

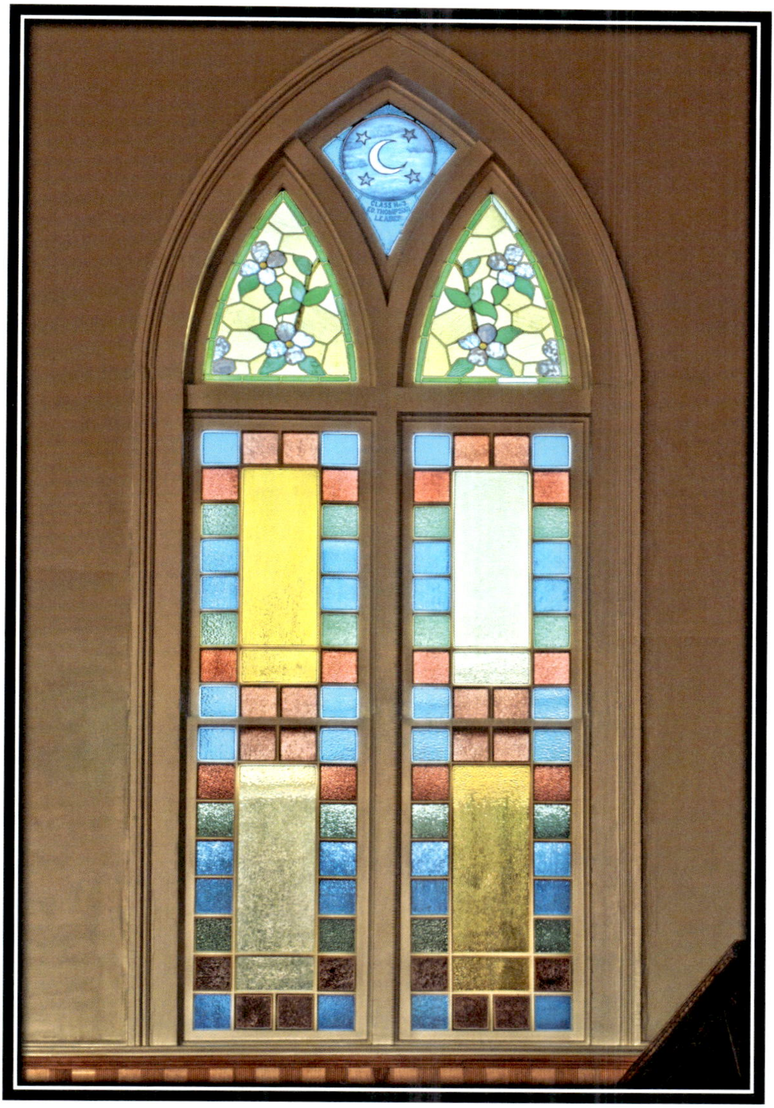

7. St. James African Methodist Episcopal Church (1848-1851)

222 N. Roman St, Tulane-Gravier
Architect undetermined; 1903 pediment replacement, Diboll & Owen

Primary pane makers undetermined. Arch sections fabricated and installed by Attenhofer's Stained Glass Studio of Metairie c.2009-2015; replicas of original panes that had aged and faded beyond repair.

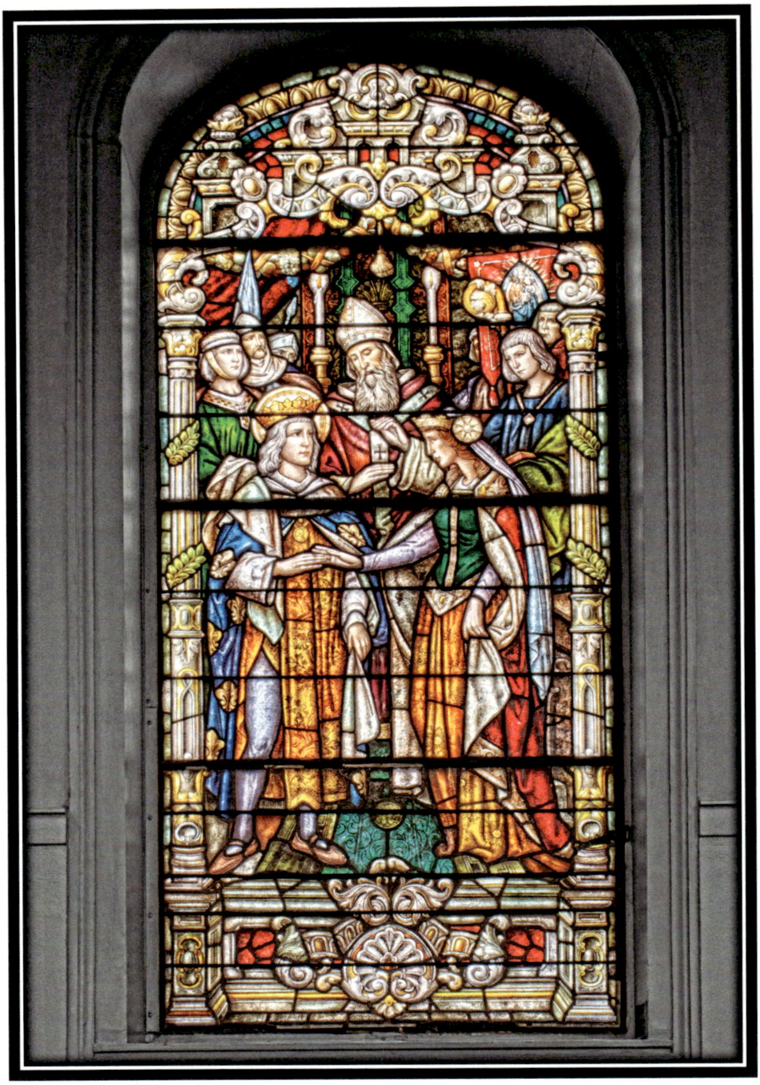

8. Cathedral-Basilica of St. Louis King of France (1849-1851)

615 Pere Antoine Alley, French Quarter
J.N.B. de Pouilly, architect

More commonly known to locals as St. Louis Cathedral. Primary nave windows [pictured] by Dr. Heinrich Oidtmann Studios of Linnich, Germany; installed c.1929. Various other designers and fabricators represented include Ruth Goliwas of New Orleans and Emil Frei Studios of St. Louis.

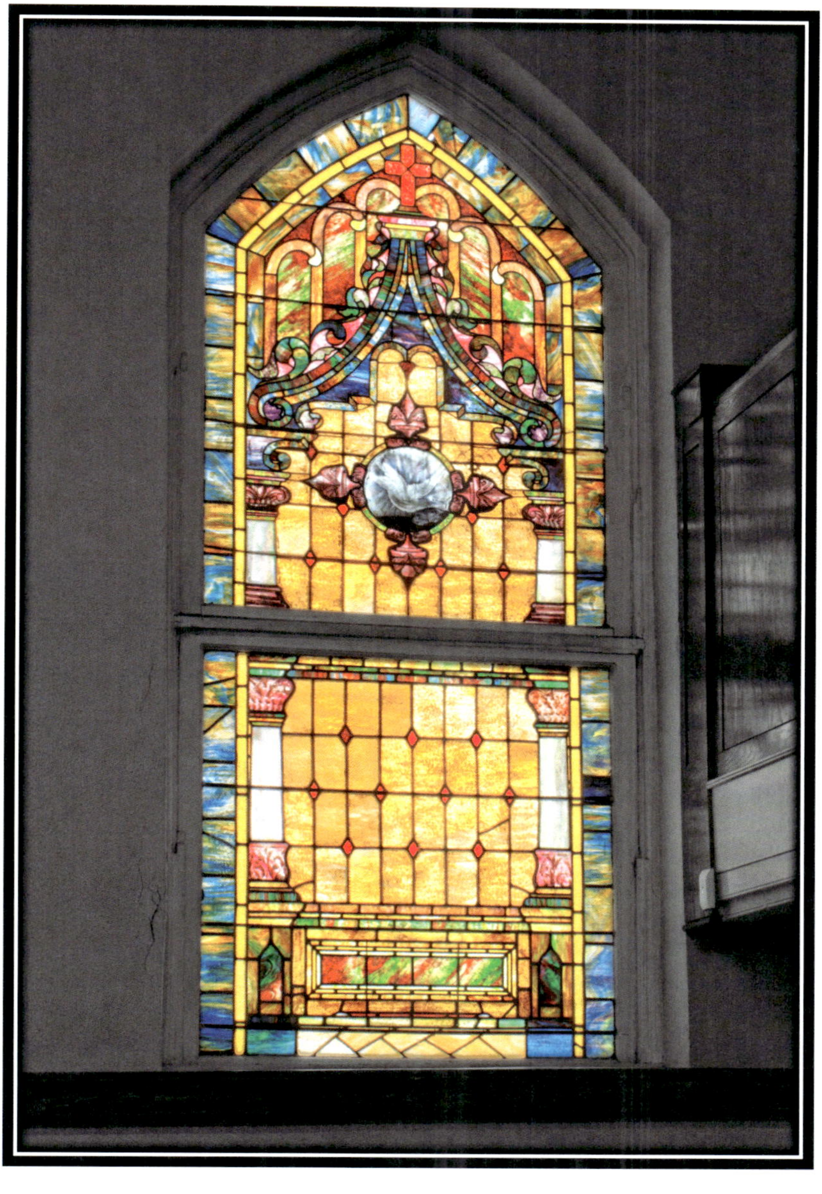

9. St. Peter Claver Catholic Church (1852)

1923 St Philip St, Tremé-Lafitte
Theodore E. Giraud, architect

Originally known as the Church of St. Anne [Catholic]. Stained glass makers undetermined; most windows installed c.1902-1912.

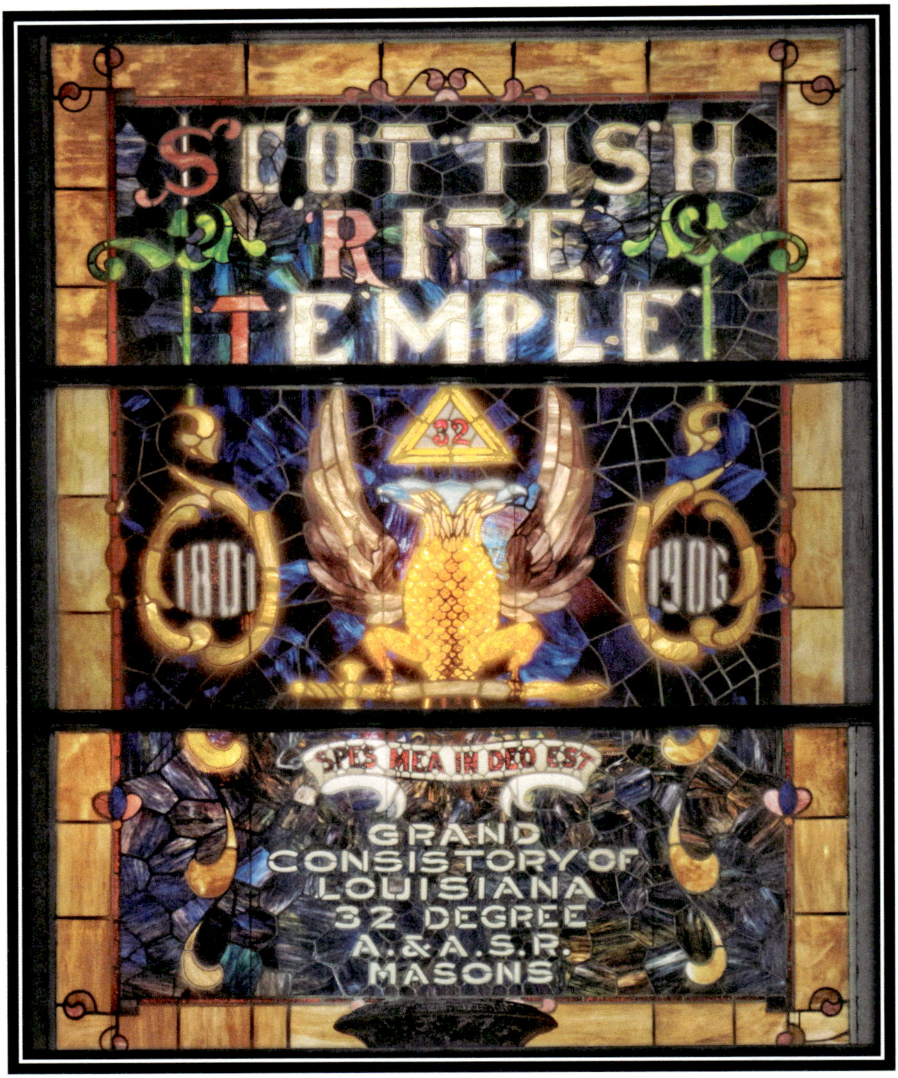

10. Scottish Rite Temple (1851-1853)

619 Carondelet St, Central Business District
George Purves, architect-builder

Originally built as Edward McGehee Methodist Episcopal Church; also known as Carondelet Street Methodist Episcopal Church. Sold and repurposed as Scottish Rite Temple in 1906. Adaptive renovation managed by Stone Brothers, architects; A. Liebe, builder. Stained glass presumably installed around that time; makers undetermined.

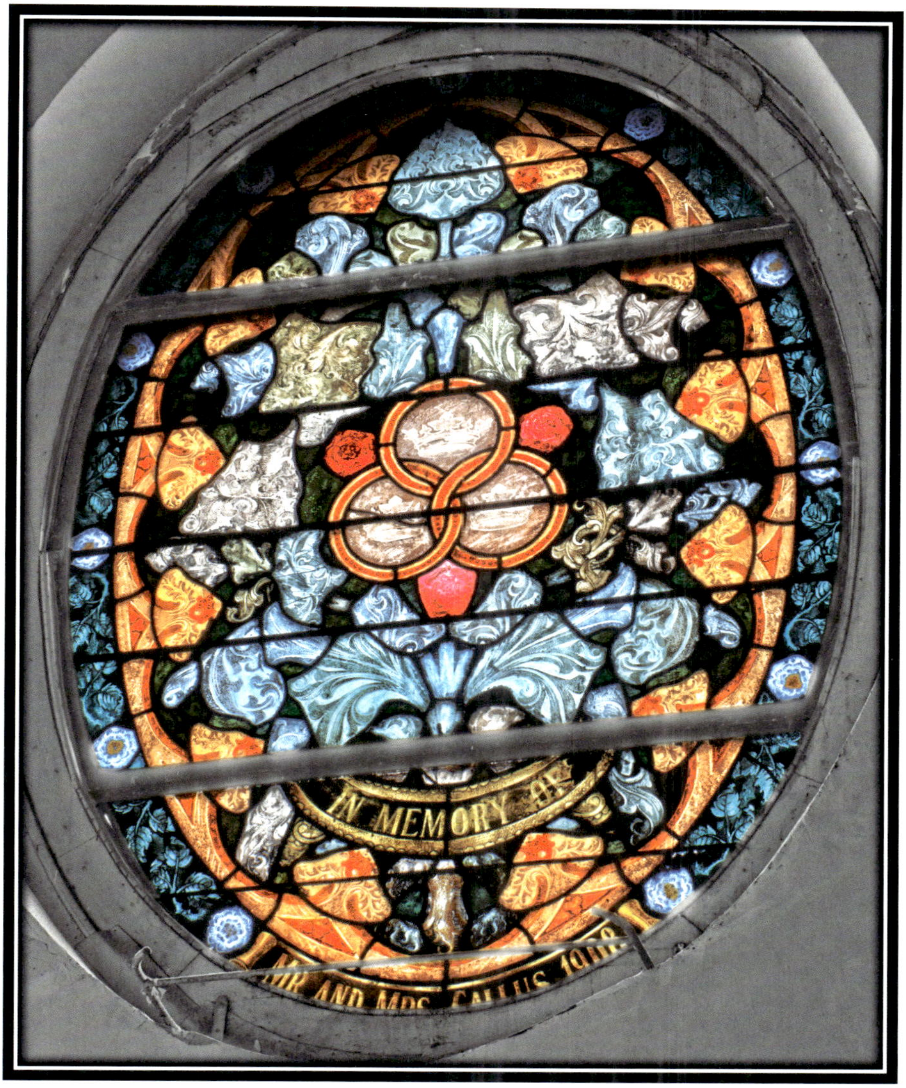

11. Holy Trinity Catholic Church (1853)

729 St Ferdinand St, Marigny
Theodore E. Giraud, architect

Deconsecrated 1997; now known as Marigny Opera House. Original lower-level nave windows transplanted to Ascension of Our Lord Catholic Church in LaPlace (*entry #126*) c.2001. Original clerestory panes remain, installed in the first decade of the 1900s; makers undetermined.

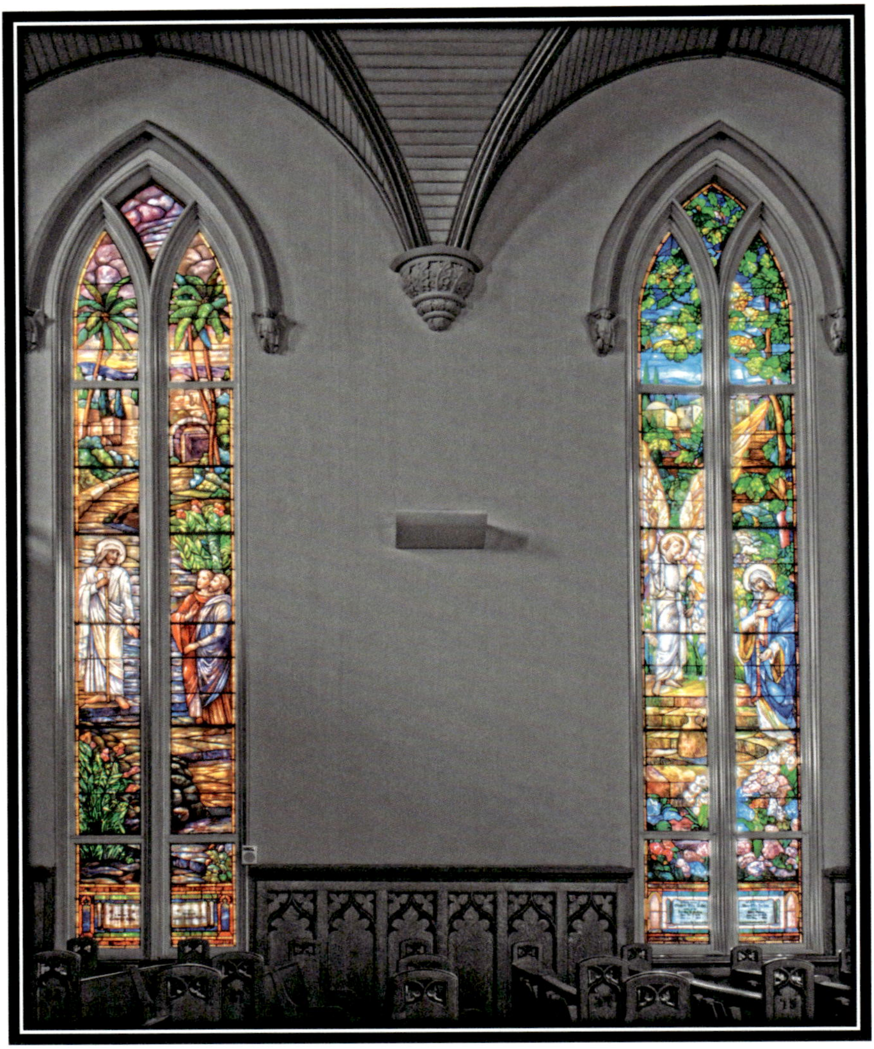

12. Trinity Episcopal Church (1852-1854)

1329 Jackson Ave, Lower Garden District
George Purves, architect-builder / 1872 tower addition: Charles L. Hillger, architect; Peter R. Middlemiss, builder

Charles J. Connick Studios of Boston and J & R Lamb Studios of New York City [pictured] are the primary window makers at this site. Other makers represented include J.P. Spencer of Montreal, Edmonston Studio of Manchester, England, Cox, Sons, Buckley & Company of New York and London, and Lavers, Barraud & Westlake of London.

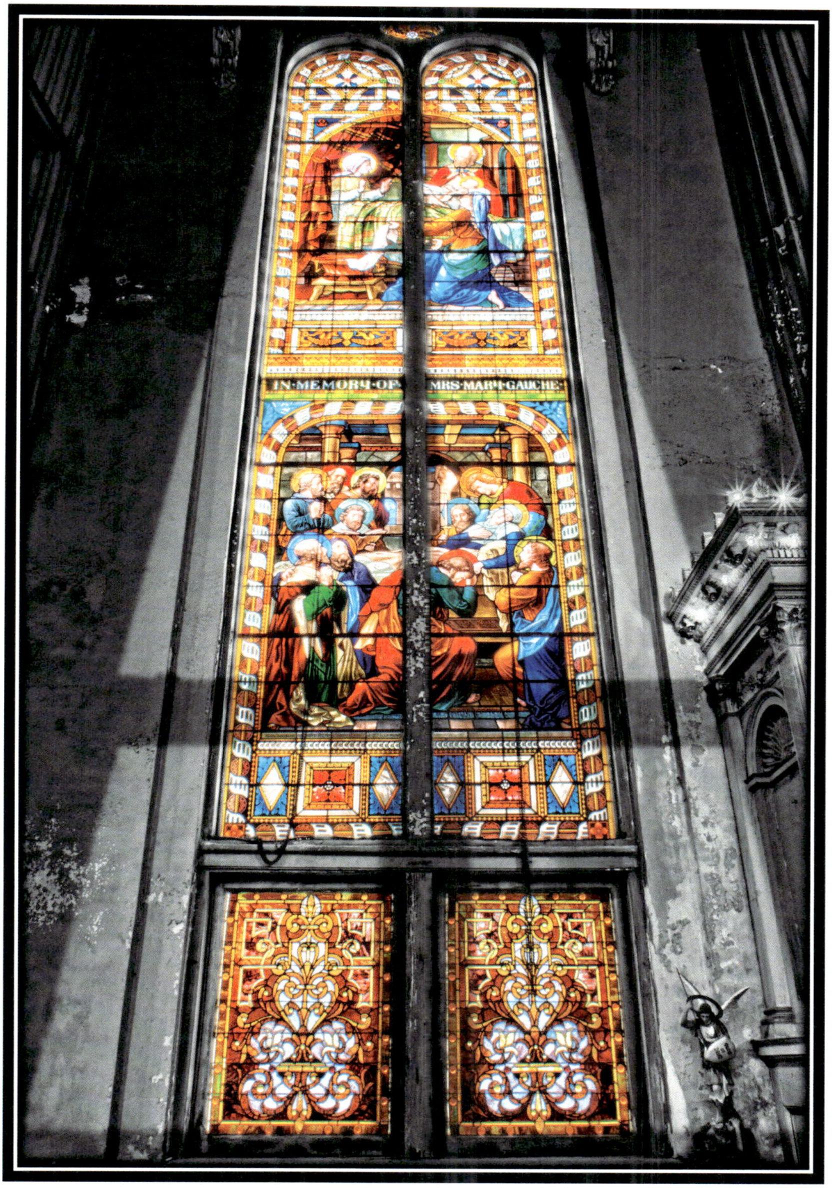

13. St. Alphonsus Catholic Church (1855-1857)

2025 Constance St, Lower Garden District
Louis L. Long, architect

Most likely built by Daniel and Thomas Mulligan. Windows by F.X. Zettler & Co. of Munich; installed 1888-1890.

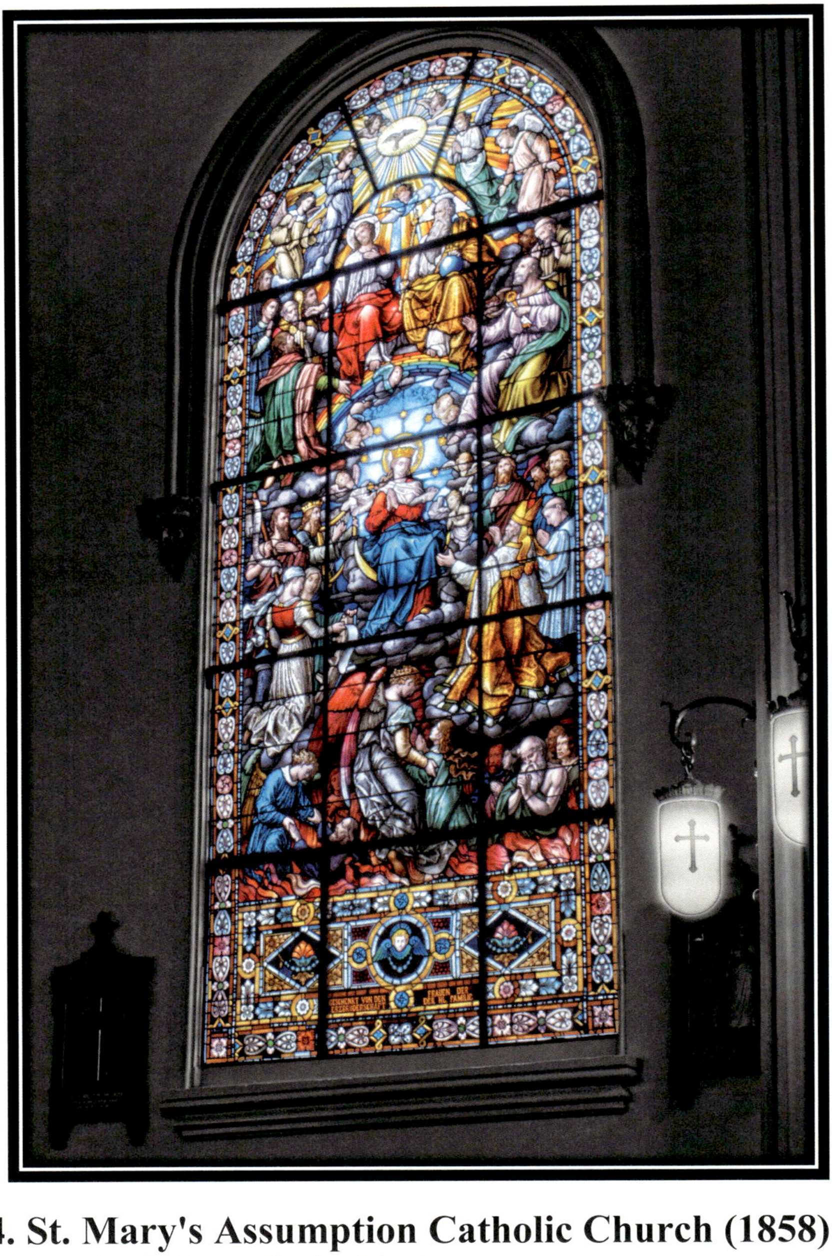

14. St. Mary's Assumption Catholic Church (1858)

923 Josephine St, Lower Garden District
Architect undetermined

This structure's design is sometimes attributed to architect Albert Diettel. Windows by F.X. Zettler & Co. of Munich; installed c.1890s.

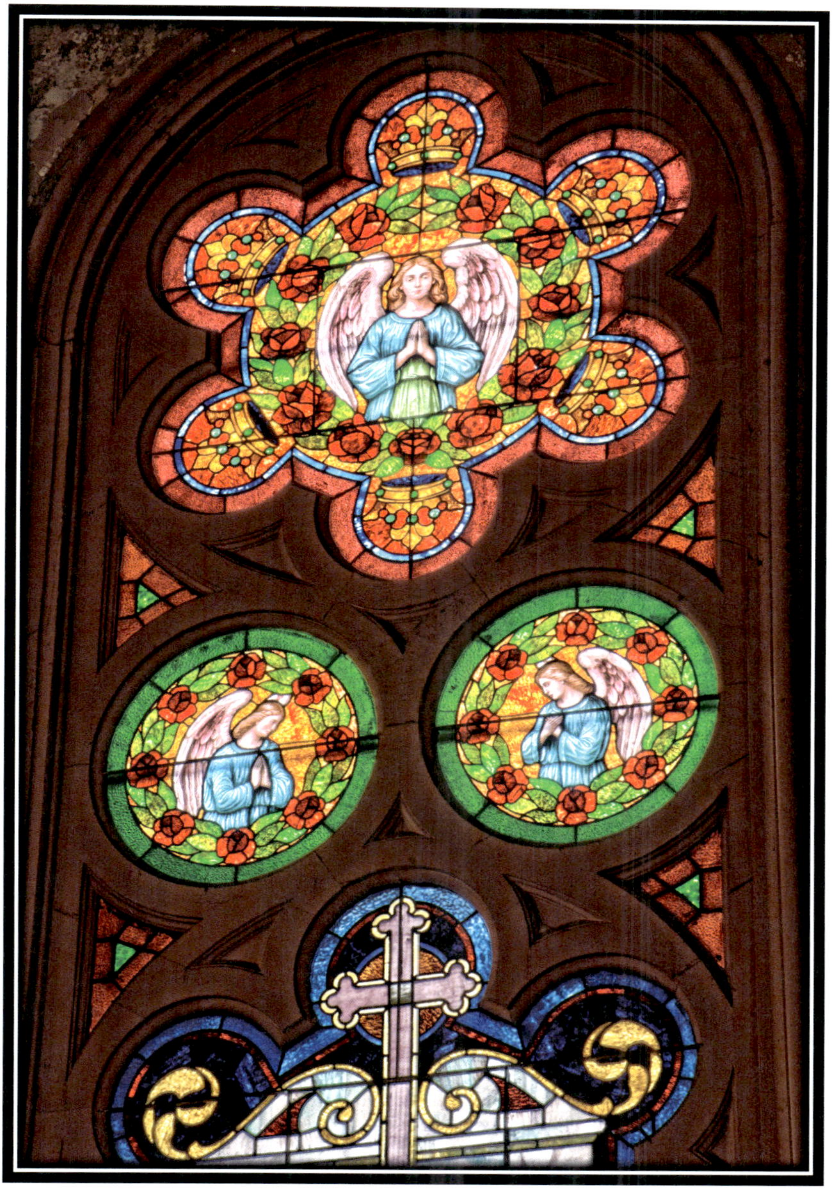

15. Ss. Peter & Paul Catholic Church (1860)

2317 Burgundy St, Marigny
Henry Howard, architect

Now known as Hotel Peter & Paul. Windows by Flanagan & Biendenweg of Chicago; installed c.1907.

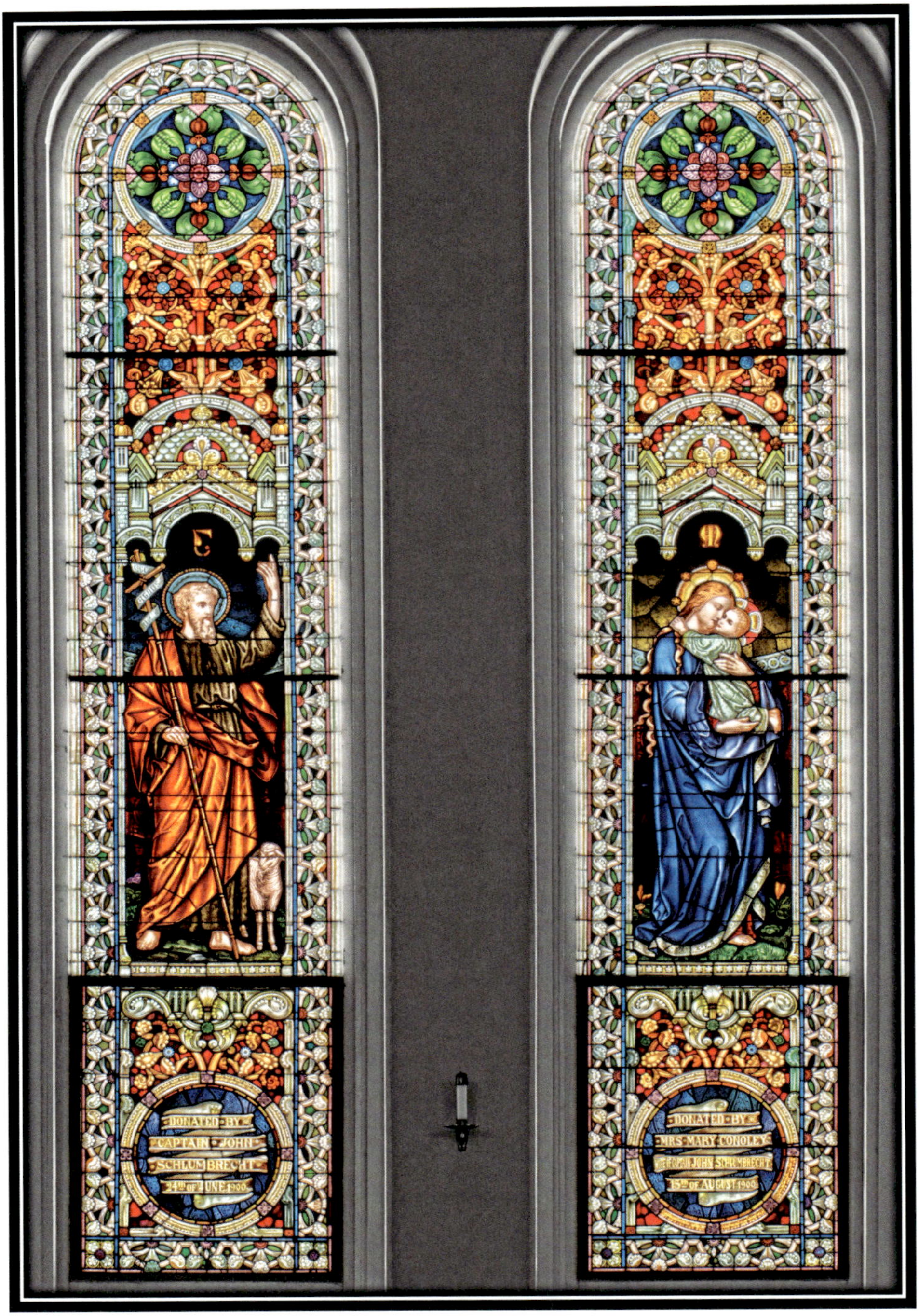
DONATED BY
CAPTAIN JOHN
SCHLUM BRECHT
24th OF JUNE 1900
DONATED BY
MRS MARY CONOLEY
15th OF AUGUST 1900

◄16. St. Vincent de Paul Catholic Church (1866)

3037 Dauphine St, Bywater
Louis E. Reynolds, architect

Now known as Blessed Francis Xavier Seelos Parish Catholic Church. Windows by Emil Frei Studios of St. Louis; installed early 1900s. Other contributors possible.

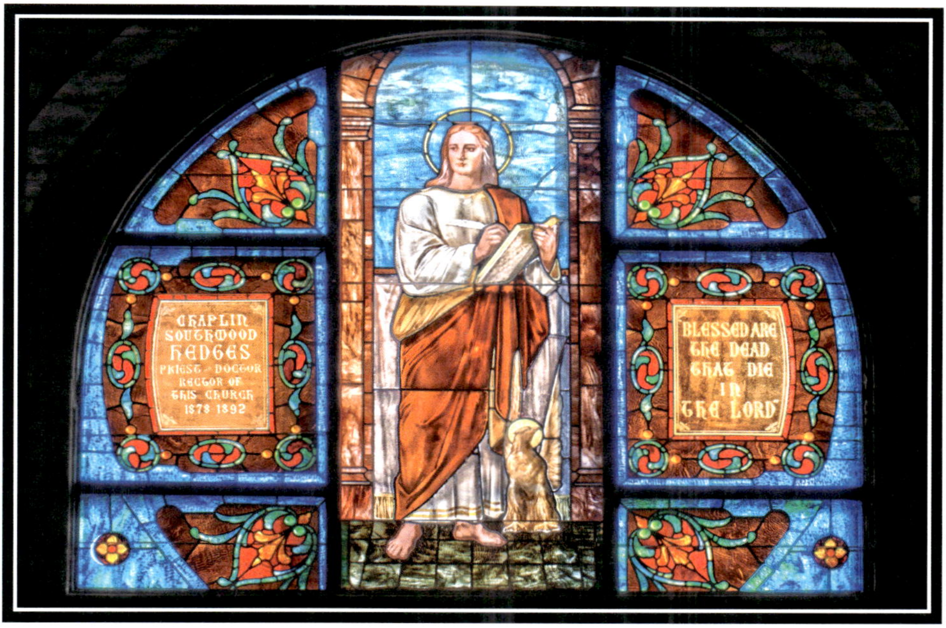

17. Mount Olivet Episcopal Church (1867)

530 Pelican Ave, Algiers Point
Architect undetermined

An historical marker affixed to this structure's façade inaccurately reports the 1854 construction date of the first Mount Olivet Church building. The present structure replaced the original church, destroyed by fire in December 1866. Stained glass makers undetermined; glass installed c.1892-1933.

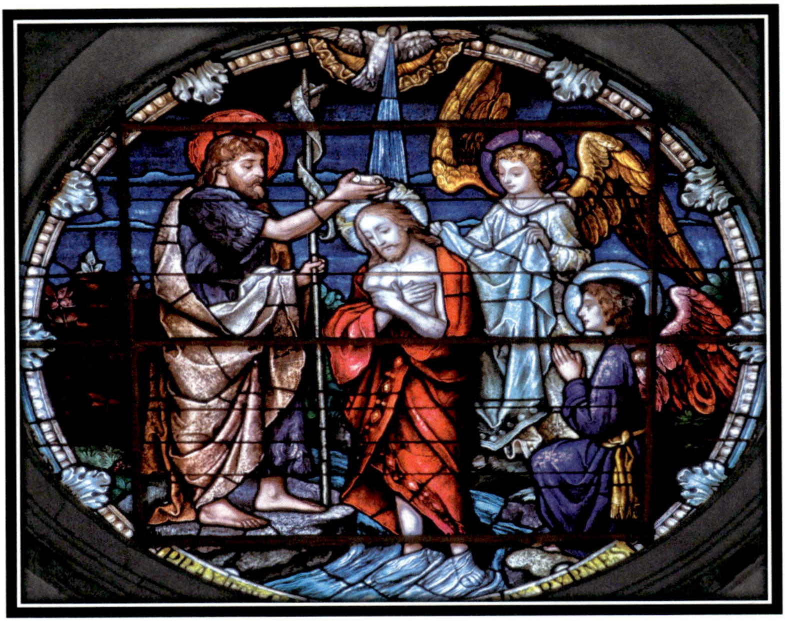

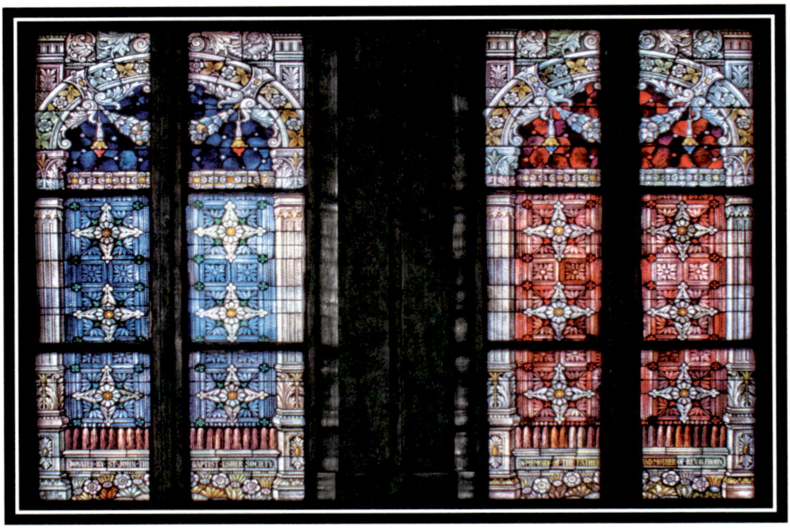

18. St. John the Baptist Catholic Church (1868-1872)

1139 Oretha Castle Haley Blvd, Central City
Albert Diettel, architect

Parish literature attributes the majority of this structure's stained glass to F.X. Zettler & Co. of Munich; other contributors are likely. Multiple eras of installation spanned the years of 1874 to 1962.

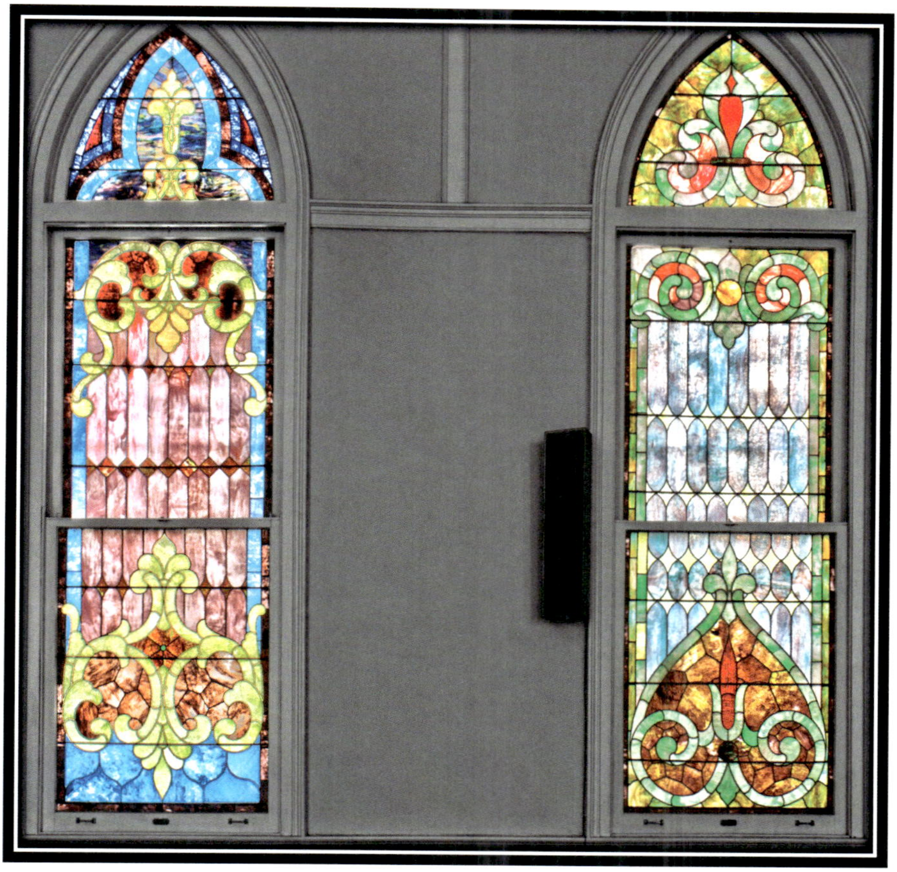

19. Zion Lutheran Church (1871-1872)

1924 St Charles Ave, Lower Garden District
Charles L. Hillger, architect

Conflicting accounts attributing this structure's design to Albert Diettel exist. I defer to the reporting of The Daily Picayune of June 16th, 1872. Stained glass makers and dates of installation are undetermined.

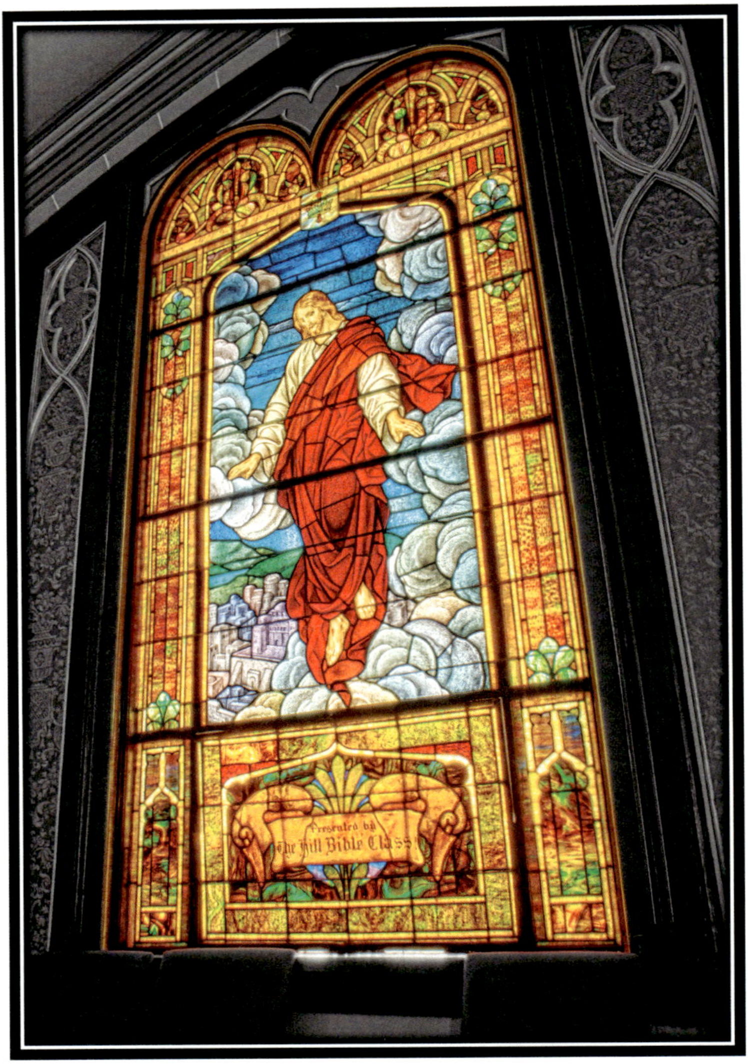

20. Rayne Memorial Methodist Episcopal Church (1875)

3900 St Charles Ave, Touro
Charles L. Hillger, architect; James Cox, builder

Originally known as St. Charles Avenue Methodist Episcopal; now known as Rayne Memorial United Methodist. According to church literature much of the stained glass at this site was made in Germany, purchased through a St. Louis firm, and installed by Henry G. Lips shortly after the New Orleans Hurricane of 1915. Post-Katrina steeple rebuild managed by Waggoner & Ball of New Orleans; Carl E. Woodward, contractor.

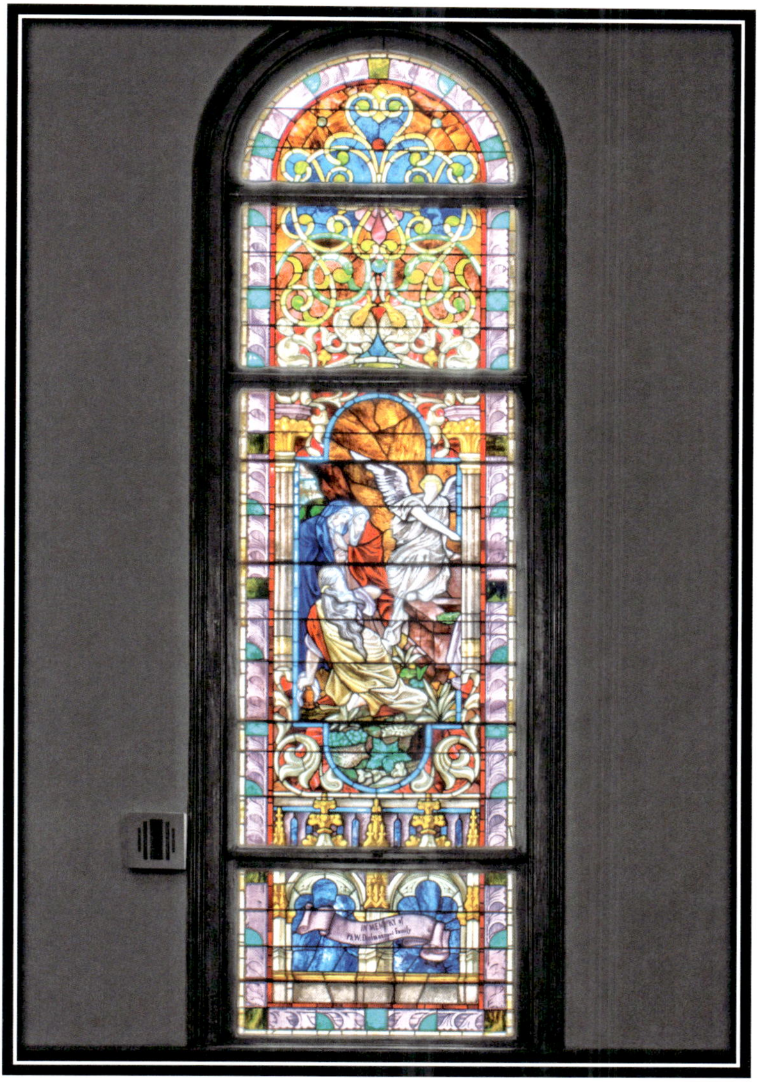

21. Jackson Avenue Evangelical Congregation (1872-1876)

2221 Chippewa St, Irish Channel
Charles L. Hillger, architect

Now known as Jackson Avenue Church. Multiple stained glass makers represented at this site include Franz Mayer Co. of Munich [pictured], Emil Frei Co. of St. Louis and Henry G. Lips' Louisiana Glass and Mirror Co. of New Orleans. Installed over multiple eras, 1902 to 1989.

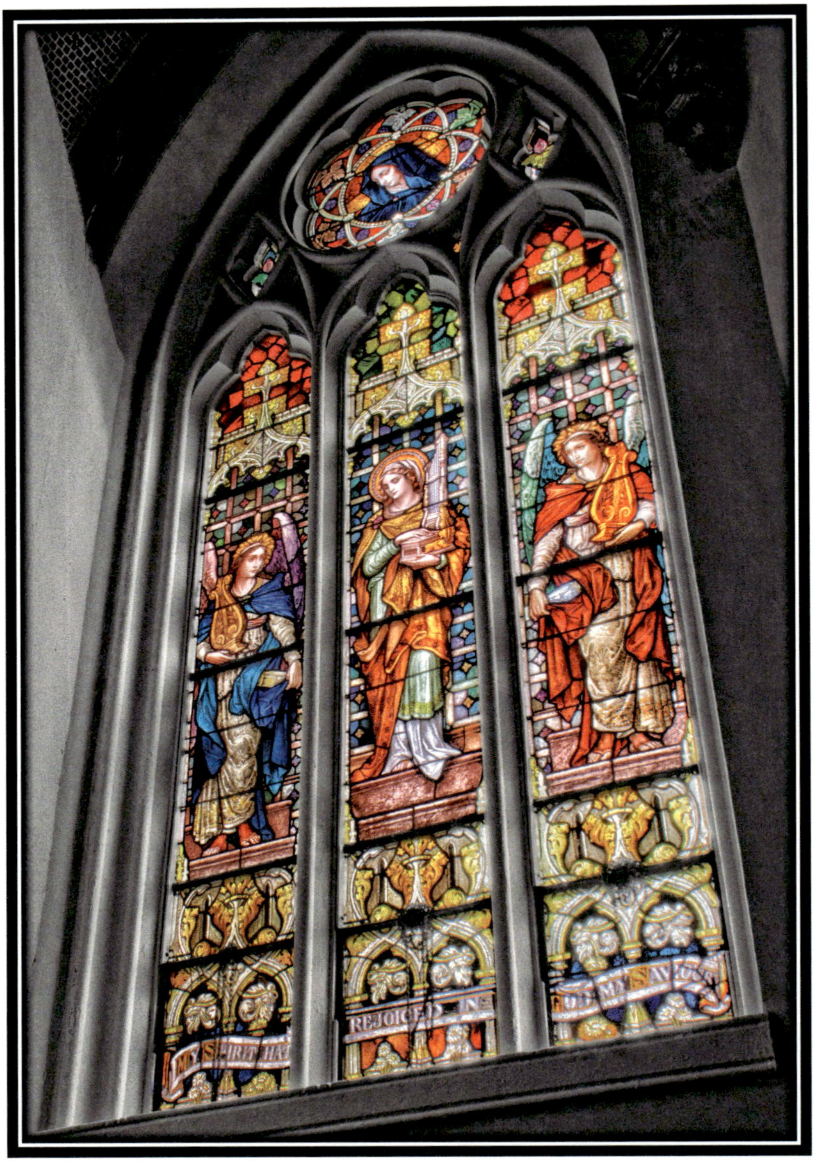

22. St. Stephen Catholic Church (1868-1887)

1025 Napoleon Ave, Touro
Thomas W. Carter, architect; Thomas O'Neil, builder / Steeple addition 1905-1908; Favrot & Livaudais, architects.

Primary windows by Emil Frei Studios of St. Louis and Franz Mayer Co. of Munich; other contributors likely.

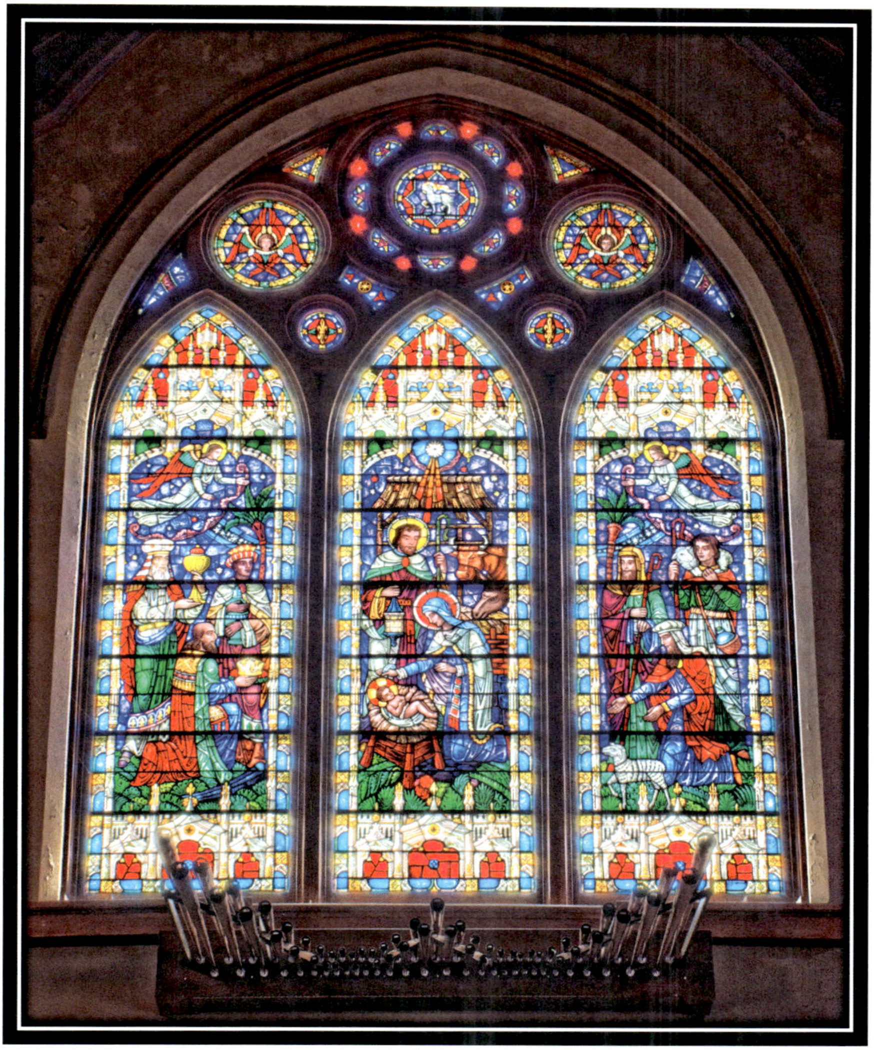

23. Christ Church Cathedral [Episcopal] (1886-1887)

2919 St Charles Ave, Central City
Lawrence B. Valk, architect; B.M. Harrod, local supervising architect

Stained glass makers represented at this site include Len R. Howard of Kent, Connecticut, Wilbur H. Burnham Studio of Boston [pictured], Willet Studios of Philadelphia and Payne Studios of Paterson, New Jersey. Dates of installation span from the 1950s to the 1980s. A triple lancet window designed in 1873 by Alphonse Friedrich & Bro. of Brooklyn was transplanted from the previous Christ Church building.

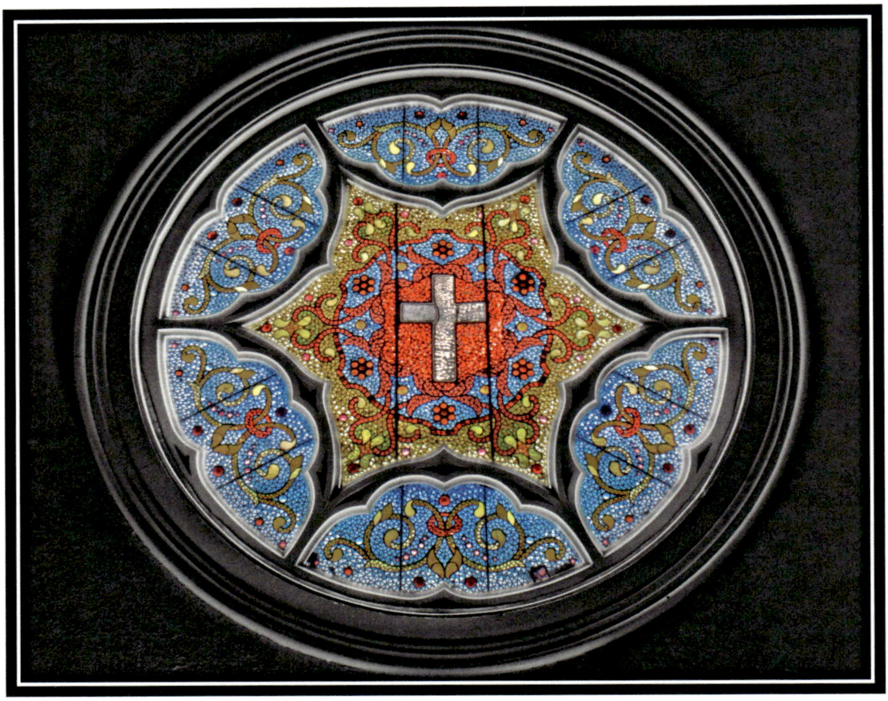

24. Christ Church Chapel [Episcopal] (1888-1889)

2919 St Charles Ave, Central City
Lawrence B. Valk, architect; Sully & Toledano, local supervising architects

Nearly all of this chapel's stained glass is by Willet Studios of Philadelphia; installed c.1960s. Most significant is a rose window by Belcher Mosaic Glass Company of Newark, NJ [pictured]. It is original to the building and now found in the choir rehearsal room as a result of alterations made during a 1940-1941 addition.

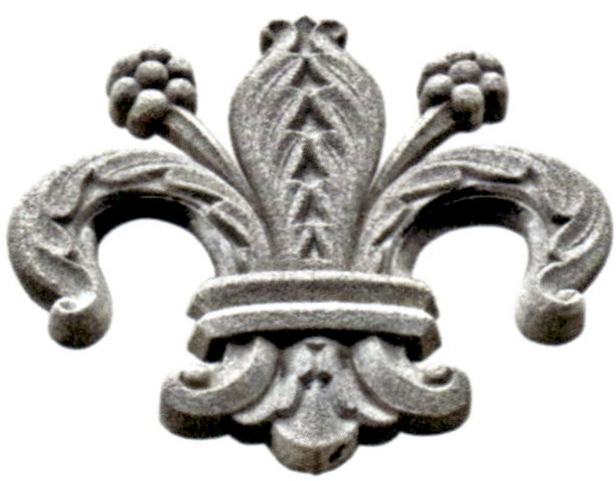

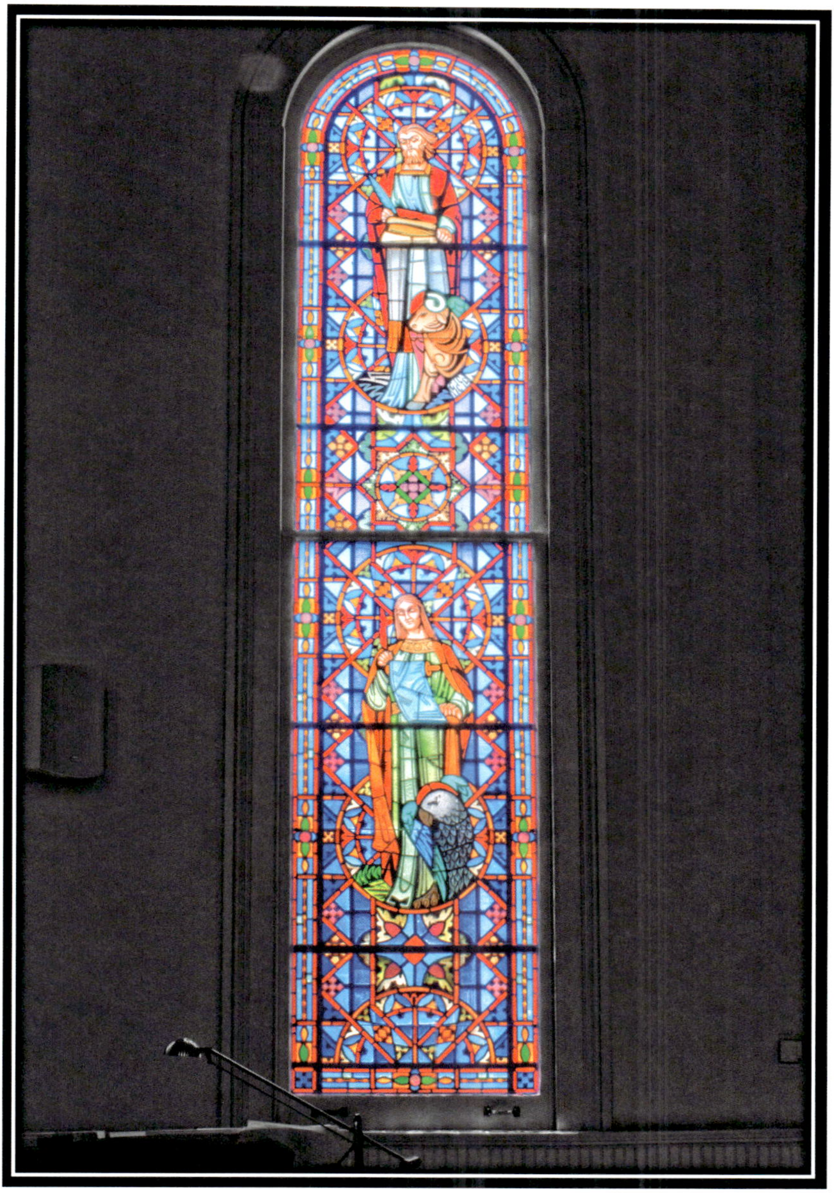

25. St. Paul Lutheran Church (1889)

2624 Burgundy St, Marigny
Architect undetermined

Stained glass designed by Rev. Adalbert R. Kretzmann of Chicago; fabricated by Giannini & Hilgart Co. of Chicago; installed 1966.

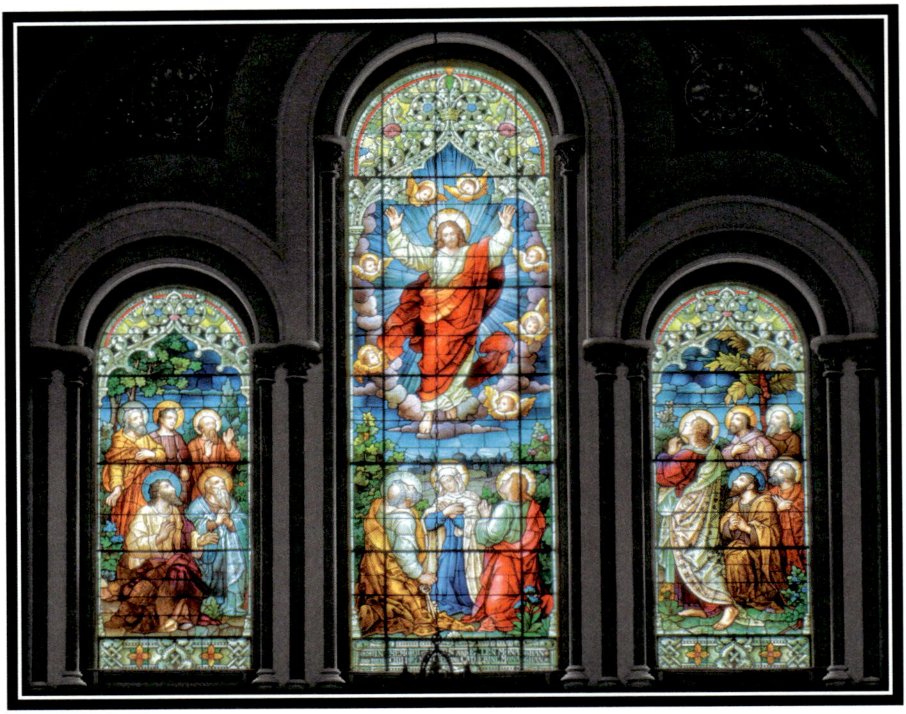

26. St. Joseph Catholic Church (1869-1892)

1802 Tulane Ave, Tulane-Gravier
Patrick Charles Keely, architect
D.M. Foley, Jr. and Thomas O'Neil, builders

Lower-level nave windows designed by the Dr. Heinrich Oidtmann Co. of Linnich, Germany. The Daily Picayune issue covering this church's 1892 dedication reports the original era of glass installed here as being fabricated at the "Royal Bavarian Stained Glass Manufactory" of Munich. PRC researchers attribute the clerestory windows specifically to Franz Mayer & Co. [pictured]. Other undetermined makers (*see page 8 and front cover*) are represented among this site's impressively broad collection.

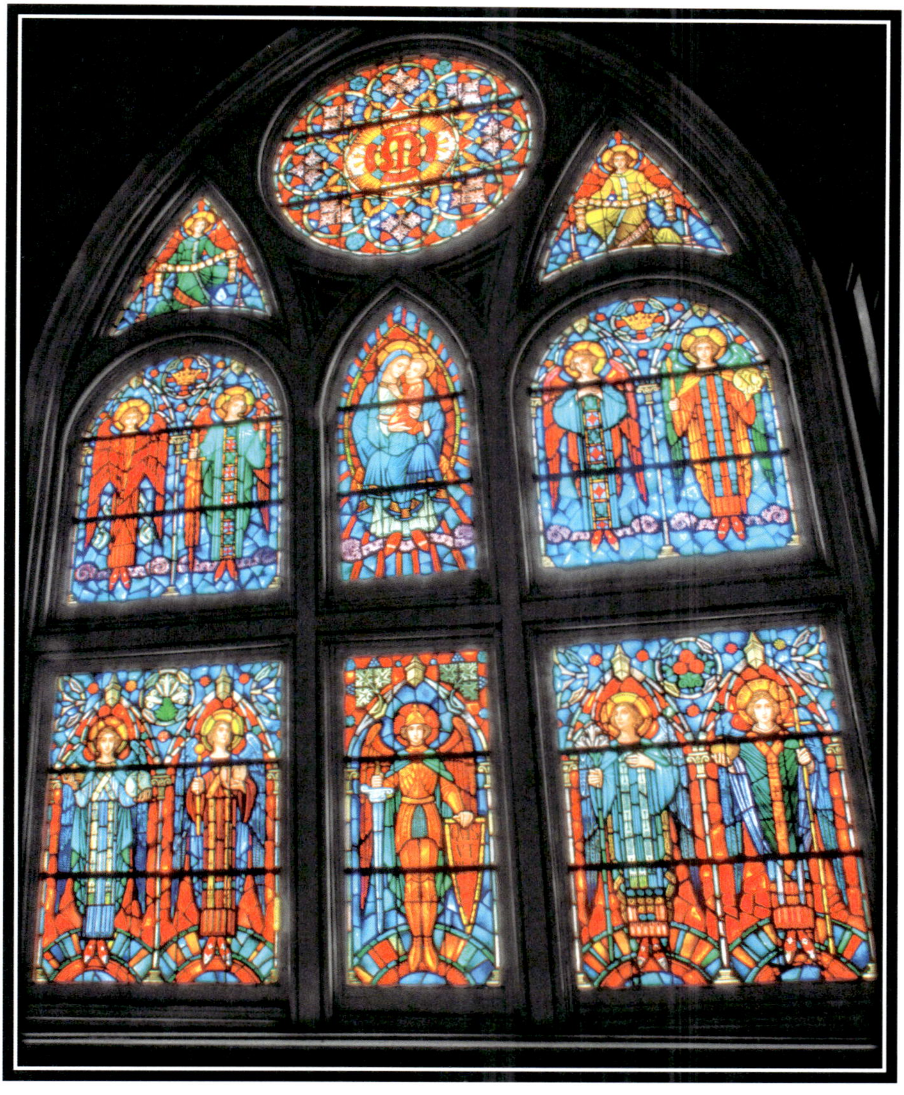

27. Our Lady of Good Counsel Catholic Church (1891-1894)

1307 Louisiana Ave, Touro
Thomas W. Carter, architect

Many of the late era windows at this site were made by Emil Frei Studios of St. Louis. Earlier installations of the 1920s are of unknown origin.

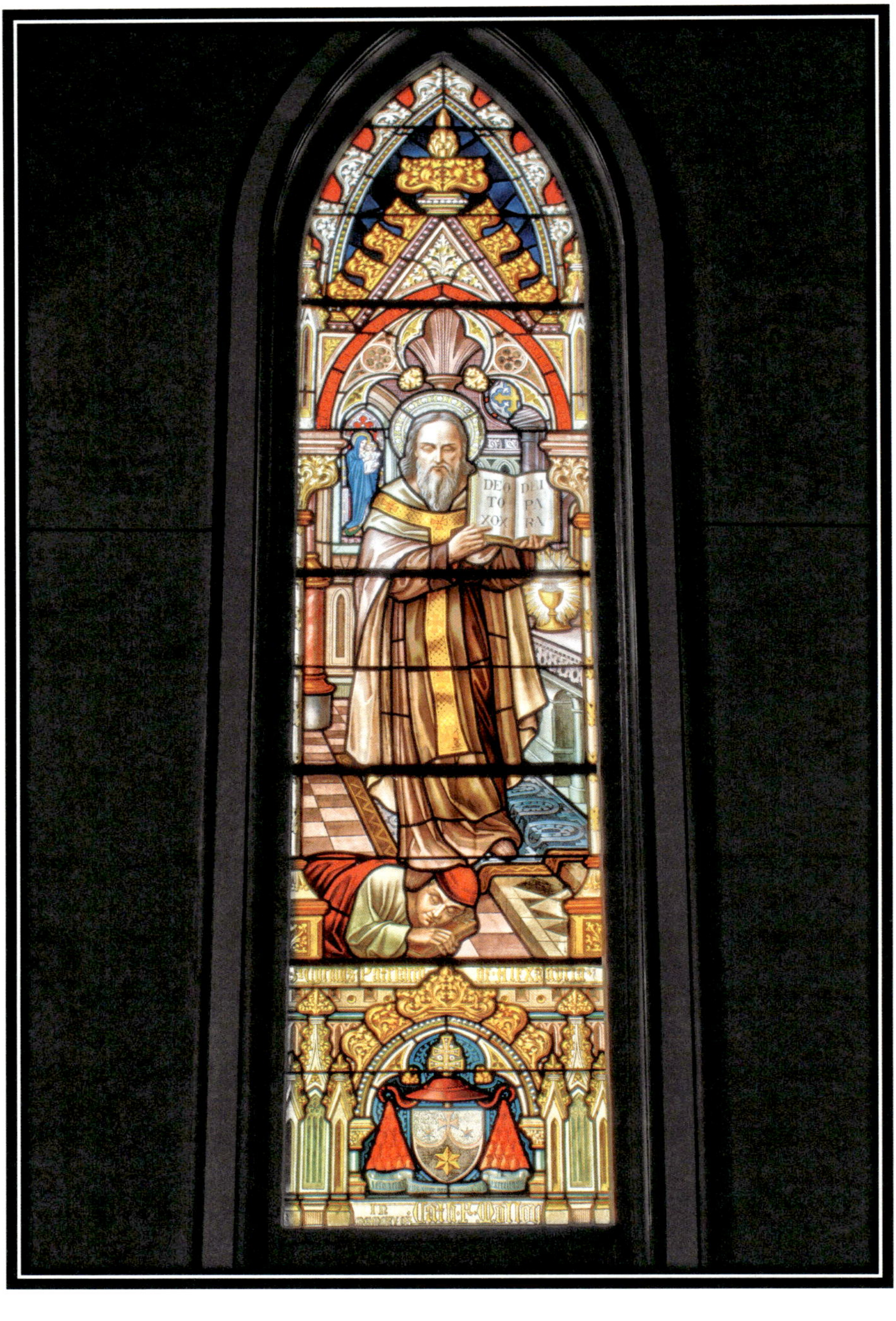
DEO
TO
XOX
DEI
PA
RA

◀28. Old Carmelite Monastery (1891-1895)

1236 N. Rampart St, French Quarter
James Freret, architect; Ferdinand Reusch, Jr., builder

Known more formally as the Monastery of St. Joseph & St. Teresa of the Discalceated Carmelite Nuns. Stained glass makers and installation dates undetermined.

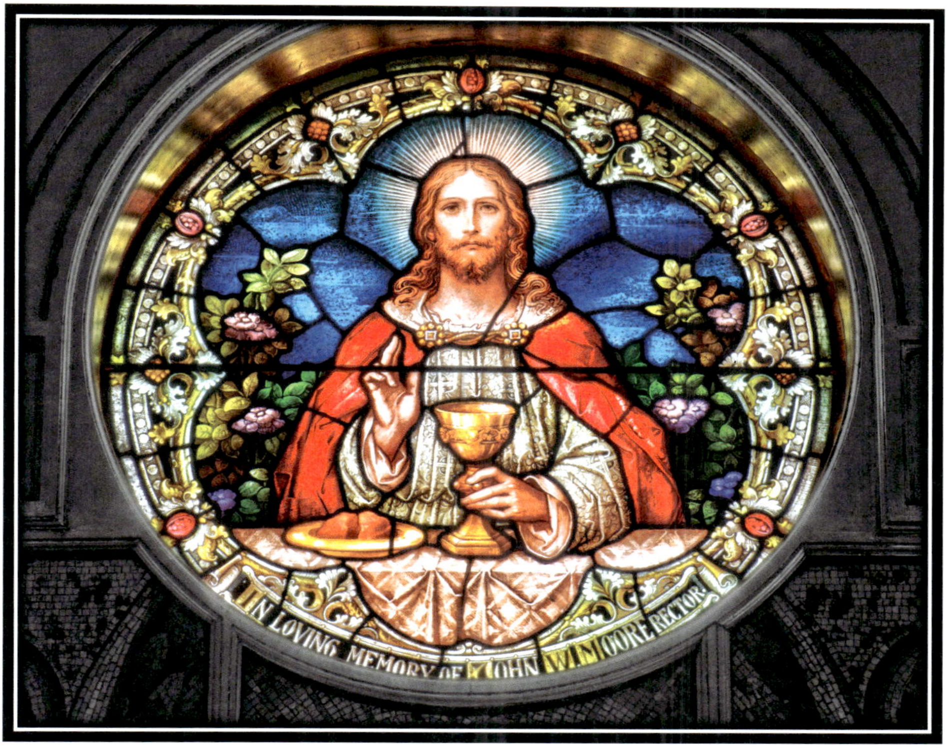

29. St. George's Episcopal Church (1899)

4600 St Charles Ave, Uptown
Southron R. Duval, architect

Find numerous panes designed by the Franz Mayer Co. of Munich [pictured] at this site. Other makers are present but undetermined. Multiple eras of installation span the years of 1900 to 1968.

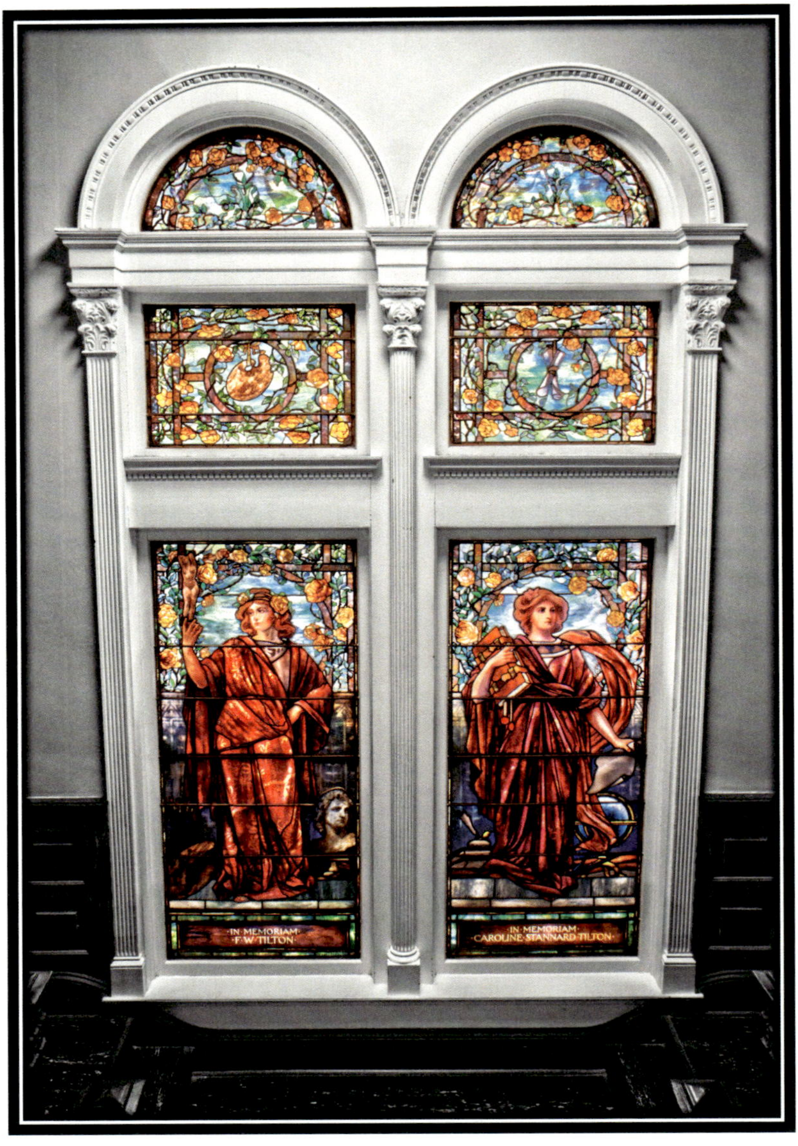

30. Tilton Memorial Library at Tulane University (1901)

6823 St Charles Ave, Audubon
Andry & Bendernagel, architects; George J. Glover, contractor

These turn-of-the-century examples by Tiffany Studios of New York City are original to the building and were installed at the time of its construction or very shortly thereafter.

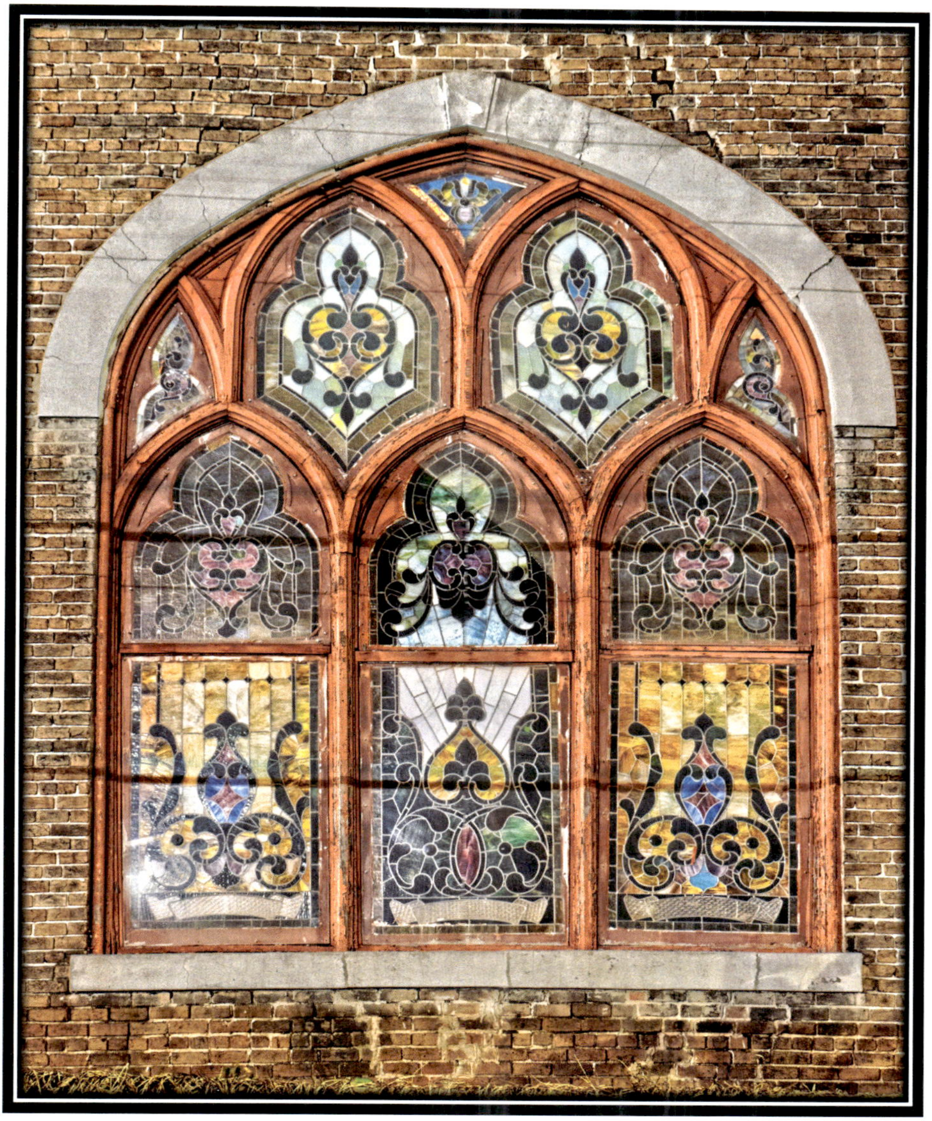

31. St. John's Evangelical Lutheran Church (1903-1904)

201 N. Prieur St, Tulane-Gravier
Spier & Rohns of Detroit, architects

Known as Grace Methodist Episcopal after 1917. Stained glass makers undetermined. Merged with First Methodist Church (*entry #78*) in 2007-2008 to form First Grace United Methodist. Structure now privately owned and inaccessible to the public.

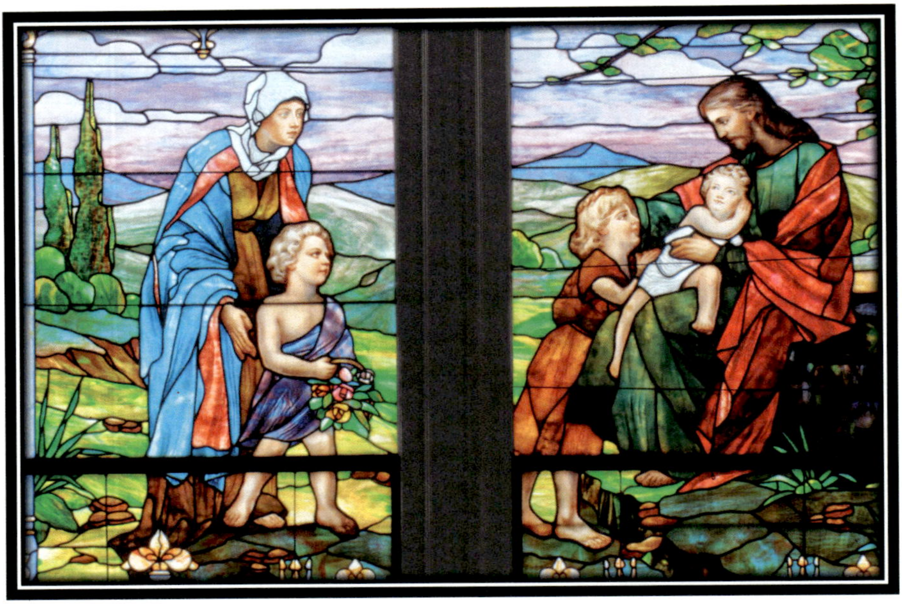

32. Salems Church [Evangelical Lutheran] (1905-1906)

4212 Camp St, Touro
Diboll & Owen, architects; J.A. Petty, builder

Primary windows by Jacoby Art Glass Company of St. Louis; installed 1908 to 1913. Other makers include the Albert H. Lips Studio of New Orleans.

---

33. Carondelet Street Evangelical Church (1906) ►

1829 Carondelet St, Central City
Diboll & Owen, architects; J.A. Petty, builder

Now known as First Emanuel Baptist Church. All available evidence strongly suggests the Jacoby Art Glass Company of St. Louis were the primary creators of the windows at this site, though the attribution is slightly less than iron clad. Other contributors are possible.

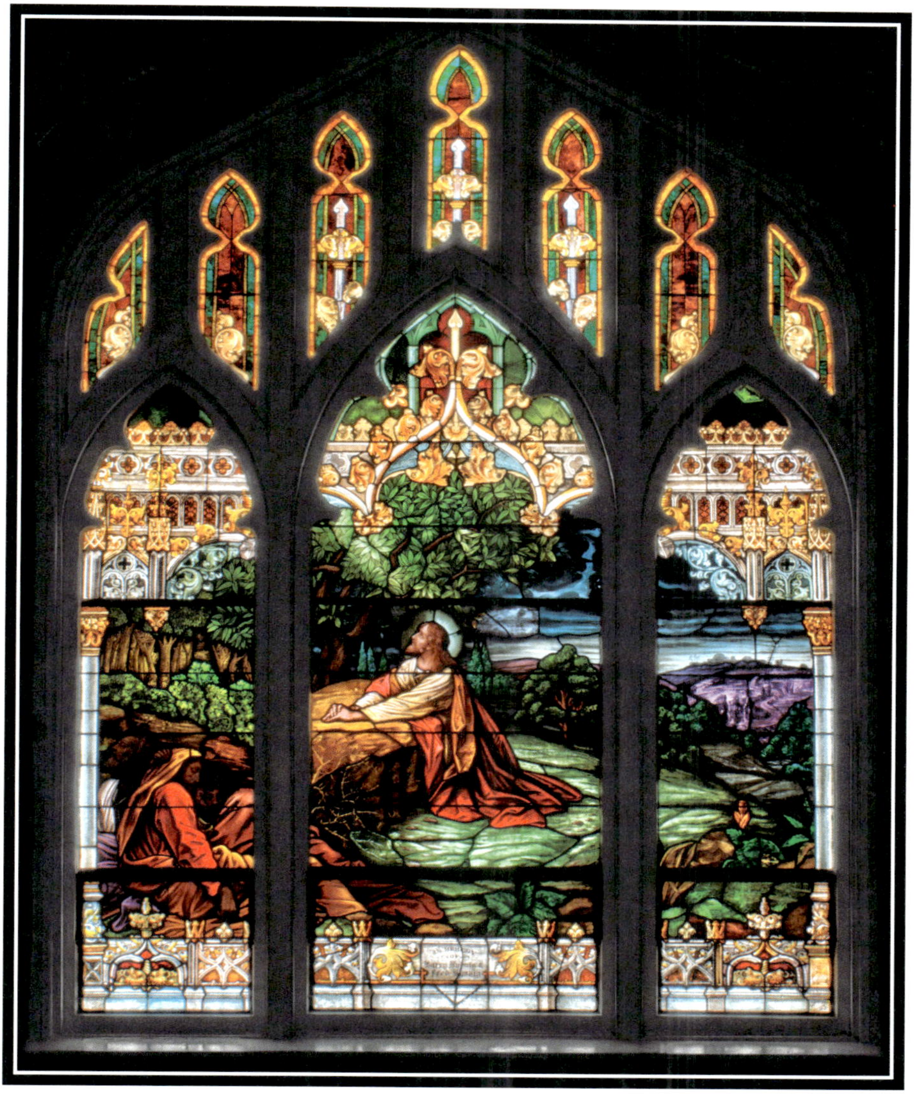

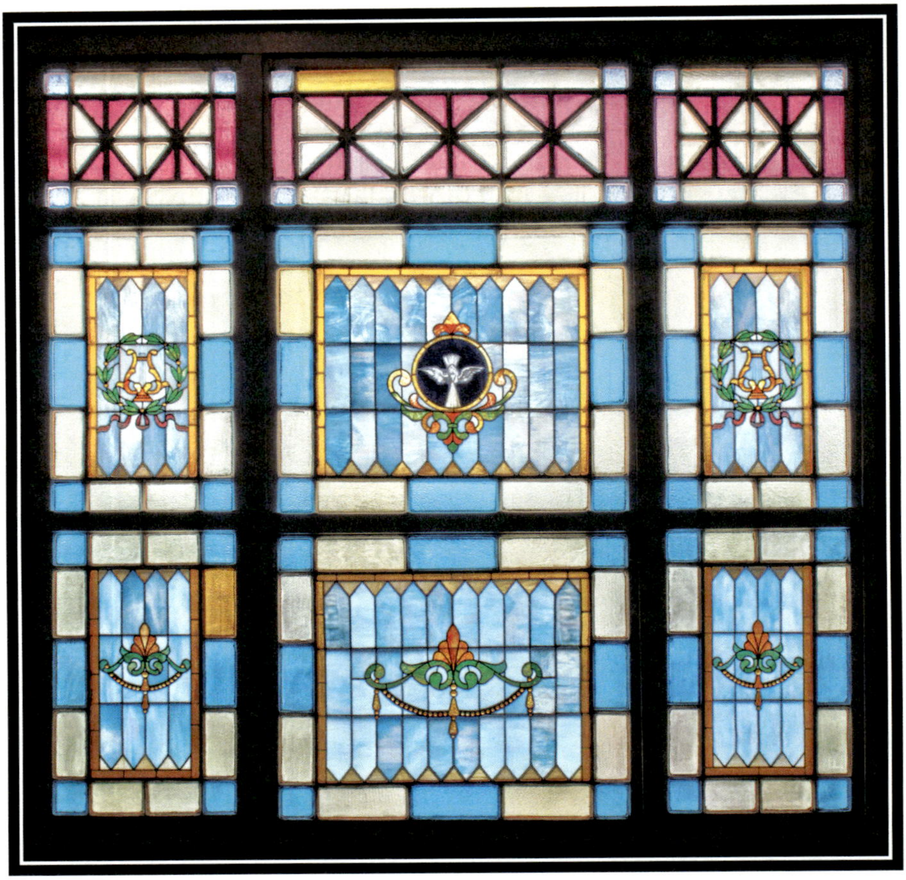

34. Second Methodist Episcopal Church, South (1907)
2525 Burgundy St, Marigny
Morris B. dePass, architect; A.W. Nyquist, builder

Now home to the architectural firm, "Perez.", the successor firm of August Perez & Associates noted in entries #205 and #208. Stained glass makers and dates of installation undetermined.

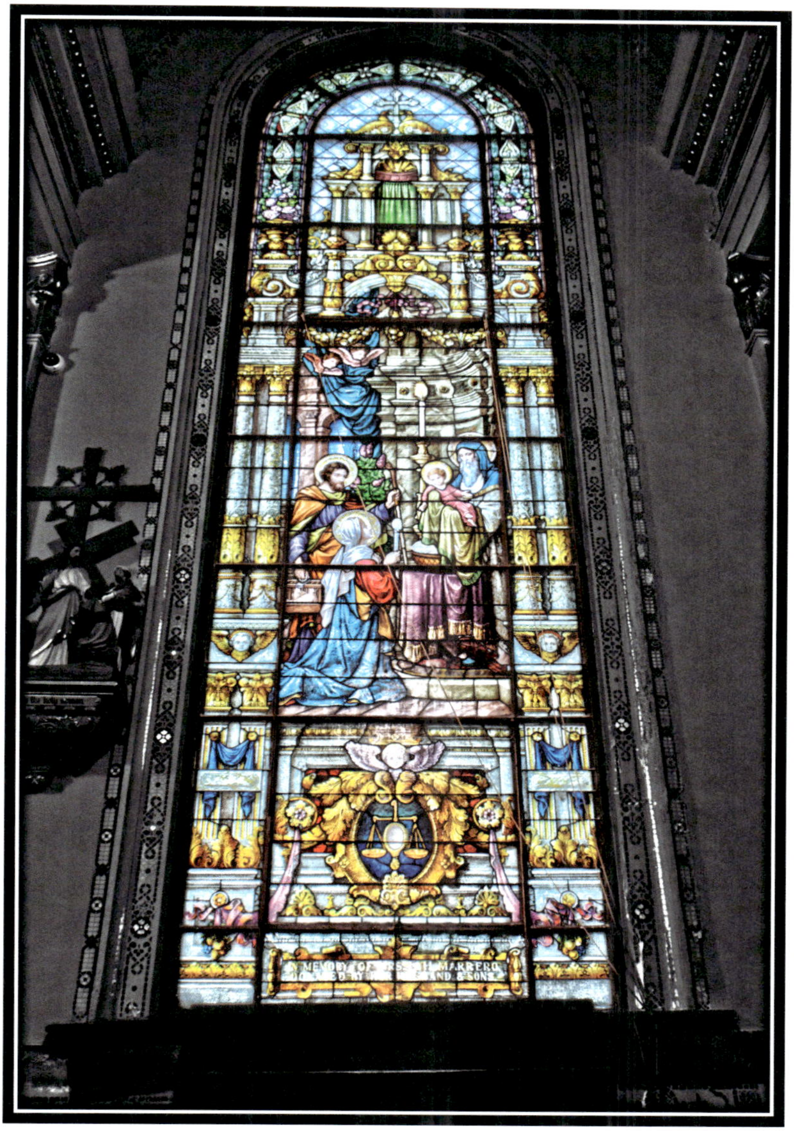

35. Mater Dolorosa Catholic Church (1908-1909)

1230 S. Carrollton Ave, Leonidas
Theodore Brune, architect; Petty & Erwin, builders

PRC researchers attribute the windows at this site to the Emil Frei Co. of St. Louis. Dates of installation are undetermined.

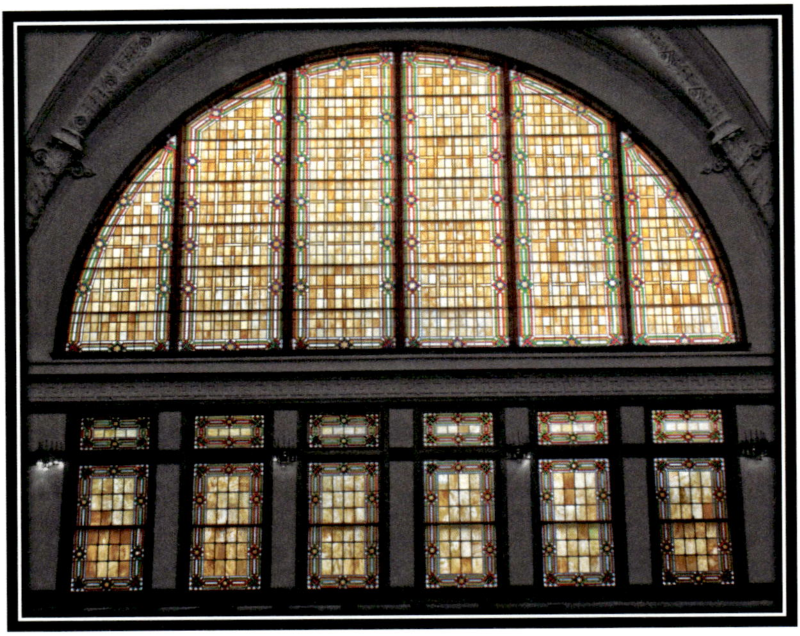

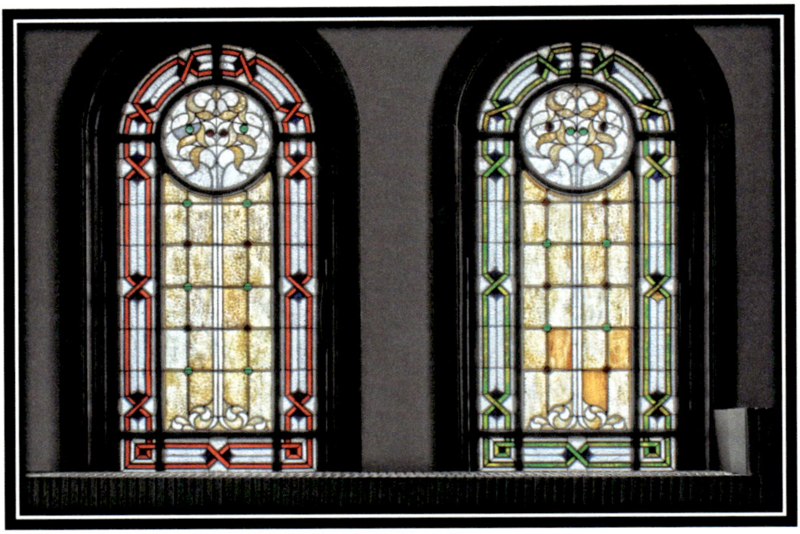

36. Touro Synagogue (1909)

4238 St Charles Ave, Touro
Emile Weil, architect; George J. Glover, builder

Primary stained glass makers undetermined. Two secondary panes by Ida Rittenberg Kohlmeyer were installed in the 1990s.

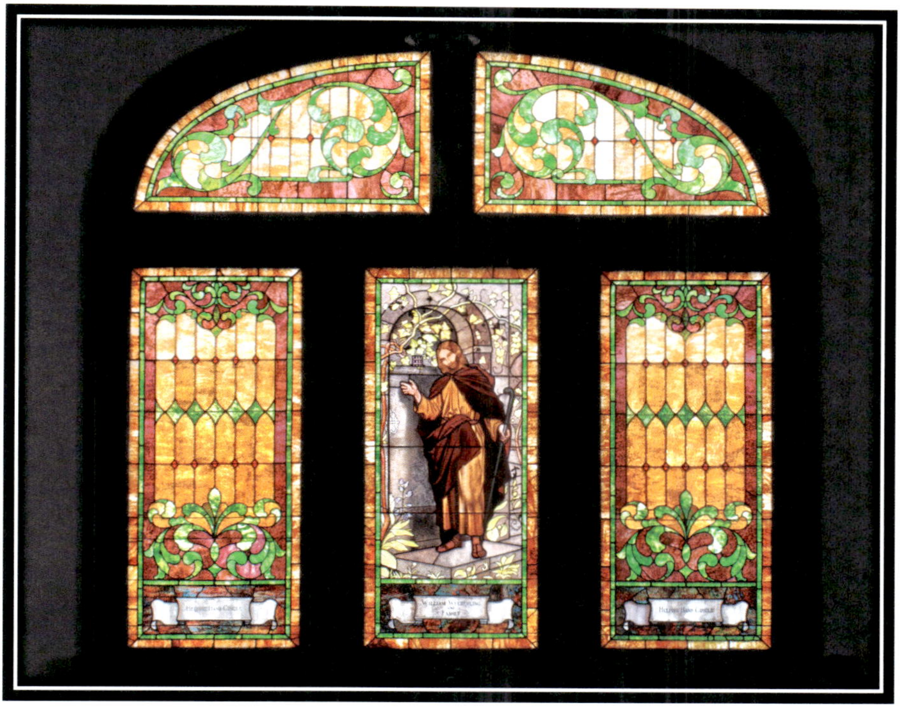

37. Trinity Lutheran Church (1911)

620 Eliza St, Algiers Point
B.W. Borne, builder

Stained glass makers and dates of installation undetermined.

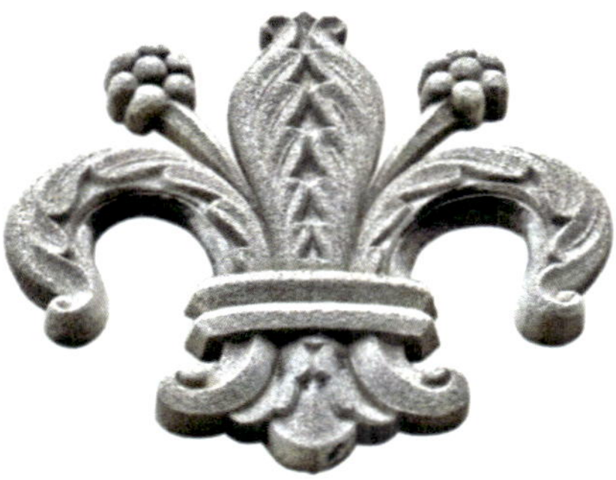

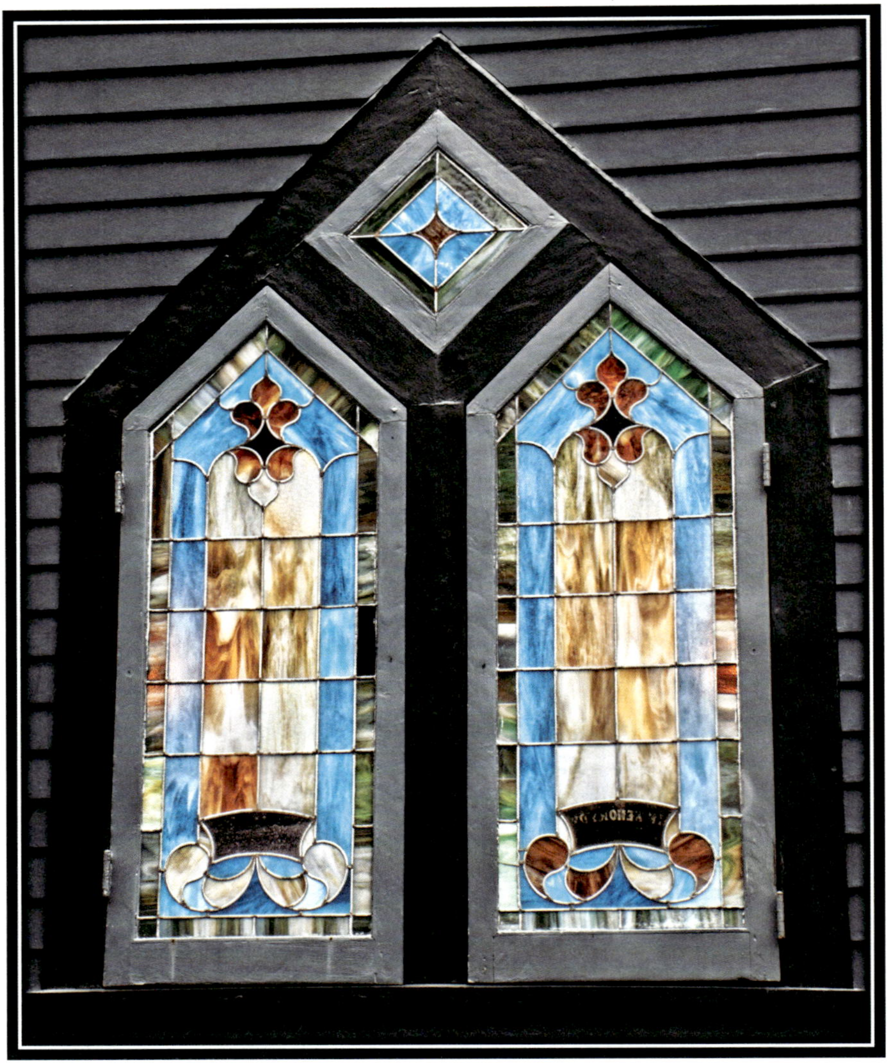

38. Mount Calvary Evangelical Lutheran Church (1912-1913)

2900 Grand Route St John St, Fairgrounds
J.H. West, architect; L. Lavie & G. Landenwetsch, builders

Now a private home, inaccessible to the public. Stained glass makers and dates of installation undetermined.

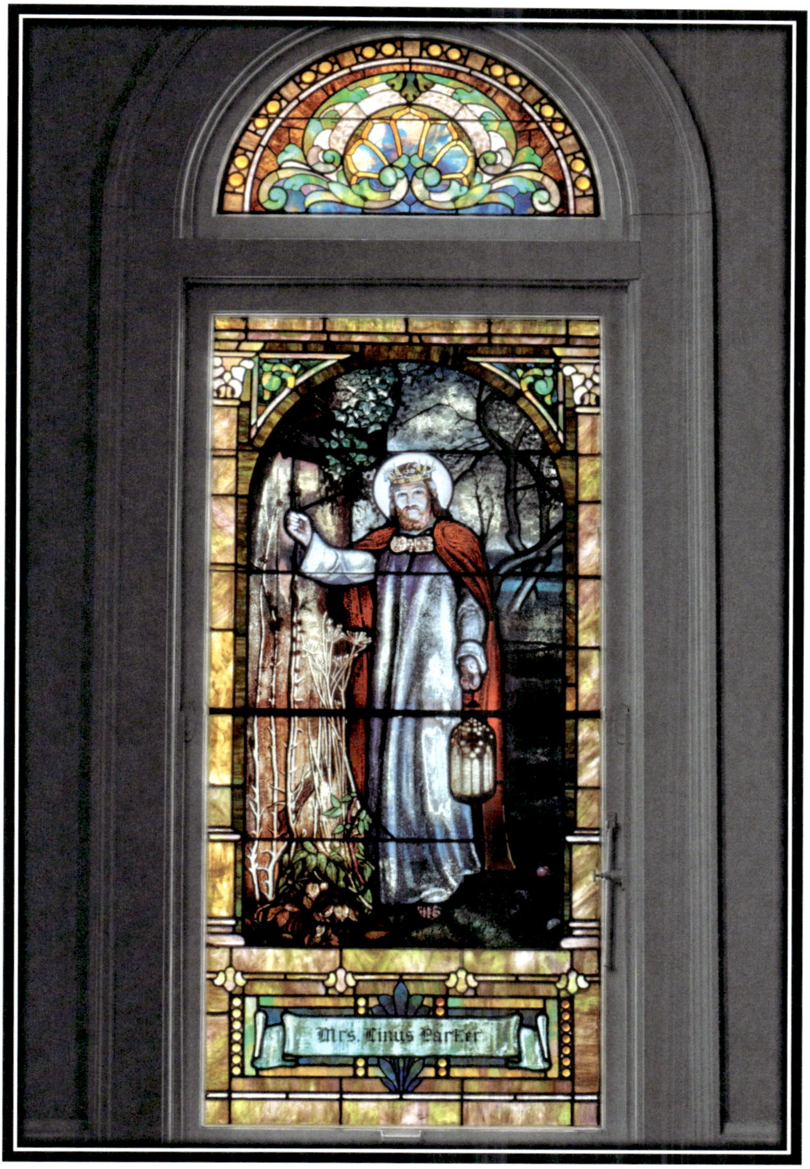

39. Carrollton Methodist Episcopal Church (1914)

921 S. Carrollton Ave, East Carrollton
Architect undetermined

Now known as Carrollton United Methodist. Stained glass makers and dates of installation undetermined.

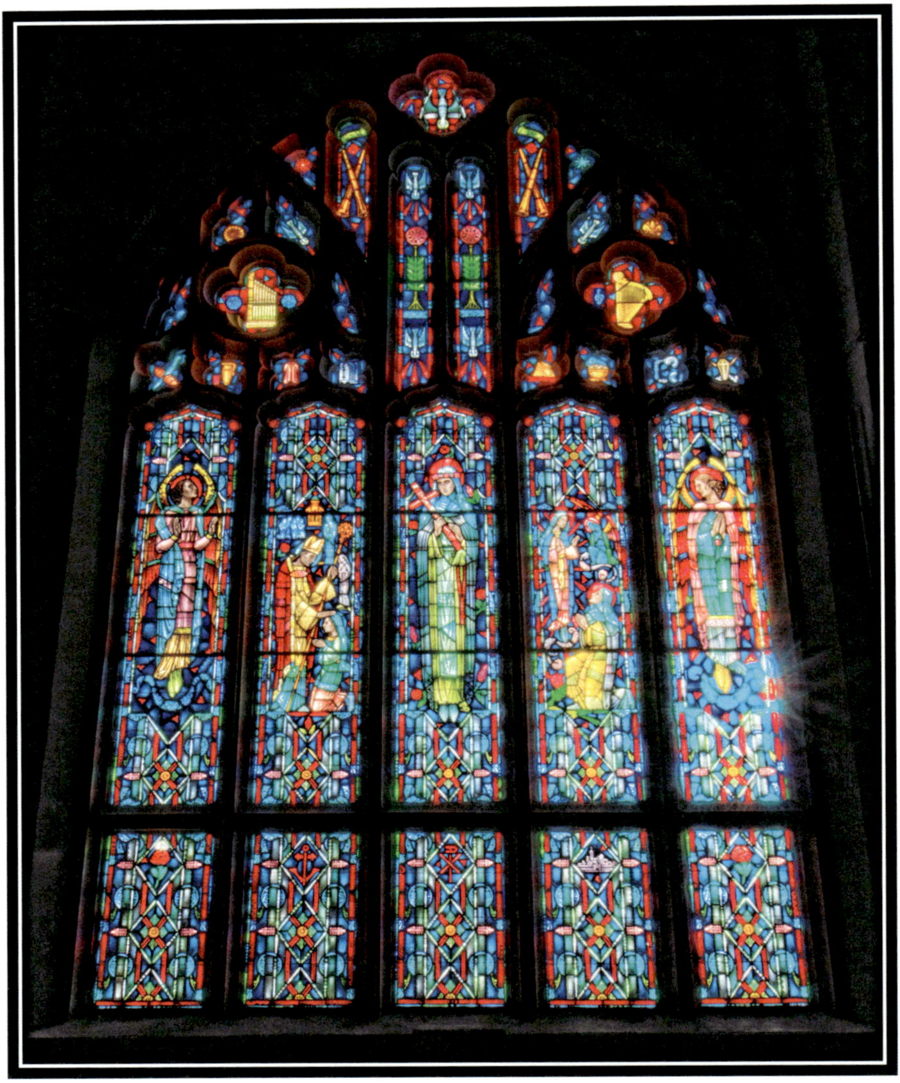

40. St. Rose de Lima Catholic Church (1914-1915)

2541 Bayou Rd, Seventh Ward
Paul Andry, architect; George J. Glover, contractor

Deconsecrated post-Katrina; now known as Southern Rep Theatre. Stained glass makers at this site include Conrad Schmitt Studios of Milwaukee [pictured], Emil Frei Inc. of St. Louis and Dr. Heinrich Oidtmann Studios of Linnich, Germany. Dates of installation are undetermined.

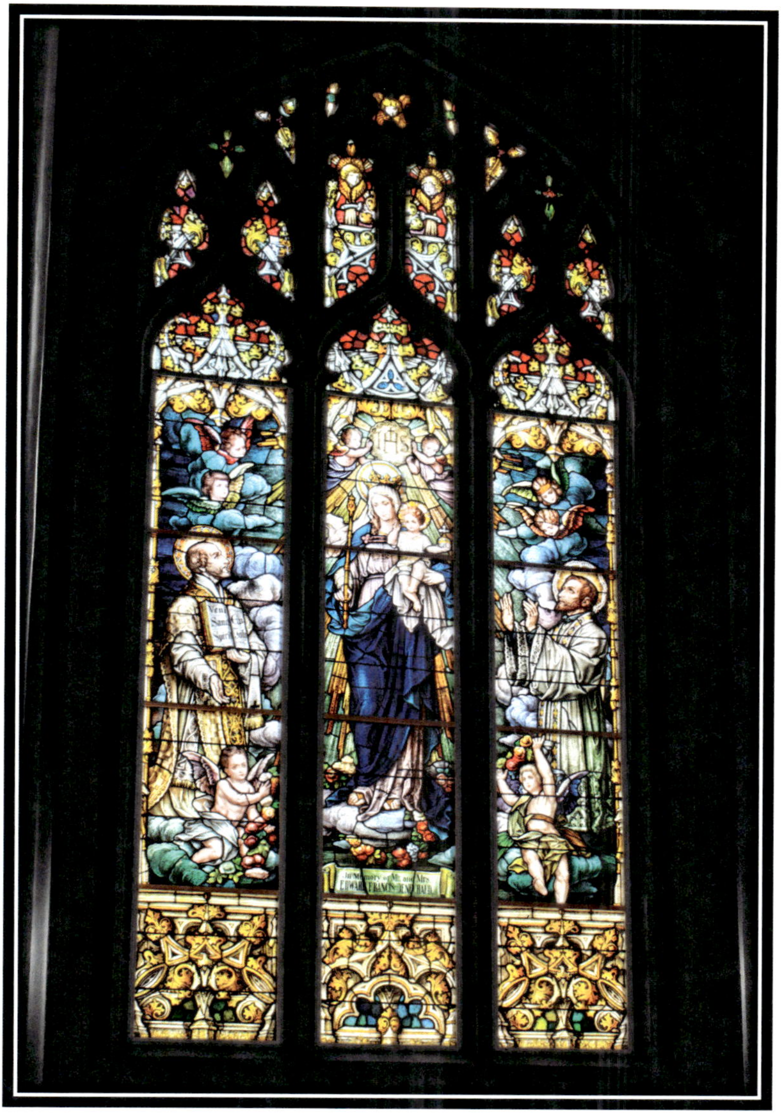

41. Church of the Most Holy Name of Jesus [Catholic] at Loyola University (1914-1918)

6367 St Charles Ave, Audubon
DeBuys, Churchill & Labouisse, architects

Nave windows by John Morgan & Sons of New York City [pictured] and Emil Frei Studios of St. Louis were installed during and shortly after construction. Clerestory windows installed in 1941.

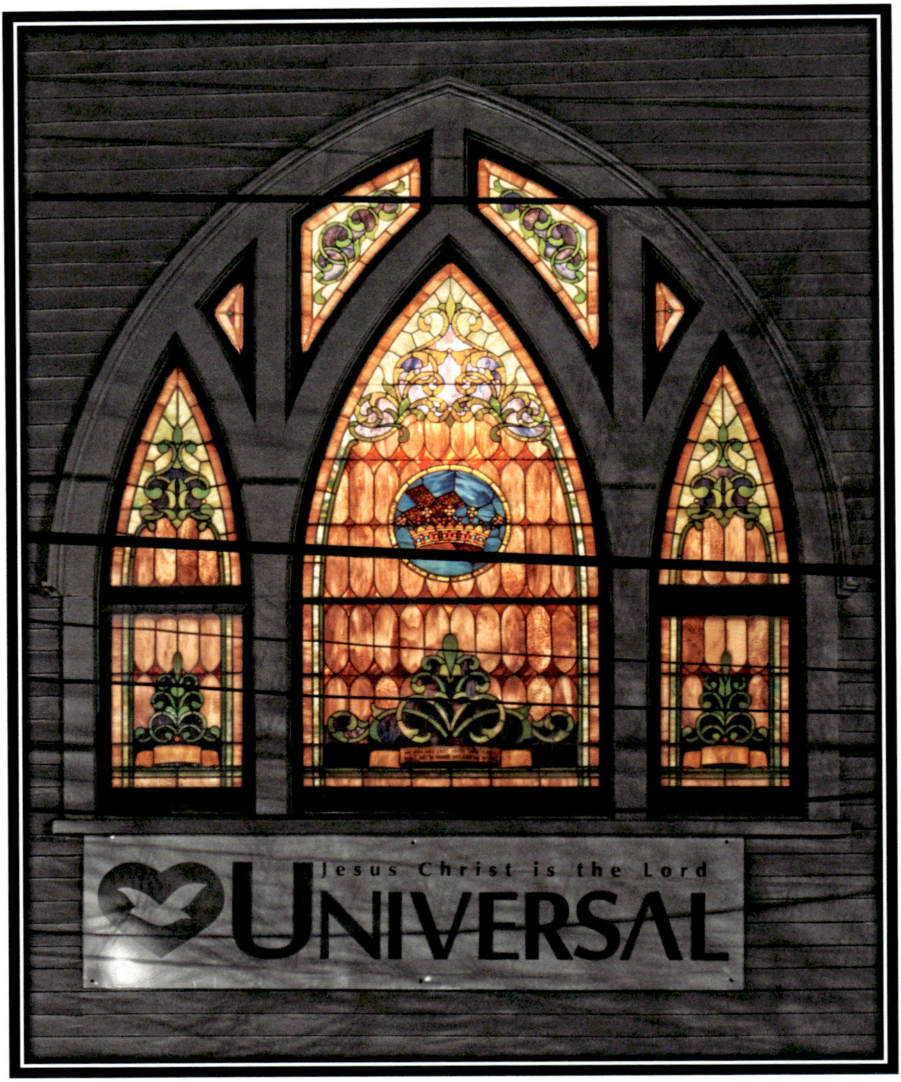

42. Immanuel Evangelical Lutheran Church (1918)

138 N. Broad St, Tulane-Gravier
G. Emile & Ernest Edward Reimann, builders

Now known as Universal Church. Stained glass makers undetermined.

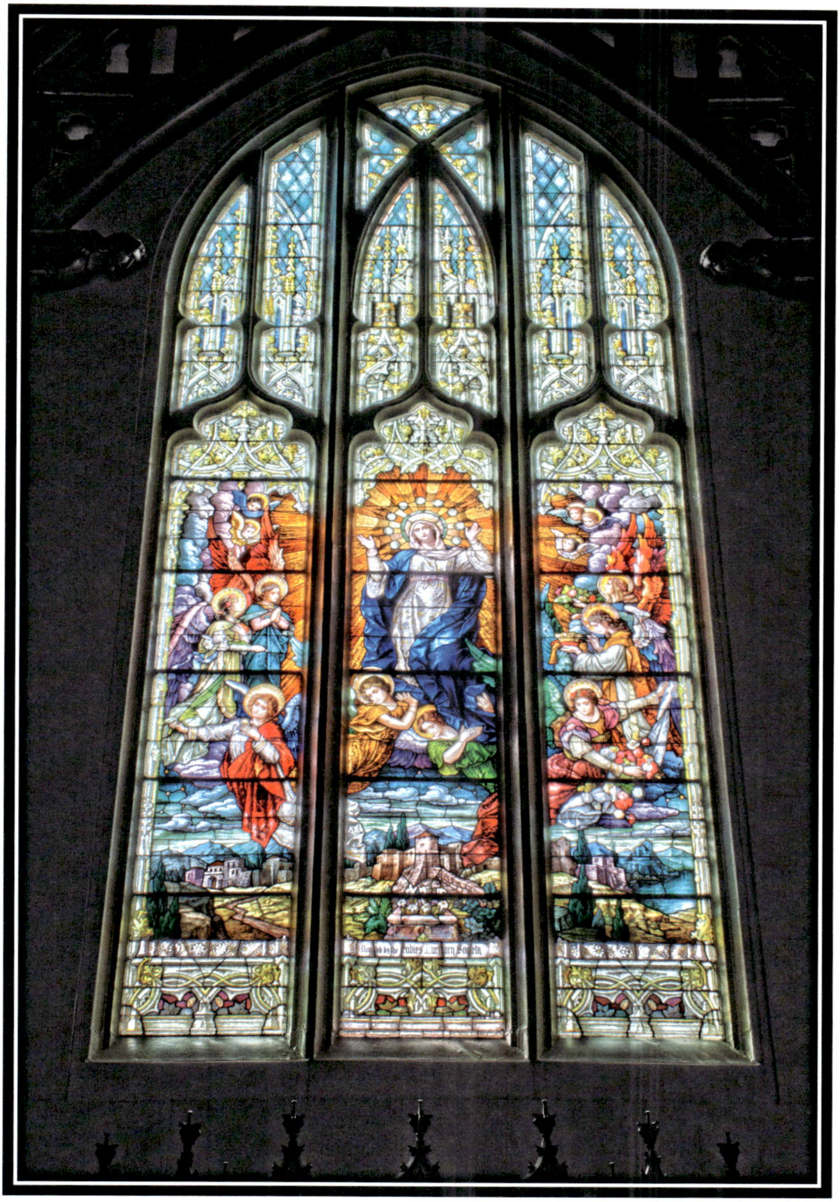

43. St. Francis of Assisi Catholic Church (1914-1921)

631 State St, West Riverside
Col. Allison Owen of Diboll & Owen, architect

Stained glass by Emil Frei Studios of St. Louis; installed 1922.

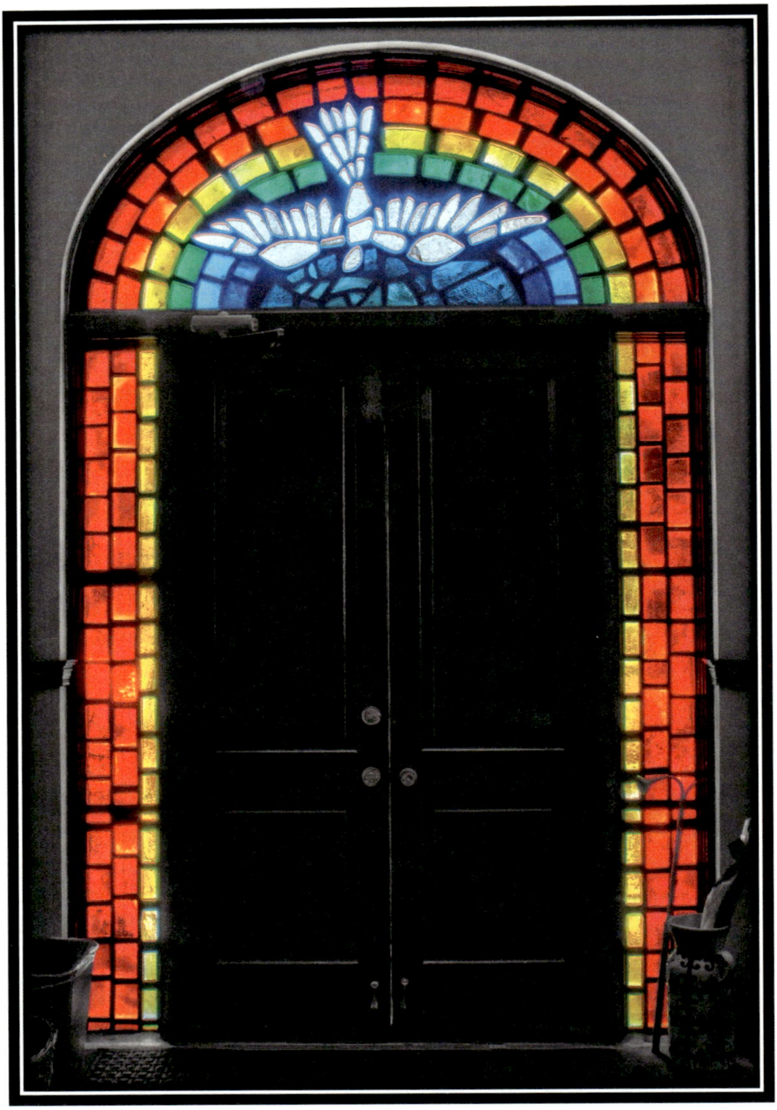

44. Algiers Methodist Episcopal Church, South (1921-1922)

637 Opelousas St, Algiers Point
T.L. Brodie, architect; J.A. Petty, general contractor

Now known as Algiers United Methodist Church. *Dalle de verre* windows designed and fabricated by Milton Pounds of Pounds Stained Glass Studio, Covington; installed 1979.

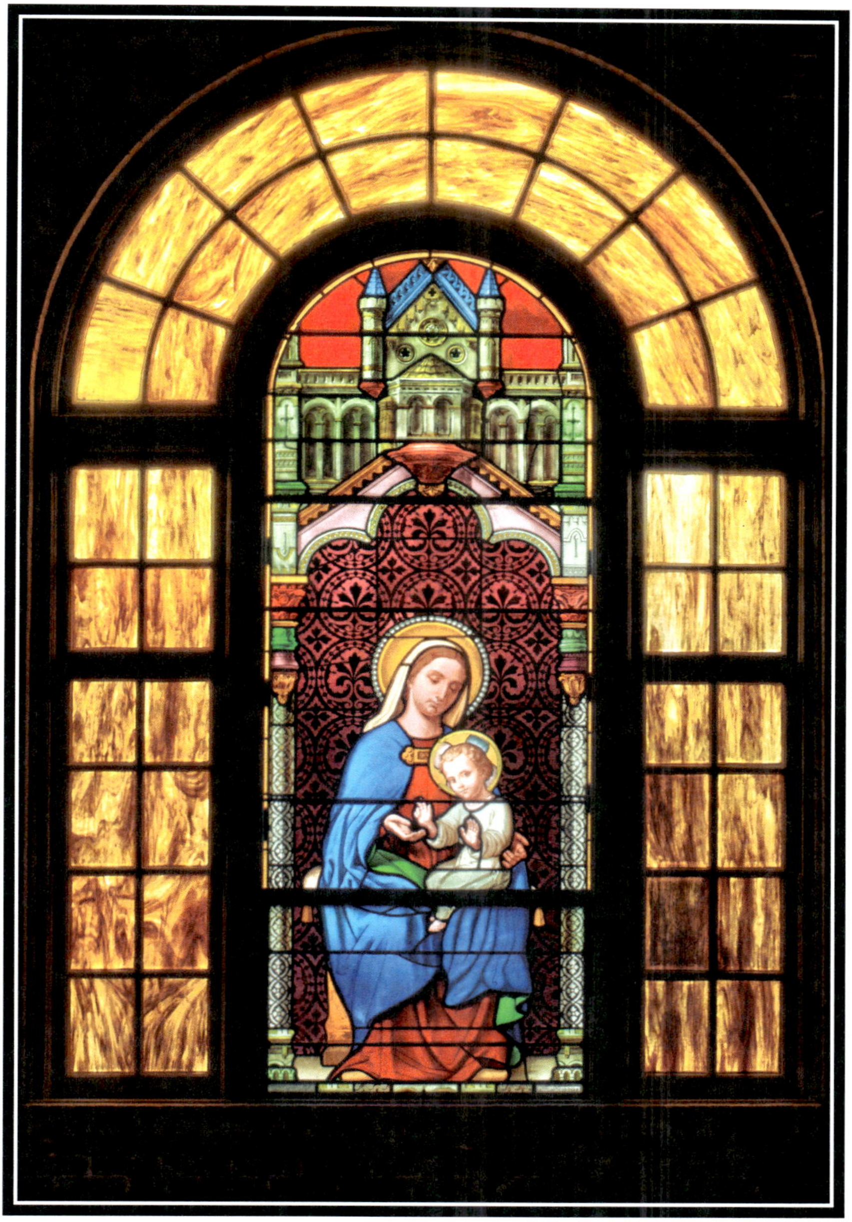

45. Annunciation Catholic Church (1922)

2301 Marais St, St. Roch
William Nash, architect

Primary panes transplanted from prior sanctuary; makers undetermined.

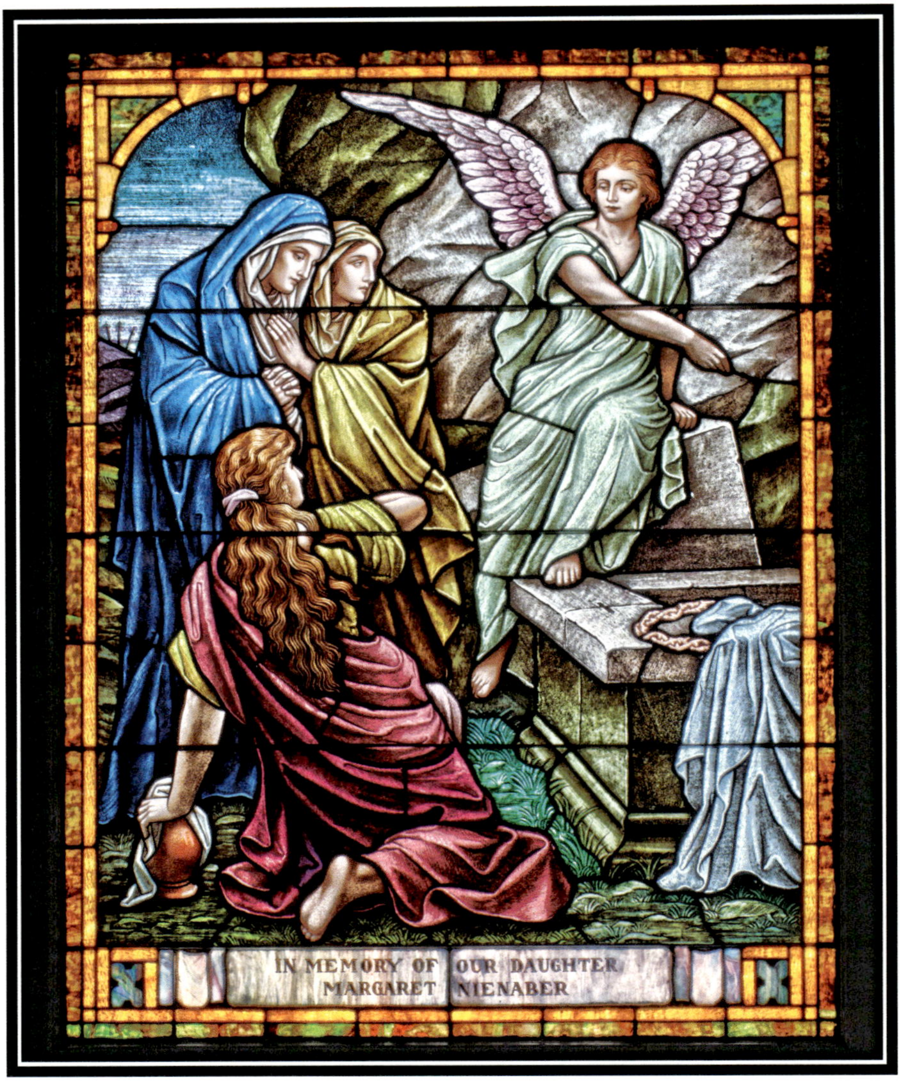

46. St. Matthew Evangelical Church (1922-1923)

1333 S. Carrollton Ave, East Carrollton
William Drago, architect; J.A. Petty, builder

Now known as Central St. Matthew United Church of Christ. Stained glass makers at this site include Emil Frei Inc. of St. Louis; other contributors are probable.

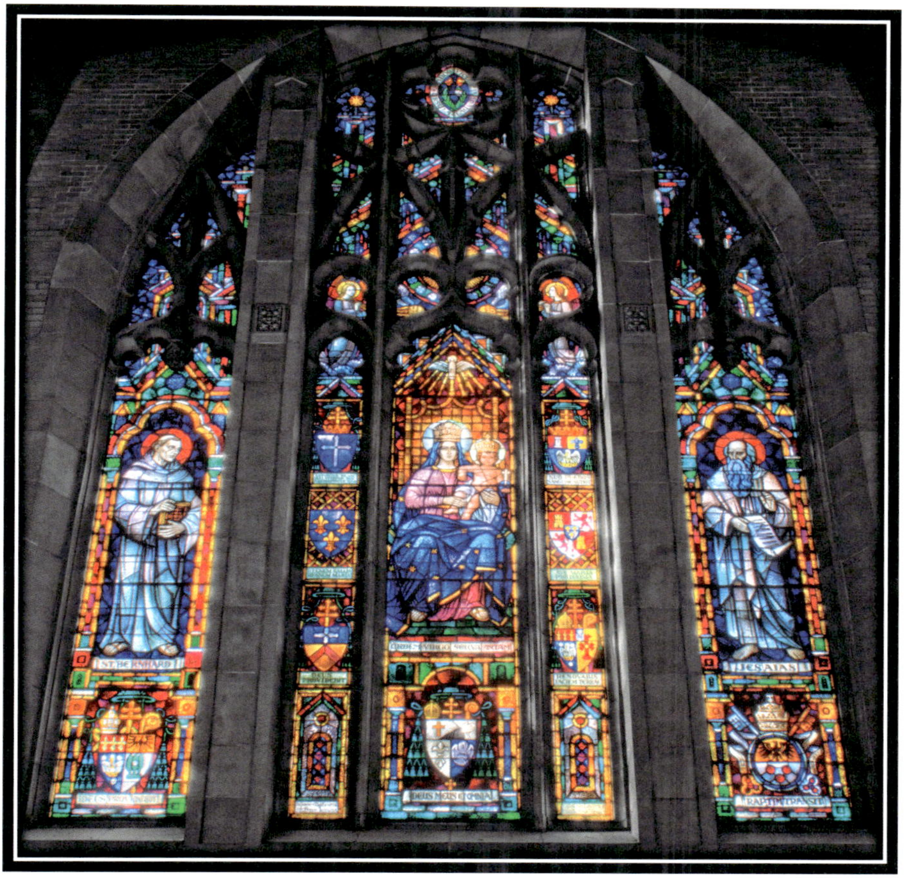

47. National Votive Shrine of Our Lady of Prompt Succor [Catholic] (1922-1923)

2701 State St, Audubon
H.L. Burton & Albert Bendernagel, architects
George J. Glover, builder

Emil Frei Studios of St. Louis [pictured] were the primary designers of the stained glass at this site. Multiple panes behind the high altar were designed by the Franz Mayer Co. of Munich in 1897 and 1902 and transplanted from the prior Shrine.

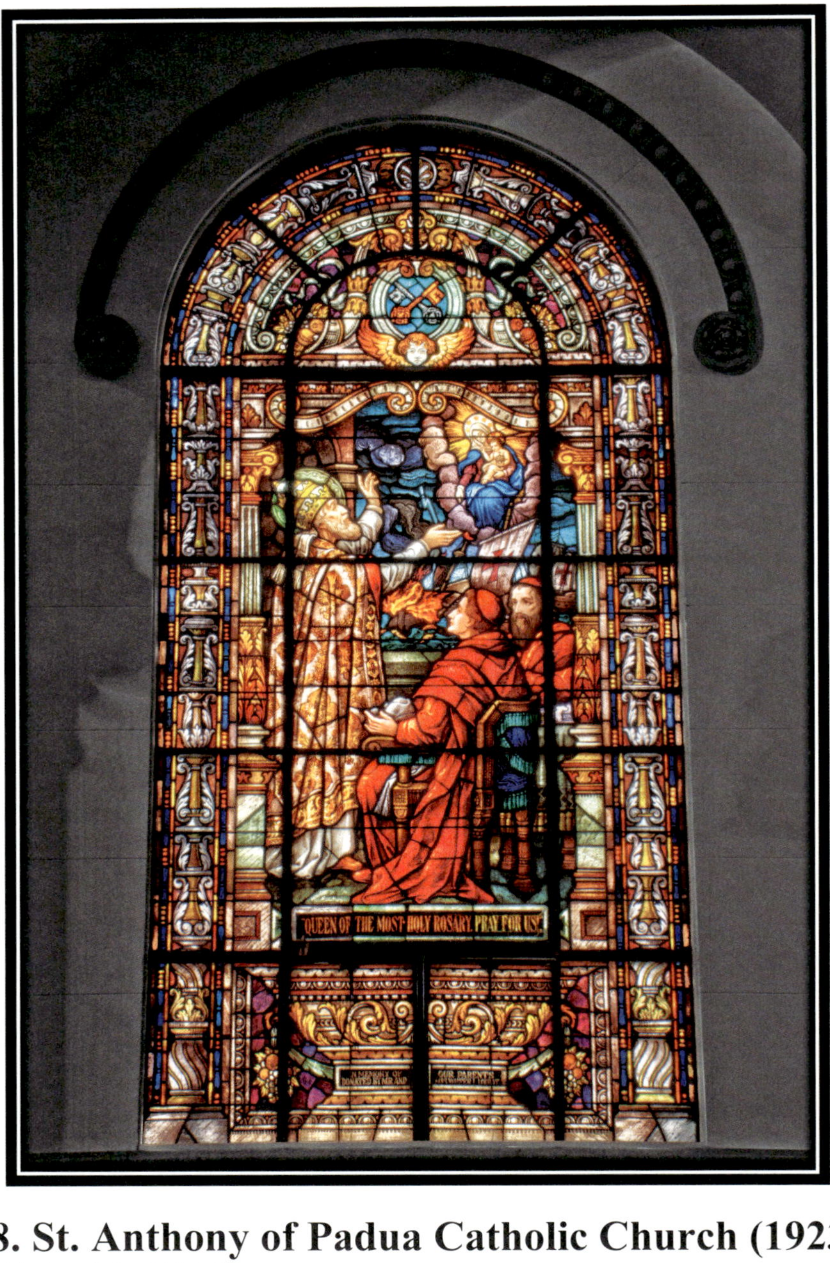

48. St. Anthony of Padua Catholic Church (1923)

4640 Canal St, Mid-City
Toledano, Wogan & Bernard, architects; Lionel F. Favret, contractor

PRC researchers attribute the windows at this site to the Emil Frei Co. of St. Louis; installed in the late 1920s.

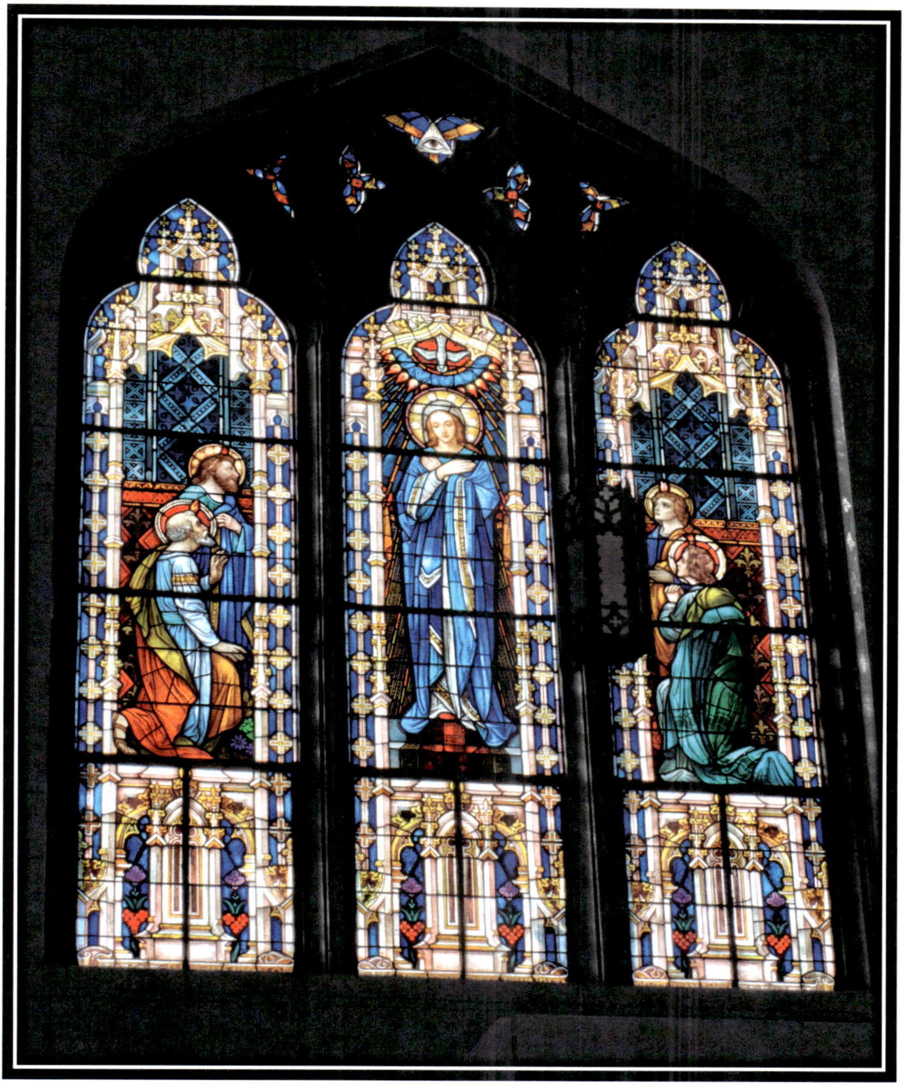

49. St. Cecilia Catholic Church (1923-1924)

1015 France St, St. Claude
Architect undetermined

Now known as PACE Catholic Charities. Stained glass makers and dates of installation undetermined.

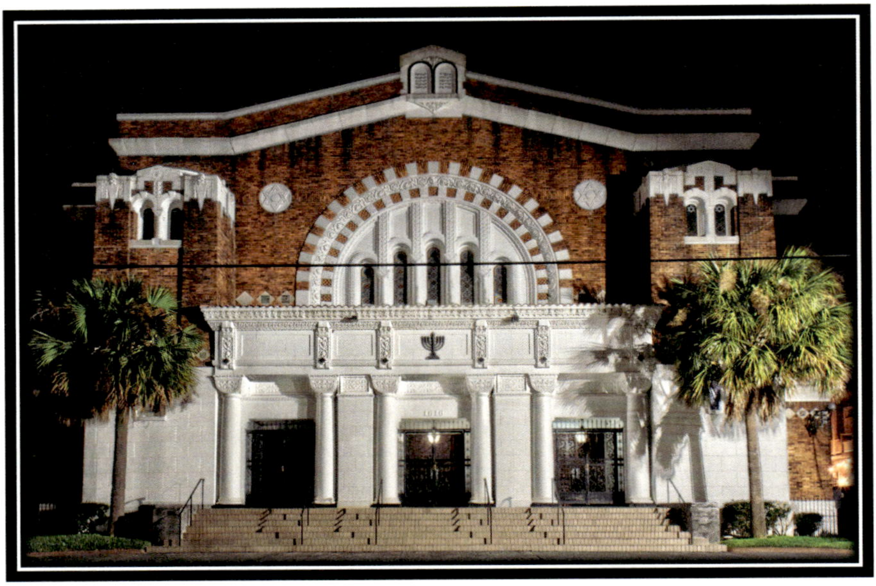

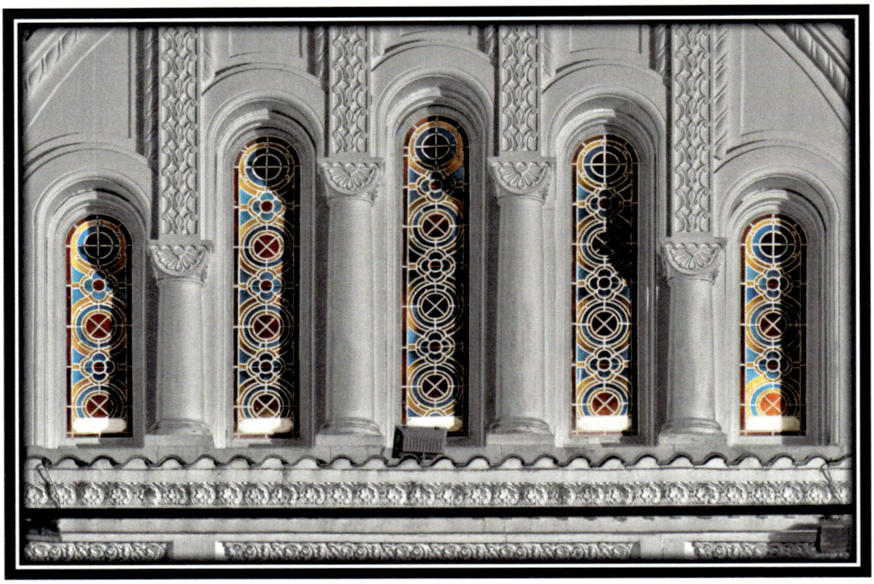

50. Beth Israel Synagogue (1924)

1613 Robert C Blakes Sr Dr, Central City
Emile Weil, architect; Charles Gibert, contractor

Now known as New Home Family Worship Center. Stained glass makers and dates of installation undetermined.

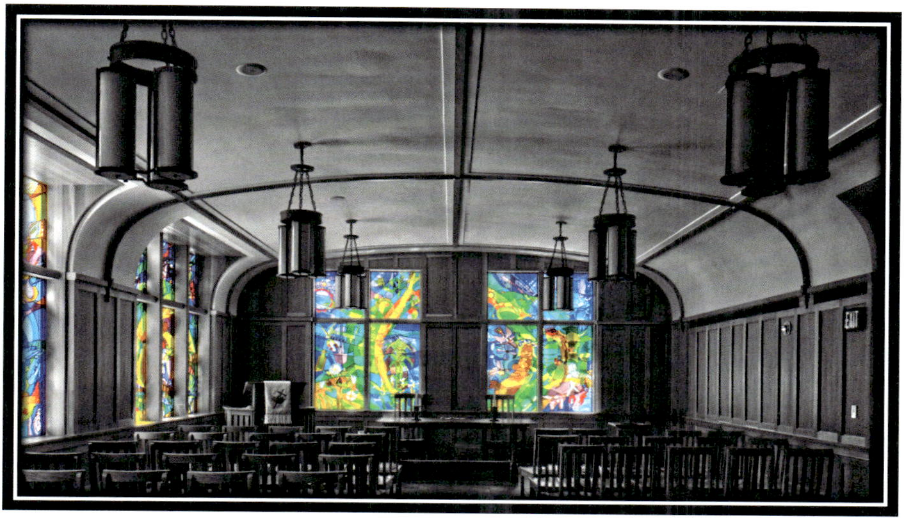

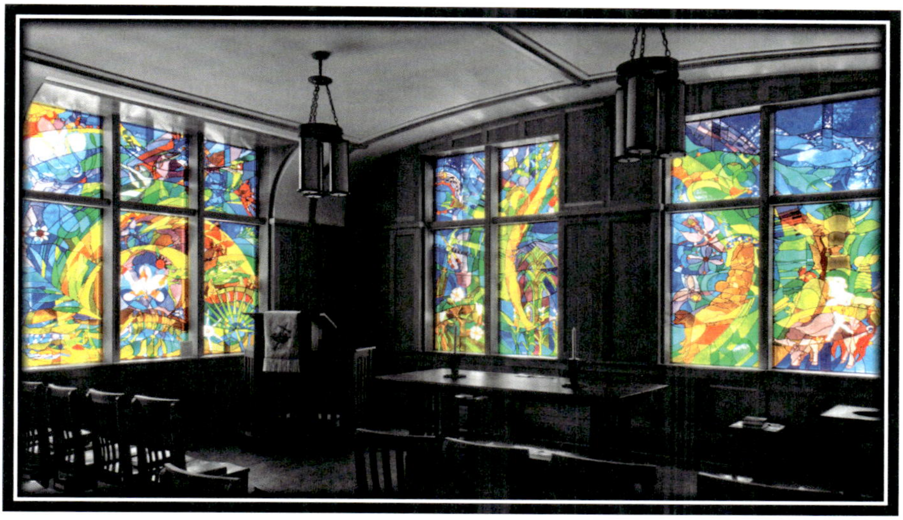

51. St. Charles Avenue Presbyterian Church ~ Sunday School Building (1923-1925)

1545 State St, Audubon
W.W. Van Meter, architect

Stained glass by Stephen Wilson of Baton Rouge; installed 2012.

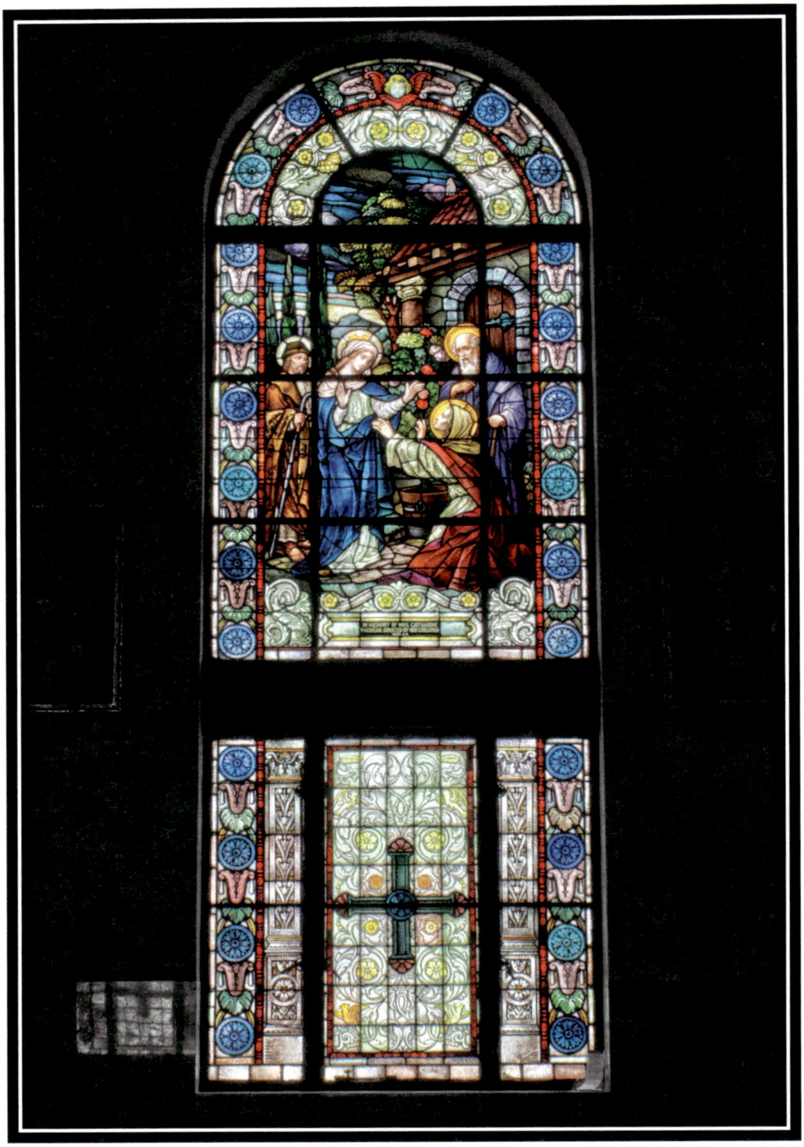

52. Our Lady of the Rosary Catholic Church (1924-1925)

3368 Esplanade Ave, Bayou St. John
Rathbone DeBuys, architect

PRC researchers attribute the primary windows at this site to Emil Frei Inc. Dome windows by Wagner Studios of New York installed in 1946.

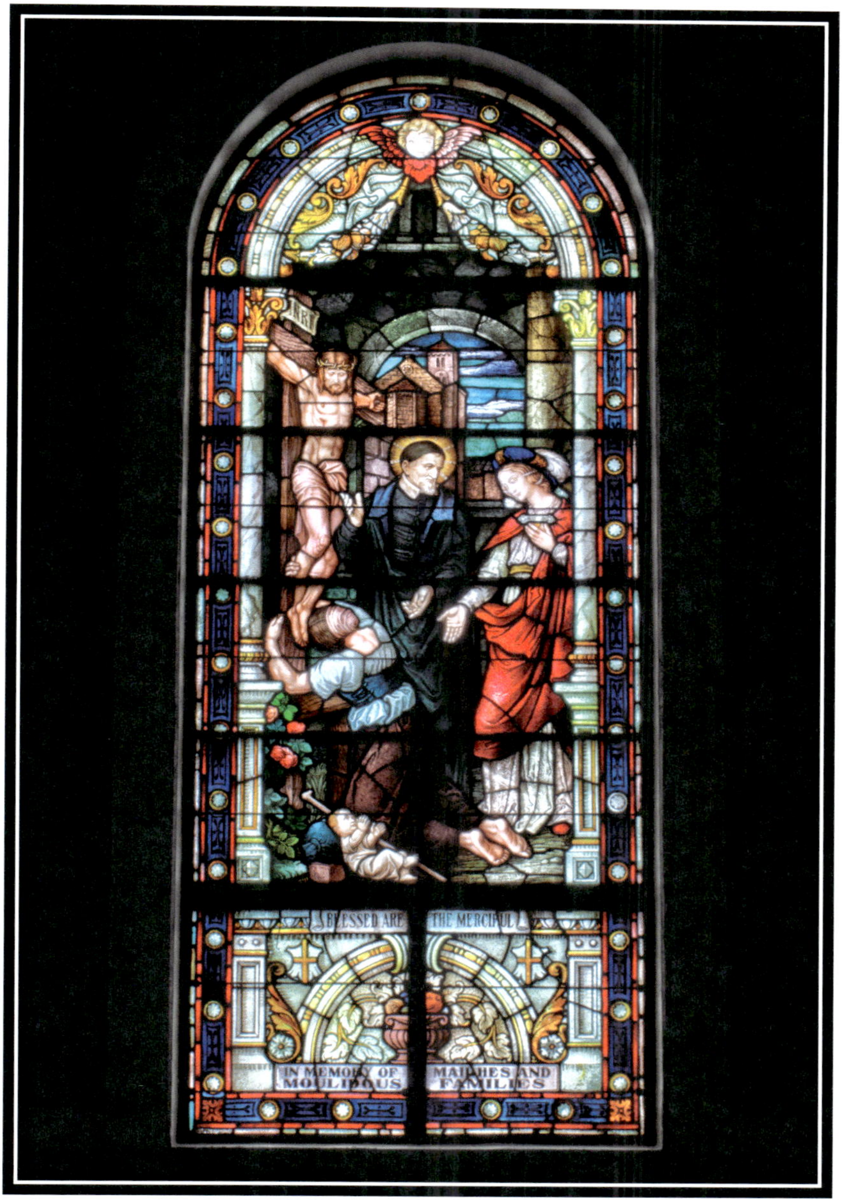

53. St. Henry's Catholic Church (1925)

812 General Pershing St, East Riverside
Diboll & Owen, architects; Lionel F. Favret, builder

Primary stained glass windows by Emil Frei Inc. of St. Louis; other contributors likely.

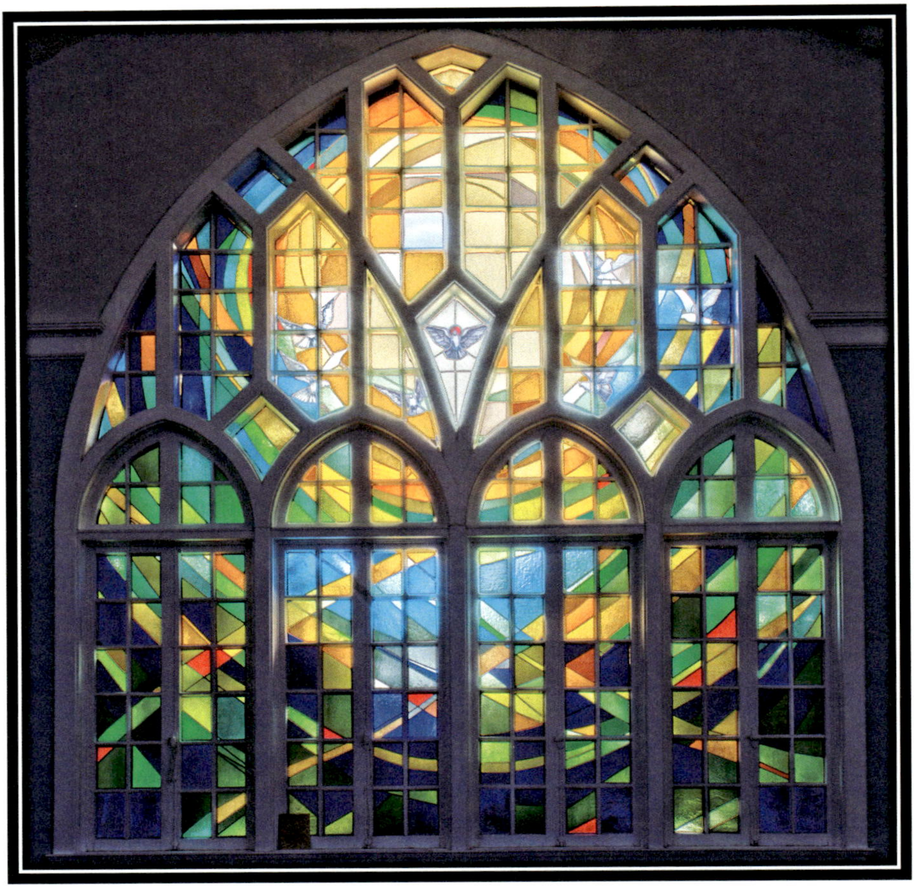

54. St. Paul's Evangelical Church (1925-1926)

600 Eleonore St, West Riverside
Edward L. Markel, architect; Henry G. DeFraites, builder

Now known as St. Paul's United Church of Christ. The designer of the window pictured is undetermined. Another major narrative window of the exact same size at this site bears an Attenhofer's corporate insignia and was fabricated and installed by Attenhofer's Stained Glass Studio of Metairie. Company founder Ken Attenhofer was most likely the designer and it was most likely installed in the 1980s or 1990s.

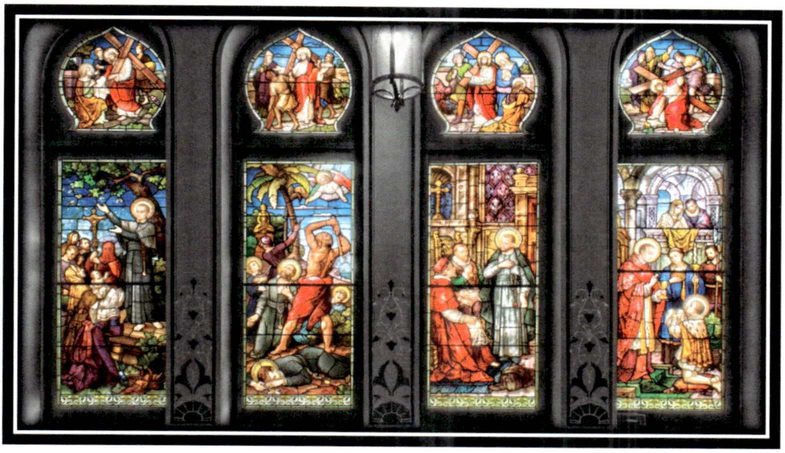

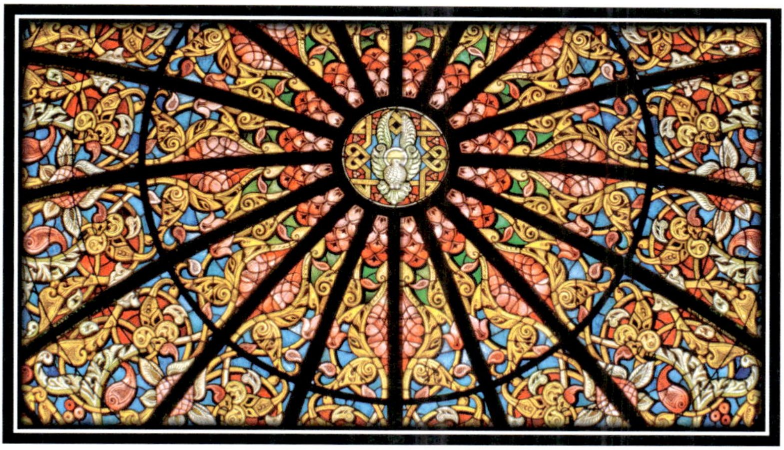

55. Chapel of the Holy Name of Jesus at Jesuit High School (1925-1926)

4133 Banks St, Mid-City
Diboll & Owen / Wogan & Bernard, architects

Also known as Thomas J. Semmes Chapel. This Diboll & Owen designed chapel was first built in 1901 as part of a major addition to the second Jesuit High School, originally located at Baronne & Common and razed in 1925 to make room for Pere Marquette Tower. The chapel, including its stained glass, was dismantled beforehand and later reconstructed on a smaller scale inside the new Wogan & Bernard designed High School building. School literature attributes the glass to the Franz Mayer Co. of Munich. One of only a few sites in this guide that are inaccessible to the general public.

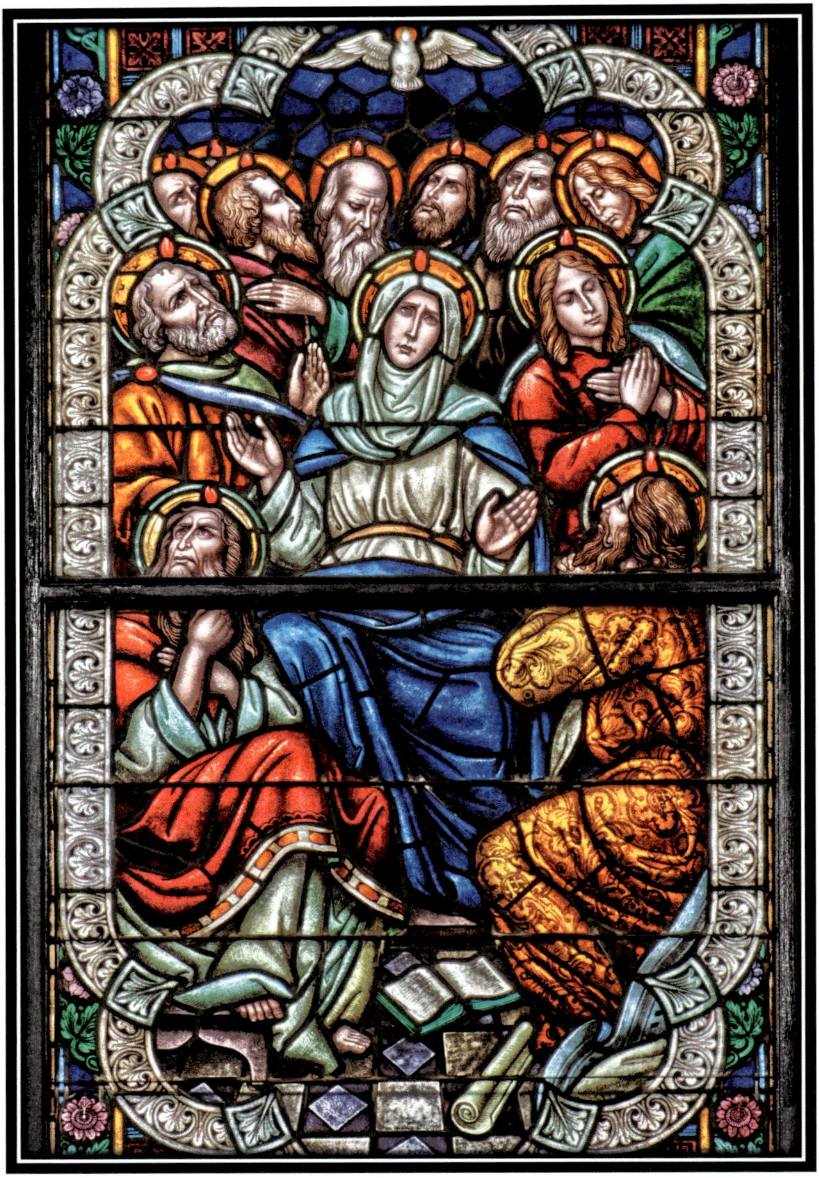

56. Holy Ghost Catholic Church (1926)

2001 Louisiana Ave, Milan
Diboll & Owen, architects; H.W. Bond & Bro., builders

Now known as St. Katharine Drexel Parish. Primary stained glass by Dr. Heinrich Oidtmann Co. of Linnich, Germany; other contributors probable.

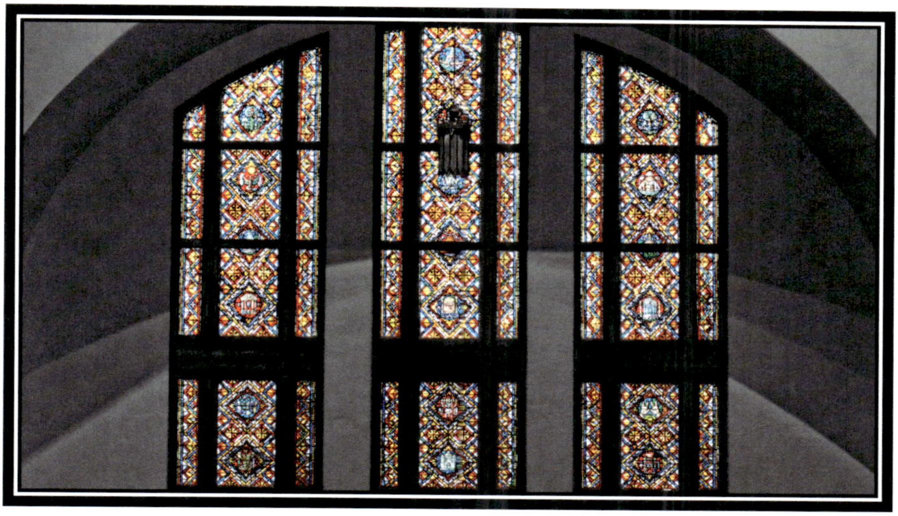

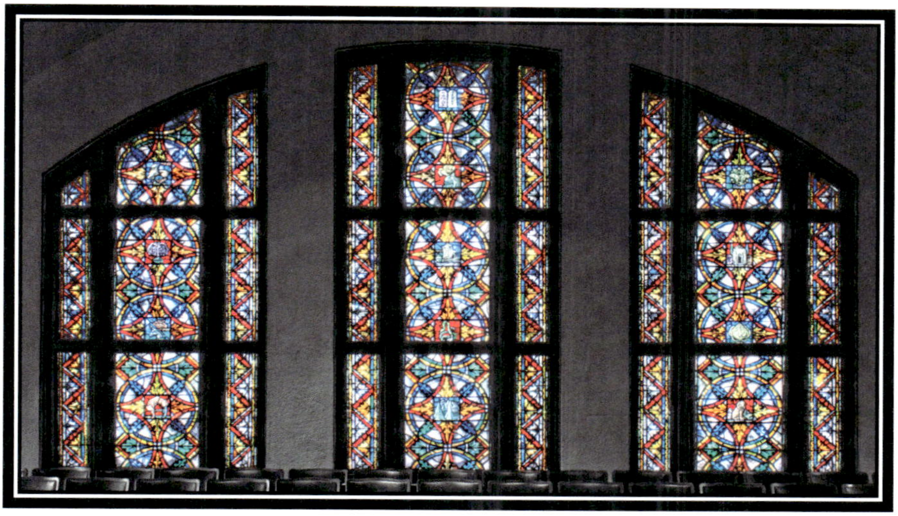

57. Temple Sinai (1927-1928)

6227 St Charles Ave, Audubon
Emile Weil; Moise H. Goldstein; Weiss, Dreyfous & Seiferth ~ associated architects; Charles Gibert, general contractor

PRC researchers attribute this synagogue's windows to Emil Frei Inc. of St. Louis; possibly executed in their Munich studio.

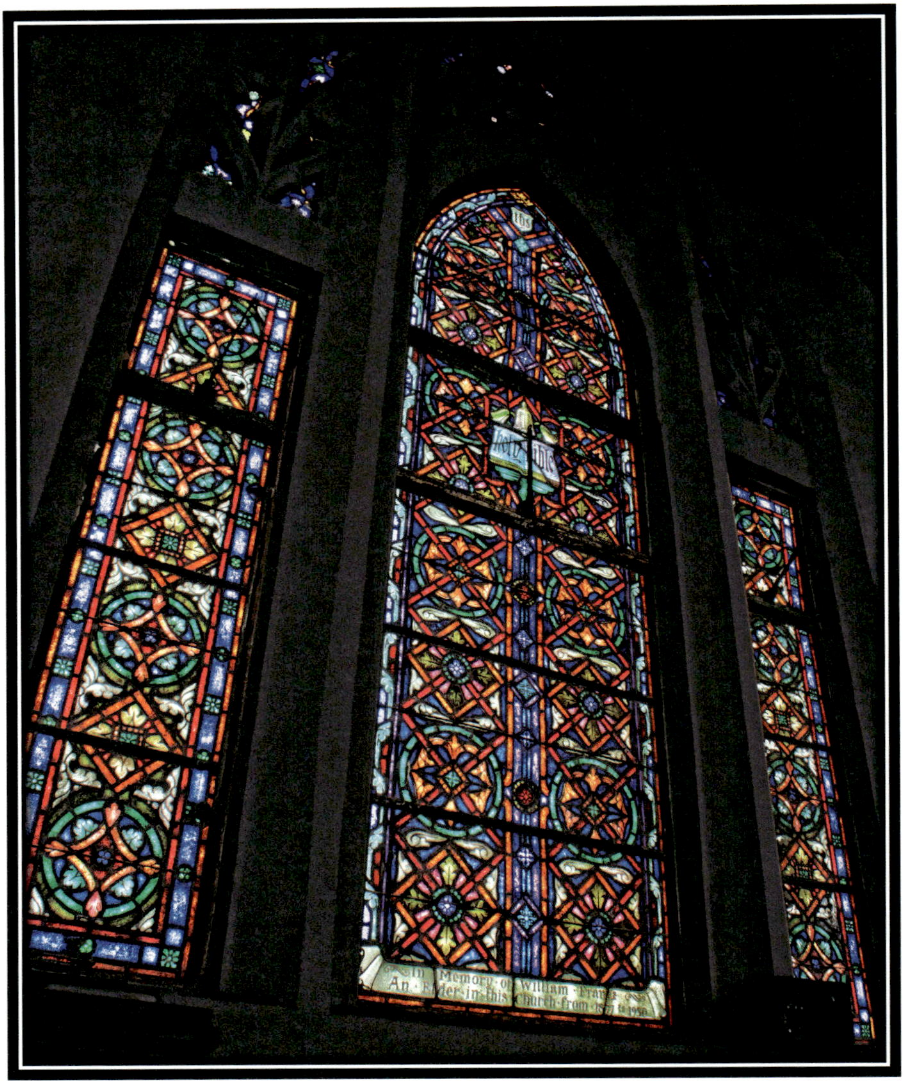

58. Canal Street Presbyterian Church (1927-1928)

4302 Canal St, Mid-City
Sam Stone, Jr. & Co., architects
G. Emile & Ernest Edward Reimann & Co., builders

Now known as Canal Street Church: A Mosaic Community. Stained glass makers and dates of installation undetermined.

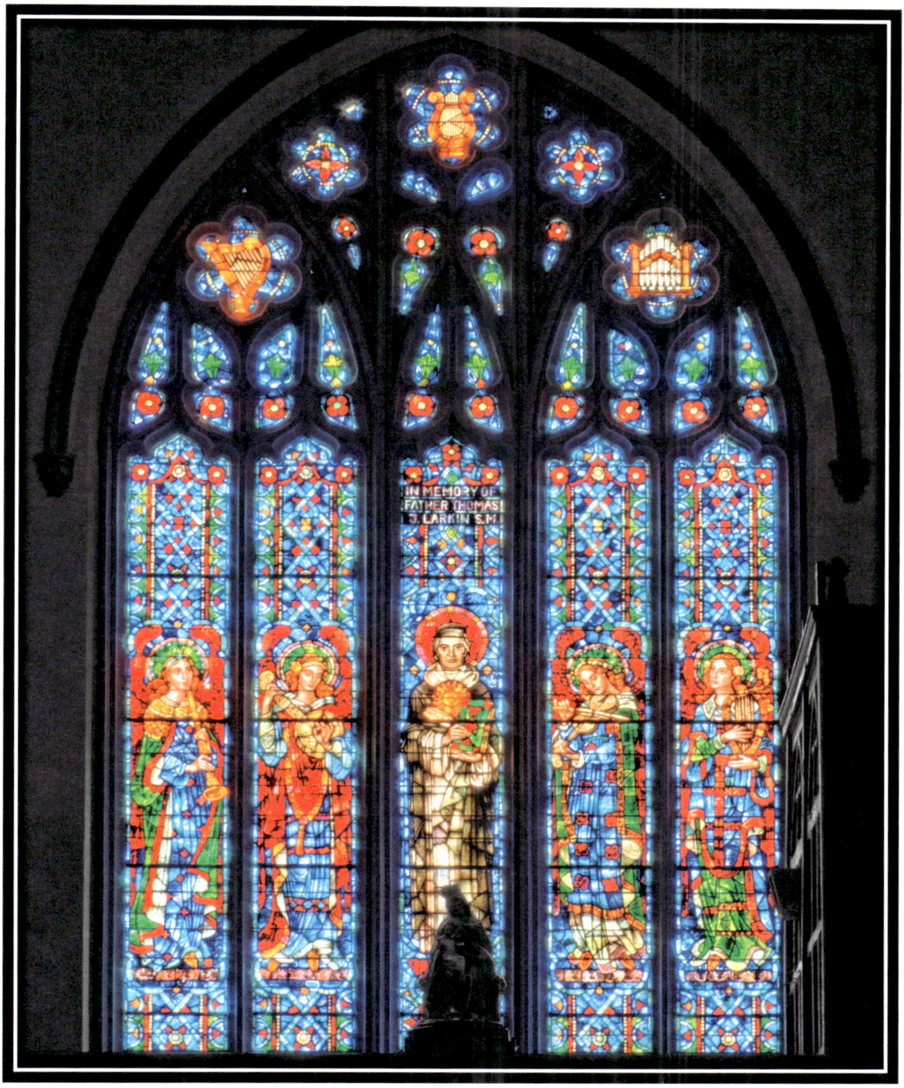

59. Church of the Holy Name of Mary [Catholic] (1928-1929)

400 Verret St, Algiers Point
Alexander W. Norman, architect; George J. Glover Company, Inc., builder

Among other undetermined makers, find five windows by Franz Mayer & Co. of Munich: two transplanted from an earlier church building, and three installed c.1959.

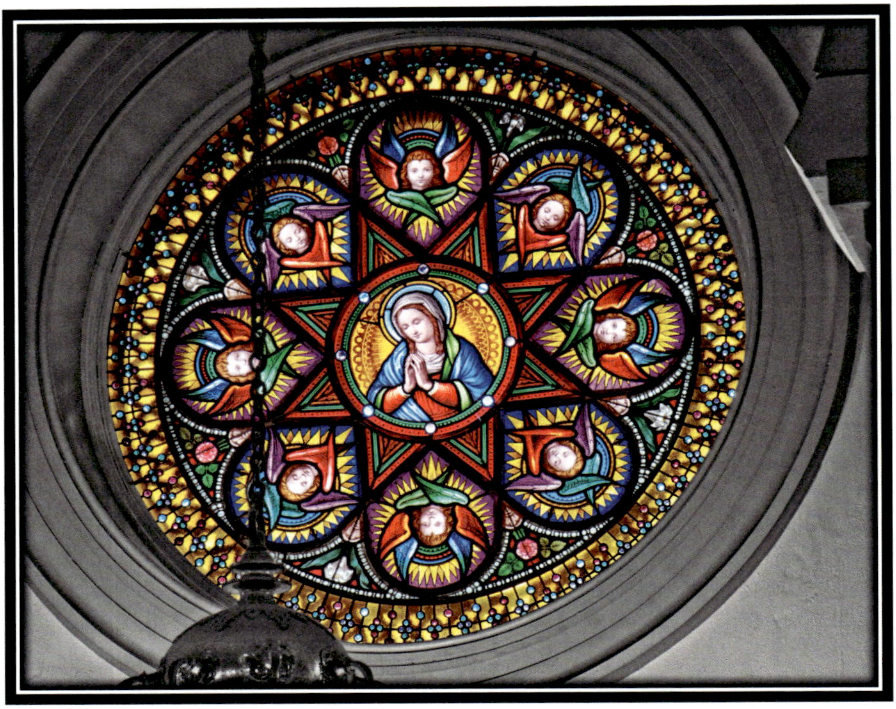

60. Immaculate Conception Jesuit Catholic Church (1928-1930)

130 Baronne St, Central Business District
Fr. John Cambiaso with Theodore E. Giraud, architects of original 1851-1857 construction / 1928-1930 rebuild managed by Wogan & Bernard

Immaculate Conception Jesuit Catholic Church, often referred to by locals as simply Jesuit Church, was first constructed 1851-1857. It was completely dismantled and rebuilt to a very similar design, using many original materials, from 1928 to 1930. Newspaper accounts of the day report that the rebuild was necessitated by bulged walls and leaning towers "threateningly out of plumb." The oldest windows at this site, made by Hucher & Rathouis of Le Mans, France, date to the late 1870s and were transplanted from the prior church building. Find also a few examples by Franz Mayer & Co. of Munich, some transplanted and some installed c.1930-1931. Other contributors are likely. The maker of the window pictured is undetermined.

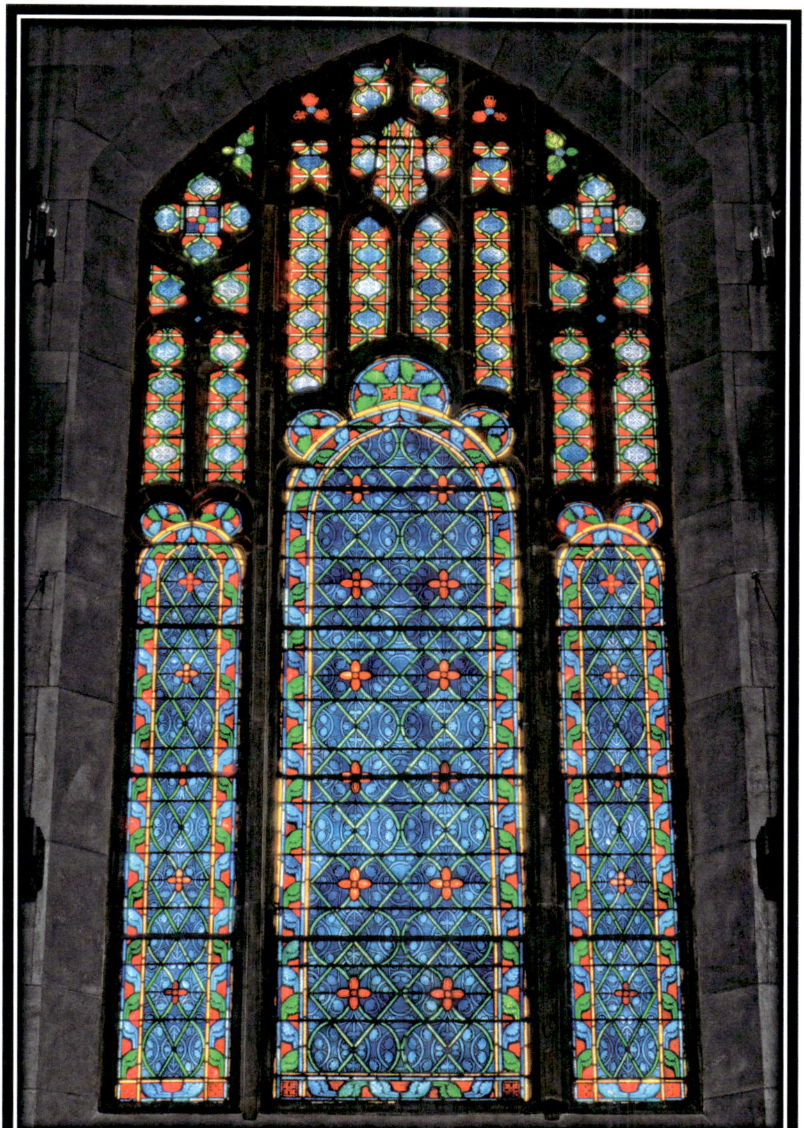

61. St. Charles Avenue Presbyterian Church (1928-1930)

1545 State St, Audubon
W.W. Van Meter, architect

Stained glass by the Dr. Heinrich Oidtmann Co. of Linnich, Germany.

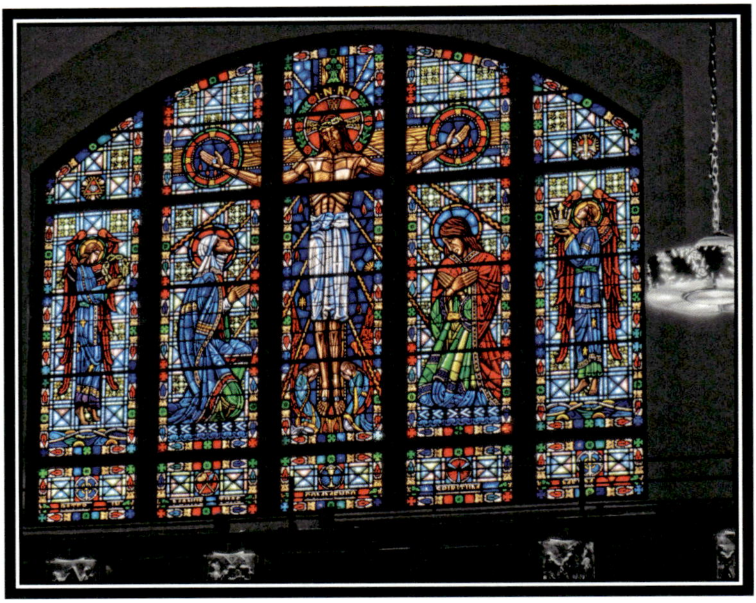

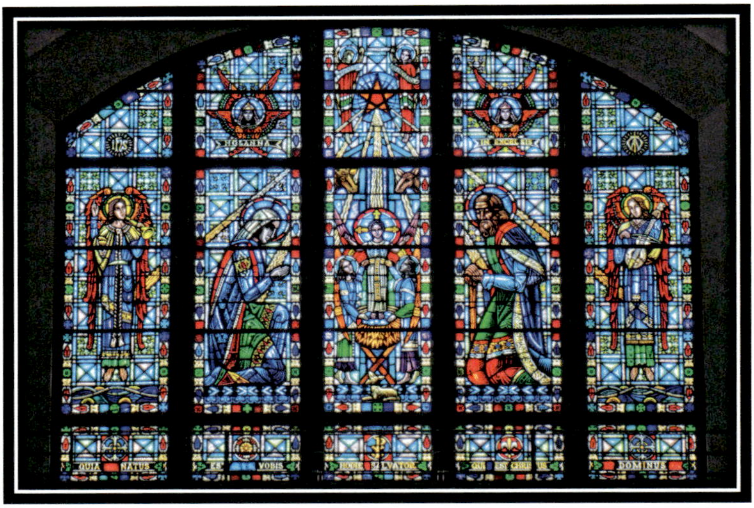

62. St. Leo the Great Catholic Church (1930)

2916 Paris Ave, Fairgrounds
Paul V. Charbonnet, architect; Gervais F. Favrot, contractor

Now known as St. Raymond & St. Leo the Great Catholic Church. According to markings upon the glass the windows at this site were designed by "Cummings Studios - R.W. Jung, Associated" of San Francisco and installed c.1941.

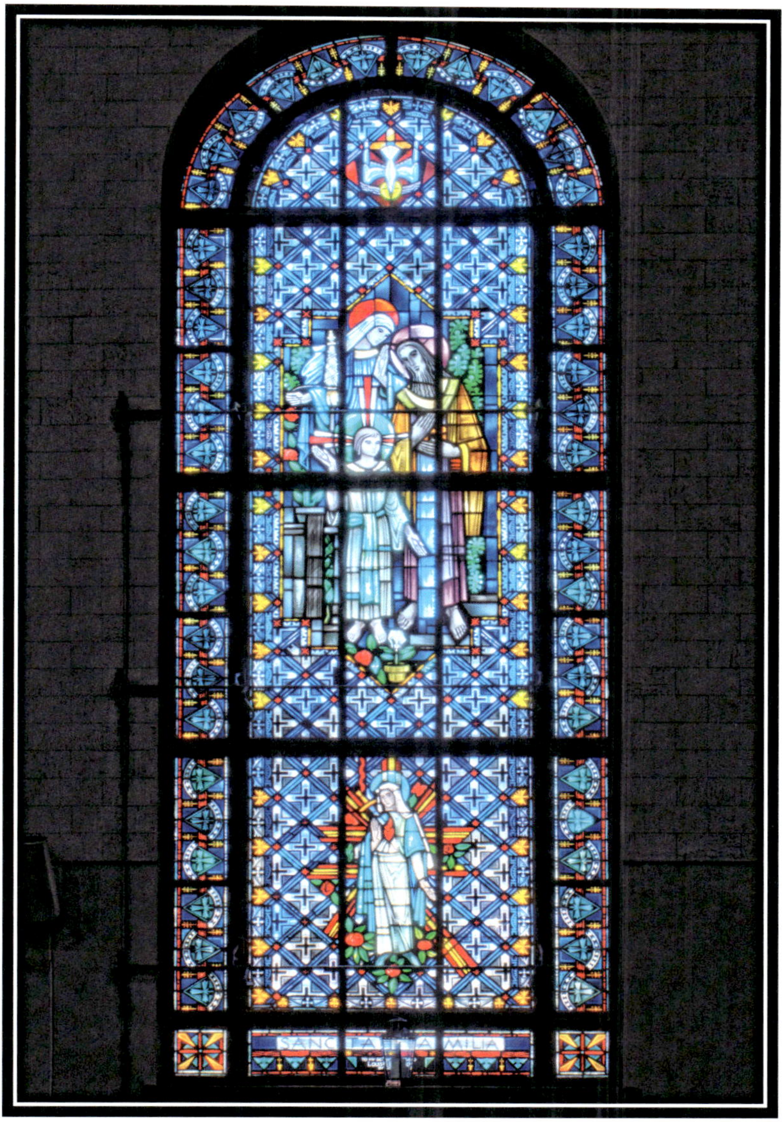

63. Our Lady Star of the Sea Catholic Church (1930-1931)

1835 St Roch Ave, St. Roch
Wogan & Bernard, architects; Gibert & Sochs, builders

Primary windows by Emil Frei Inc. of St. Louis [pictured]; two secondary panes by Franz Mayer & Co. of Munich. All installed in the 1930s.

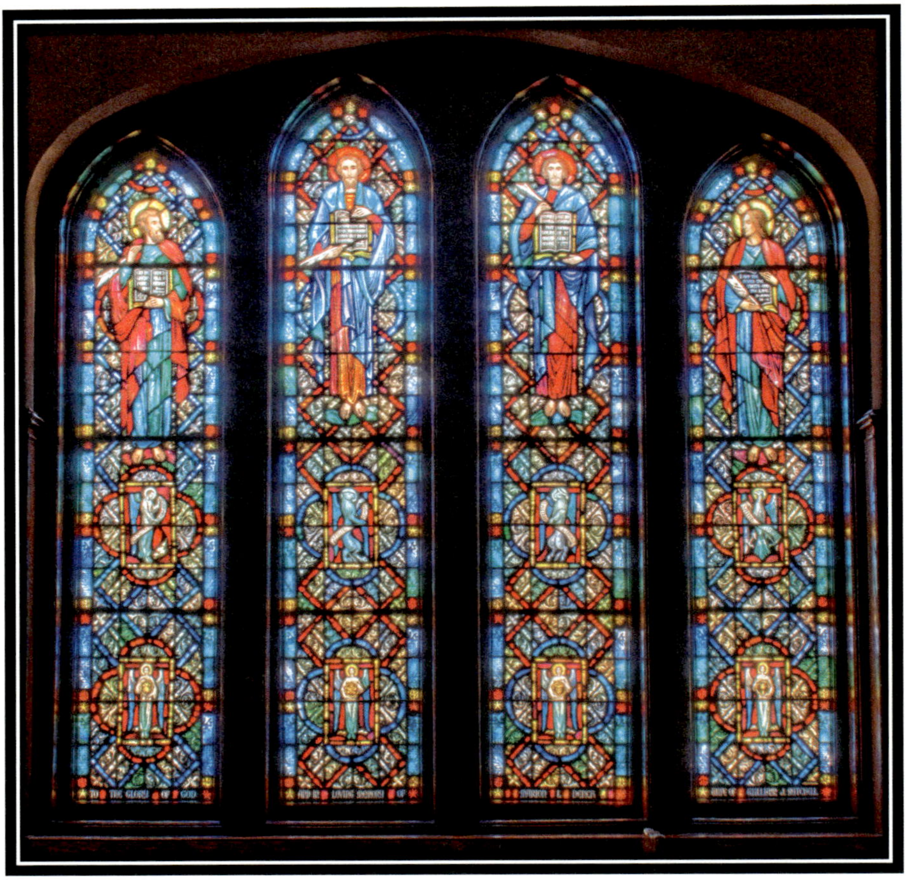

64. Trinity Episcopal Church ~ Chapel Addition (c.1928-1932)

1329 Jackson Ave, Lower Garden District
Richard Koch, architect

Stained glass by Charles J. Connick Studios of Boston; installed 1930s to 1950s.

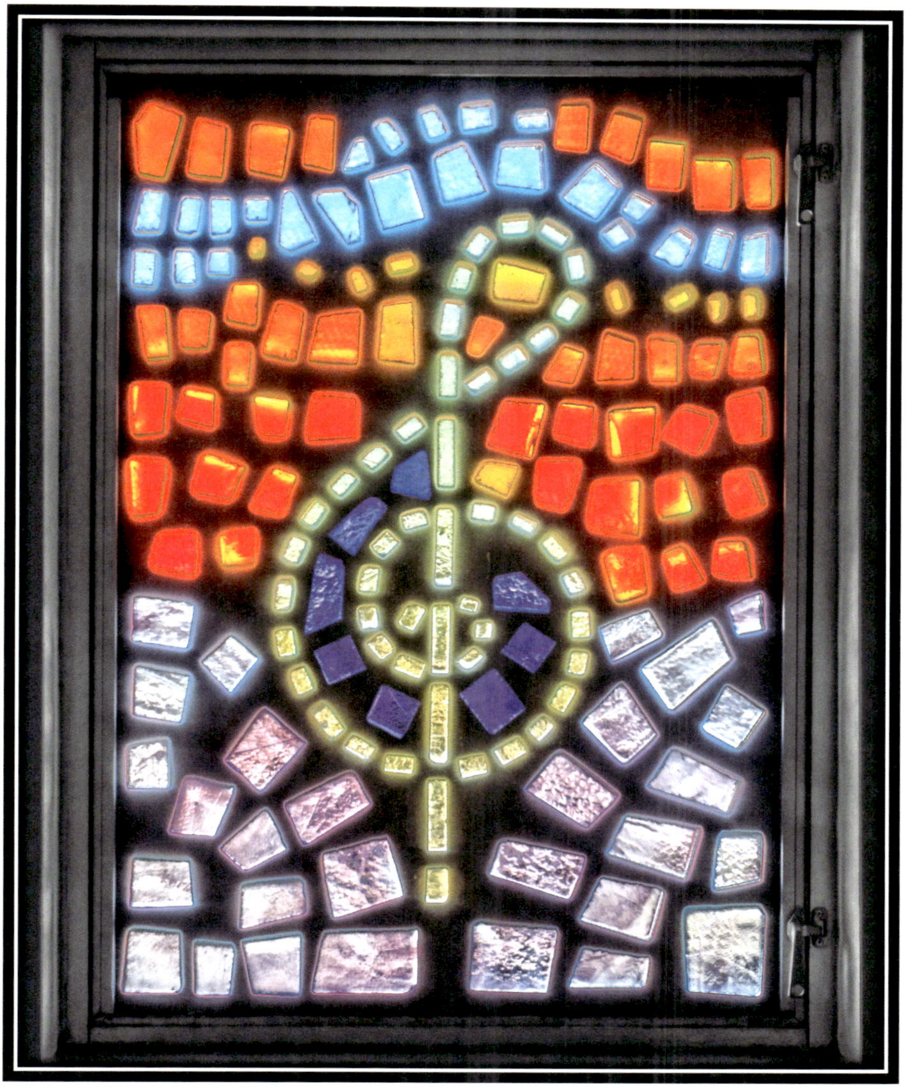

65. St. David Catholic Church (1937)

5625 St Claude Ave, Lower Ninth Ward
Architect undetermined

Dalle de verre window makers undetermined; installed c.1992.

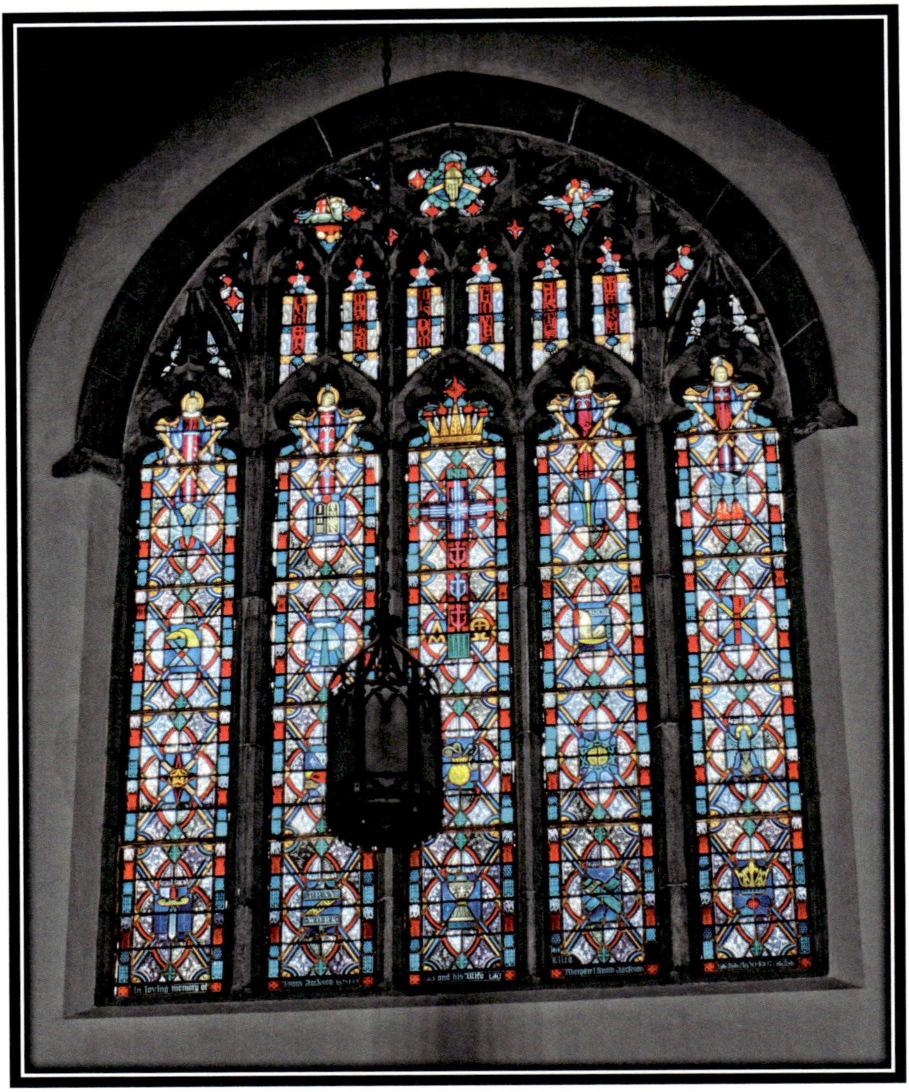

66. First Presbyterian Church (1938-1939)

5401 S. Claiborne Ave, Marlyville-Fontainebleau
Sam Stone, Jr. & Douglass V. Freret, architects

Emil Frei Inc. designed the window pictured, located above the high altar. Clerestory windows transplanted from prior church.

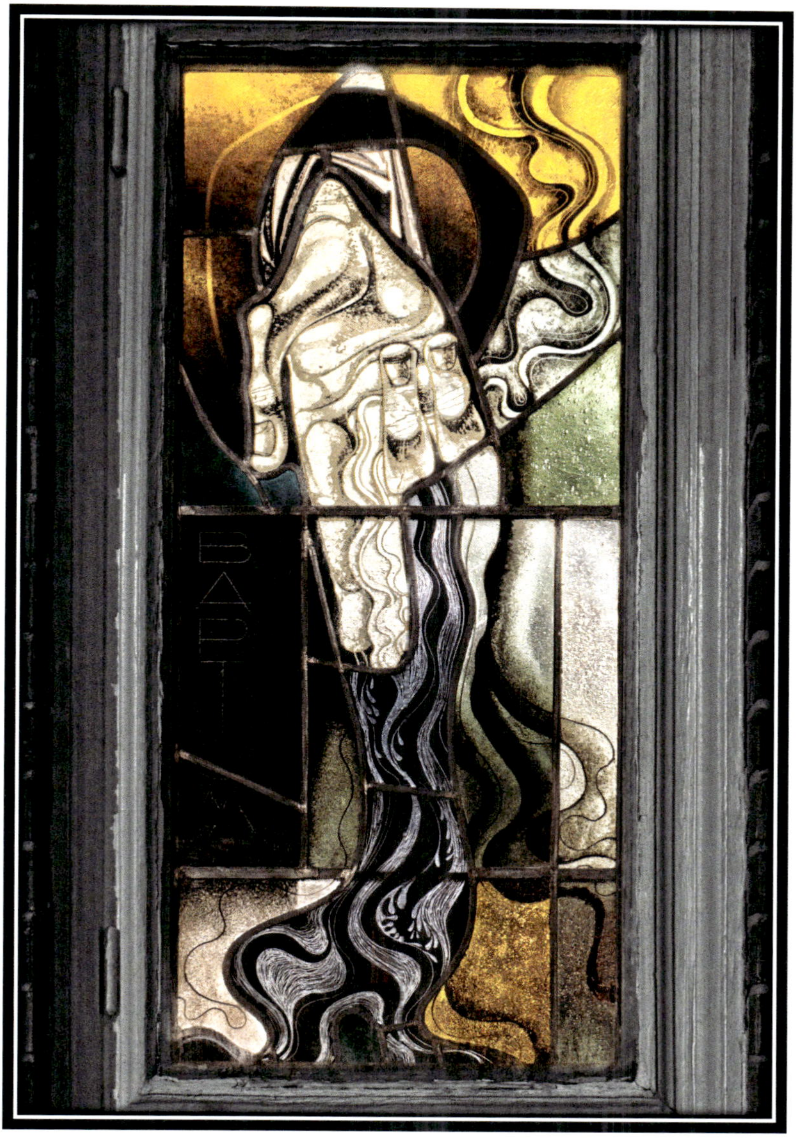

67. Redeemer Evangelical Lutheran Church (1950)

1300 Alvar St, St. Claude
Favrot, Reed, Mathes & Bergman, architects
R.P. Farnsworth & Co., contractors

According to PRC researchers, most of the stained glass at this site was designed by Siegfried Reinhardt and fabricated by Emil Frei Inc. [pictured]; installed 1951-1969.

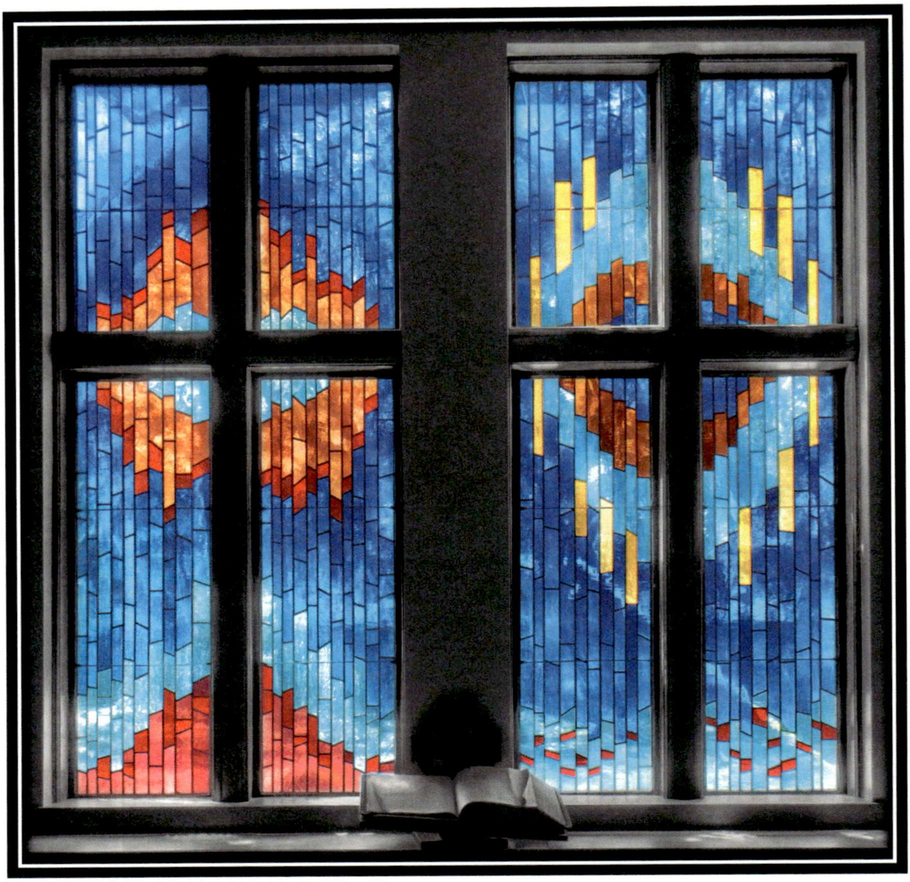

68. St. Charles Avenue Presbyterian Church ~ Education Building (1949-1951)

1545 State St, Audubon
Favrot, Reed, Mathes & Bergman, architects
Keller Construction Co., builder

Stained glass designed by David Dew Bruner; fabricated and installed by Trudy L. Richie, 1979.

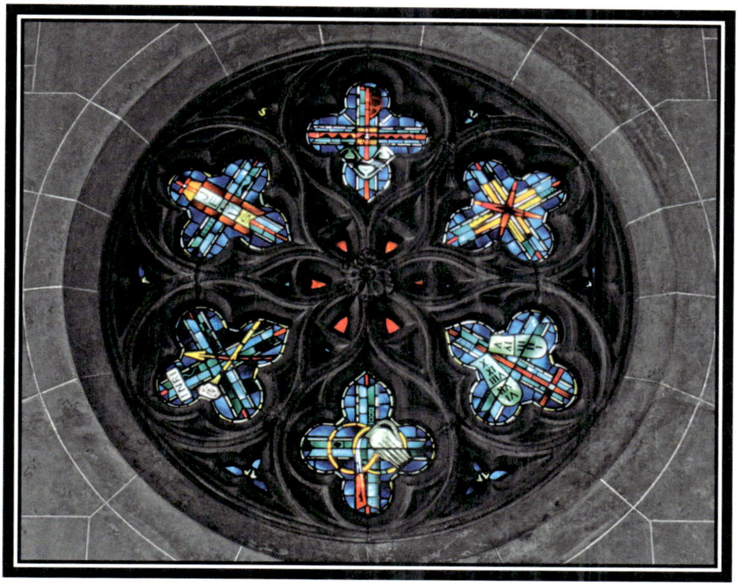

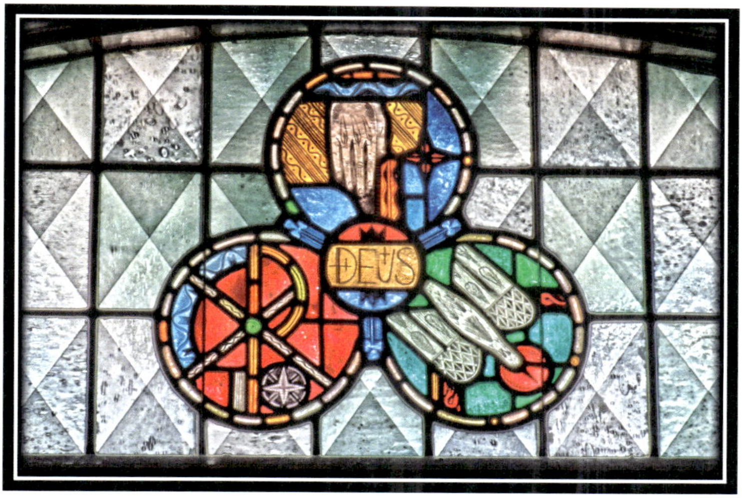

69. First Evangelical & Reformed Church (1950-1951)

5212 S. Claiborne Ave, Freret
Carl L. Olschner & Associates, architects; Chris Larsen Co., contractors

Now known as First Unitarian Universalist Church. Of special note at this site is the Gordon Window, designed by George Gugert and fabricated by Willet Studios of Philadelphia in the 1930s. It was transplanted from the congregation's prior church. Makers of other windows [pictured] are undetermined.

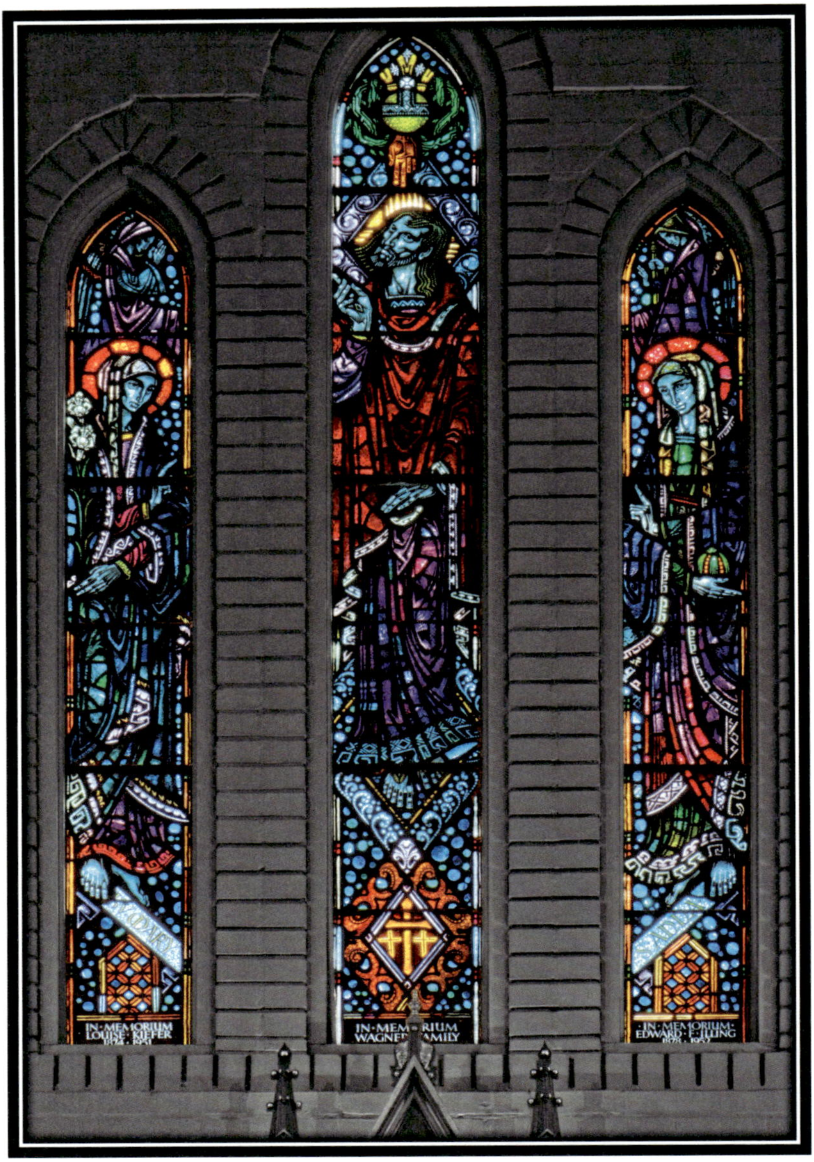

70. St. Anna's Episcopal Church (1951-1952)

1313 Esplanade Ave, Seventh Ward
Claude E. Hooton, architect

PRC researchers attribute this church's nave windows, installed in 1956, to William Morris Studio of London. Makers and dates of installation of the primary panes [pictured] are undetermined.

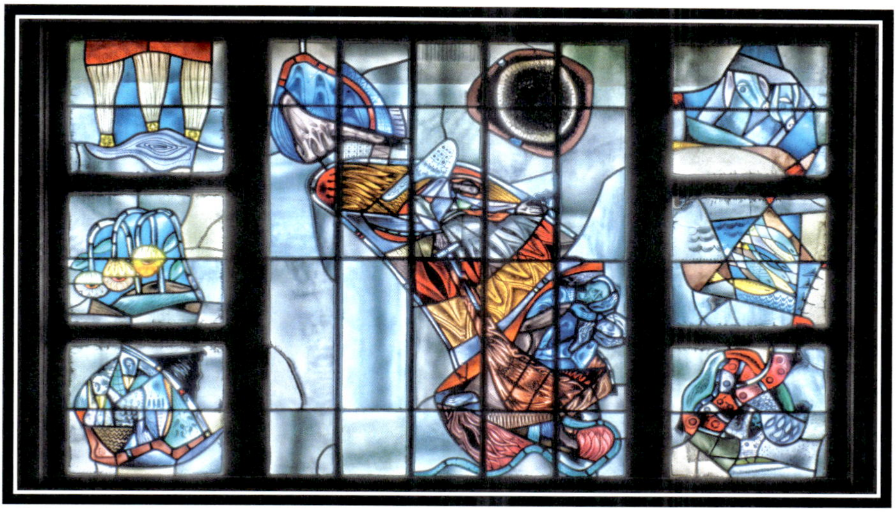

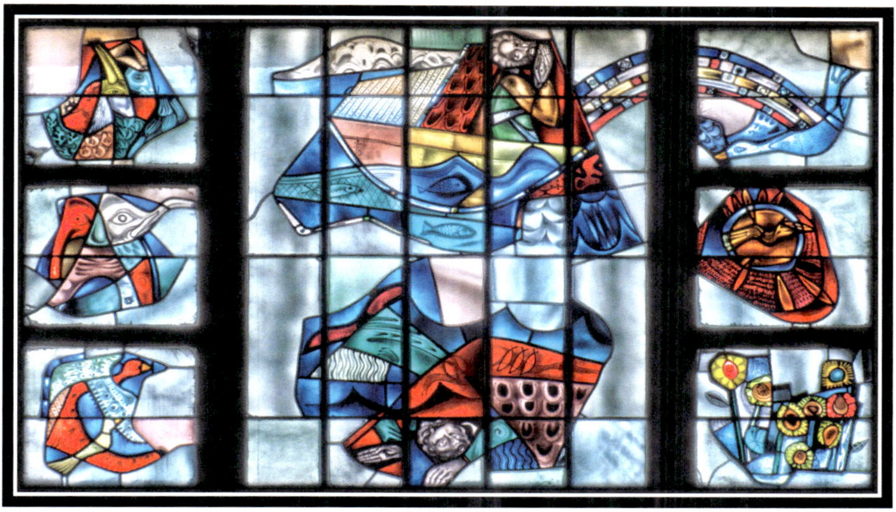

71. St. James Major Catholic Church (1951-1952)

3736 Gentilly Blvd, Gentilly Terrace
Thomas Byrd Burk, architect

According to PRC researchers, the stained glass at this site was designed by Robert Harmon, fabricated by Emil Frei Inc. of St. Louis and installed by the Henry J. Lips Glass Co. of New Orleans in the early 1960s.

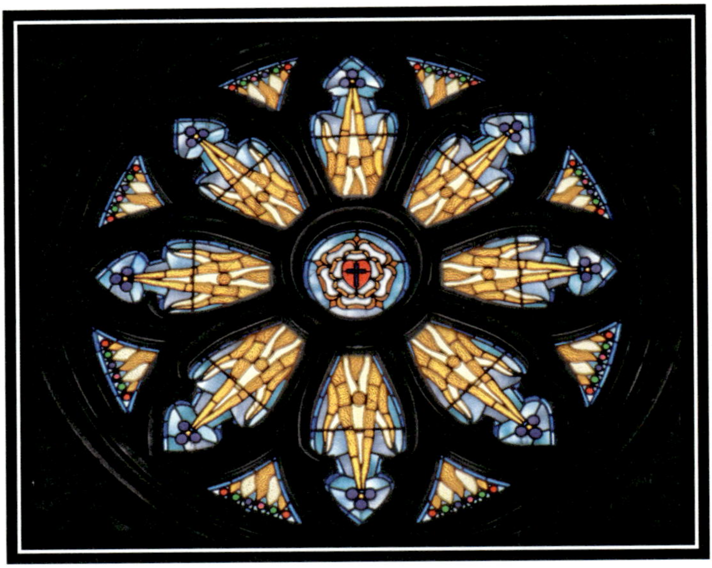

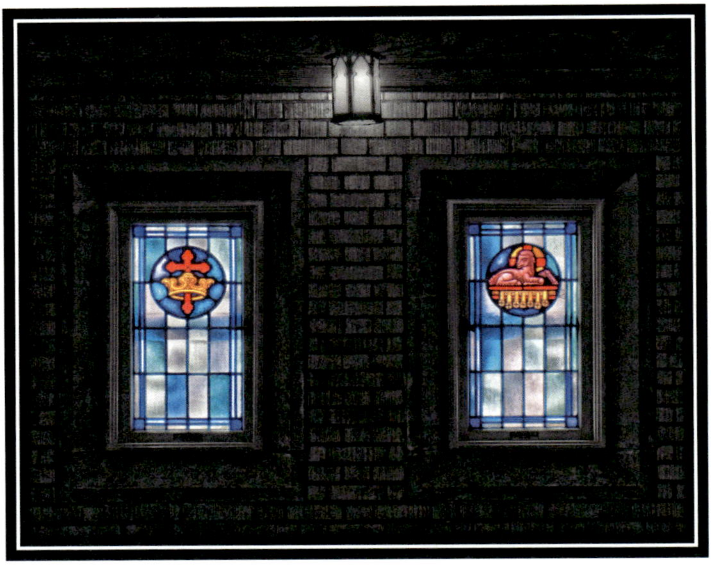

72. Gloria Dei Lutheran Church (1951-1953)

2021 S. Dupre St, Broadmoor
Freret, Wolf & Umbach, architects
Milton Helmke, builder

Now known as Broadmoor Community Church. Stained glass makers and dates of installation undetermined.

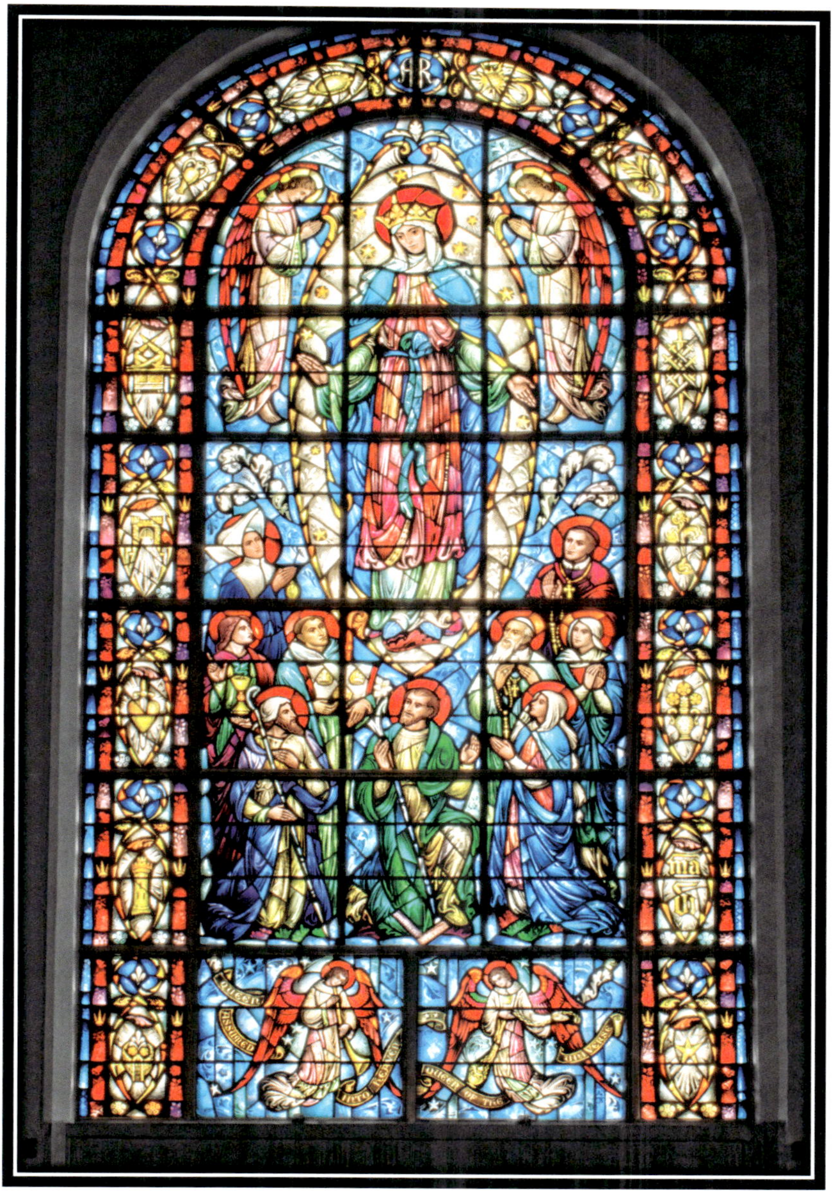

73. St. Rita Catholic Church (1952-1953)

2729 Lowerline St, Marlyville-Fontainebleau
Bendernagel & Cazale, architects
Gervais F. Favrot, builder

Stained glass by Charles J. Connick Studios of Boston; installed c.1957.

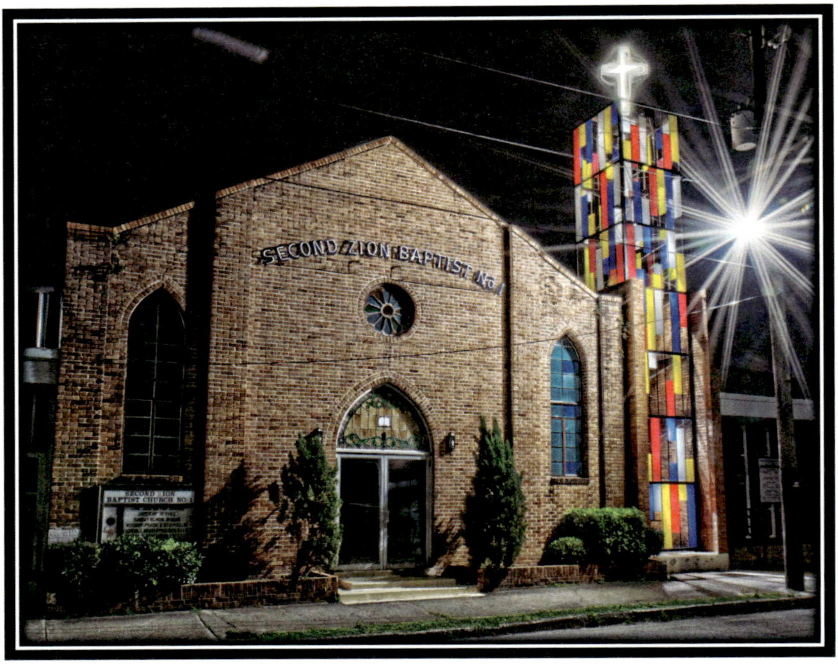

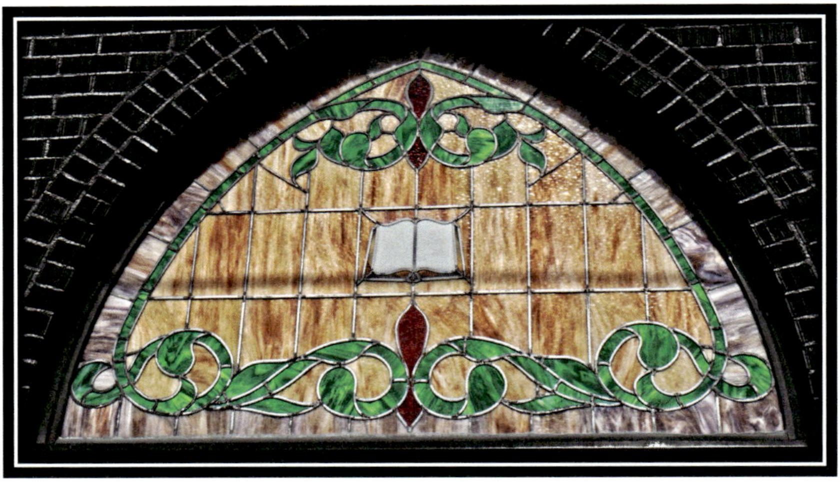

74. Second Zion Baptist Church No. 1 (1954)

2929 Second St, Central City
Architect undetermined

Stained glass and plexiglass tower makers undetermined.

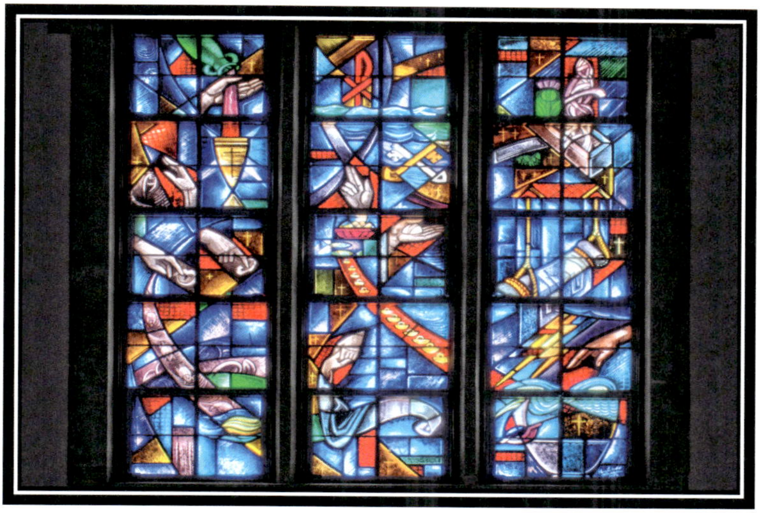

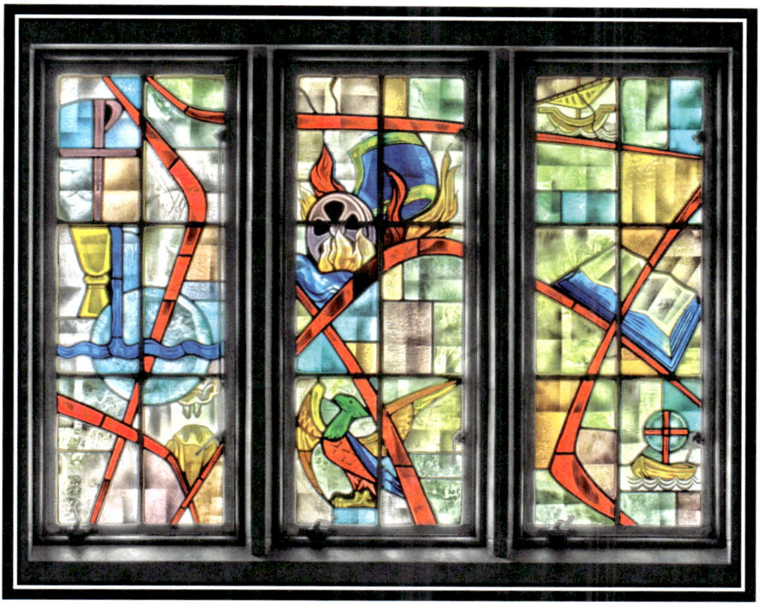

75. St. Andrew's Episcopal Church (1954-1955)

1101 S. Carrollton Ave, East Carrollton
Jones, Roessle & Von Osthopp, architects
R.P. Farnsworth & Co., contractors

Stained glass designed by Henry Lee Willet of Willet Studios, Philadelphia, installed c.1958.

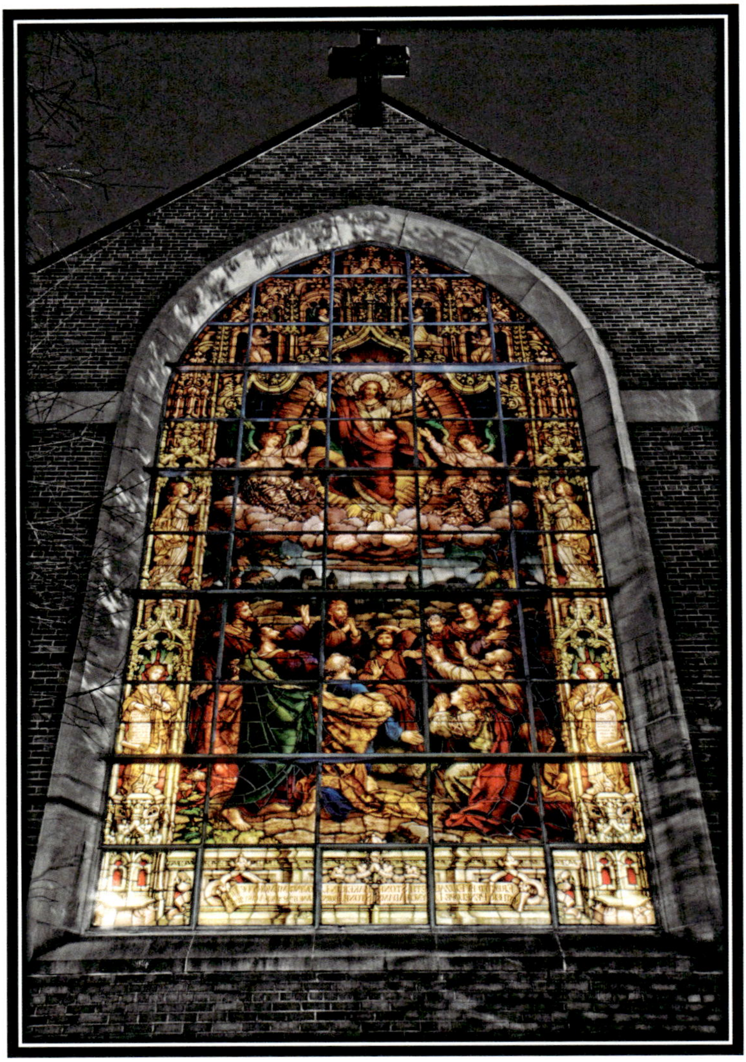

76. St. Paul's Episcopal Church (1956-1957)

6249 Canal Blvd, Lakeview
Jones, Roessle & Von Osthopp, architects
Haase Construction Co., Inc., general contractors

PRC researchers report at this site a handful of windows made by Franz Mayer & Co. of Munich, some transplanted from the congregation's prior church, plus three windows made by J. Wippel & Co. of Great Britain, installed in 1984. The Ascension window [pictured] was made by Emil Frei Inc. of St. Louis.

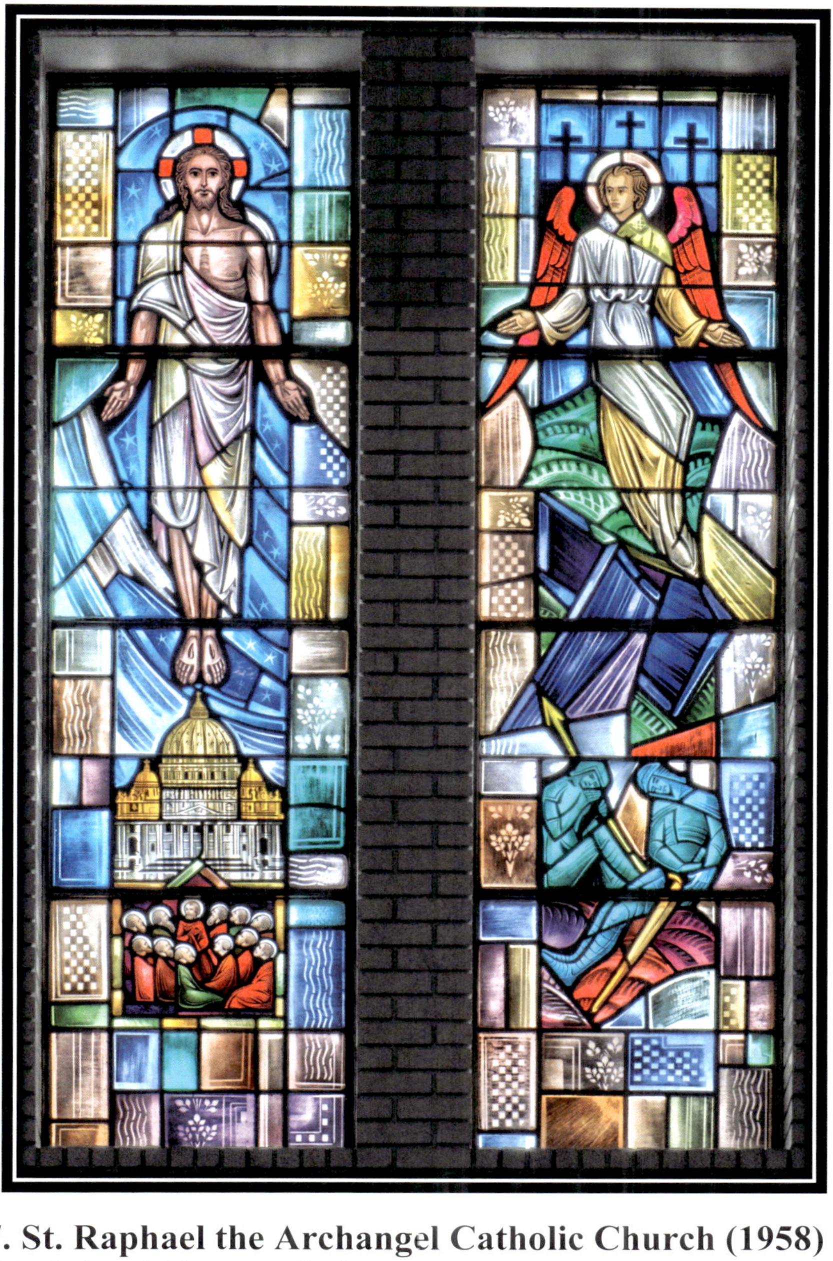

77. St. Raphael the Archangel Catholic Church (1958)

5621 Elysian Fields Ave, Milneburg
Irvin J. Kohler, architect; Gervais F. Favrot Co., Inc., contractors

Now known as Transfiguration of the Lord Catholic Church. Stained glass by Charles J. Connick Studios of Boston; installed c.1961.

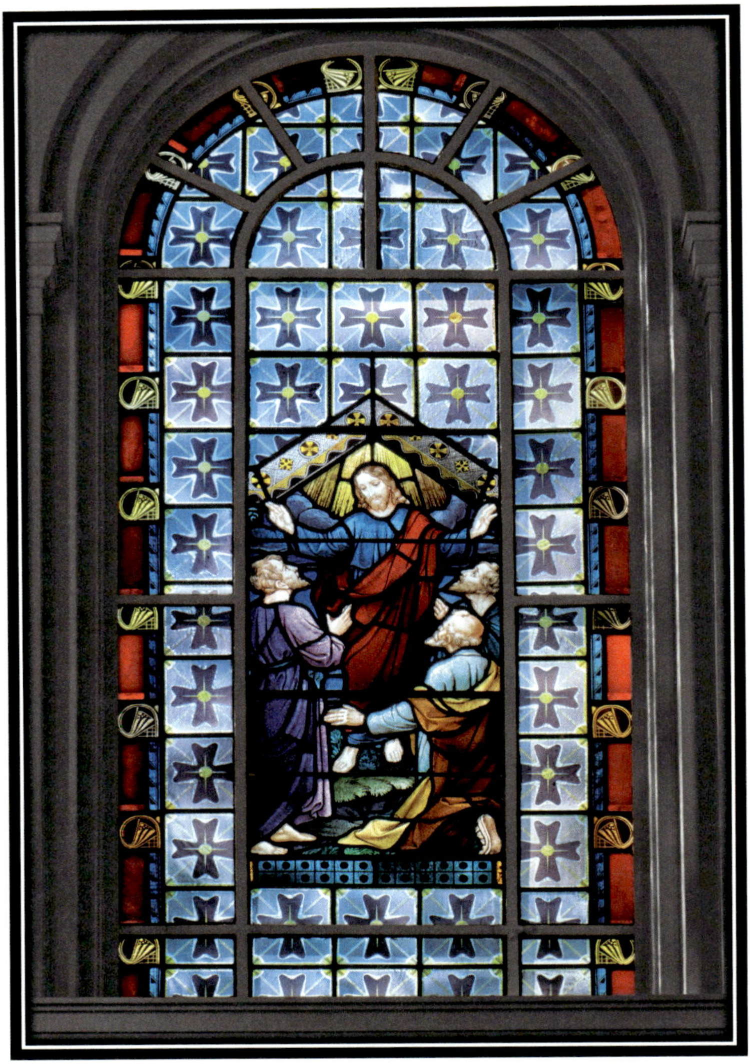

78. First Methodist Church (1959-1960)

3401 Canal St, Mid-City
Carl L. Olschner & Associates, architects
R.P. Farnsworth & Co., contractors

Merged with Grace Methodist Episcopal (*entry #31*) in 2007-2008 to become First Grace United Methodist. Two major windows at this site by Franz Mayer & Co. of Munich were transplanted from the prior First Methodist Church building. Six more identically trimmed major windows [pictured] are of undetermined origin.

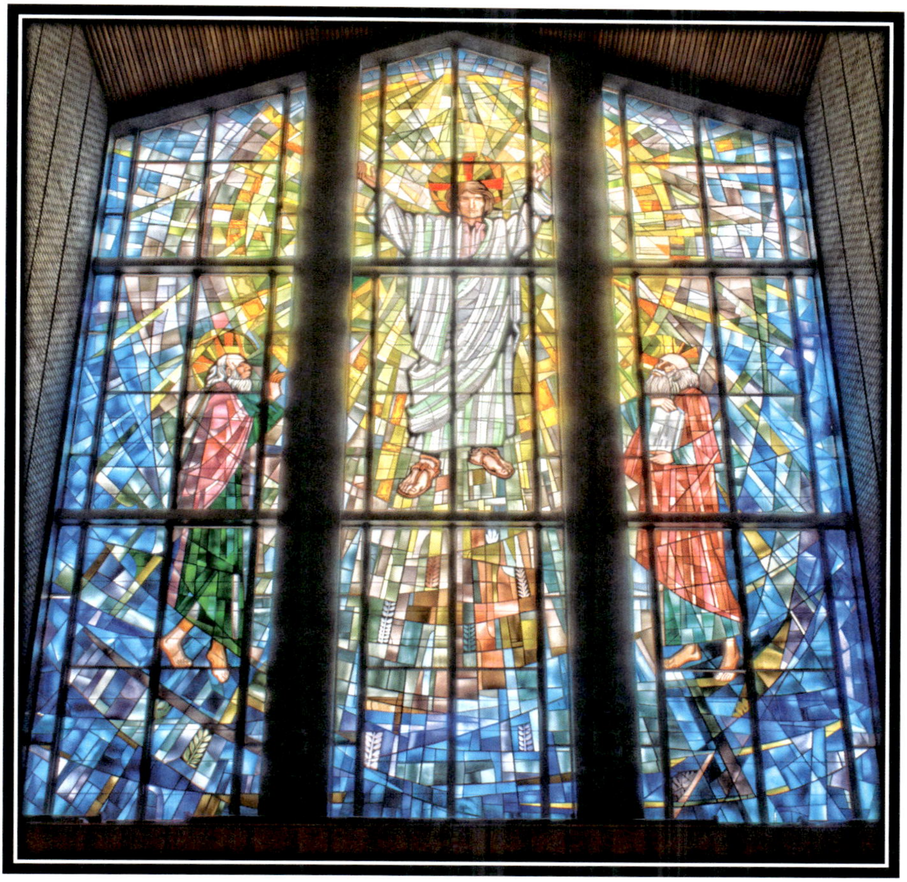

79. St. Dominic Catholic Church (1959-1961)

775 Harrison Ave, Lakeview
Irvin J. Kohler, architect; Tellepsen Construction Co., builders

Multiple stained glass makers represented at this location include Franz Pauli of Germany, John Chase of New Orleans [pictured], and Botz & Miesen of Cologne, Germany. Chase's window was installed in 1974. Other installation dates are undetermined.

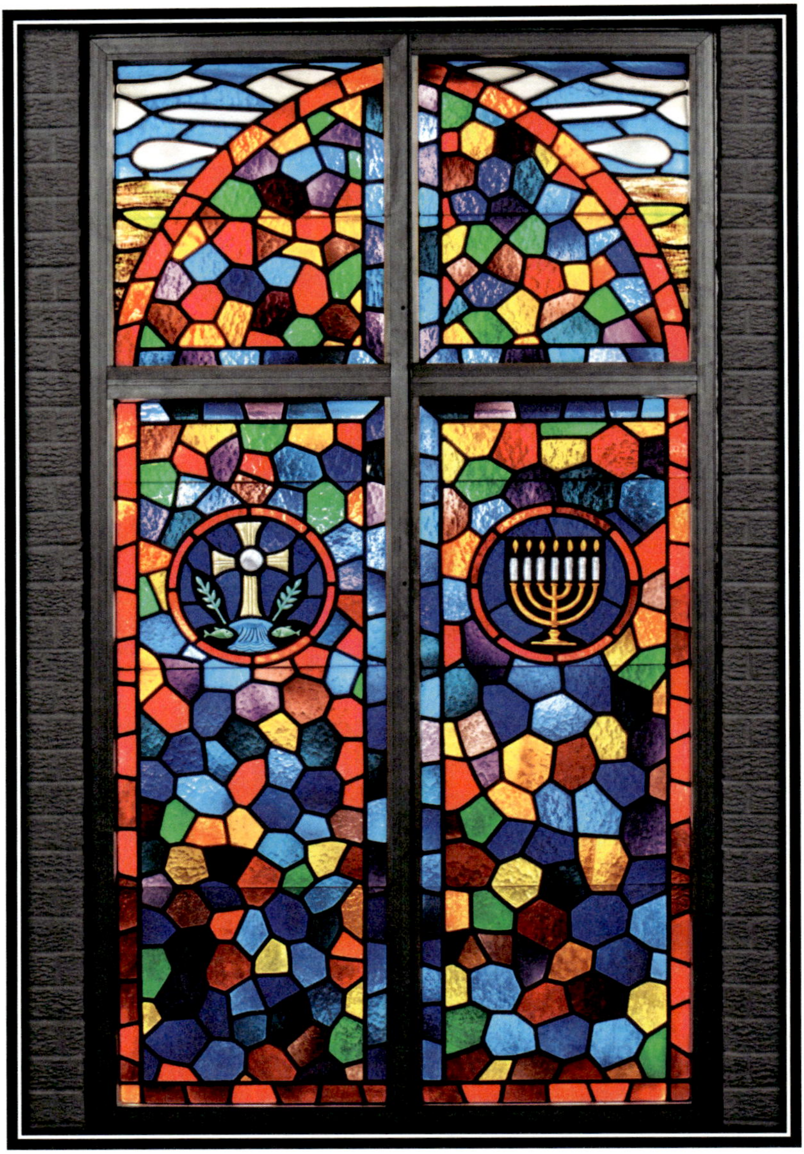

80. Hannah Chapel at Rayne Memorial United Methodist Church (1968)

3910 St Charles Ave, Touro
John Dart, Jr., builder

According to PRC researchers, this chapel's windows were made by Emil Frei Inc. of St. Louis with the assistance of Henry J. Lips of New Orleans.

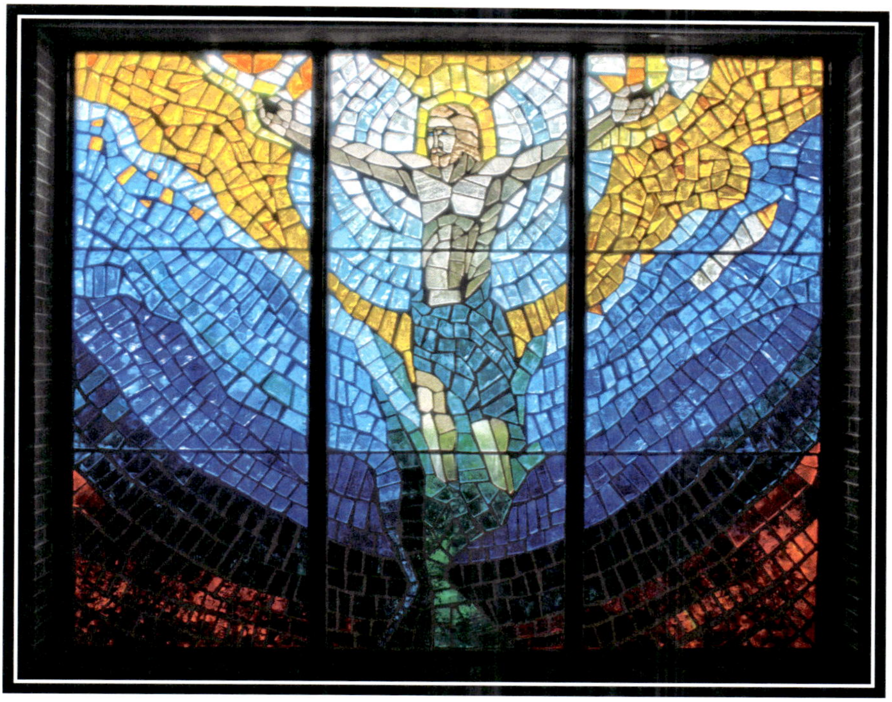

81. Aurora United Methodist Church (1975)

3300 Eton St, Old Aurora
James P. Oubre, architect; Building Construction Co., general contractor

Dalle de verre windows designed and fabricated by Milton Pounds of Pounds Stained Glass Studio, Covington.

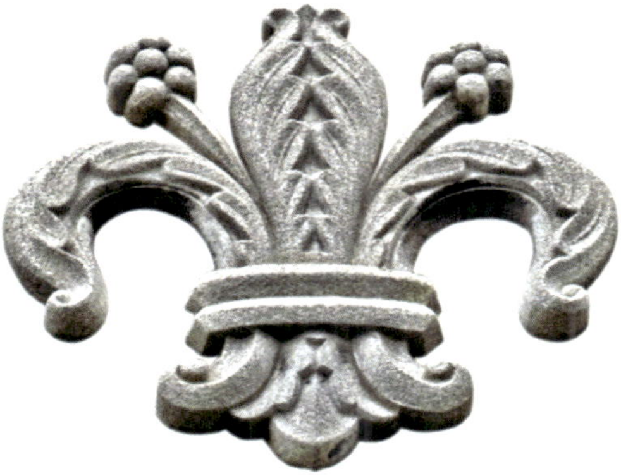

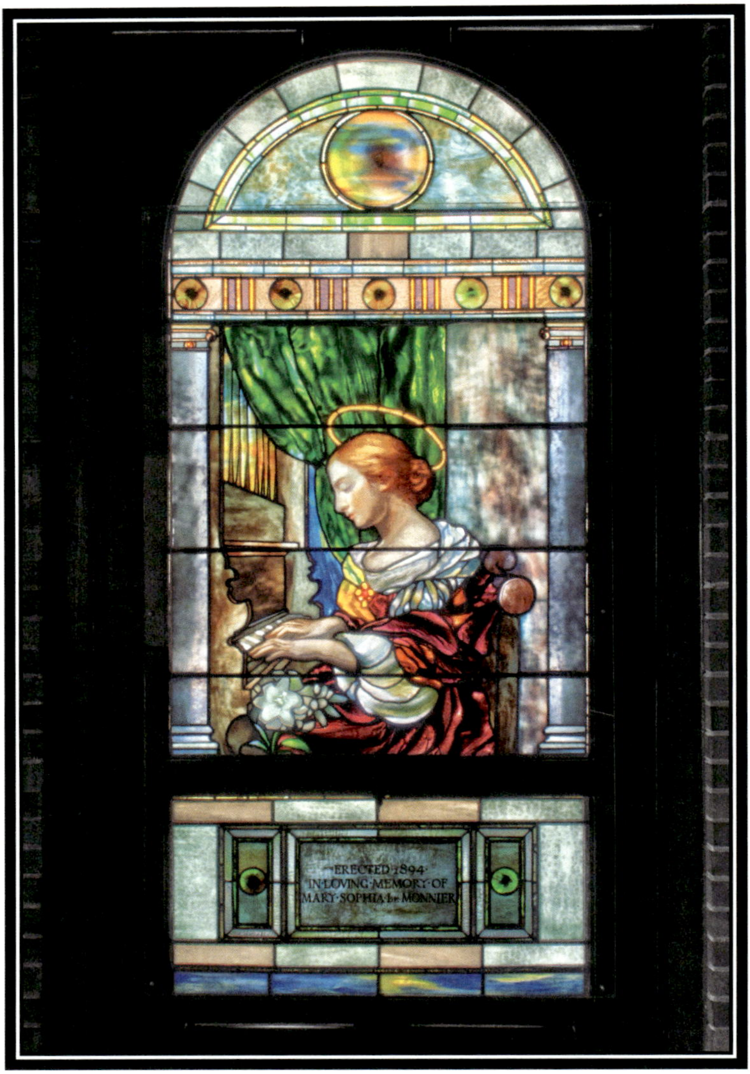

82. Myra Clare Rogers Memorial Chapel at Tulane University (1976)

1229 Broadway St, Audubon
Douglass V. Freret & John Desmond, architects

Find four radius windows and one rose window at this location, all designed and fabricated by Tiffany Studios of New York City between 1894 and 1911 and originally installed at the Newcomb College Chapel that formerly stood near Chestnut and Sixth Street in the Garden District.

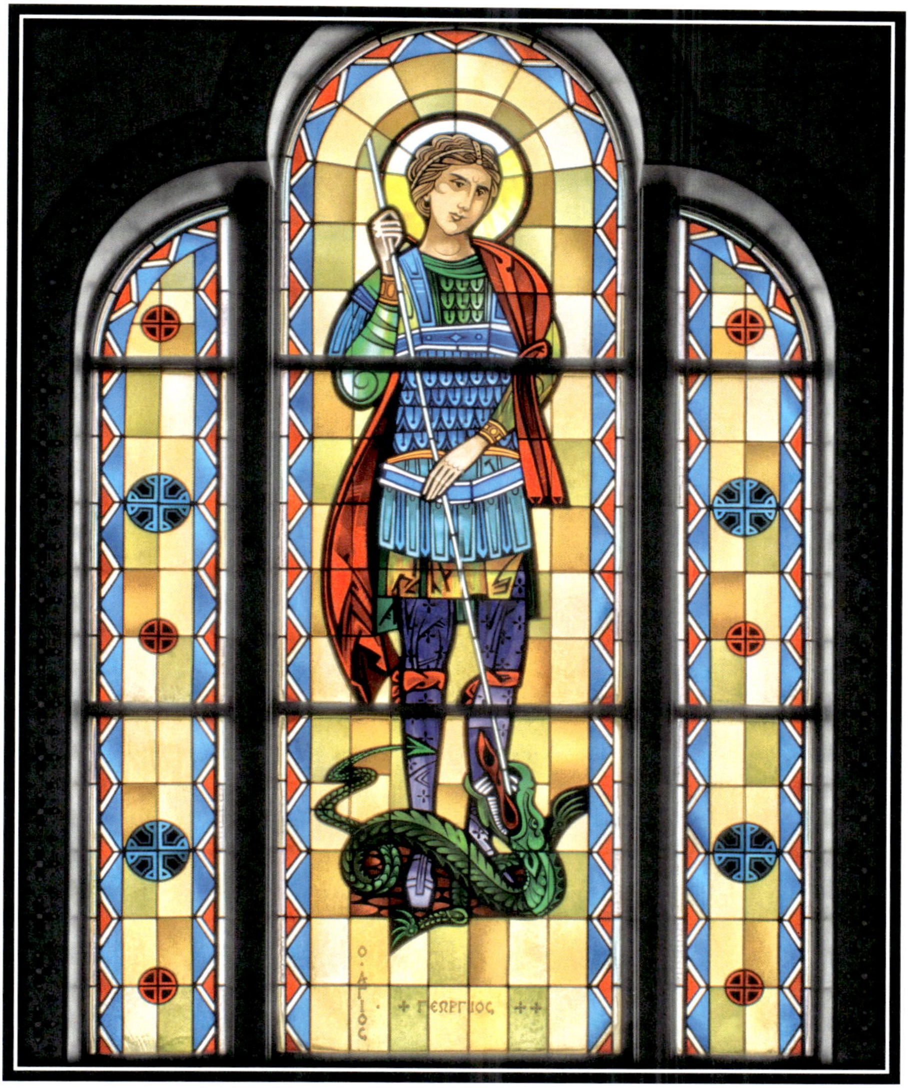

83. Holy Trinity Greek Orthodox Cathedral (1985)

1200 Robert E Lee Blvd, Fillmore
Frank Nicoladis & John C. Yemelos of N-Y Associates, Inc., architect-planners; Amoss Construction Co., contractor

Stained glass by Conrad Schmitt Studios of New Berlin, WI.

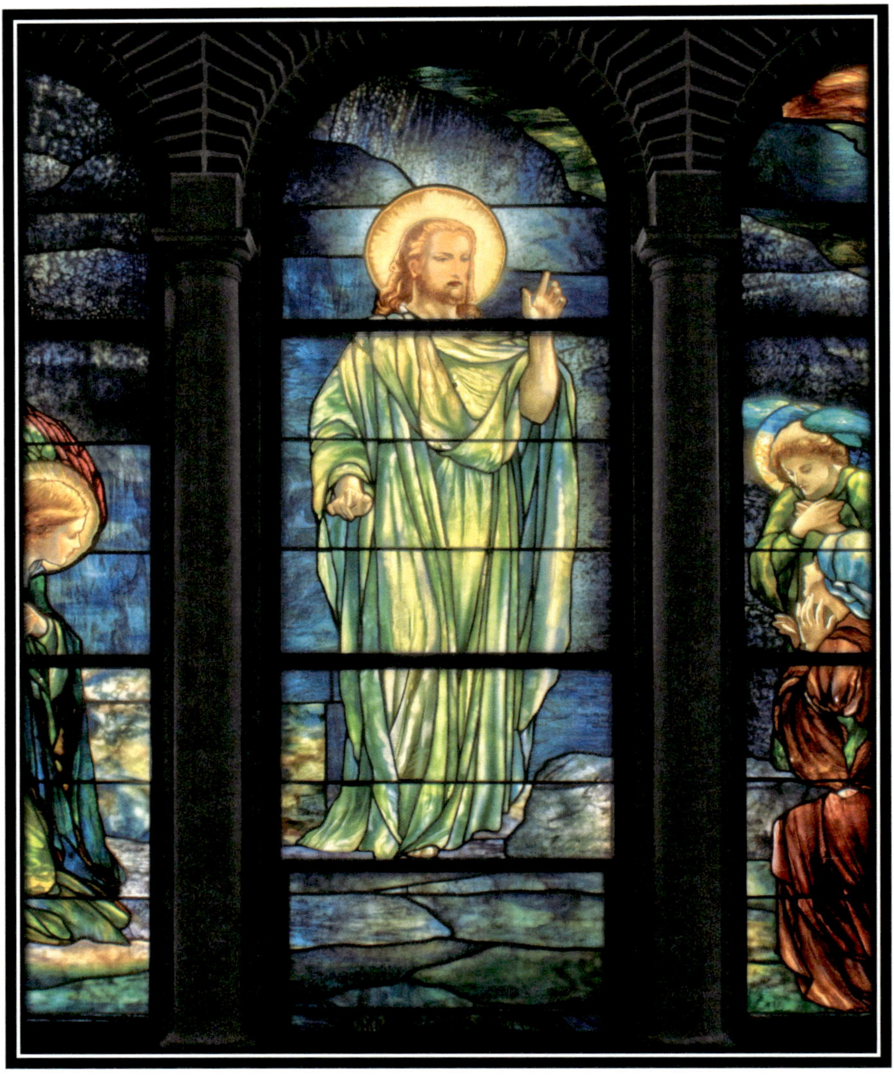

84. Woldenberg Art Center at Tulane University (1995-1996)

Newcomb Cir, Audubon
Hartman-Cox, architects

Find two triptych windows designed and fabricated by Tiffany Studios of New York City at this site, one depicting the Resurrection [pictured] and one depicting the Supper at Emmaus *(see page 5)*; both originally installed in the Chapel of Newcomb College's Garden District campus in the mid-1890s.

PART TWO

THE SUBURBS

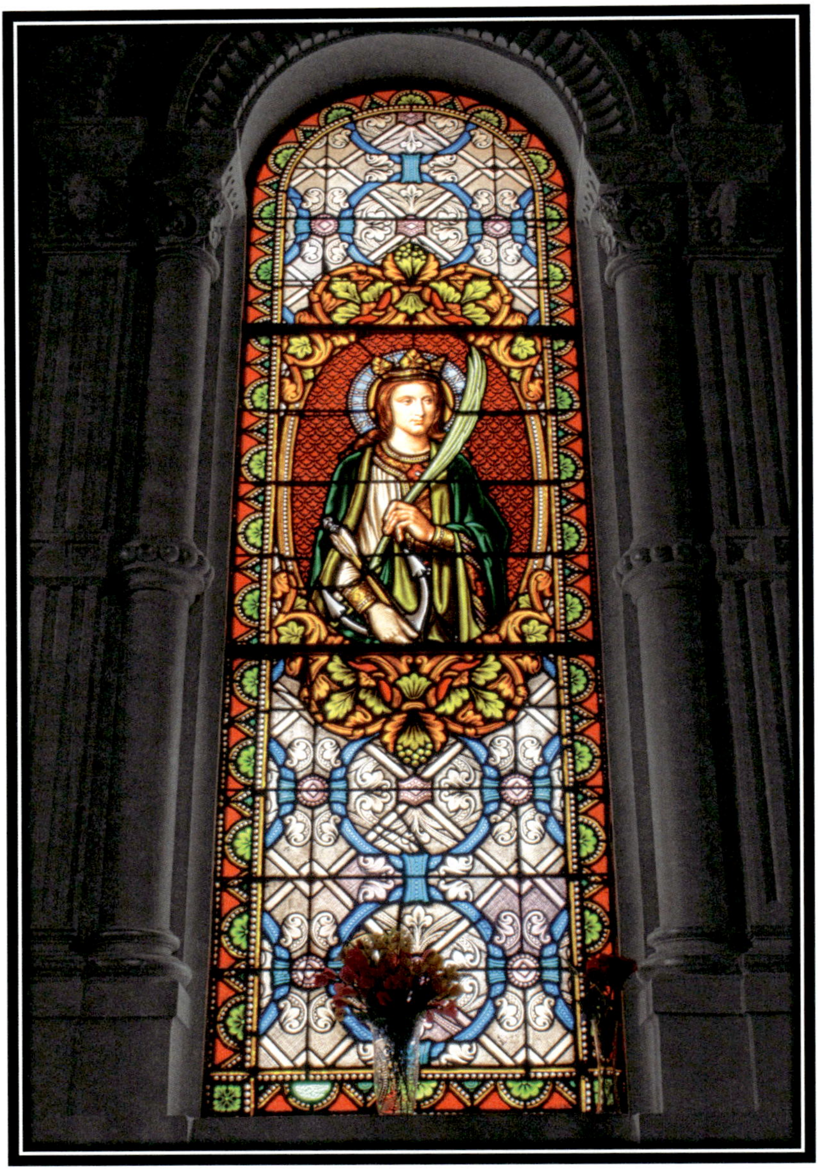

85. St. Michael the Archangel Catholic Church (1831-1833)

6476 LA-44, Convent
Florian P. Dicharry, architect; Christopher Colomb, master mason

Stained glass makers and dates of installation undetermined.

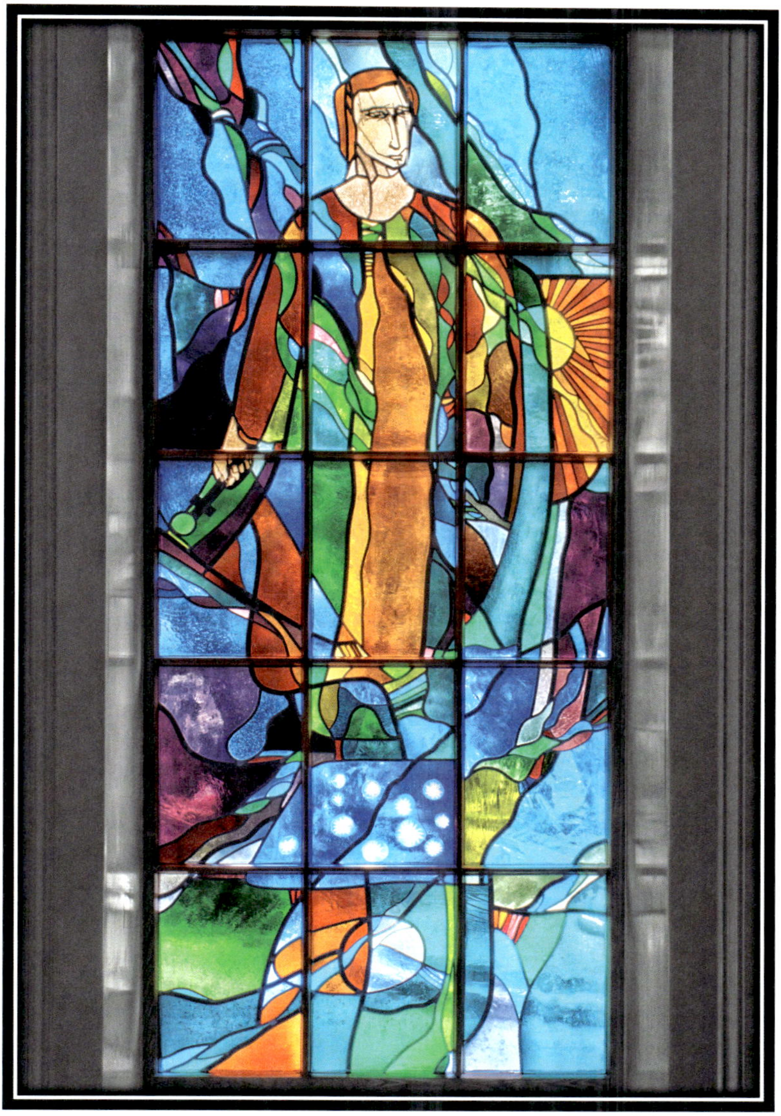

86. St. Joseph Chapel at Manresa House of Retreats (1842)

5858 LA-44, Convent
Architect undetermined

Located in the Main Building. In 1987, stained glass by Samuel J. Corso of Dufour/Corso Studios of Baton Rouge was installed during an extensive interior renovation that included the construction of this chapel.

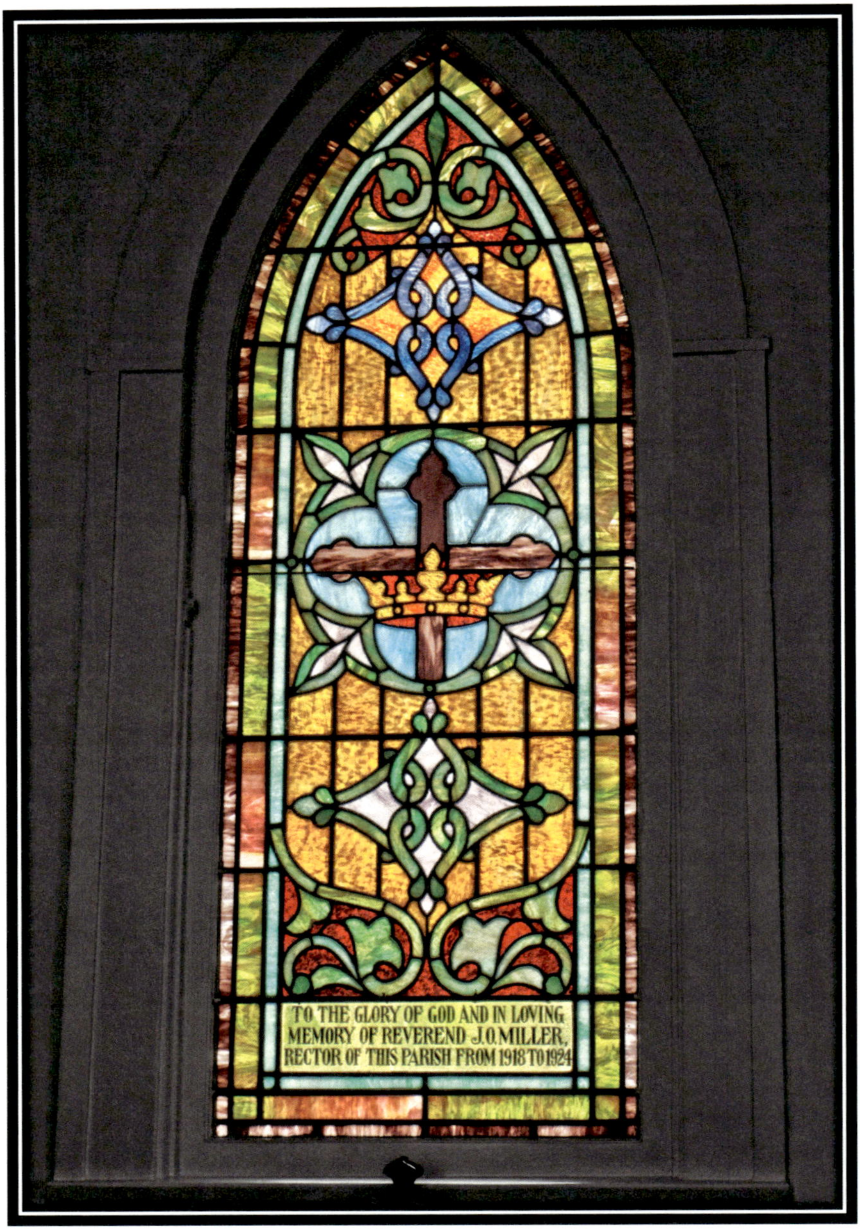

87. Old Christ Episcopal Church (1846)

120 S. New Hampshire St, Covington
Jonathan Arthur, builder

Stained glass makers undetermined; installed c. 1924.

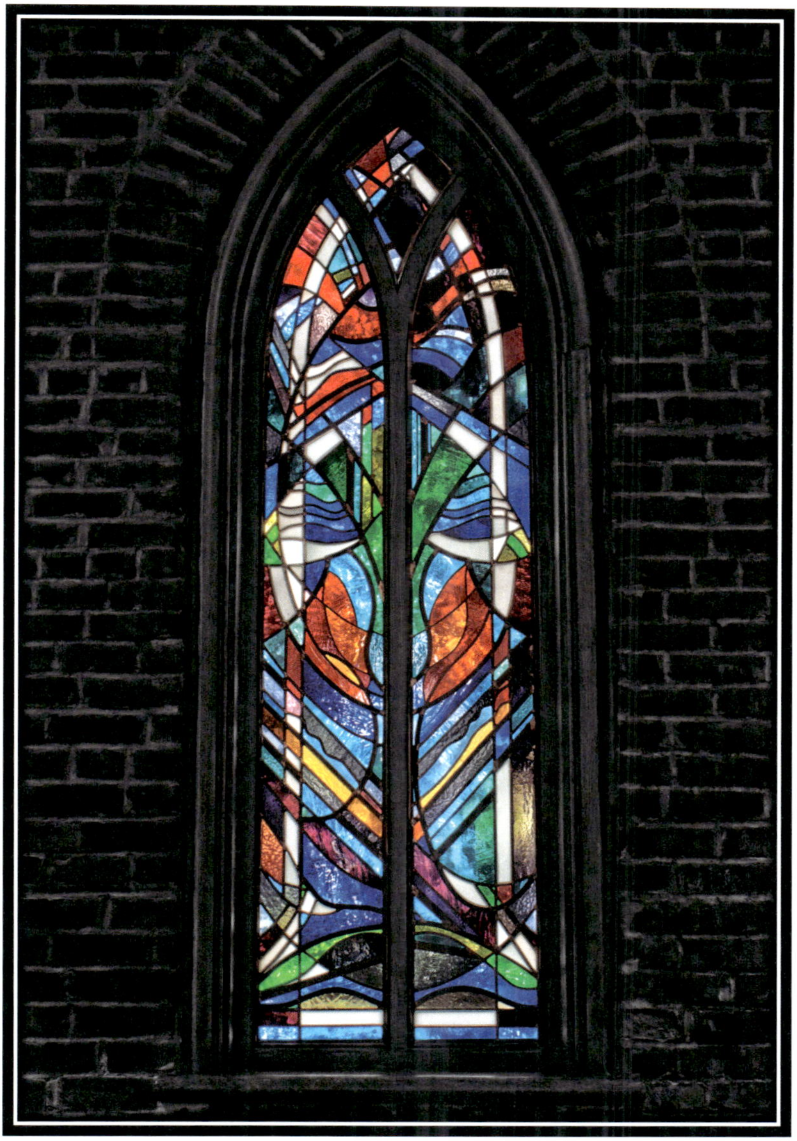

88. Sacred Heart Chapel at Manresa House of Retreats (1859)

5858 LA-44, Convent
Architect undetermined

Stained glass by Samuel J. Corso of Dufour/Corso Studios, Baton Rouge; installed 1985.

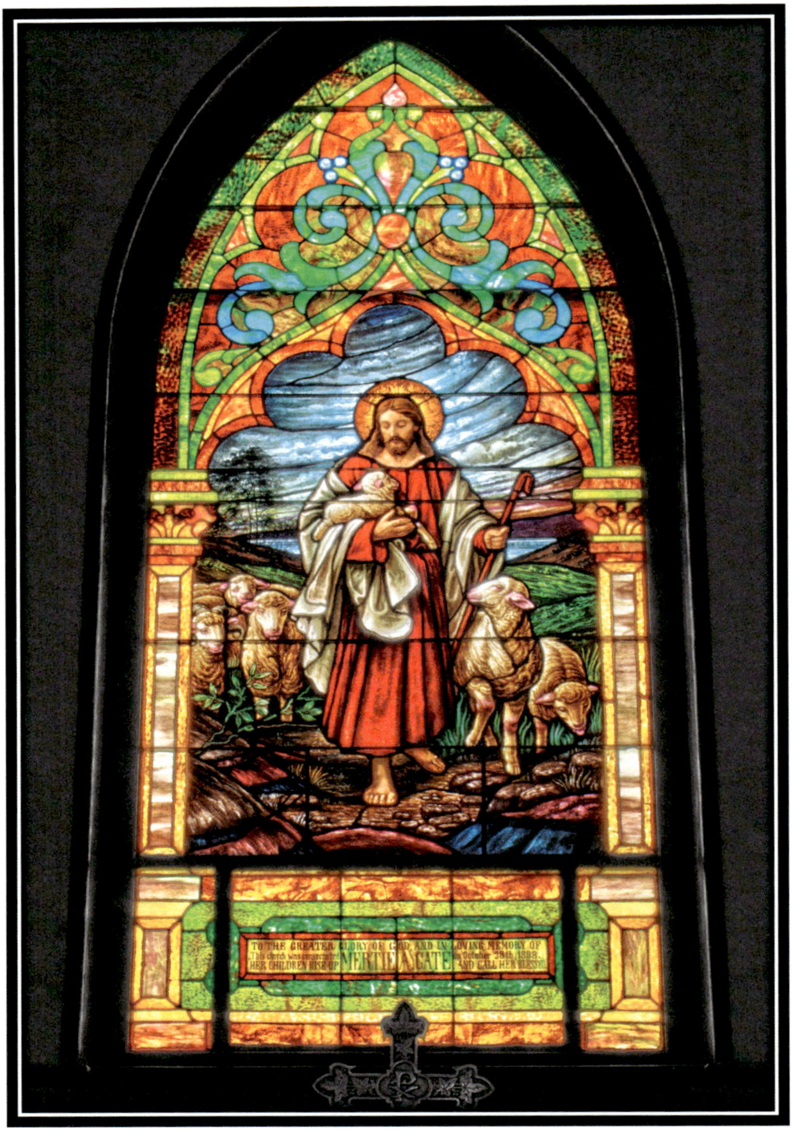

89. Grace Memorial Episcopal Church (1876)

100 W. Church St, Hammond
Architect undetermined

Primary window makers undetermined; wide ranging dates of installation from c.1888 to c.1978. One secondary lancet window by Cynthia Courage, Frankie Ostello and Anthony Fontana of Attenhofer's Stained Glass Studio in Metairie was installed c.2002.

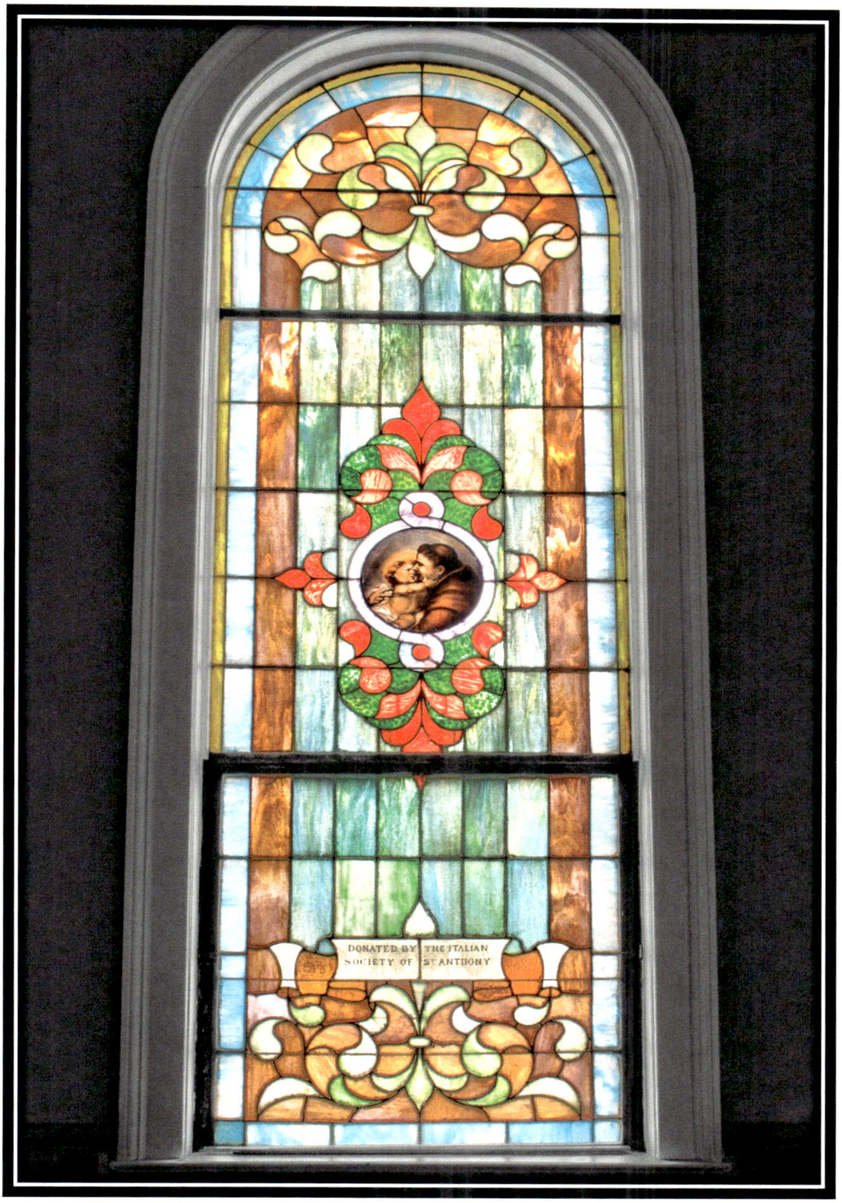

90. Old Holy Ghost Catholic Church (1902)

515 N. Oak St. Hammond
Architect undetermined

Stained glass makers and dates of installation undetermined.

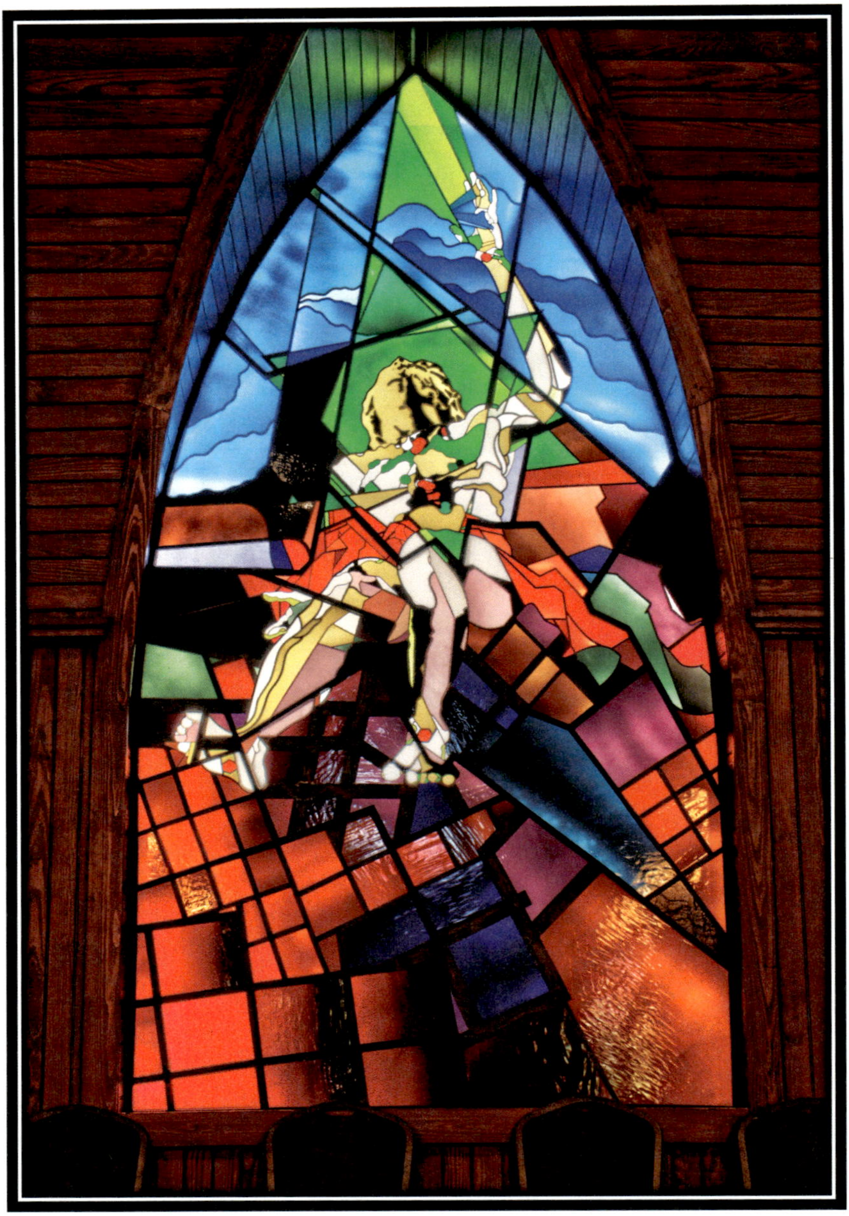

91. Covington Presbyterian Church (1902-1903)

222 S. Jefferson Ave, Covington
W.H. Krone, architect/builder

Stained glass by Stephen Wilson of Baton Rouge; installed 1982.

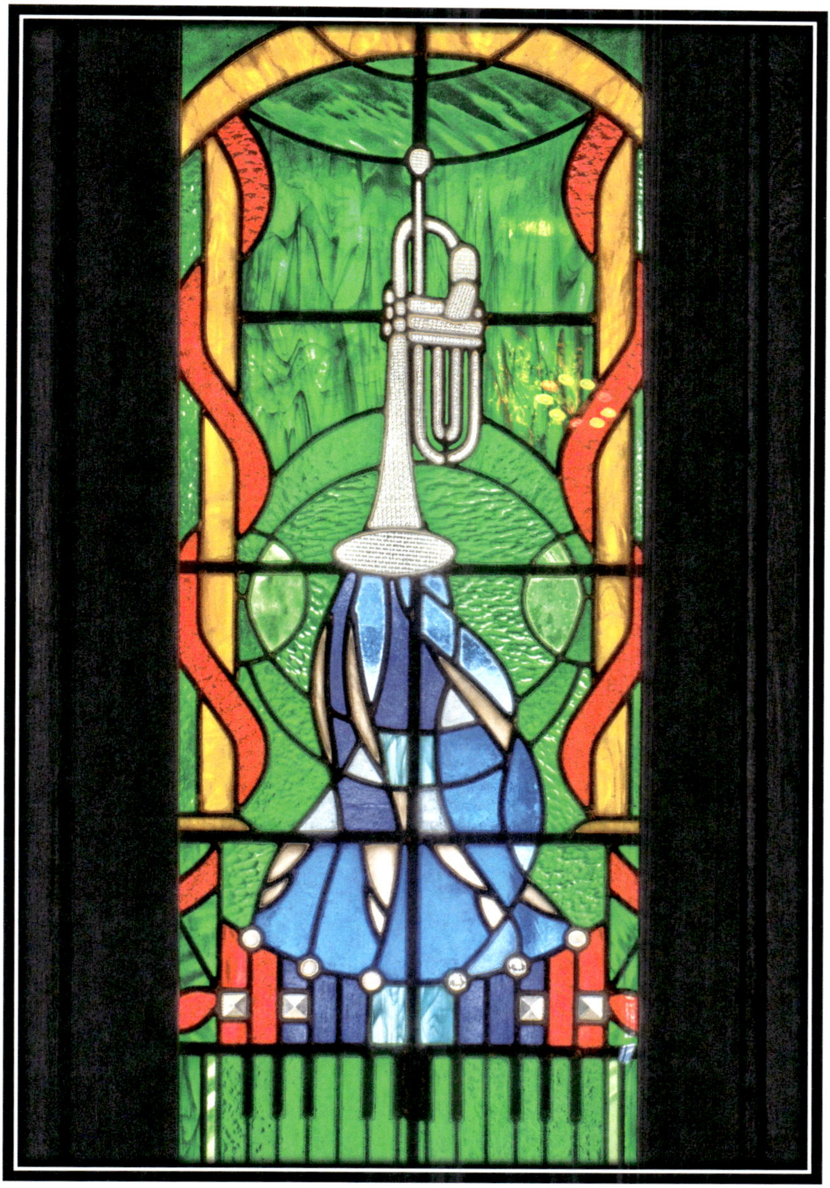

92. Wharton's (c.1914)

521 E. Boston St, Covington
Architect/builder undetermined

Also known as The Green Room. Stained glass designed and fabricated by John West of Jarreau, LA; installed 2007.

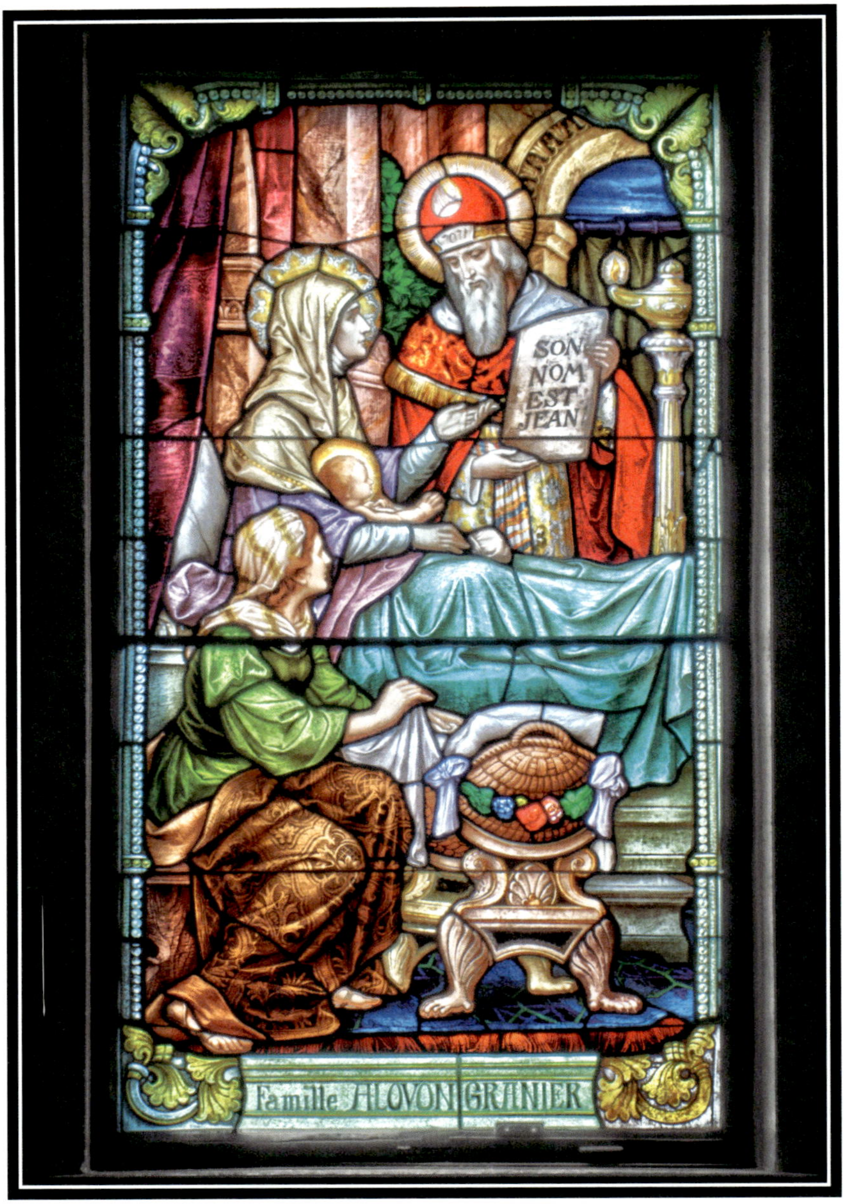

93. St. John the Baptist Catholic Church (1920)

2349 LA-18, Edgard
Favrot & Livaudais, architects

Stained glass makers and dates of installation undetermined.

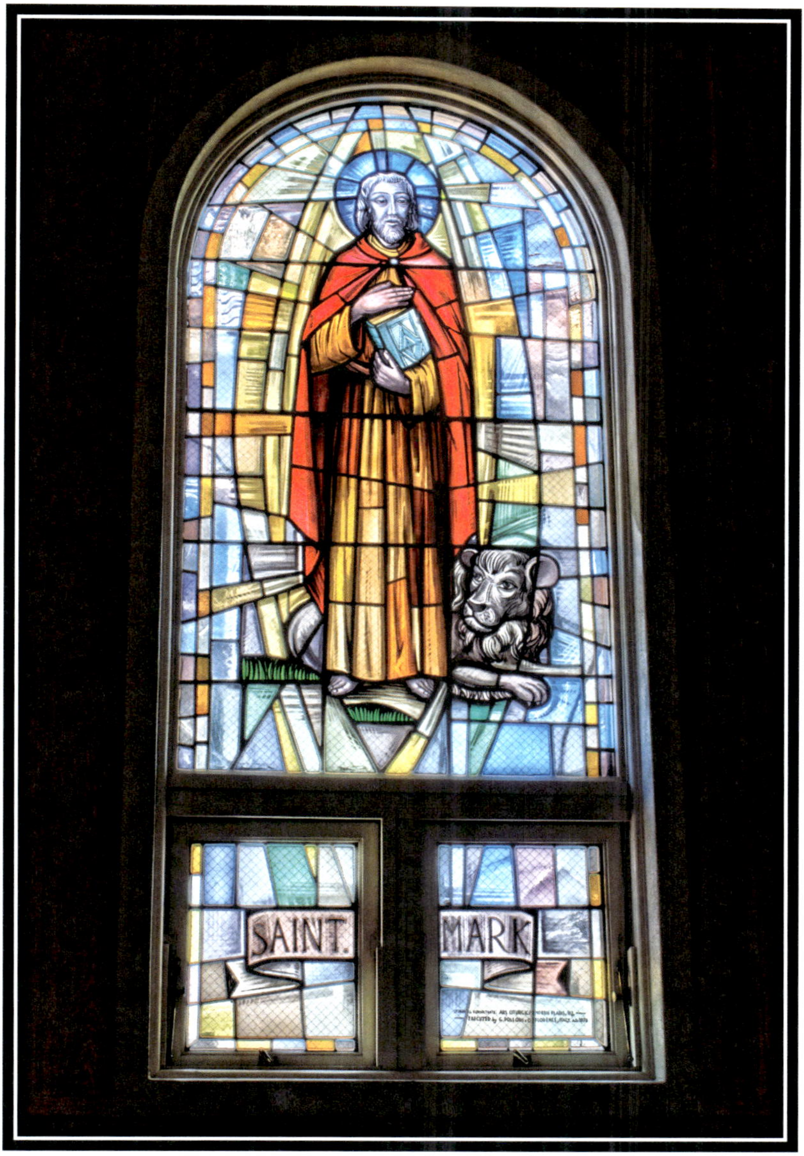

94. St. Charles Borromeo Catholic Church (1921)

13396 River Rd, Destrehan
H.L. Burton & Albert Bendernagel, architects
A.C. Babin's Sons, builders

Stained glass fabricated by Guido Polloni & Co. of Florence, Italy; Ars Liturgica of Morris Plains, NJ, consultants; installed c.1978.

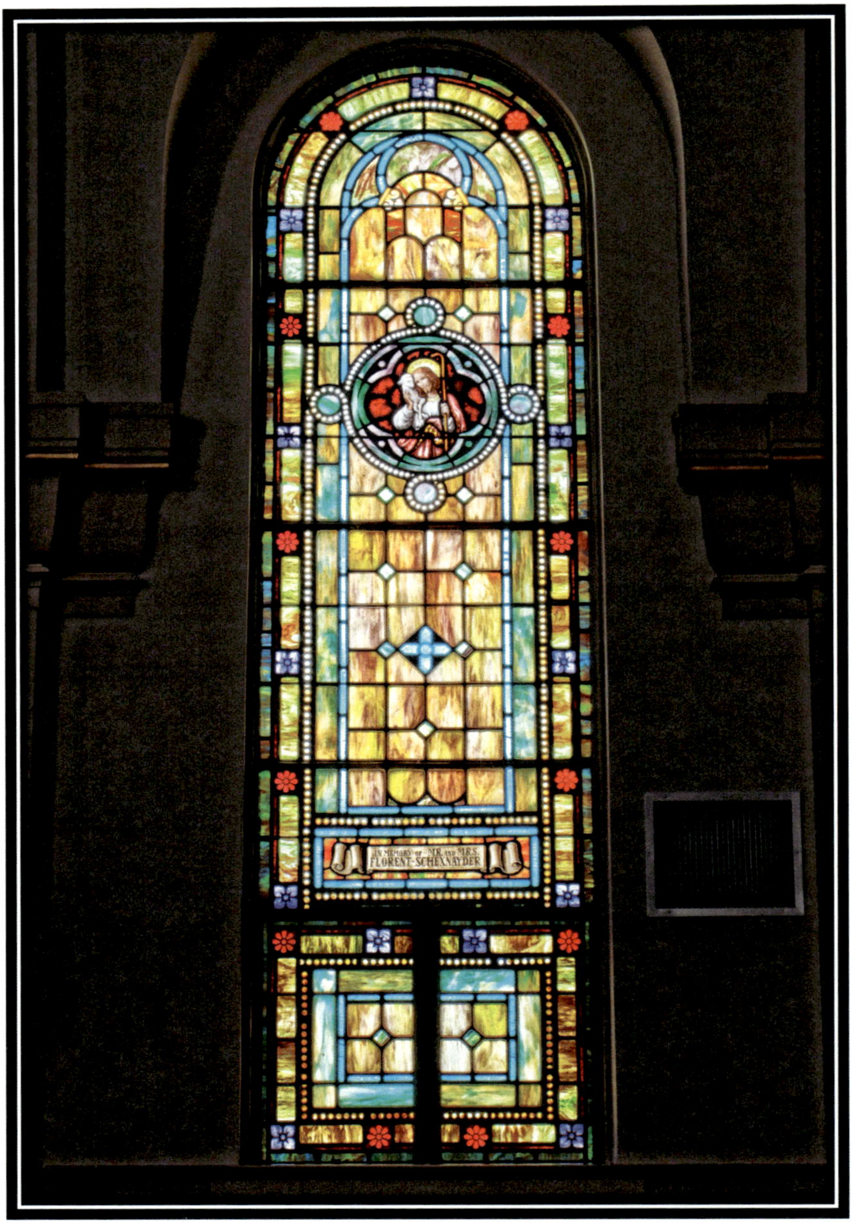

95. St. Joseph Catholic Church (1921)

2130 Rectory St, Paulina
Architect undetermined

Stained glass makers and dates of installation undetermined.

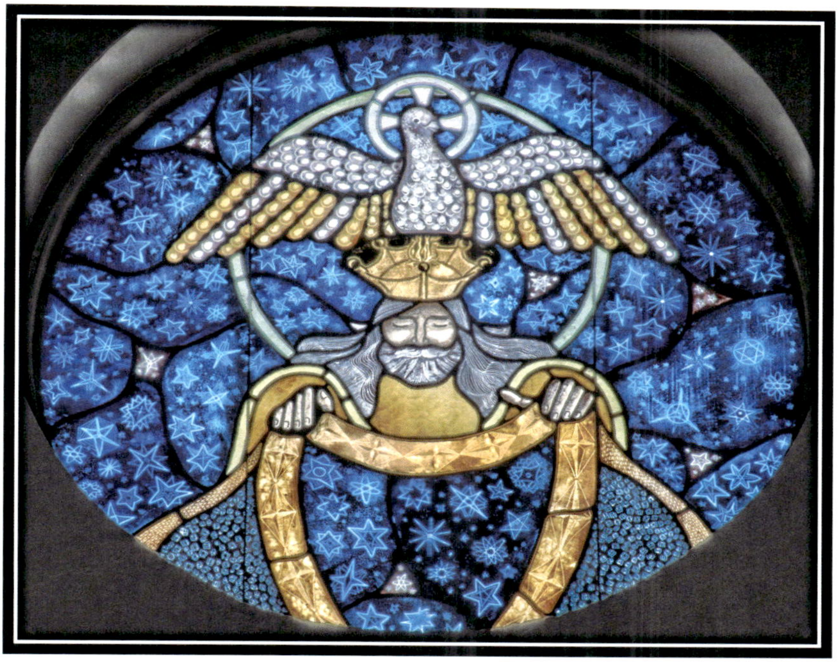

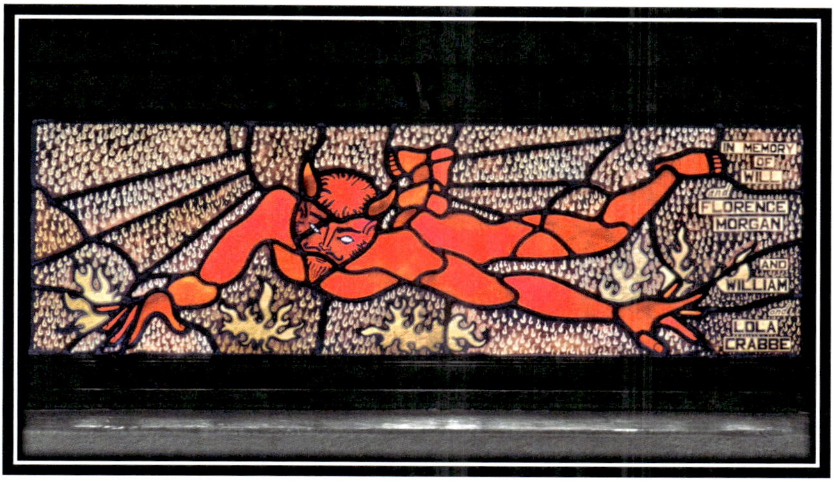

96. St. Jane de Chantal Catholic Church (1923-1924)

72040 Maple St, Abita Springs
Theodore Brune, architect; J.A. Hardoin, builder

Primary stained glass windows designed and fabricated by the Monks of the Abbey of Our Lady of the Holy Ghost, Conyers, GA. Installed in the latter half of the twentieth century; exact dates undetermined.

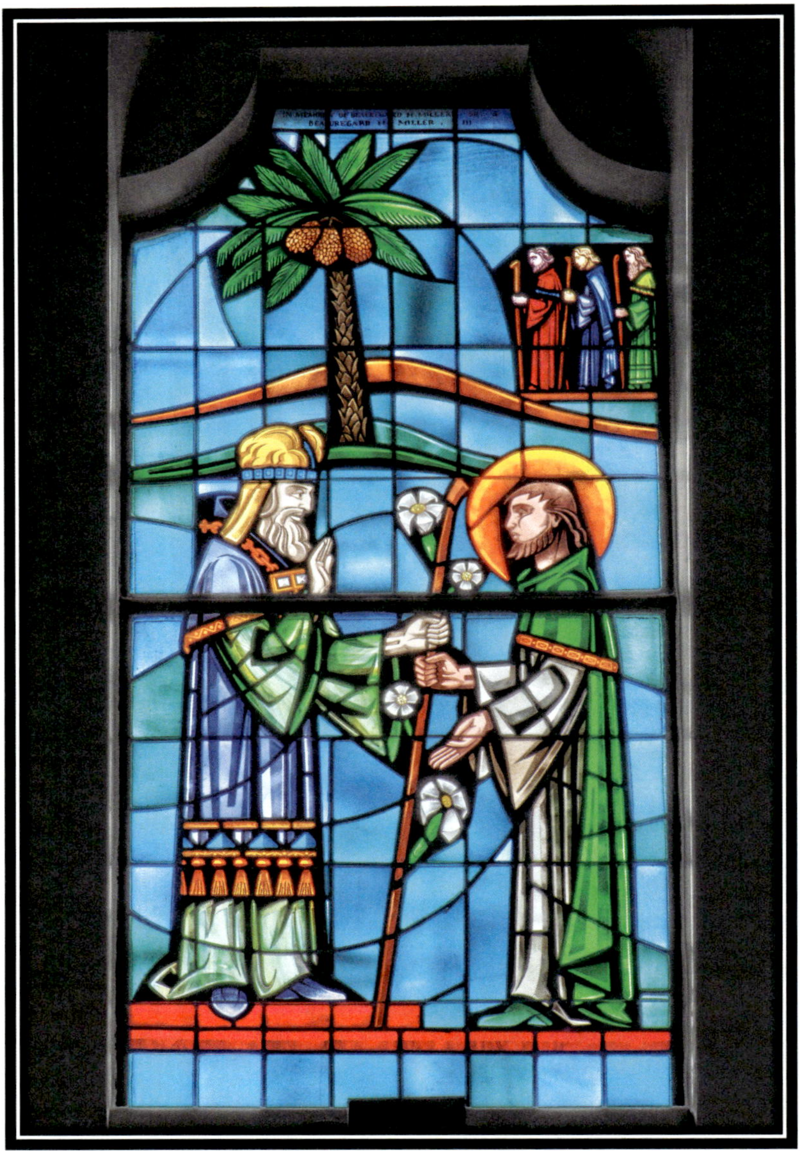

97. St. Joseph Catholic Church (1926-1927)

610 Sixth St, Gretna
William Richard Burk, architect; Joseph Fromherz Inc., contractor

According to PRC researchers, St. Joseph's primary windows were designed by Bernard O. Gruenke and fabricated by Conrad Schmitt Studios of New Berlin, Wisconsin; installed in the 1980s.

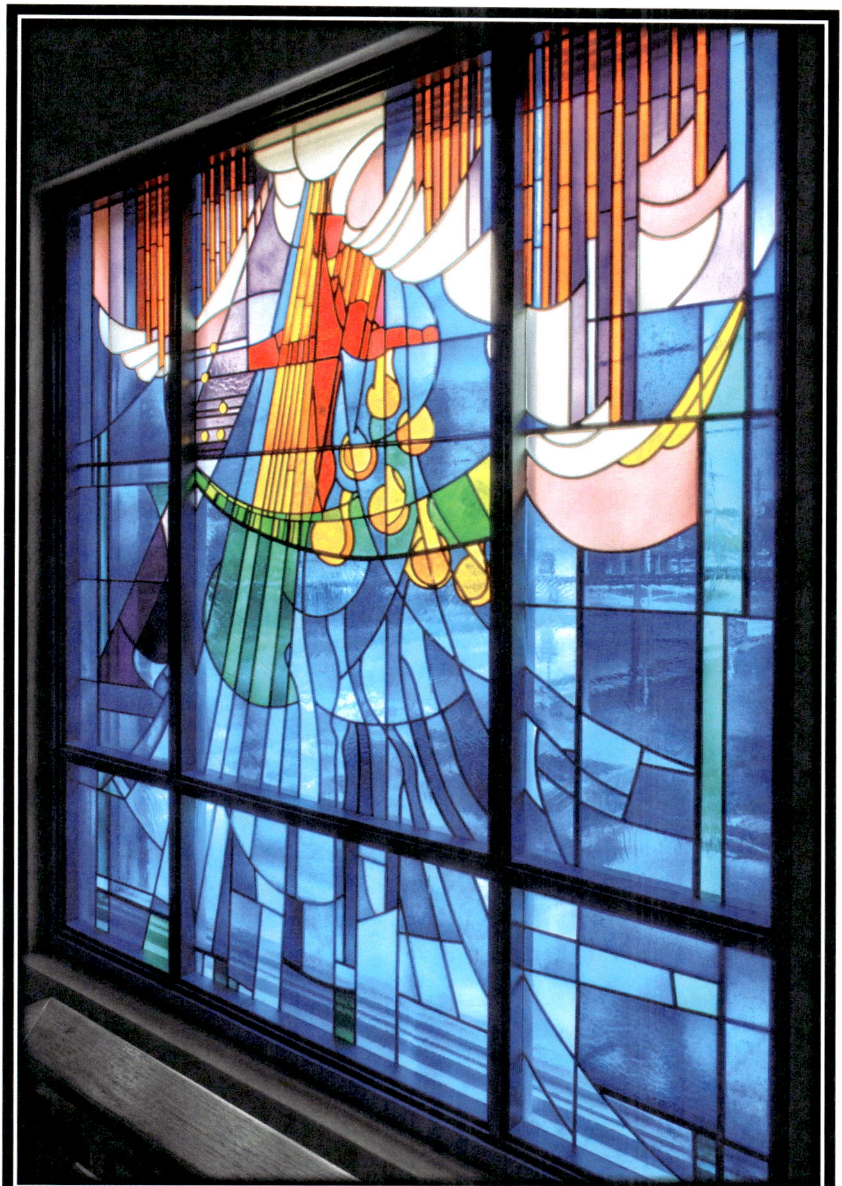

98. First Baptist Church (1929)

401 W. Morris Ave, Hammond
Architect/builder undetermined

Stained glass by Stephen Wilson of Baton Rouge; installed 1988.

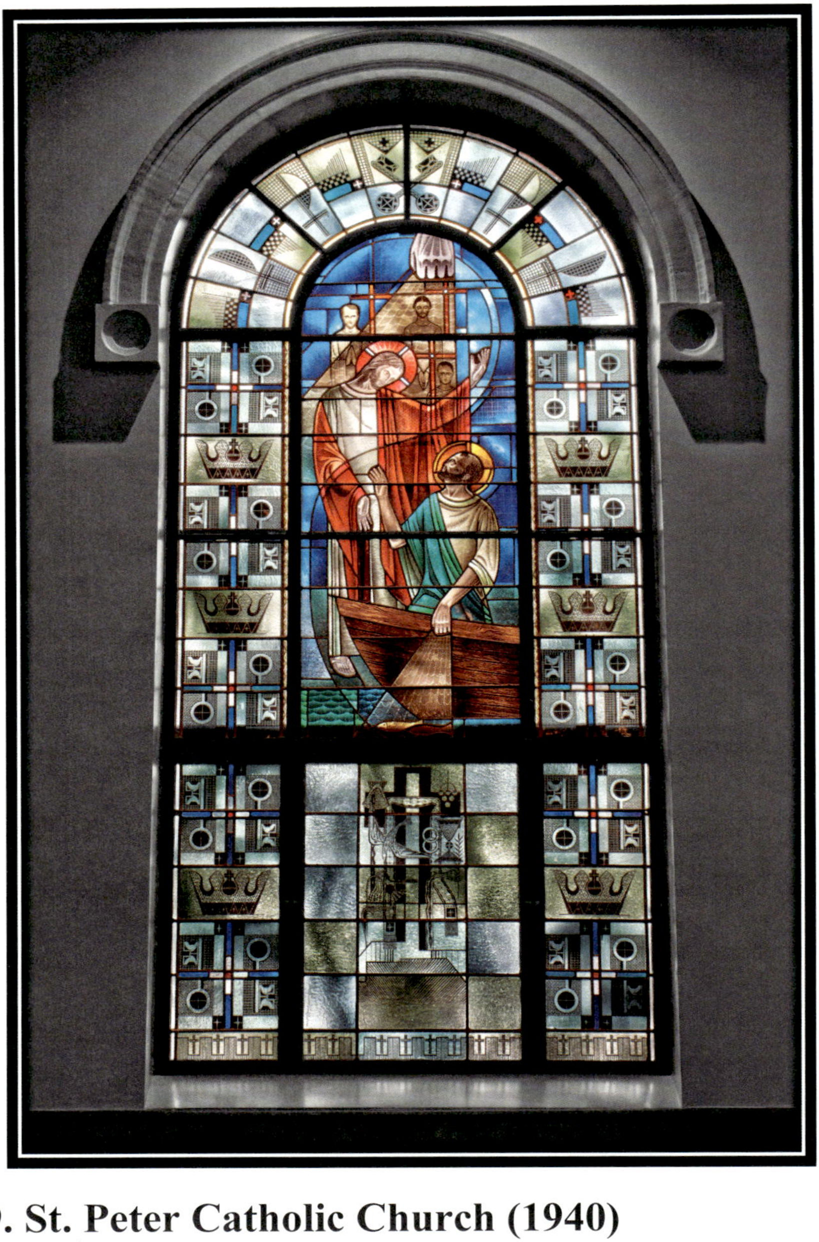

99. St. Peter Catholic Church (1940)

125 E. 19th Ave, Covington
Wogan & Bernard, architects

Stained glass by Emil Frei Studios of St. Louis; installed in two eras, 1940s and 1960s.

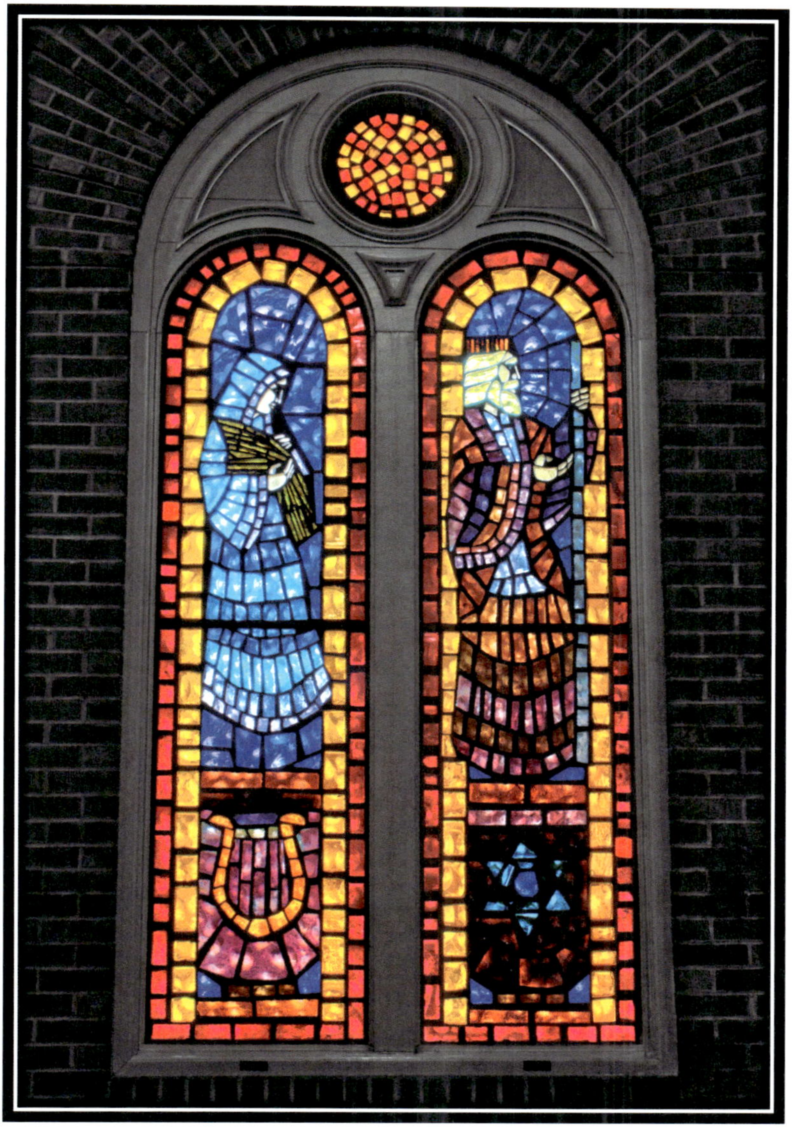

100. Metairie Baptist Church (1949-1950)

401 Codifer Blvd, Metairie
Favrot & Reed, architects; R.P. Farnsworth & Co., contractors

Primary *dalle de verre* windows [pictured] designed and fabricated by Milton Pounds of Pounds Stained Glass Studio, Covington; installed 1981. Window over high altar by Stan Gall Stained Glass of Crowley, LA; installed c.2000.

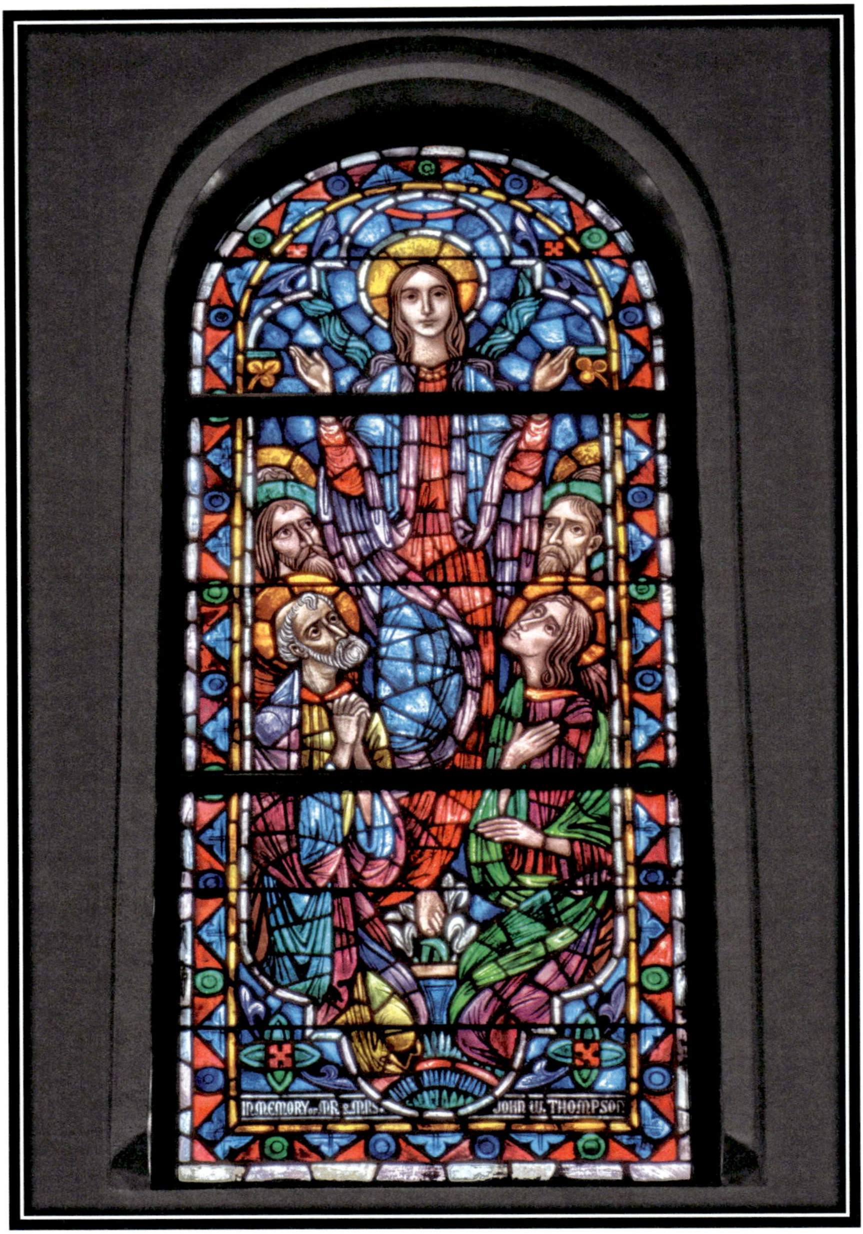

101. Our Lady of the Lake Catholic Church (1951-1953)
395 Lafitte St, Mandeville
Philip P. Cazale, architect; Lawrence P. Smith, builder

Stained glass made by Franz Mayer Co. of Munich; installed 1954-1958.

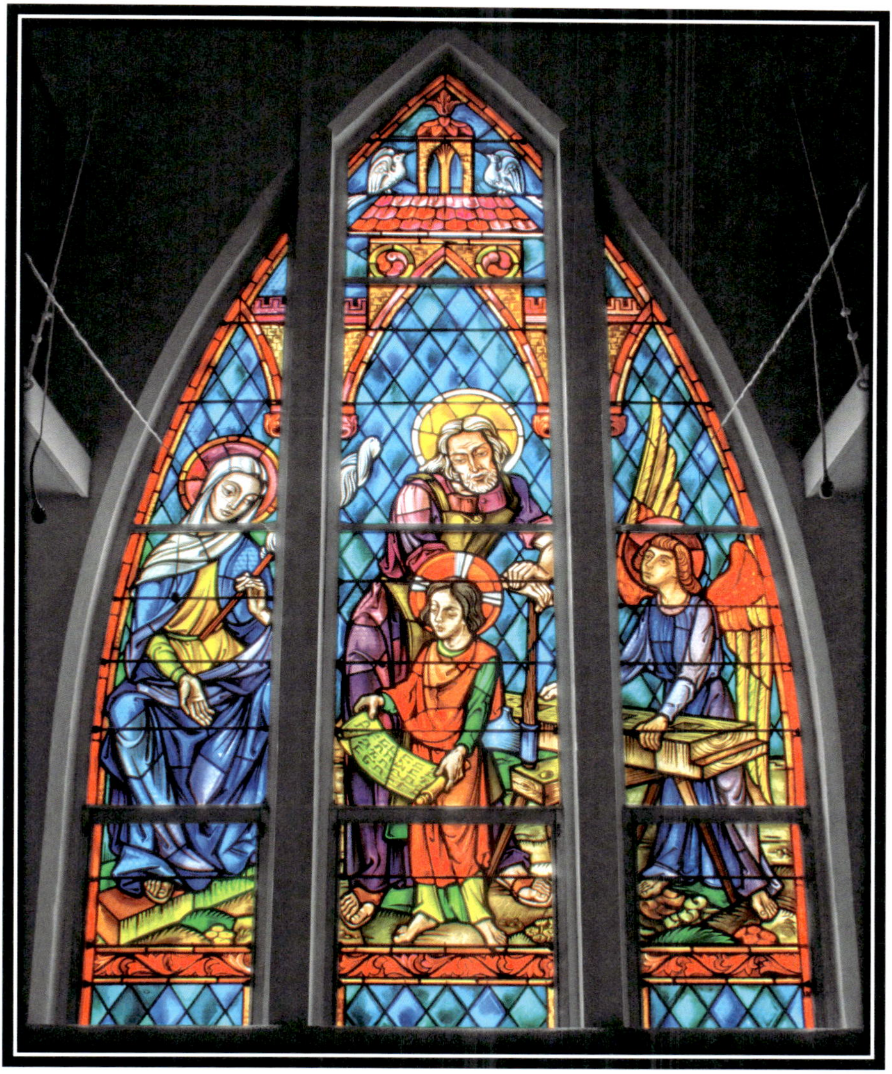

102. Most Sacred Heart of Jesus Catholic Church (1955)

616 E. Main St, Gramercy
Philip P. Cazale, architect; Charles Carter and Co., builders

Stained glass designed by Glasmalerei O. Peters Studio of Paderborn, Germany; installed c.1957.

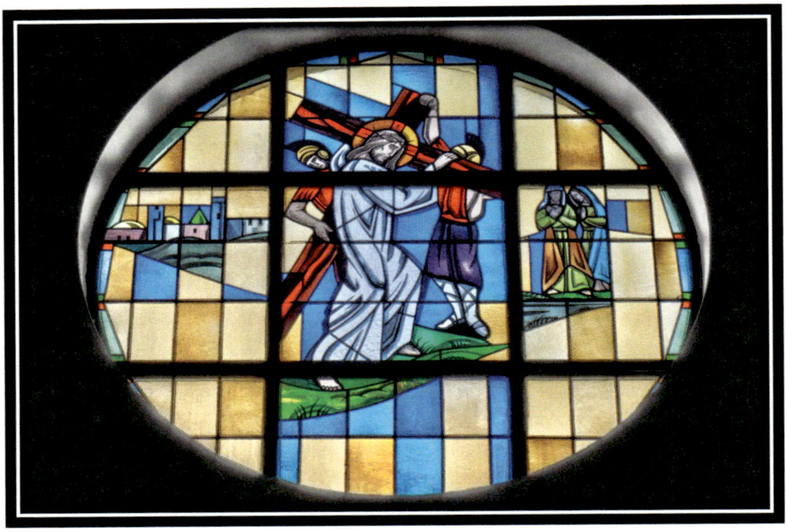

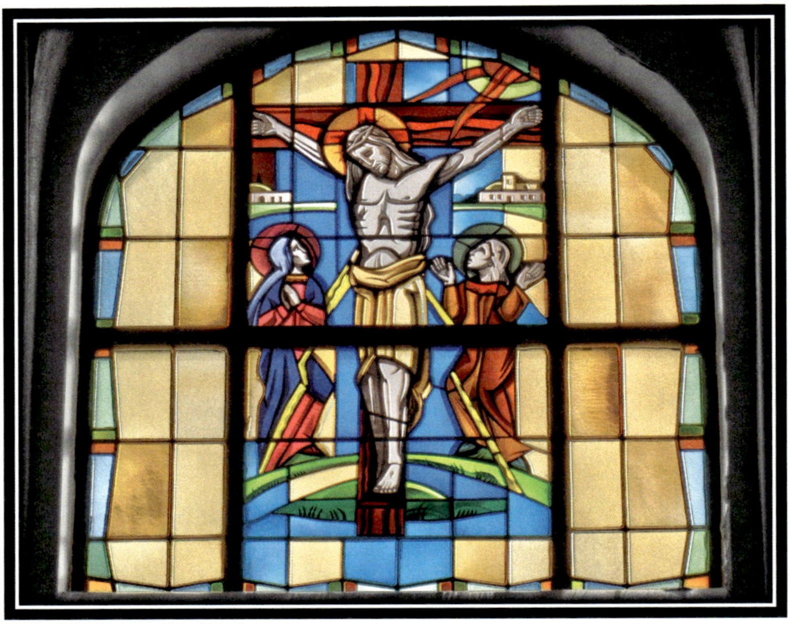

103. Our Lady of Prompt Succor Catholic Church (1955-1956)

146 Fourth St, Westwego
Diboll-Kessels & Associates, architects

Glass makers and dates of installation undetermined.

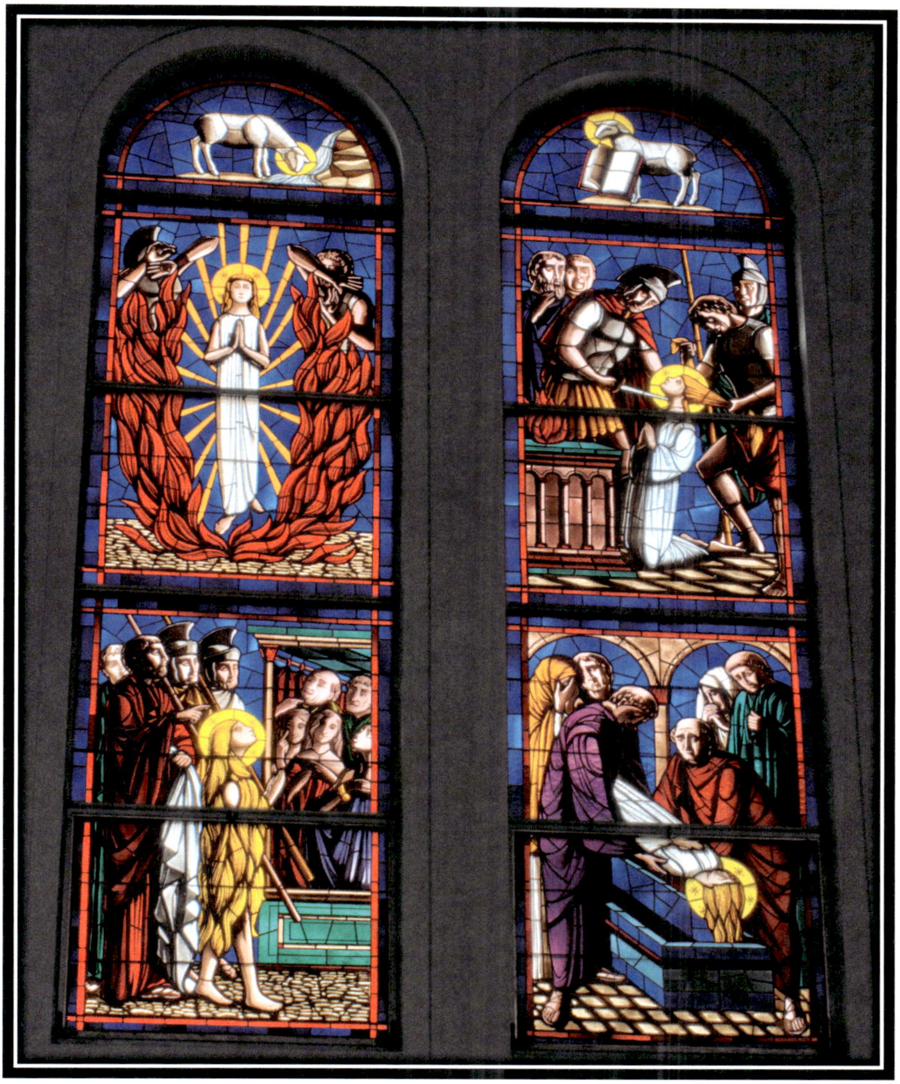

104. St. Agnes Virgin and Martyr Catholic Church (1956-1957)

3310 Jefferson Hwy, Jefferson
D.D. Albert Bendernagel, Jr. & John M. Lachin, Jr., architects
Perrilliat-Rickey & Co., contractors

Stained glass by Studio D'Arte Tolleri of Florence, Italy.

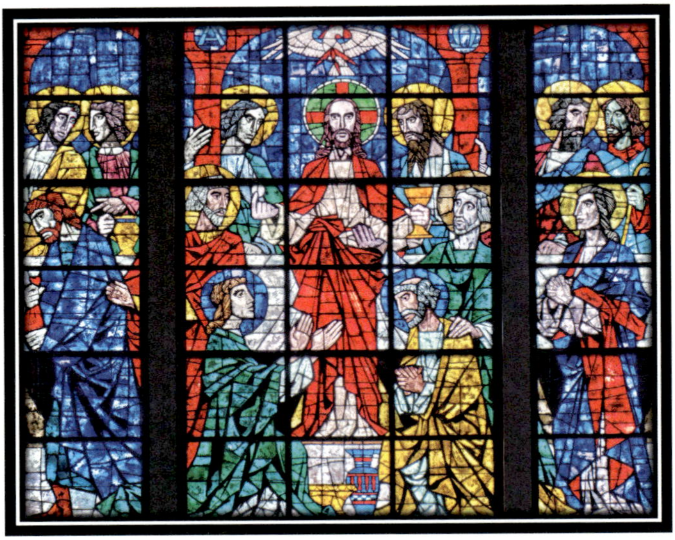

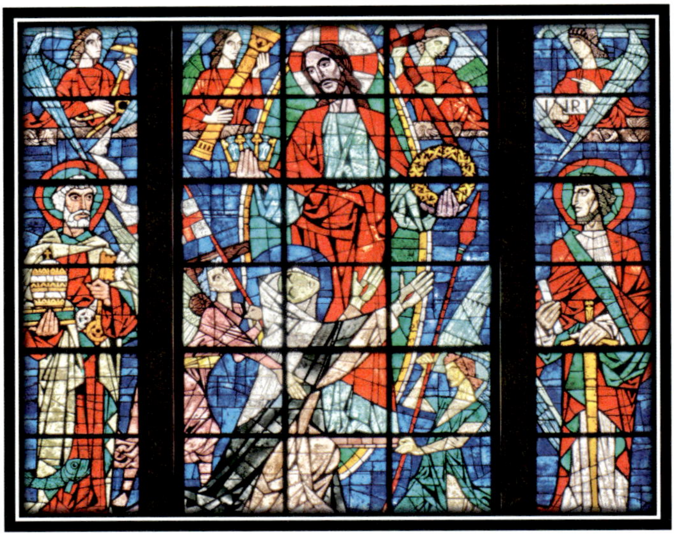

105. St. Catherine of Siena Catholic Church (1956-1957)

105 Bonnabel Blvd, Metairie
Burk, LeBreton & Lamantia, architects
Lionel F. Favret Co., Inc., general contractor

Stained glass designed by Franz X. W. Braunmiller; fabricated by Franz Mayer Co. of Munich.

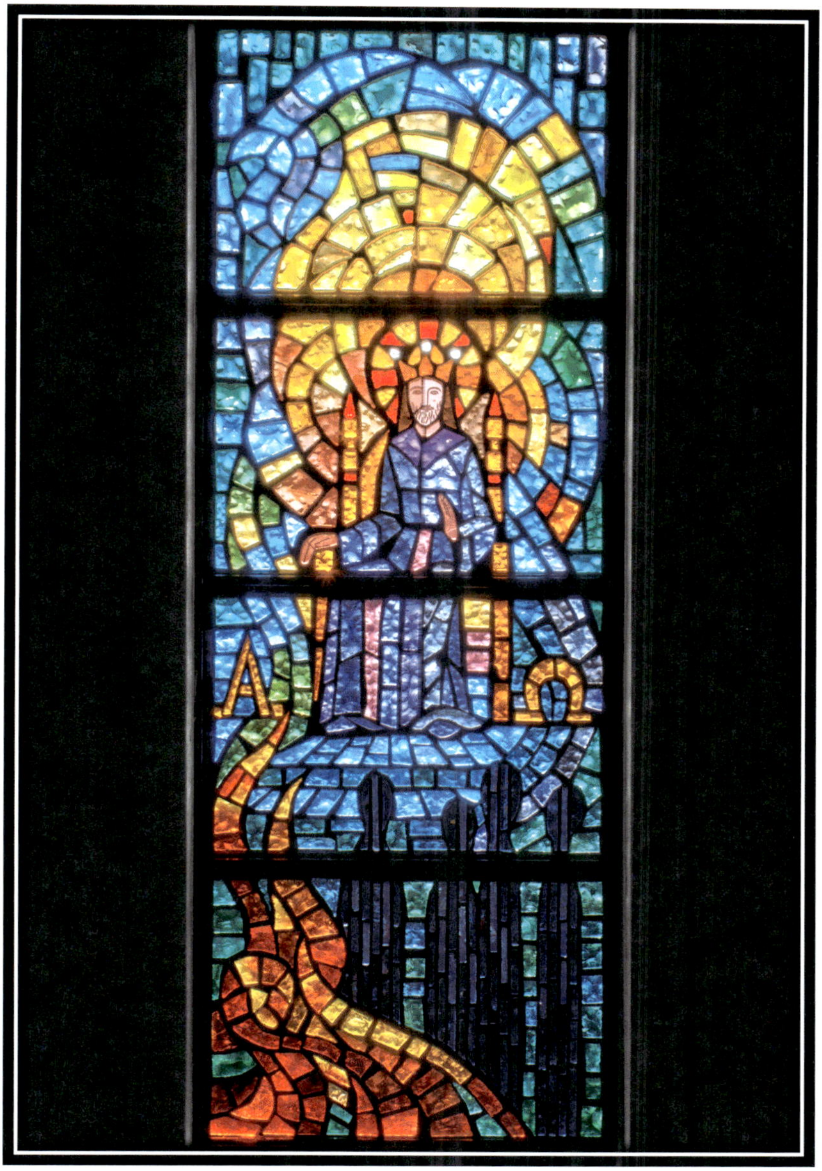

106. St. Christopher the Martyr Catholic Church (1957)

3900 Derbigny St, Metairie
Philip P. Cazale, architect; George J. Glover, Inc., general contractor

Primary *dalle de verre* windows designed by the Cavallini Company of San Antonio, TX [pictured]; installed during a 1981 renovation. Find also one leaded, hexagonal window fabricated by Franz Mayer Co. of Munich in 1960.

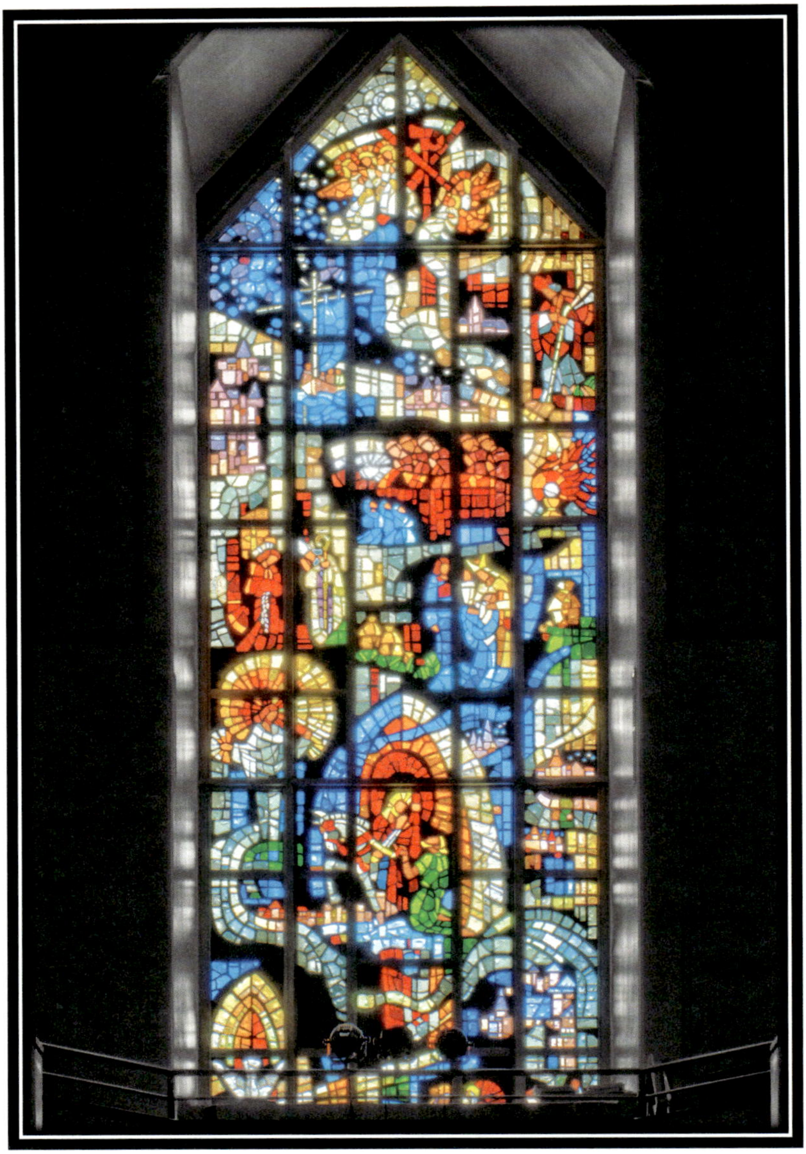

107. St. Martin's Episcopal Church (1958-1959)

2216 Metairie Rd, Metairie
Ricciuti Associates, architects

Dalle de verre windows designed by Gabriel and Jacques Loire of Loire Atelier, Chartres, France. Nave windows installed 1968-1969; choir balcony window, 2004.

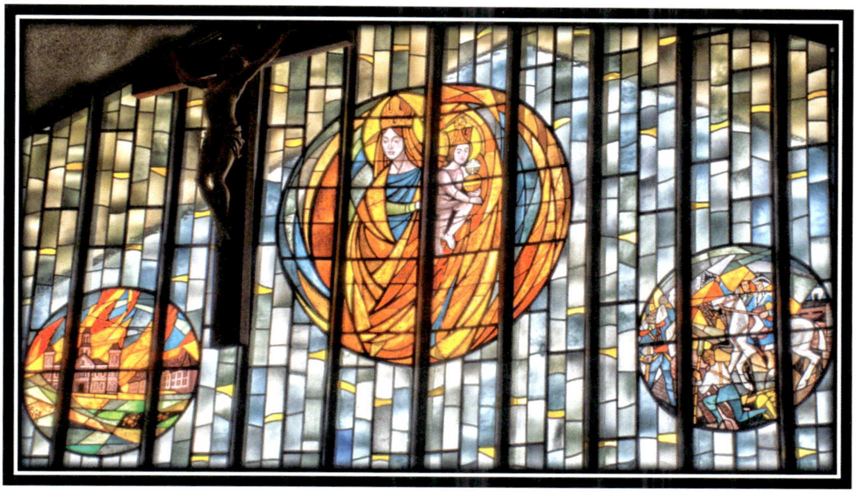

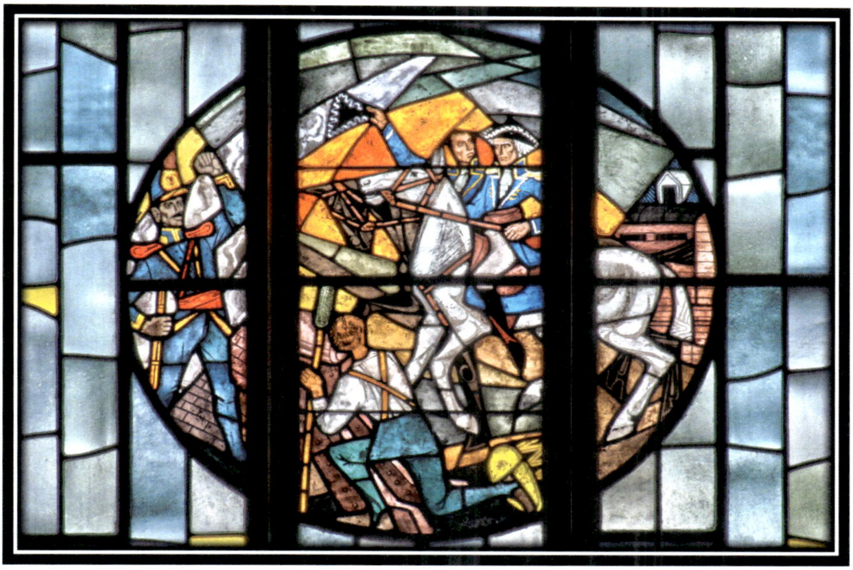

108. Our Lady of Prompt Succor Catholic Church (1958-1959)

2320 Paris Rd, Chalmette
Burk, LeBreton & Lamantia, architects
Bartley, Inc., general contractor

PRC researchers attribute the stained glass at this site to the A. Henry Lips Company of Chalmette.

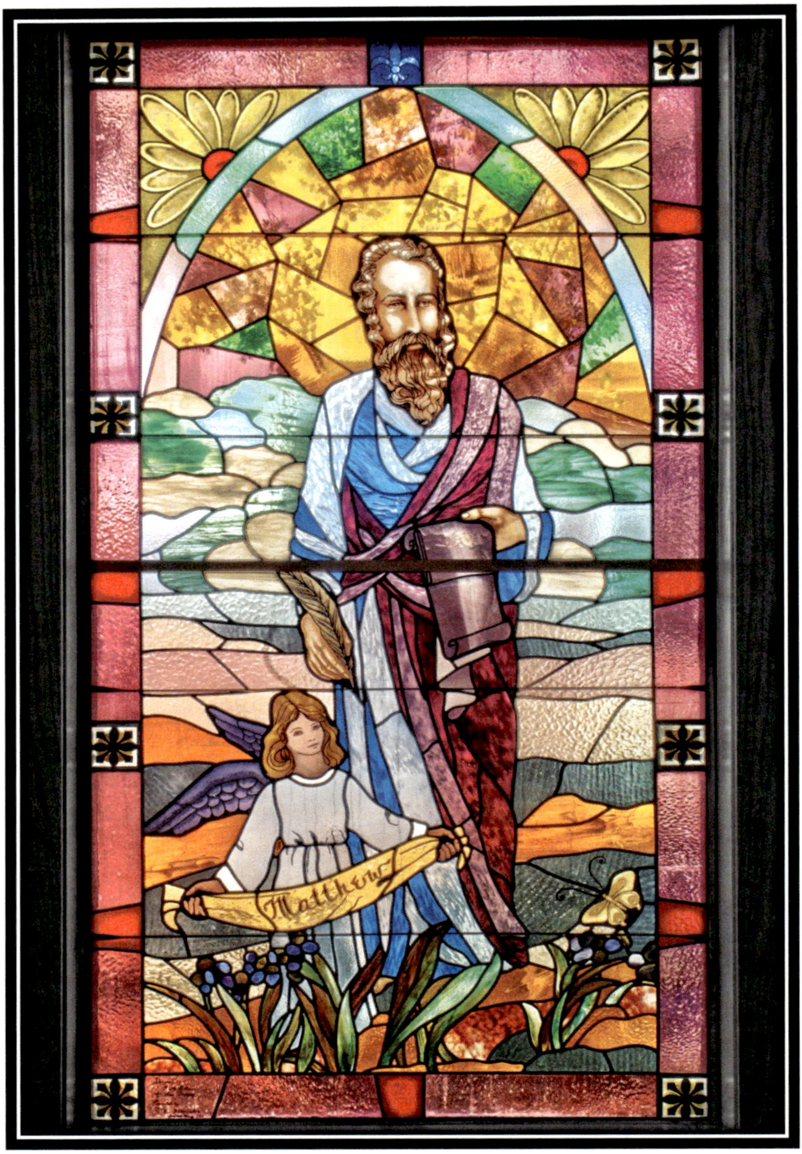

109. St. Matthew the Apostle Catholic Church (1960)

10021 Jefferson Hwy, River Ridge
John M. Lachin, Jr. & Fernand T. Picou, architects
Perrilliat-Rickey & Co., contractors

Stained glass designed by Ruth Goliwas of Alon Company, New Orleans; fabricated by Attenhofer's Stained Glass Studio of Metairie; installed c.1982.

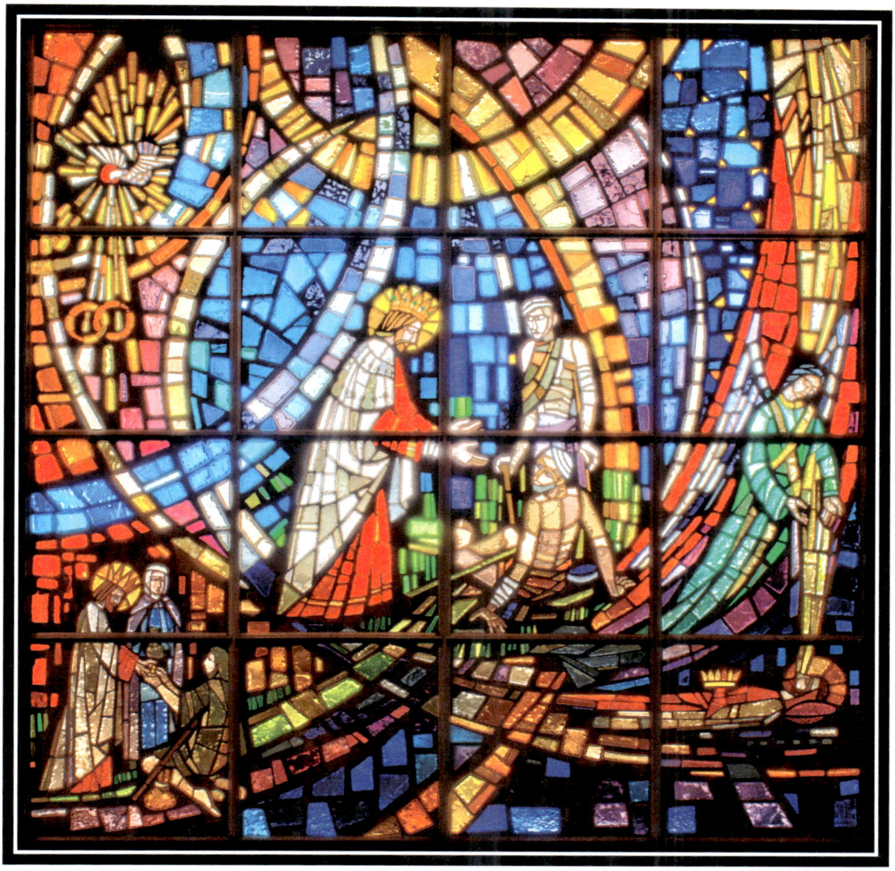

110. St. Edward the Confessor Catholic Church (1964)
4921 W. Metairie Ave, Metairie
J. Buchanon Blitch, architect

Dalle de verre windows made by Guido Polloni & Co. of Florence, Italy; Ars Liturgica of Morris Plains, NJ, consultants; installed c.1982.

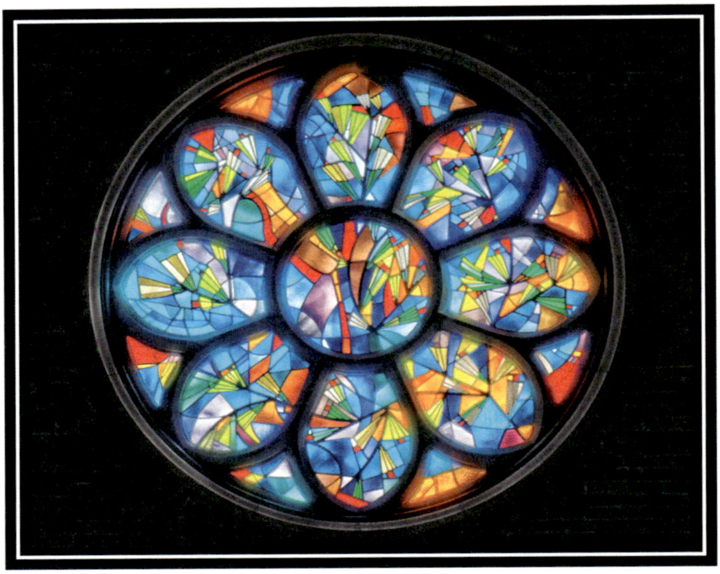

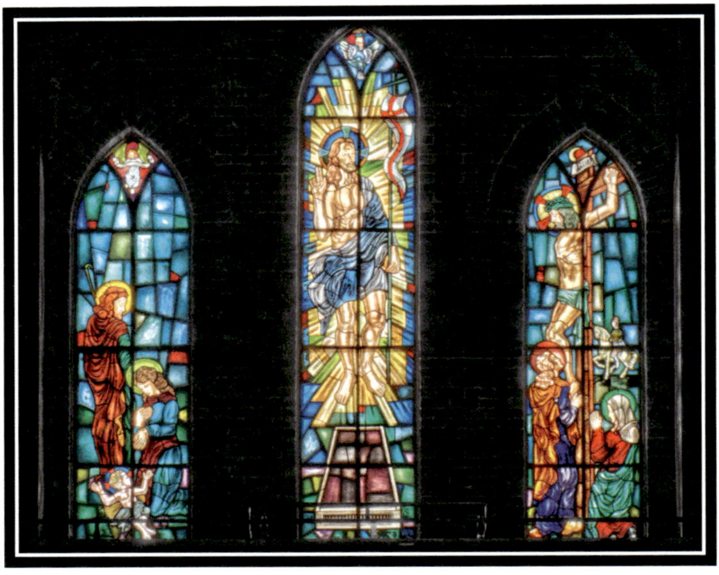

111. Christ Episcopal Church (1967)

120 S. New Hampshire St, Covington
Douglass V. Freret, architect

Rose window by Paul Dufour of Dufour/Corso Studios, Baton Rouge; installed c.1980s. Makers and installation dates of choir balcony windows undetermined.

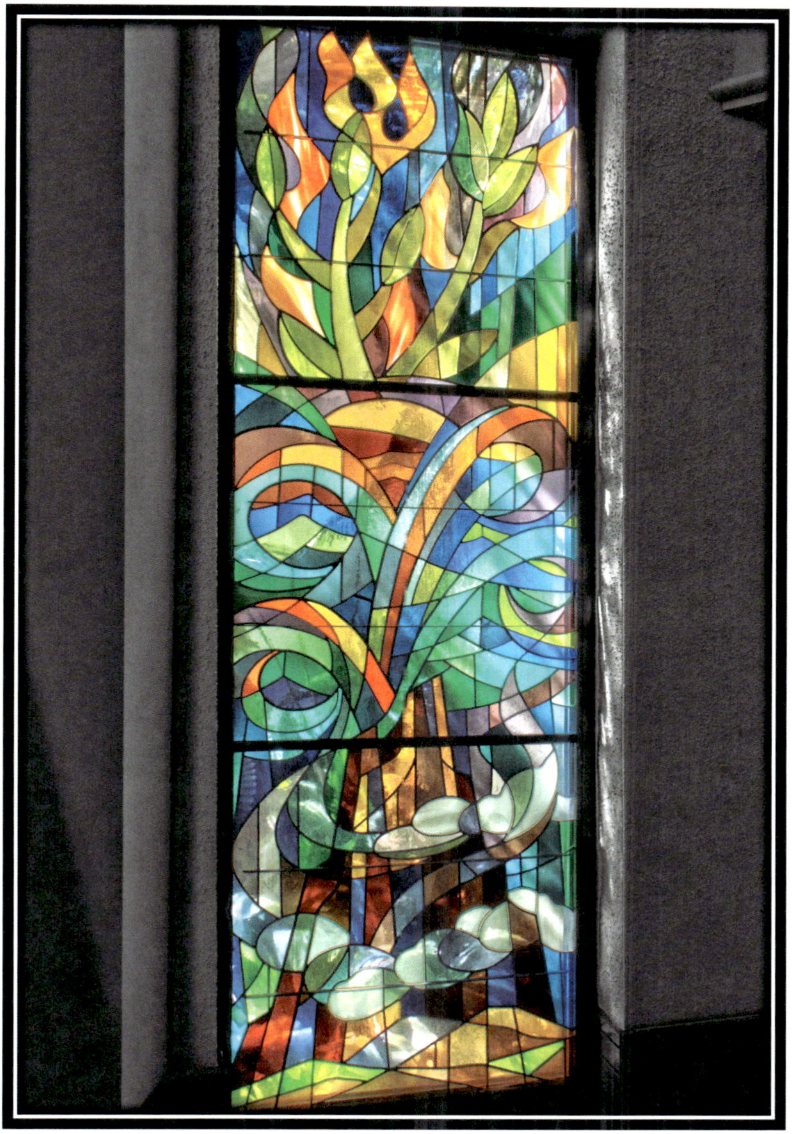

112. Congregation Gates of Prayer Synagogue (1974-1975)

4000 W. Esplanade Ave, Metairie
Caldwell & Bedikian, architects; Bernard Bennett, general contractor

PRC researchers attribute this site's stained glass to David Ascalon of Tel Aviv and New Jersey.

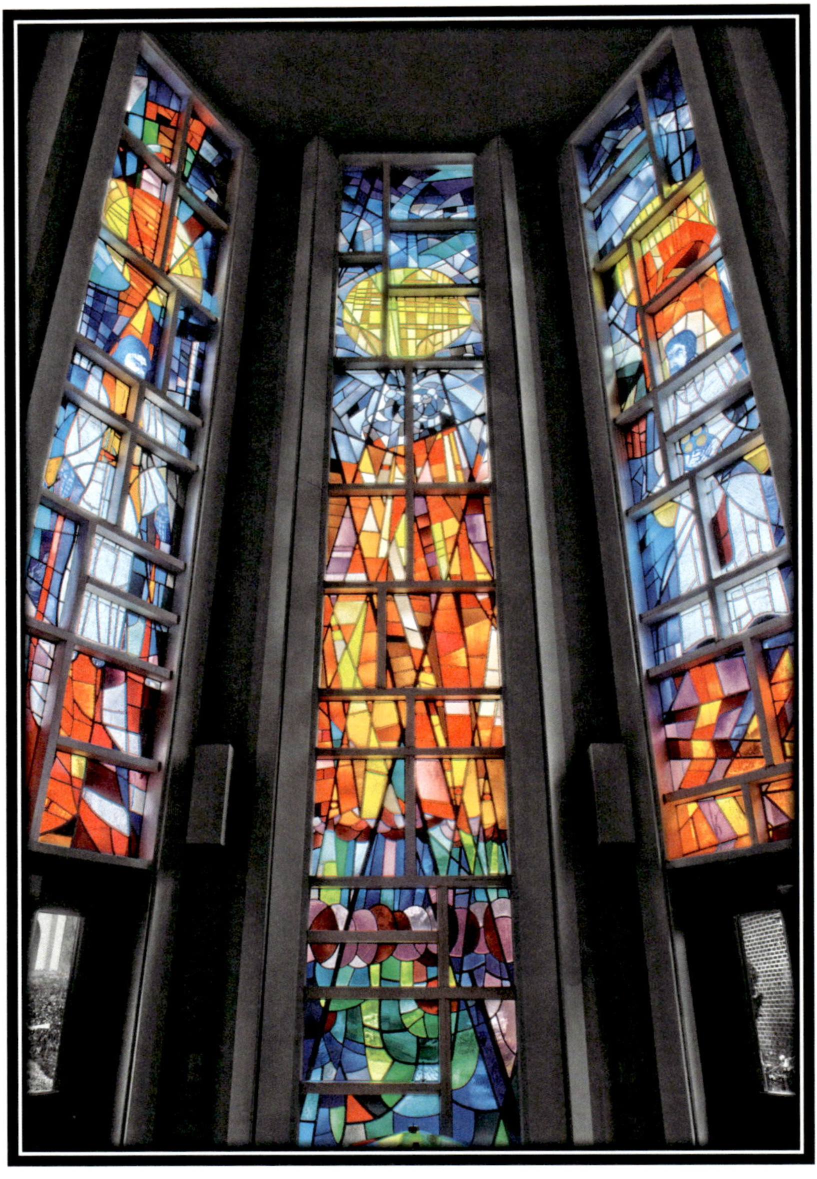

113. Old Holy Ghost Catholic Church ~ Chapel Addition (1975)

515 N. Oak St, Hammond
Architect undetermined

Stained glass by Paul A. Dufour of Dufour/Corso Studios, Baton Rouge.

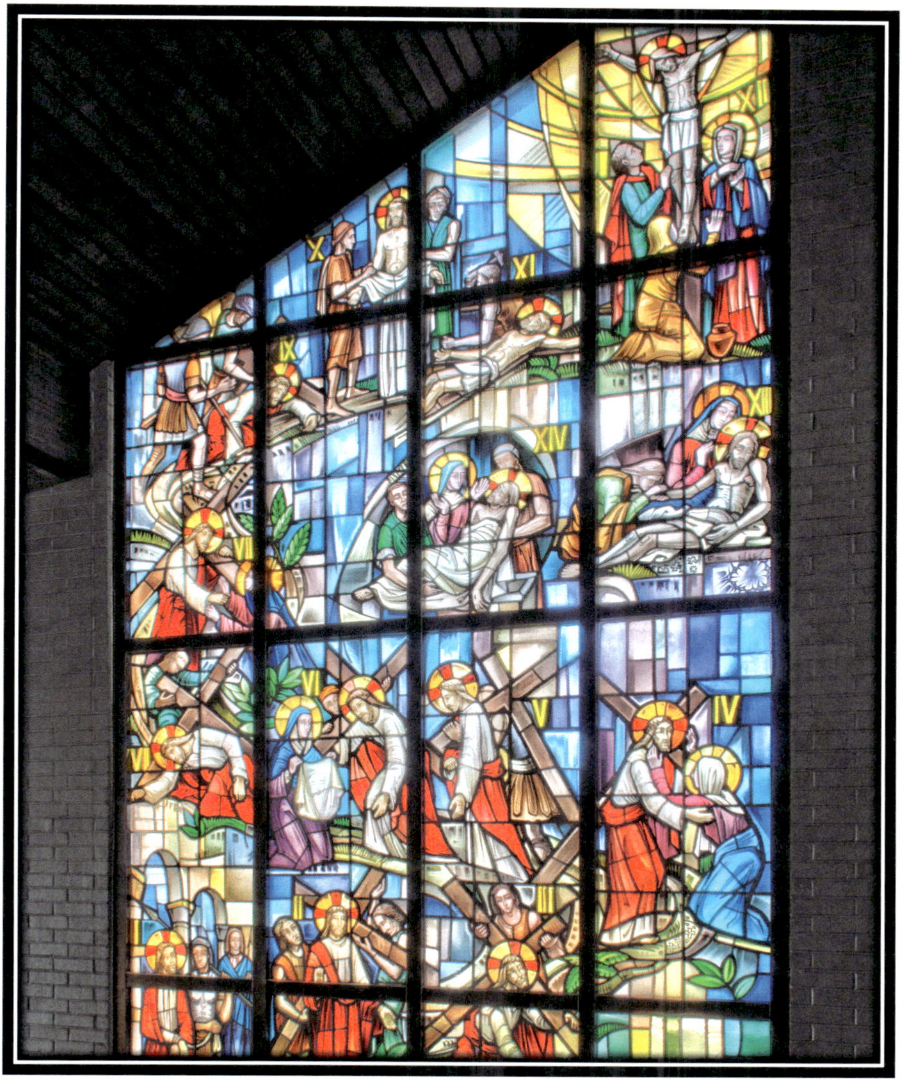

114. St. Ann Catholic Church & National Shrine (1976)
3601 Transcontinental Dr, Metairie
Architect and builder undetermined

Stained glass by Guido Polloni & Co. of Florence, Italy; Ars Liturgica of Morris Plains, NJ, consultants; installed 1977.

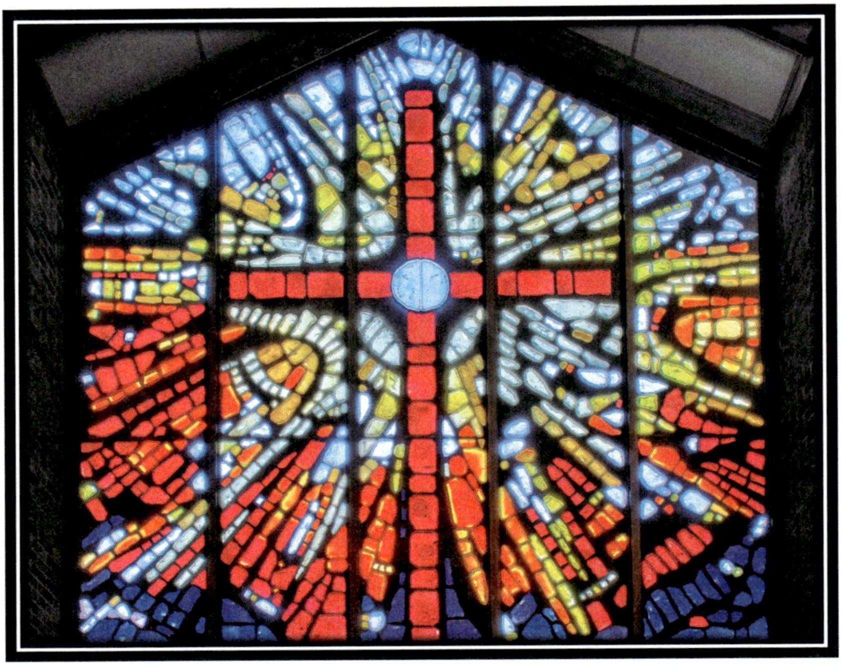

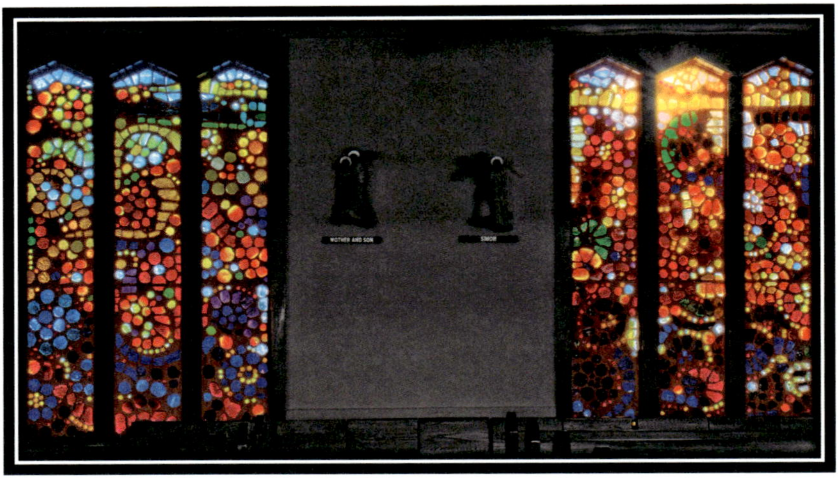

115. St. Margaret Mary Catholic Church (1977)

1050 Robert Blvd, Slidell
Architect undetermined

Dalle de verre windows designed and fabricated by Milton Pounds of Pounds Stained Glass Studio of Covington.

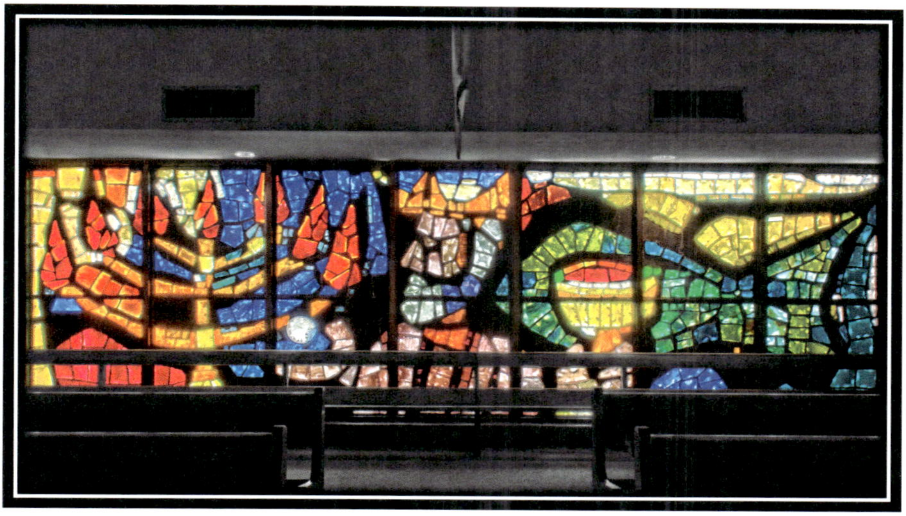

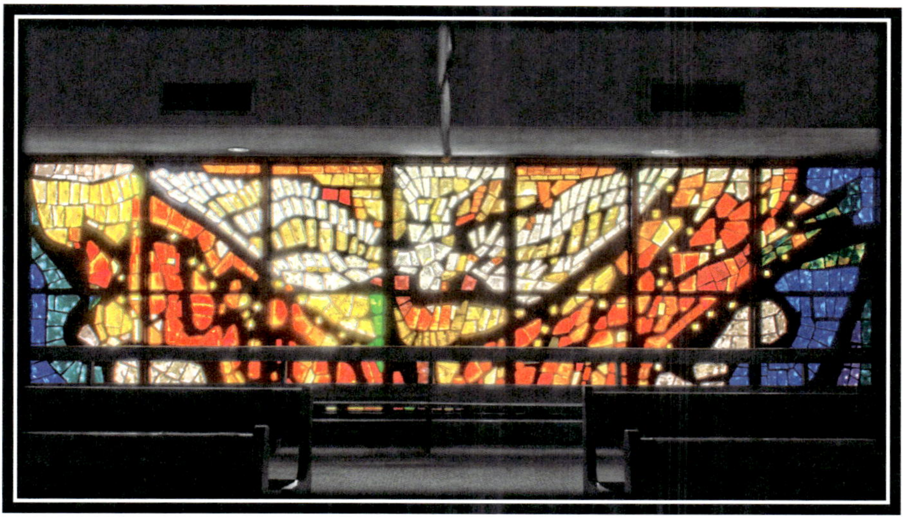

116. St. Philip Neri Catholic Church (1978-1979)

6500 Kawanee Ave, Metairie
Rock & Galloway, architects
Brice Building Co., Inc., general contractor

Dalle de verre windows designed and fabricated by Milton Pounds of Pounds Stained Glass Studio, Covington.

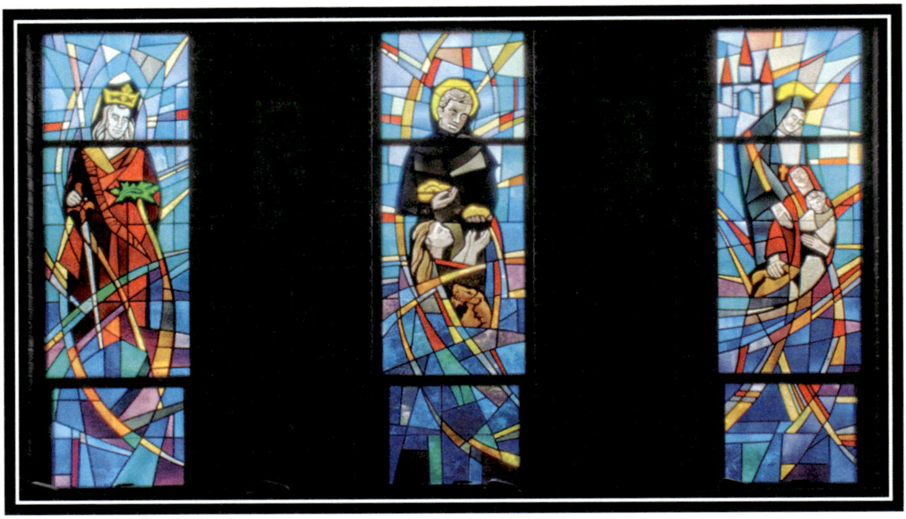

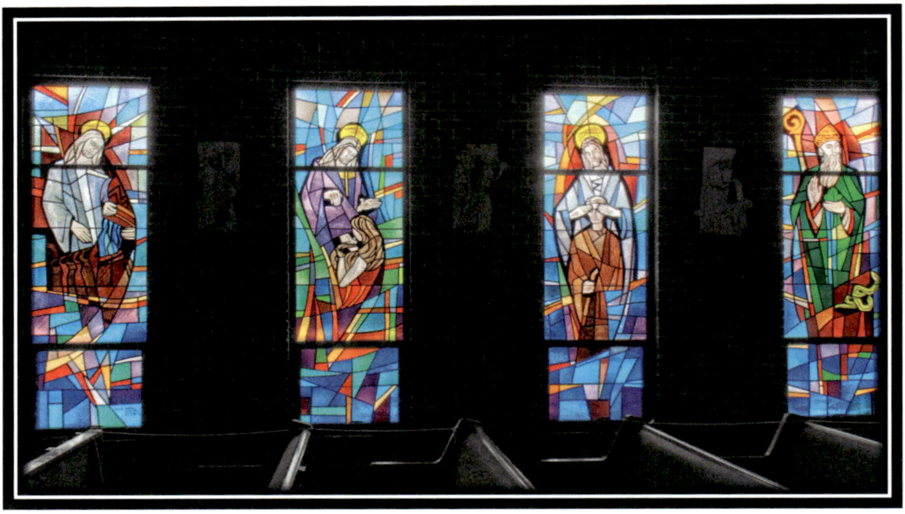

117. St. Clement of Rome Catholic Church (1980)

4317 Richland Ave, Metairie
Joseph T. Fulco, architect

Primary stained glass designed by Herbert Gunther Studio Inc. of New York City [pictured]. *Dalle de verre* window maker undetermined.

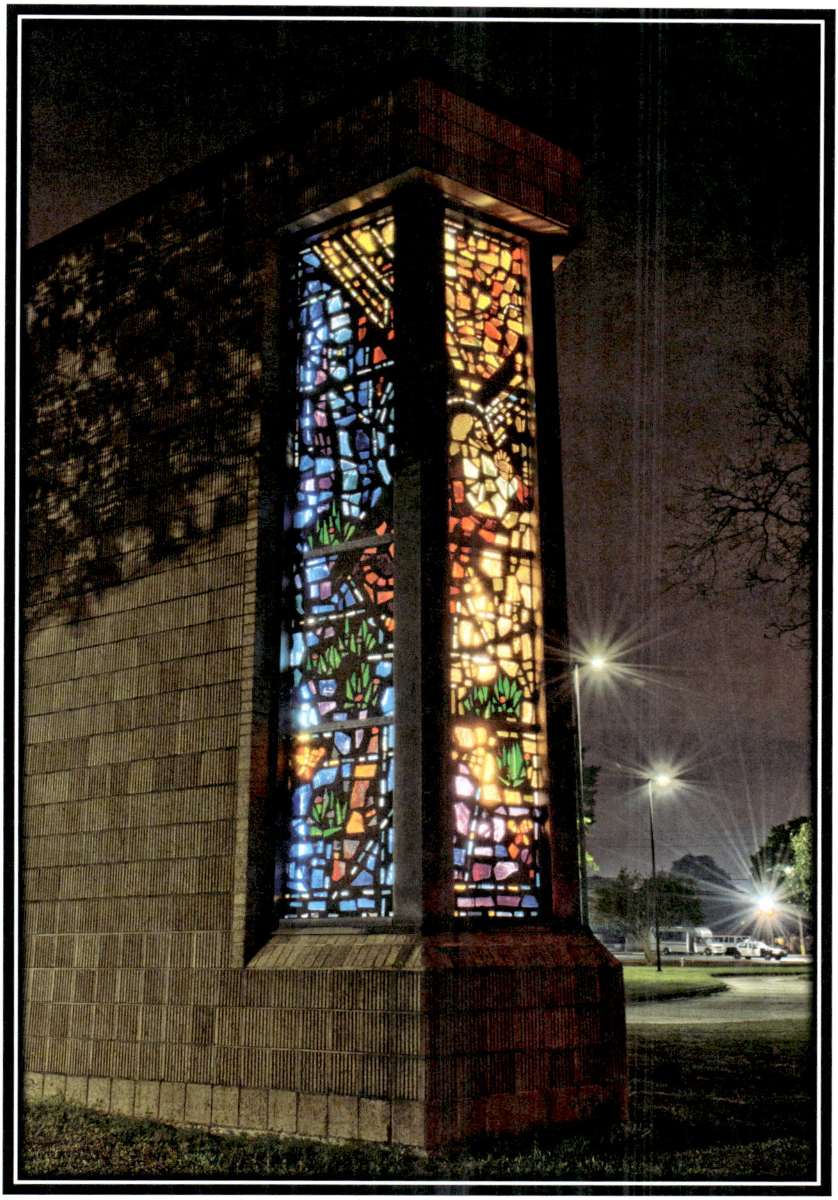

118. First Baptist Church (1983)

1400 Williams Blvd, Kenner
Ellerbe Architects

Dalle de verre windows designed by Inge Pape Trampler; fabricated by Rohlf Studio, Inc. of Mount Vernon, NY.

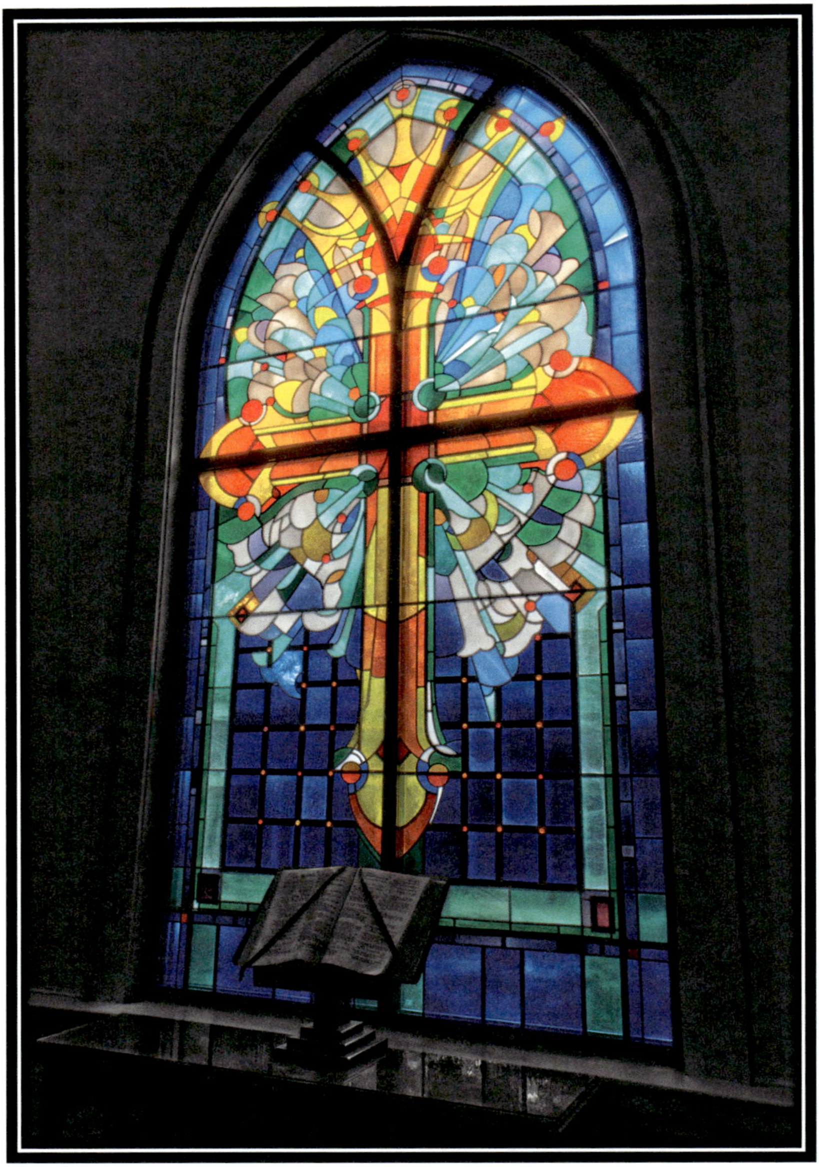

119. New Covenant Evangelical Presbyterian Church (1984-1985)
4375 LA-22, Mandeville
Morton and Associates, architects; Gulf Builders, Inc., general contractor

Stained glass by Stephen Wilson of Baton Rouge.

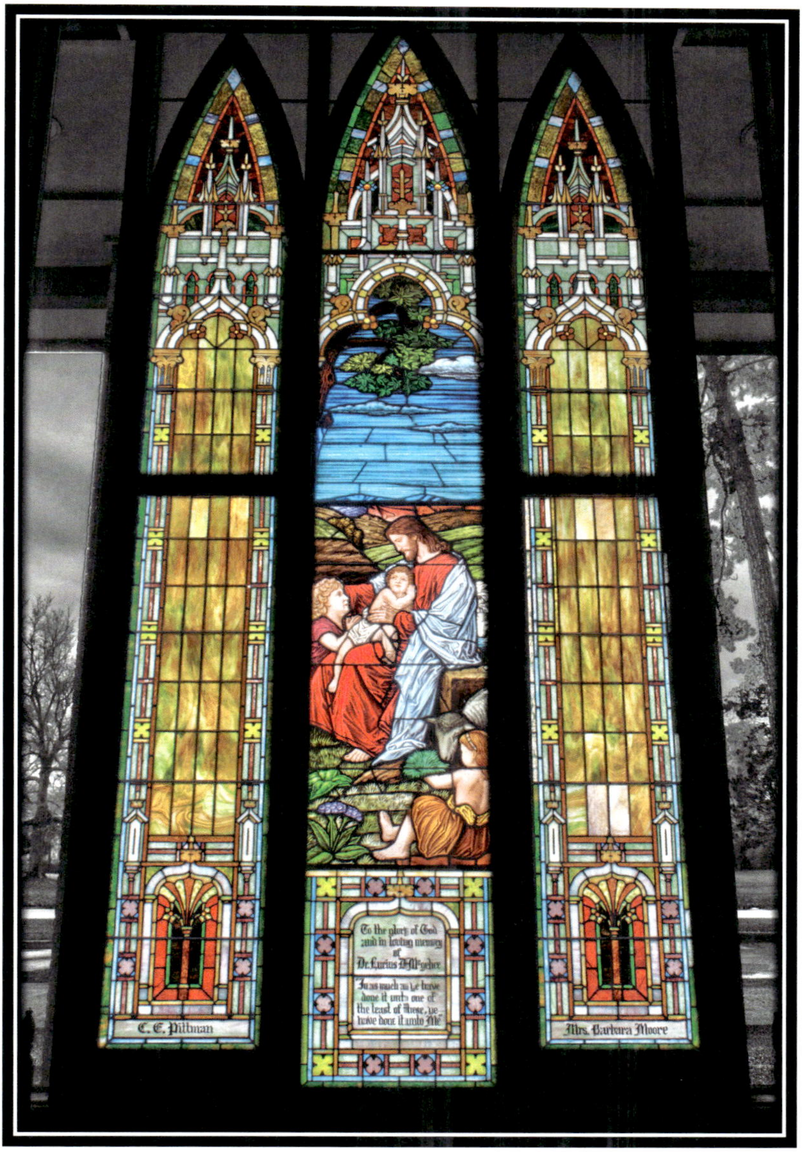

120. First United Methodist Church (1985)

2200 Rue Denise, Hammond
Architect undetermined

Three large windows at this site were transplanted from First United Methodist's previous church building. Their makers and dates of manufacture are undetermined.

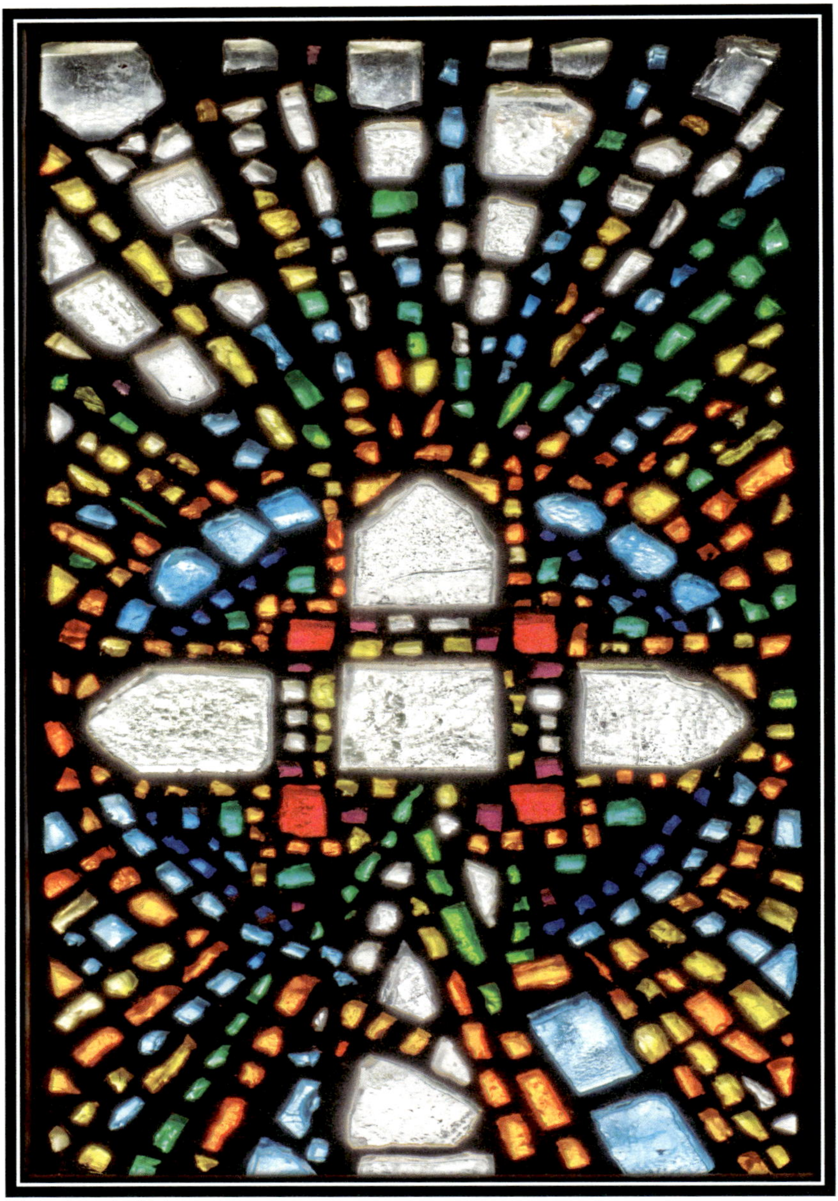

121. Bethany Lutheran Church (1988)

1340 Eighth St, Slidell
Fred Wagner, architect; Robert Carter, contractor

Now known as Open Arms Ministries. *Dalle de verre* windows by Stephen Wilson of Baton Rouge.

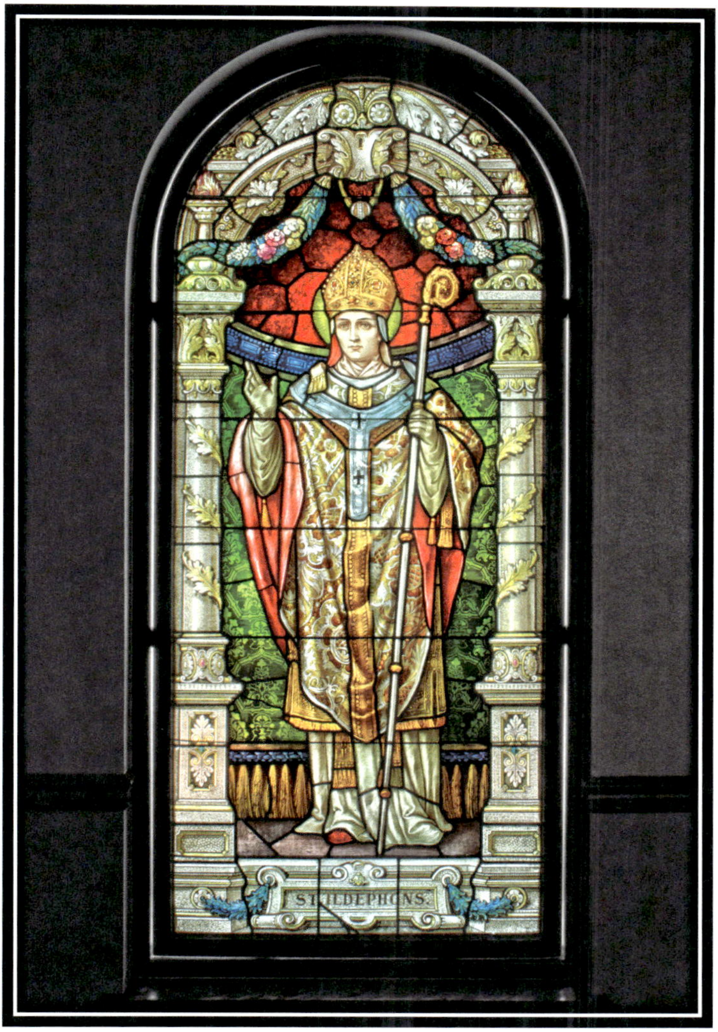

122. Sacred Heart of Jesus Catholic Church (1995-1996)

28088 Main St, Lacombe
Rathe Construction Co., contractors

Times-Picayune reporting from 1996 states that this church's windows are German in origin and have been with the parish since the 1880s. The parish website's *History* page reports no chronologically corresponding constructions and states that the windows were a gift from St. Scholastica Academy in Covington. The full history of these windows remains elusive.

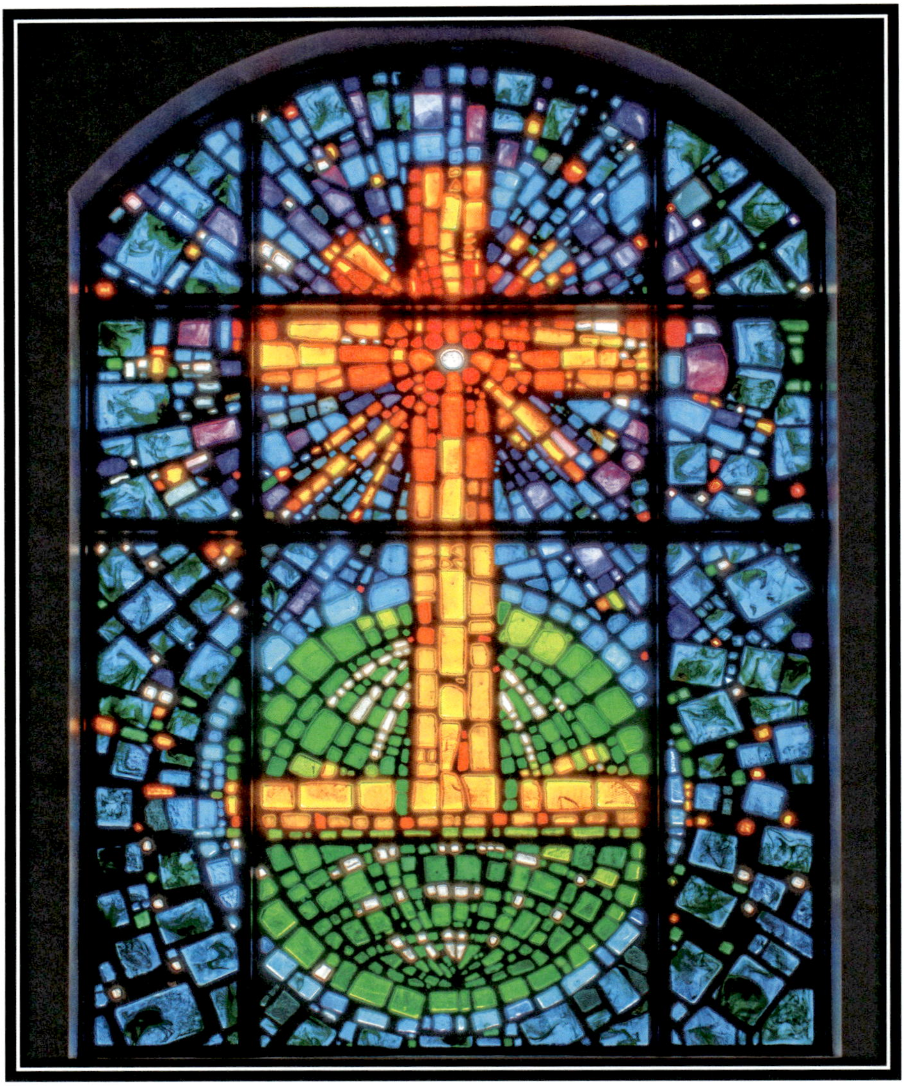

123. Parkview Baptist Church (1997)

6301 Camphor St, Metairie
Architect and builder undetermined

Dalle de verre windows by Stephen Wilson of Baton Rouge.

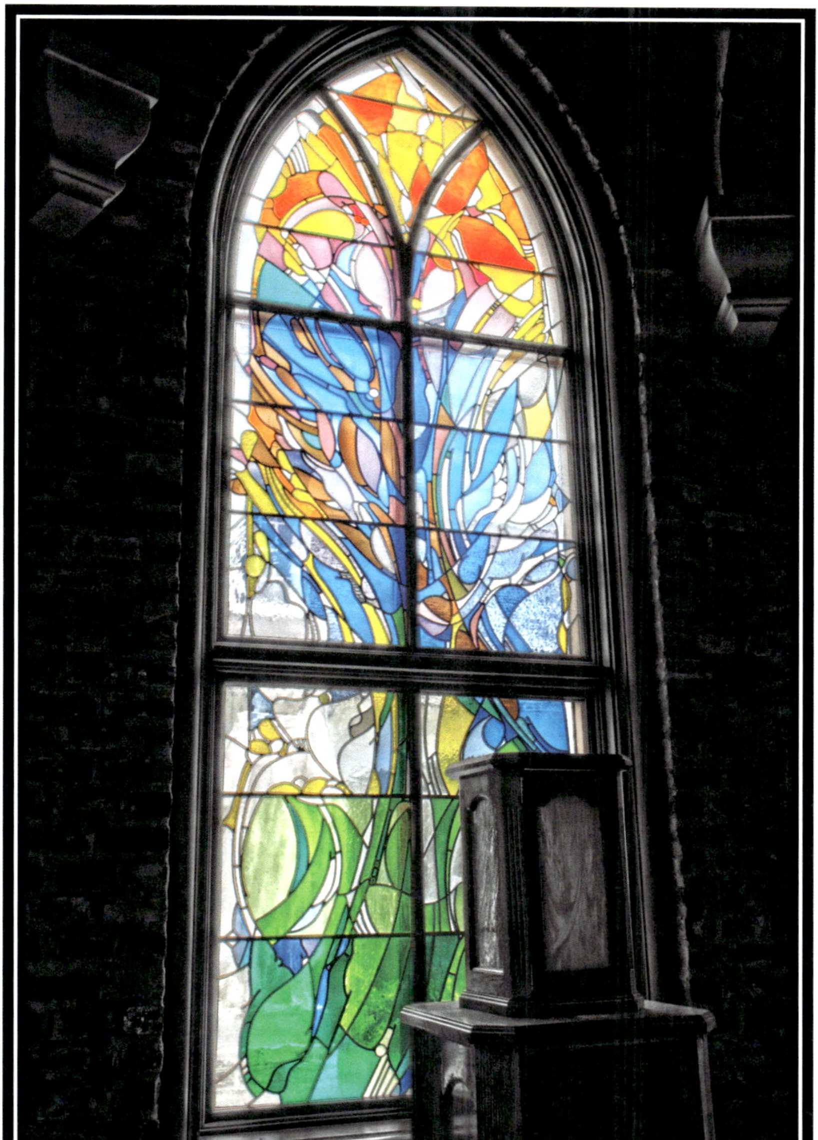

124. Holy Name of Jesus Chapel at Manresa House of Retreats (1999-2001)

5858 LA-44, Convent
Architect and builder undetermined

Located inside Loyola Hall. Stained glass by Stephen Wilson of Baton Rouge.

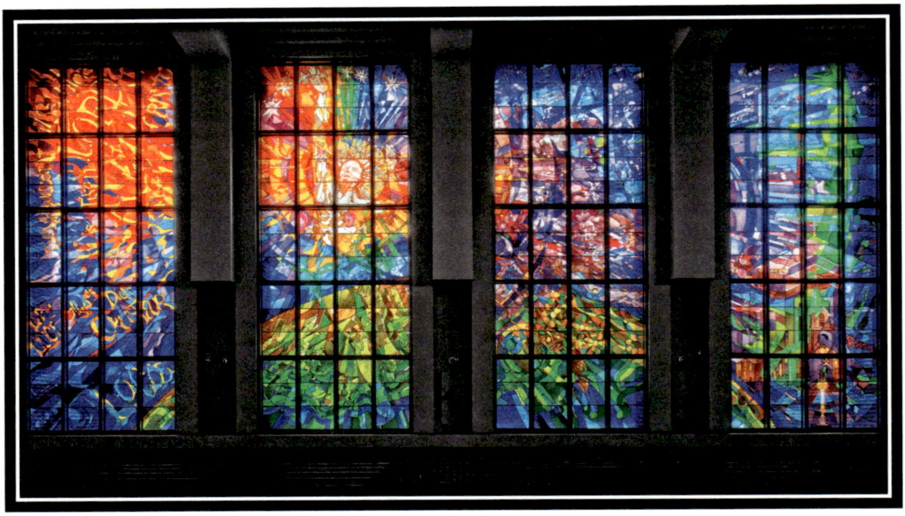

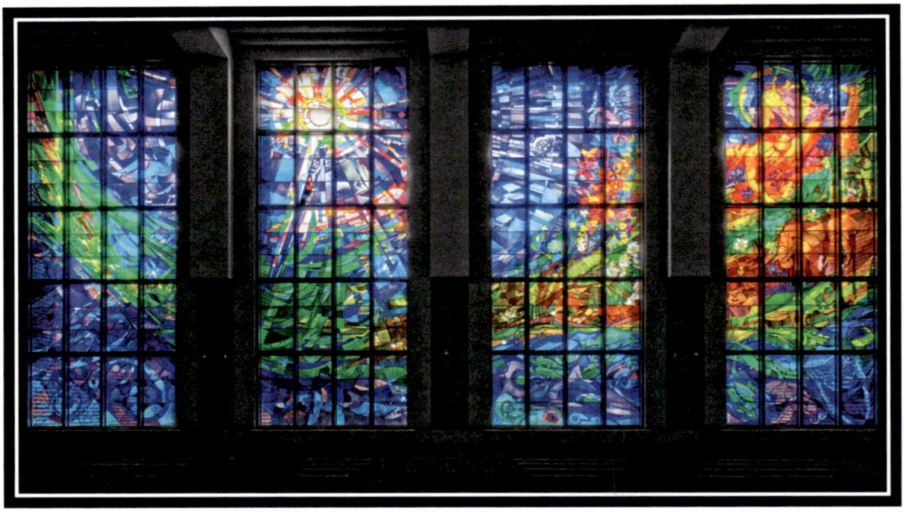

125. Holy Ghost Catholic Church (2000-2001)

600 N. Oak St, Hammond
Holly & Smith Architects
Stafford Construction Co., builders

Stained glass by Stephen Wilson of Baton Rouge.

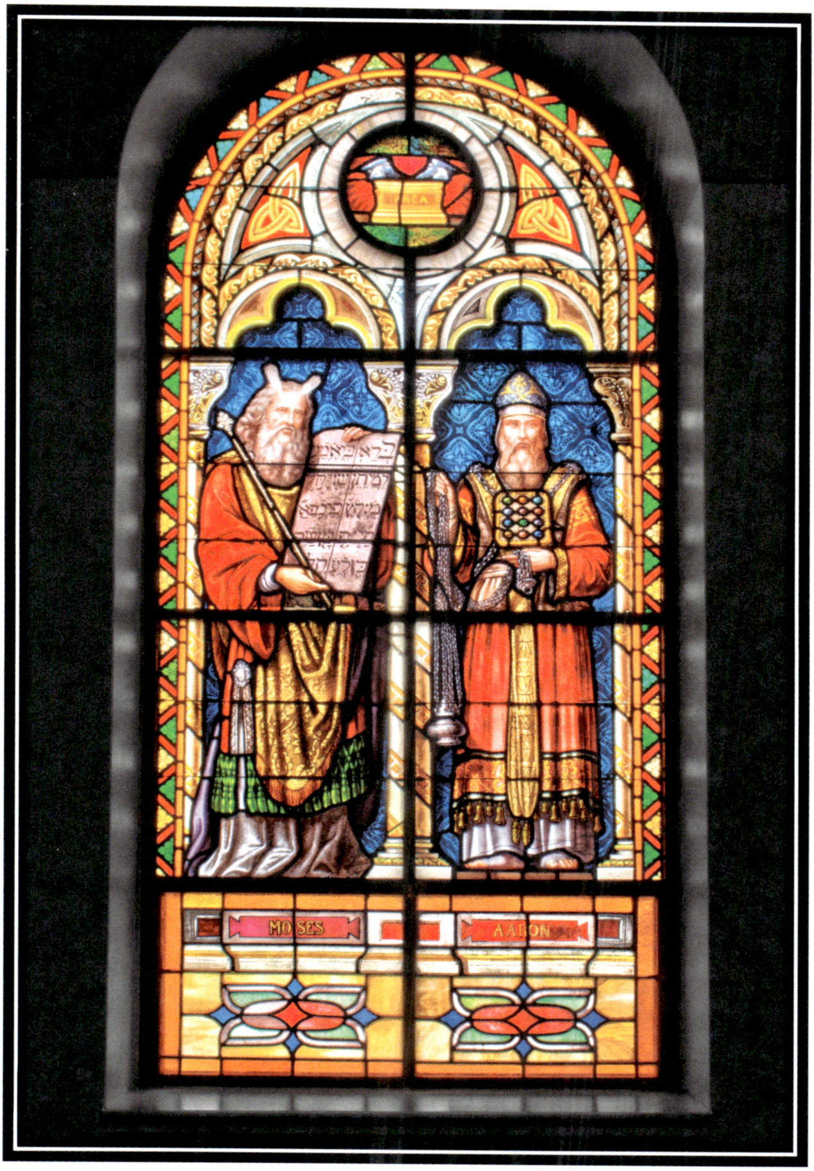

126. Ascension of Our Lord Catholic Church (2001)

1900 Greenwood Dr, LaPlace
Blitch-Knevel Architects

Windows dating to the 1870s transplanted from Holy Trinity, New Orleans (*entry #11*) in 2001. Made by Charles des Granges of Clermont-Ferrand, France.

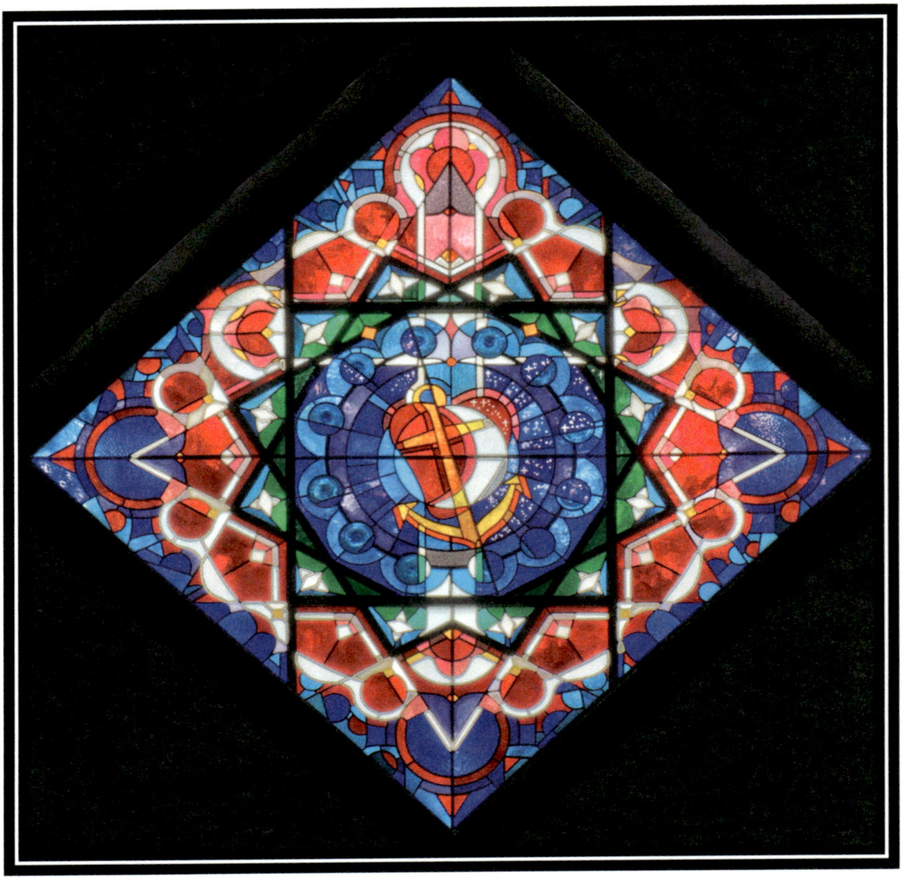

127. Faith Presbyterian Church (c.2005)

16330 LA-1085, Covington
Architect and builder undetermined

Stained glass by Stephen Wilson of Baton Rouge.

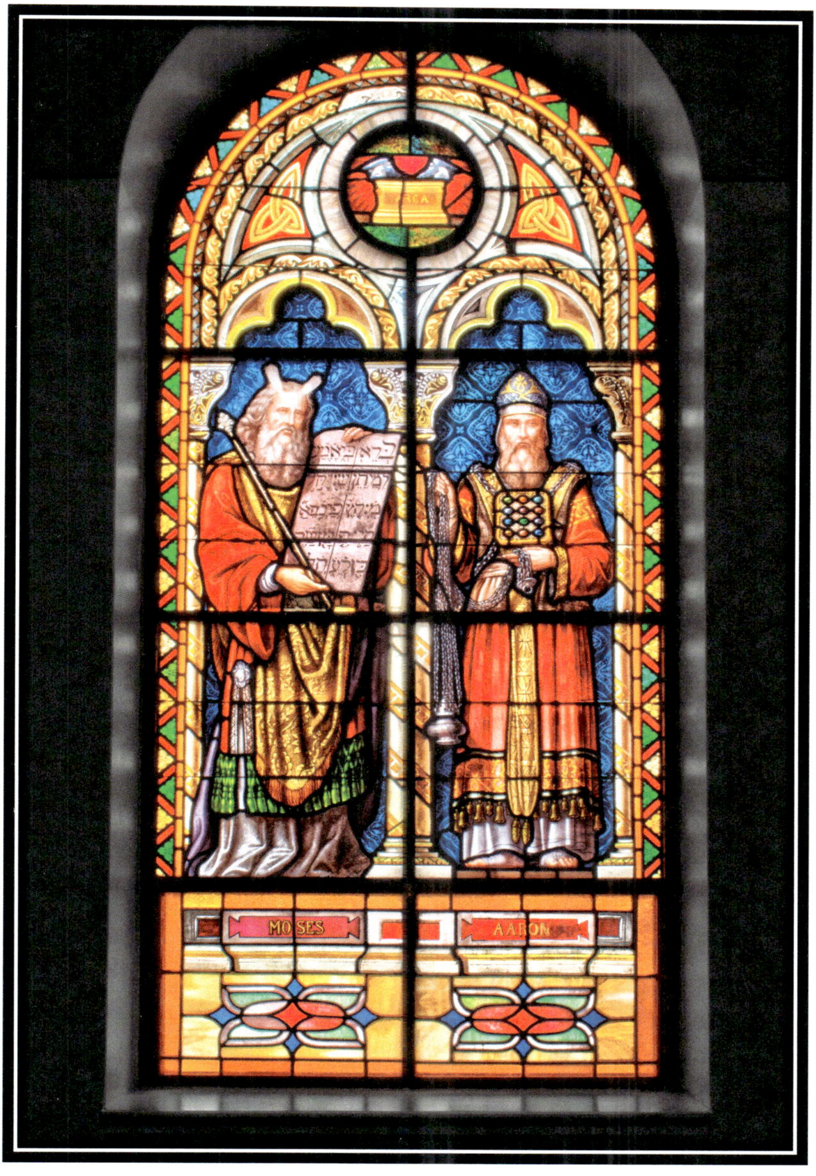

126. Ascension of Our Lord Catholic Church (2001)

1900 Greenwood Dr, LaPlace
Blitch-Knevel Architects

Windows dating to the 1870s transplanted from Holy Trinity, New Orleans (*entry #11*) in 2001. Made by Charles des Granges of Clermont-Ferrand, France.

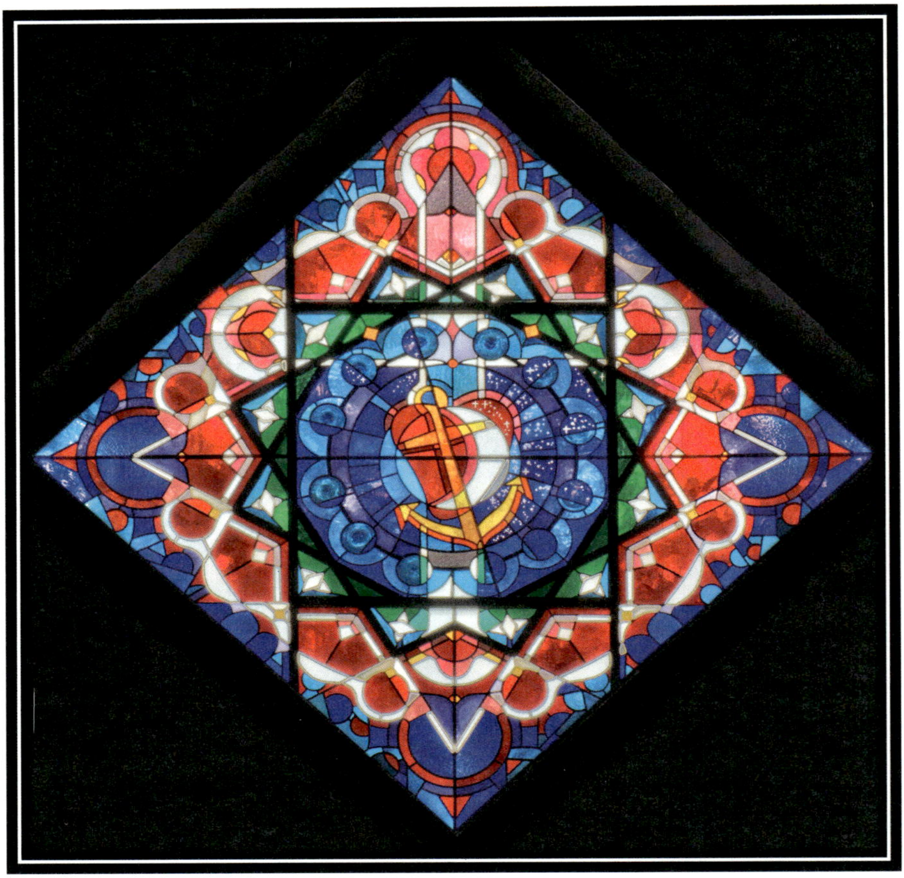

127. Faith Presbyterian Church (c.2005)

16330 LA-1085, Covington
Architect and builder undetermined

Stained glass by Stephen Wilson of Baton Rouge.

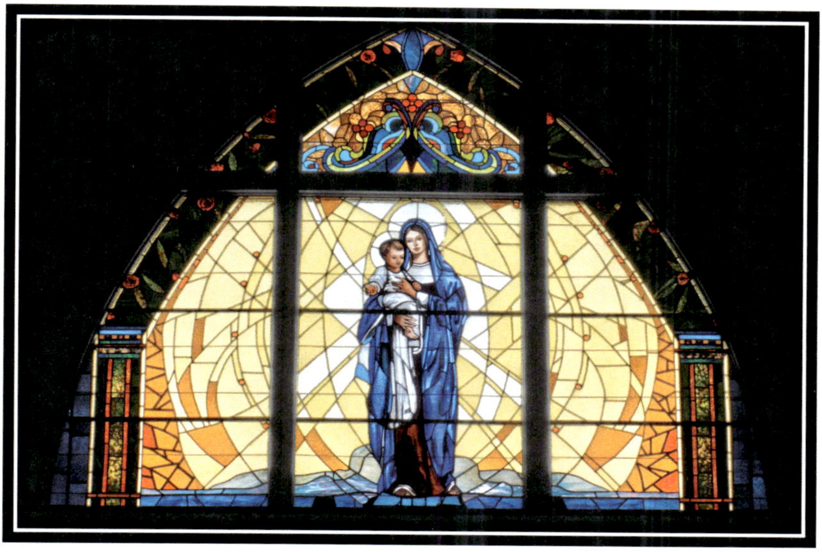

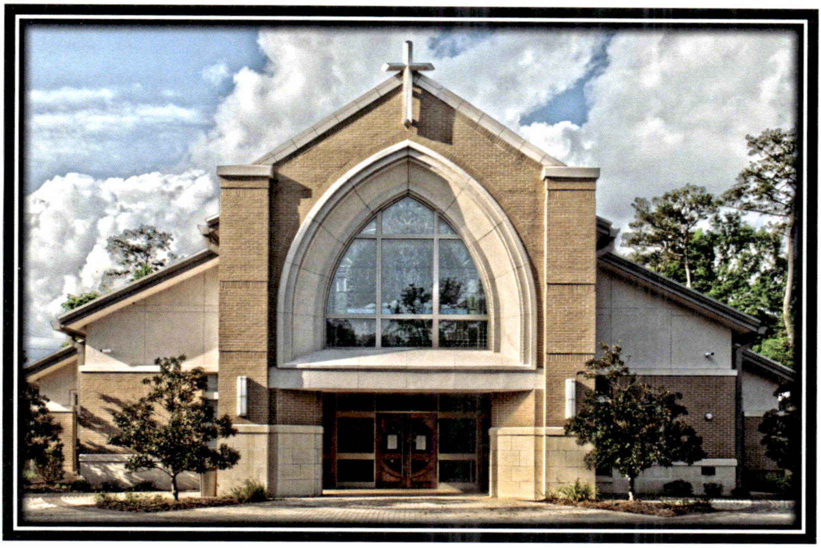

128. Mary Queen of Peace Catholic Church (2007-2008)

1501 West Causeway Approach, Mandeville
fl+WB Architects (aka Fauntelroy, Latham, Weldon & Barré)
F.H. Myers Construction, general contractor

Stained glass designed by Ruth Goliwas of New Orleans.

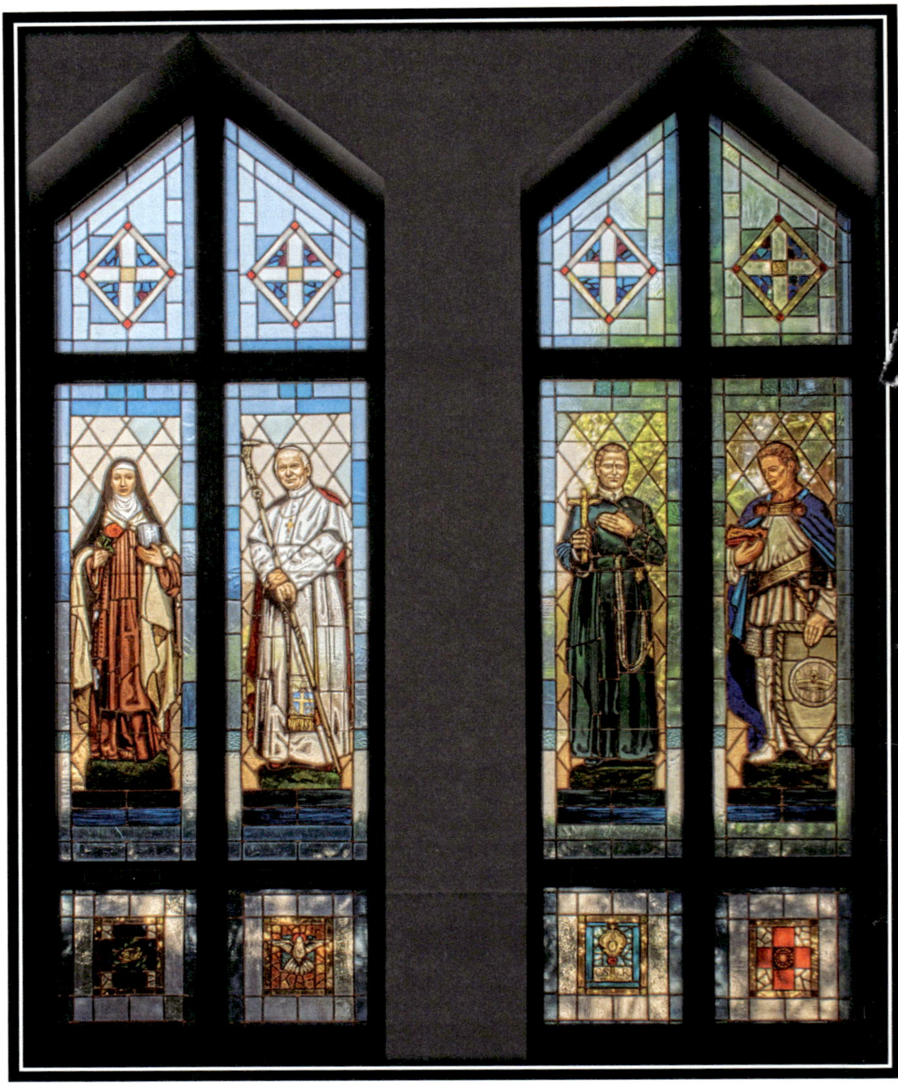

129. St. Francis Xavier Catholic Church (2008-2010)

444 Metairie Rd, Metairie
Nano Turchi, architect
Tim Held, contractor

Stained glass designed by Ruth Goliwas of New Orleans.

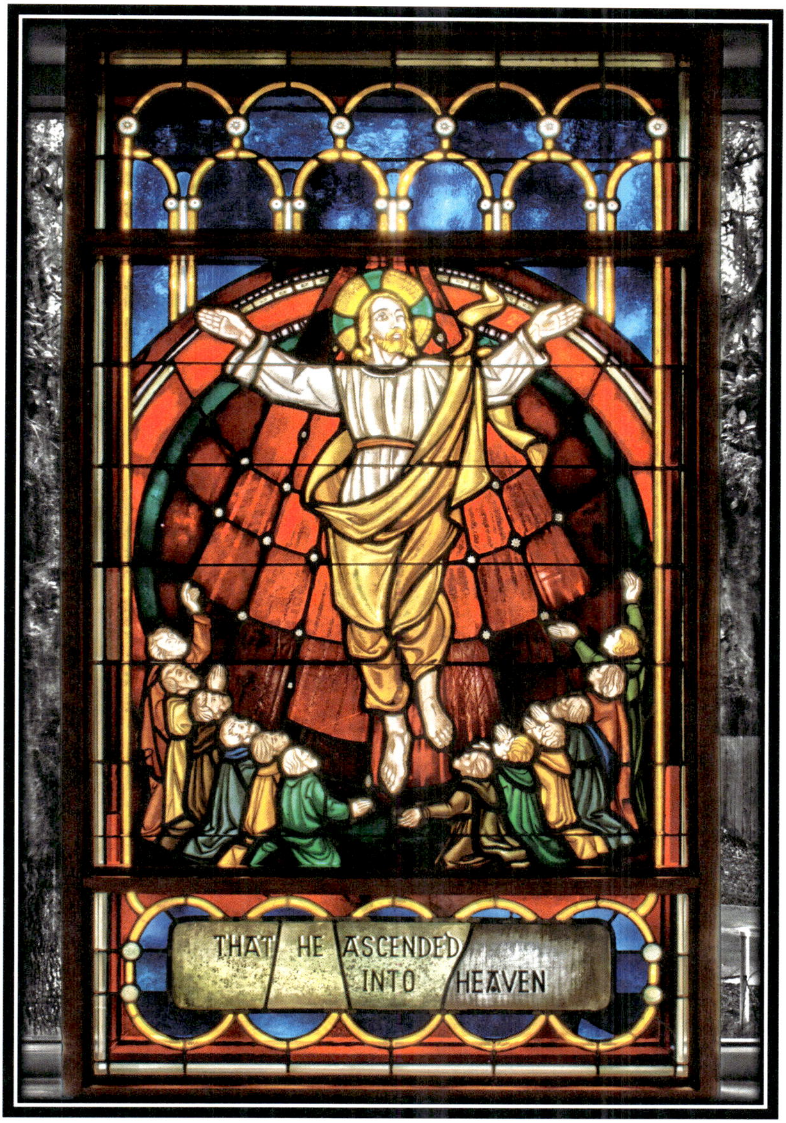

130. St. Genevieve Catholic Church (2010-2012)

58203 LA-433, Bonfouca
Argus Architecture Engineering, architects
Voelkel-McWilliams Construction, builders

Stained glass fabricated by Botz & Miesen of Cologne, Germany for Ecclesiastical Art of Dallas, Texas; transplanted from prior church destroyed by Hurricane Katrina.

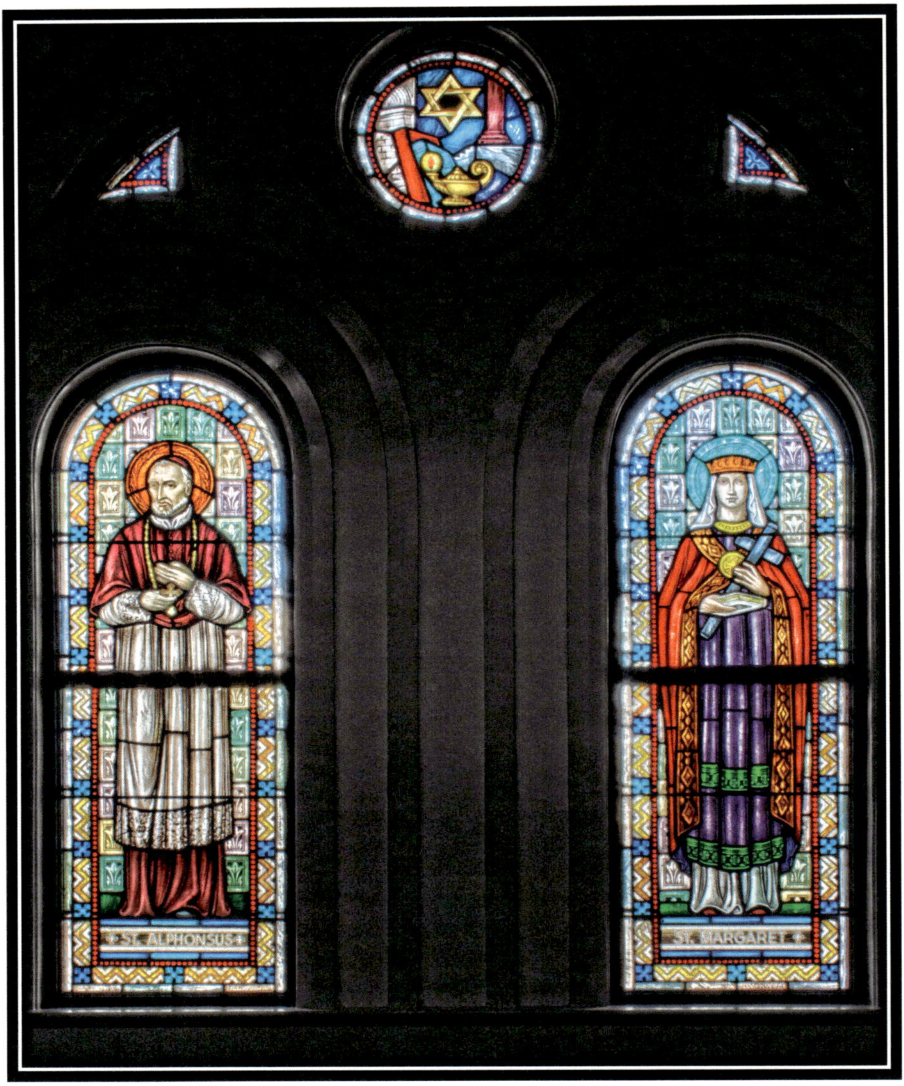

131. Most Holy Trinity Catholic Church (2016)

501 Holy Trinity Dr, Covington
fl+WB Architects (aka Fauntelroy, Latham, Weldon & Barré)
DonahueFavret, contractors

Primary windows [pictured] transplanted from St. Maurice (*entry #185*) c.2016; makers undetermined. Trinity rose window by Attenhofer's Stained Glass Studio of Metairie.

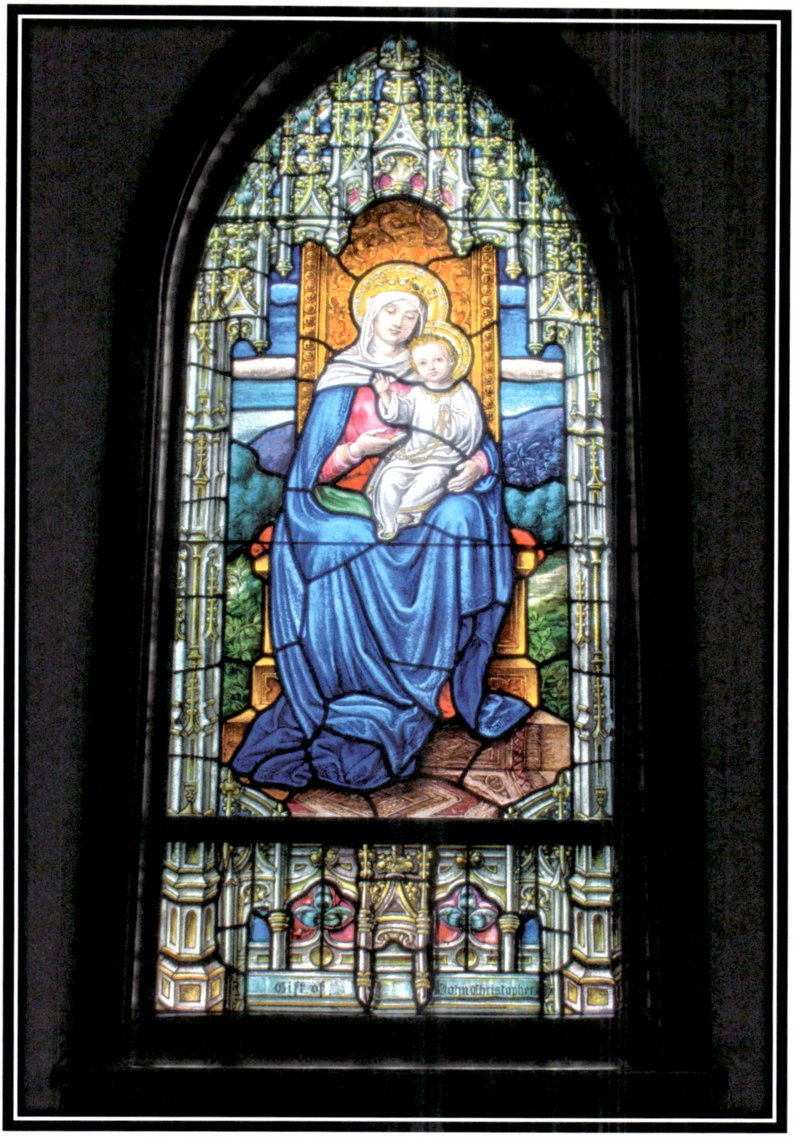

132. Our Lady of Fatima Latin Mass Church (2016)

66110 Vortisch Rd, Lacombe
K.B. Kaufmann & Co., builders

Knowledgeable parishioners report the stained glass at this site as German in origin and transplanted from a deconsecrated Catholic church in western, upstate New York.

PART THREE

METAIRIE and LAKE LAWN CEMETERIES

Of the many aesthetically striking cemeteries in the city of New Orleans, only Metairie and Lake Lawn can brag of extensive stained glass collections. Find Metairie Cemetery at 5100 Pontchartrain Blvd and Lake Lawn at 5454. Both are located in the Lakewood neighborhood. Designers and fabricators of stained glass windows found within private mausoleums at both Metairie and Lake Lawn are undetermined except where otherwise noted.

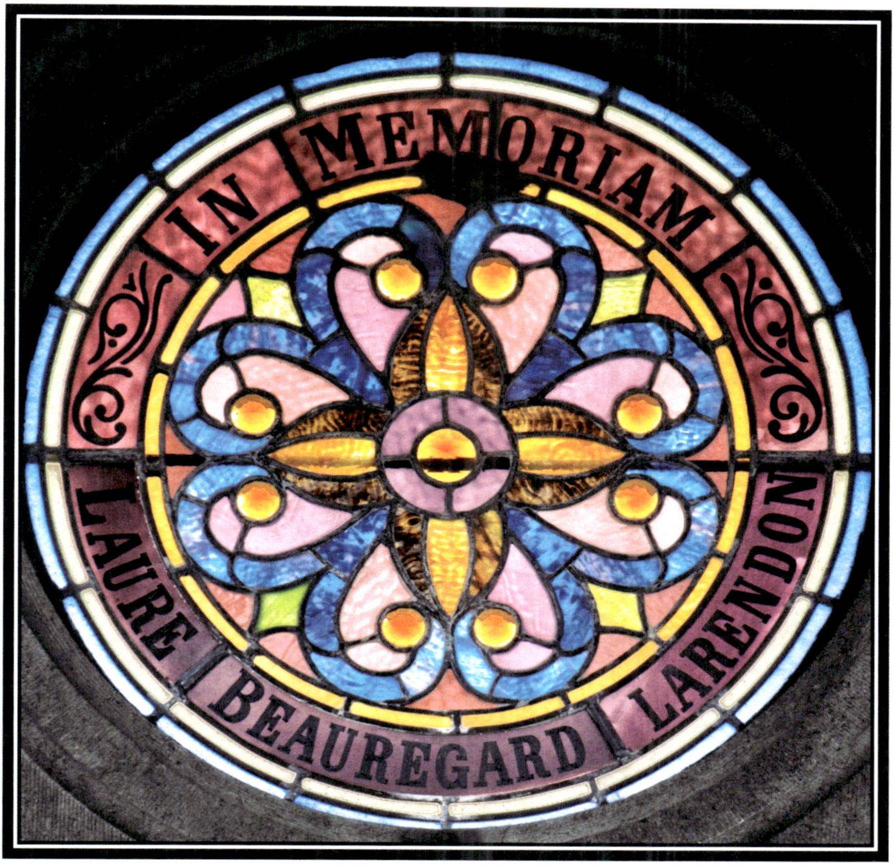

133. "Laure T. Beauregard-Larendon" Mausoleum (1885)

Metairie Cemetery, Section 128

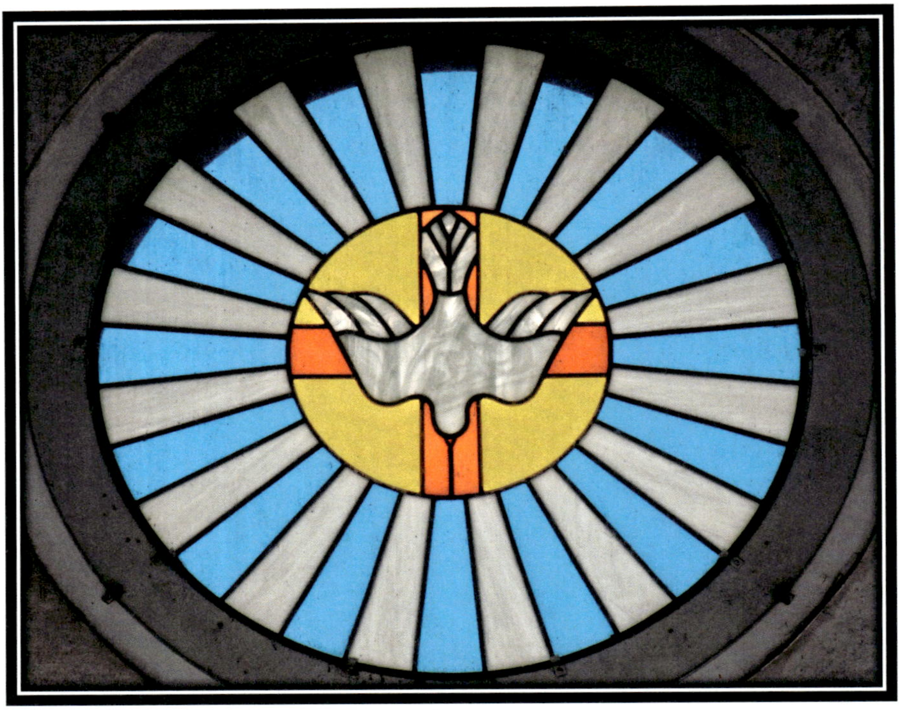

134. "Societa Italiana Di Beneficenza Contessa Entellina" Mausoleum (c.1886)
Metairie Cemetery, Section 86

---

135. "Chas. & Thos. Smith" Mausoleum (c.1890)►
Metairie Cemetery, Section 112

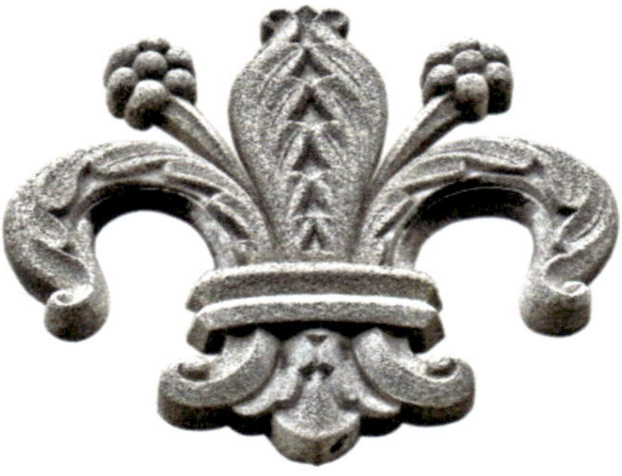

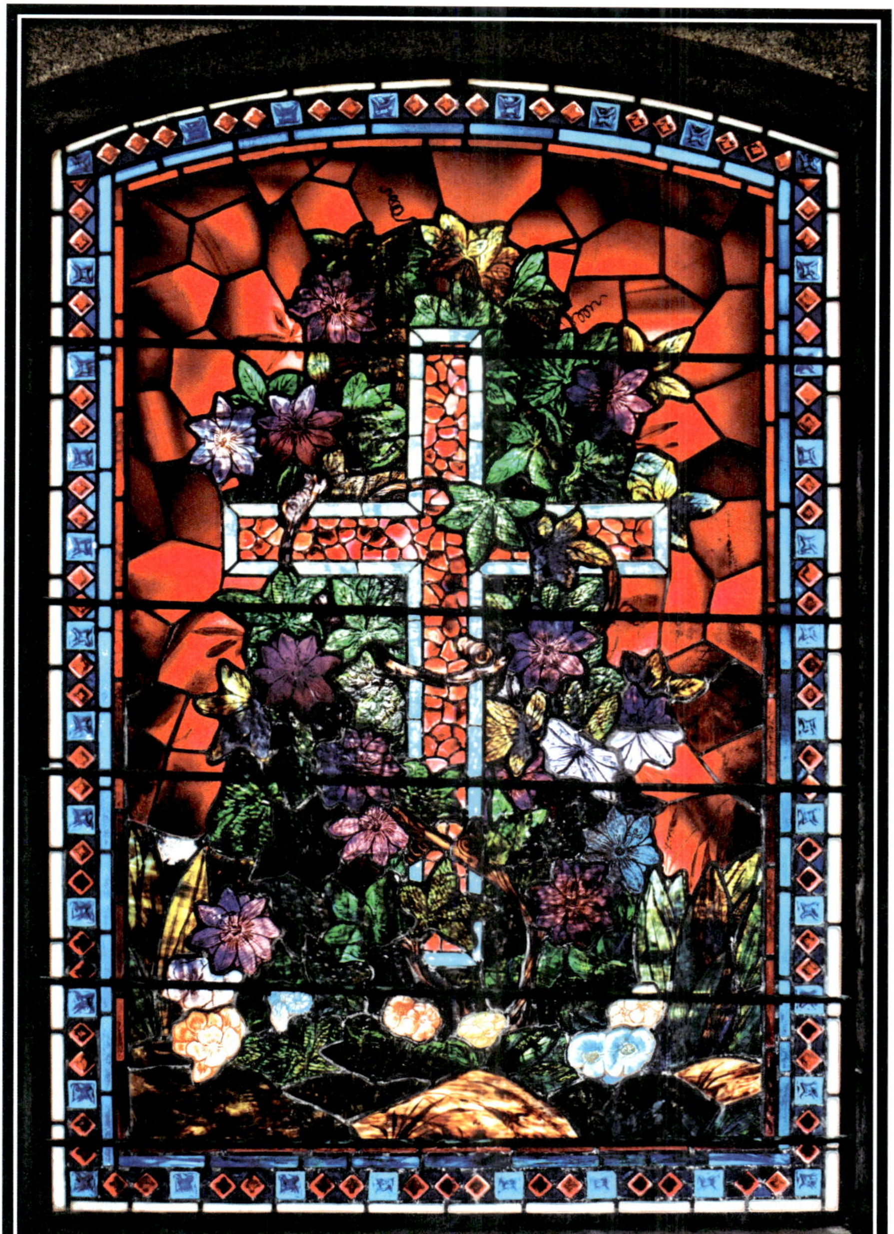

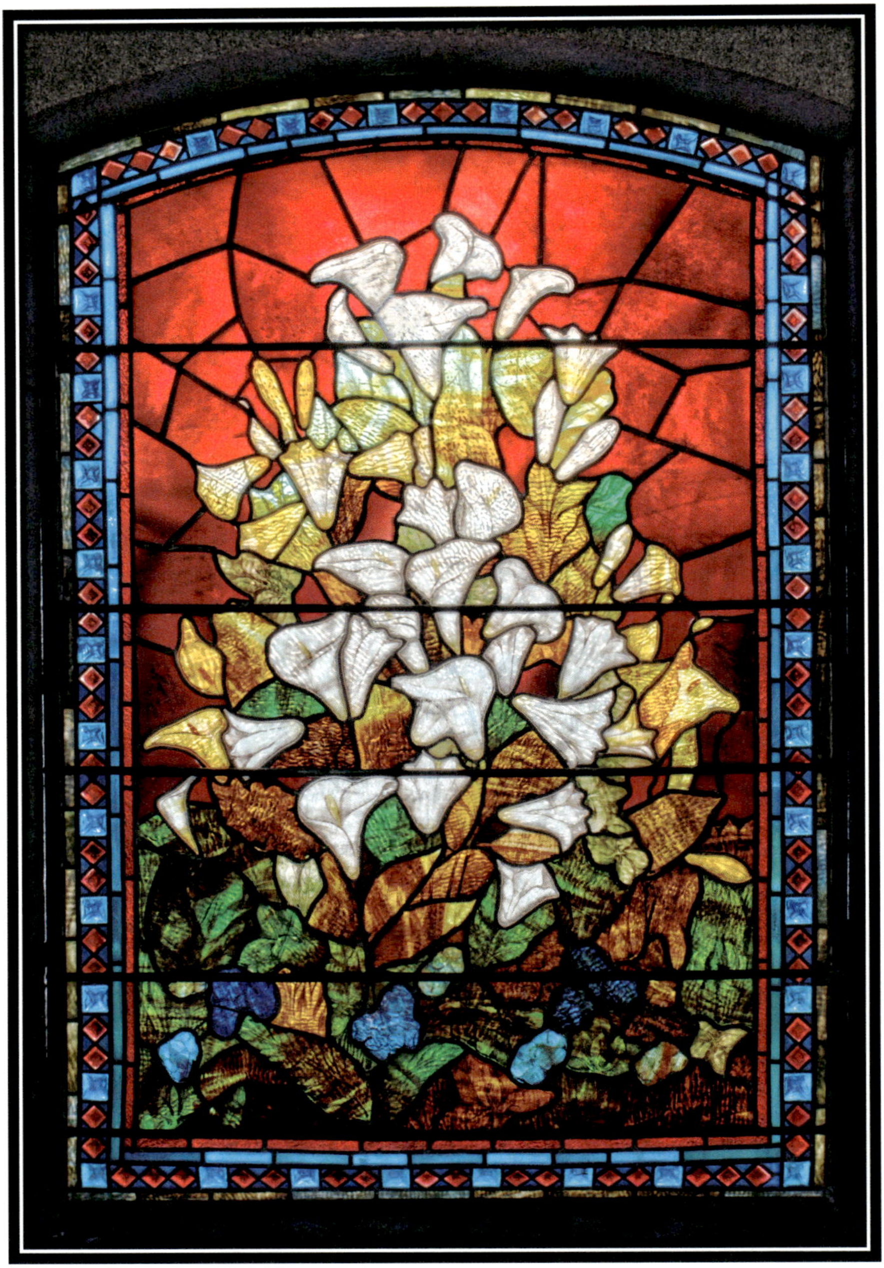

136. "F.W. Tilton" Mausoleum (c.1890)
Metairie Cemetery, Section 112

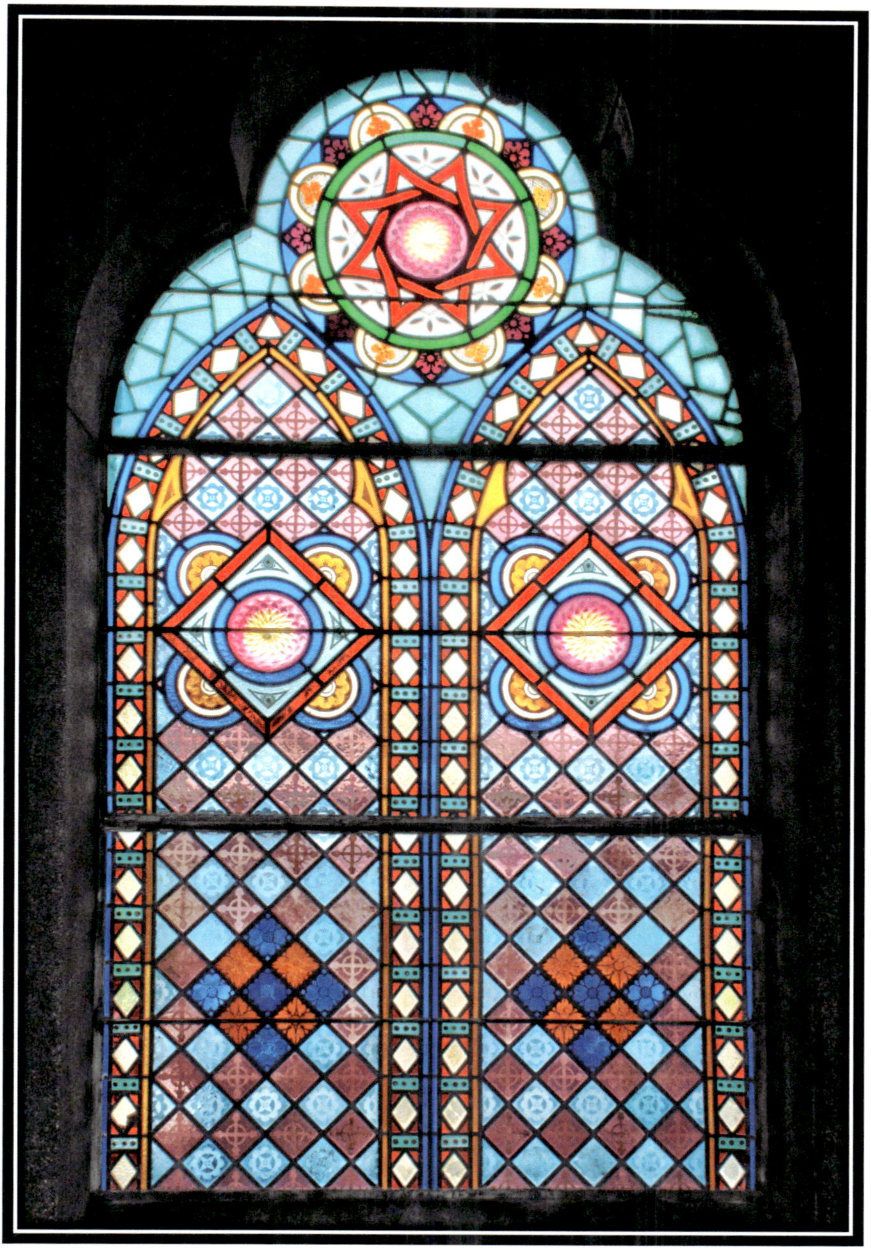

137. "McCan" Mausoleum (c.1893)
Metairie Cemetery, Section 116
Theodore Brune, architect; Charles A. Orleans, builder

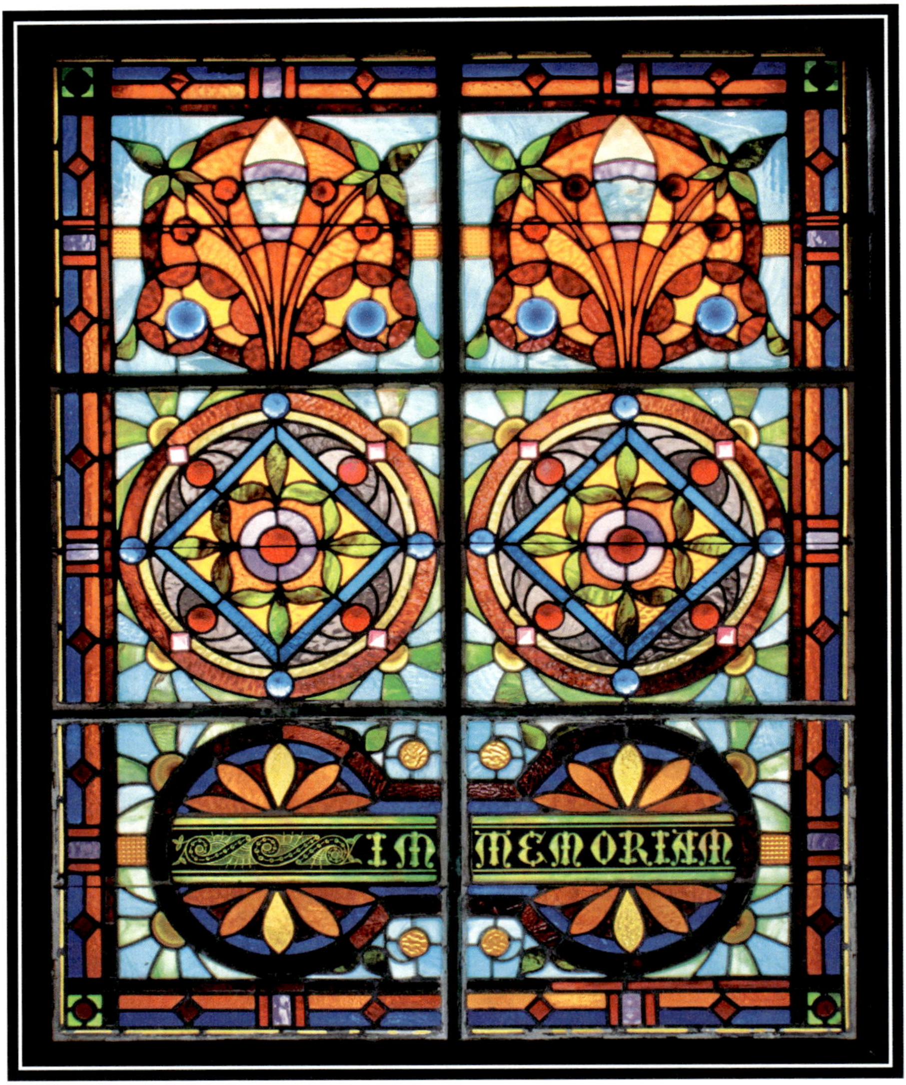

138. "F.M. Ziegler" & "W.B. Schmidt" Mausoleums (c.1901)

Metairie Cemetery, Section 123

These two mausoleums feature identical stained glass designs.

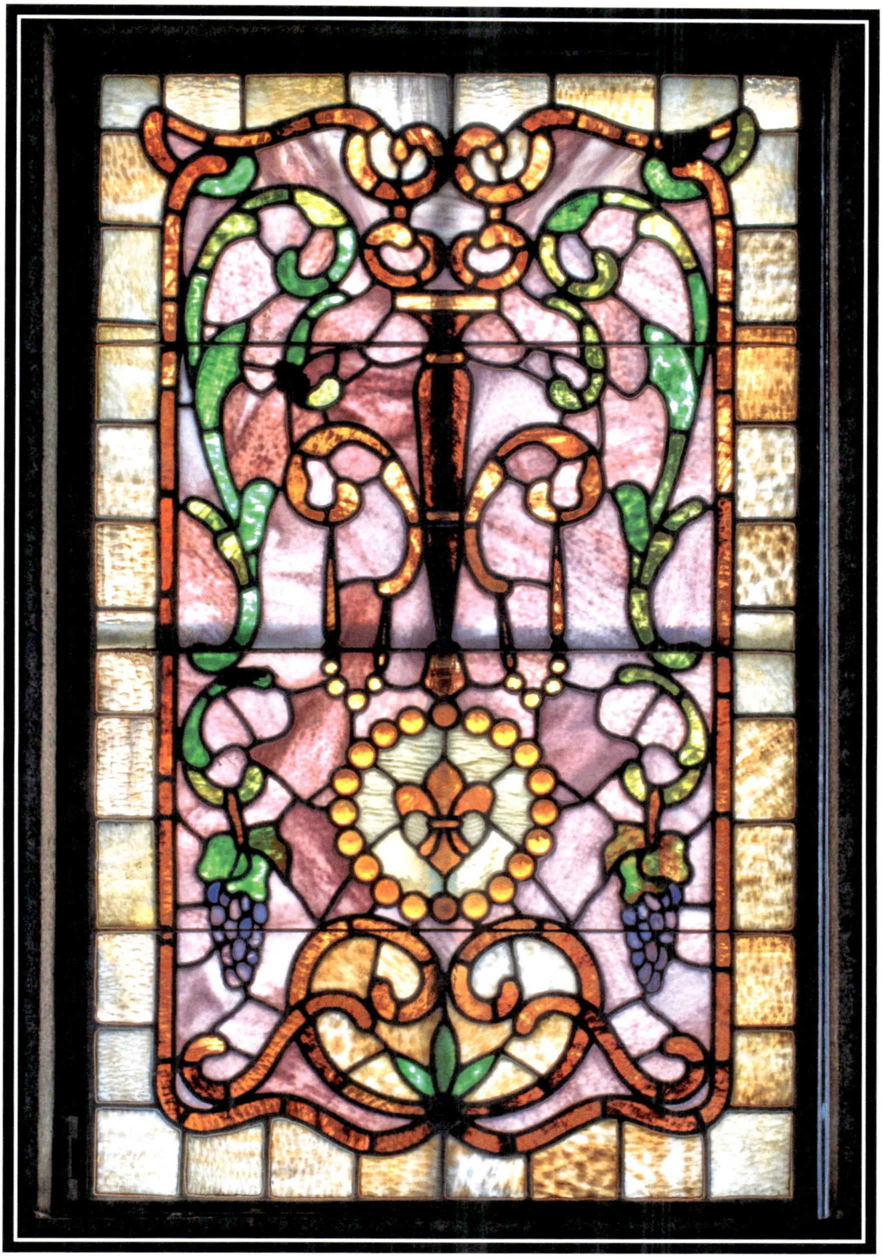

139. "Menge" Mausoleum (c.1905)
Metairie Cemetery, Section 113

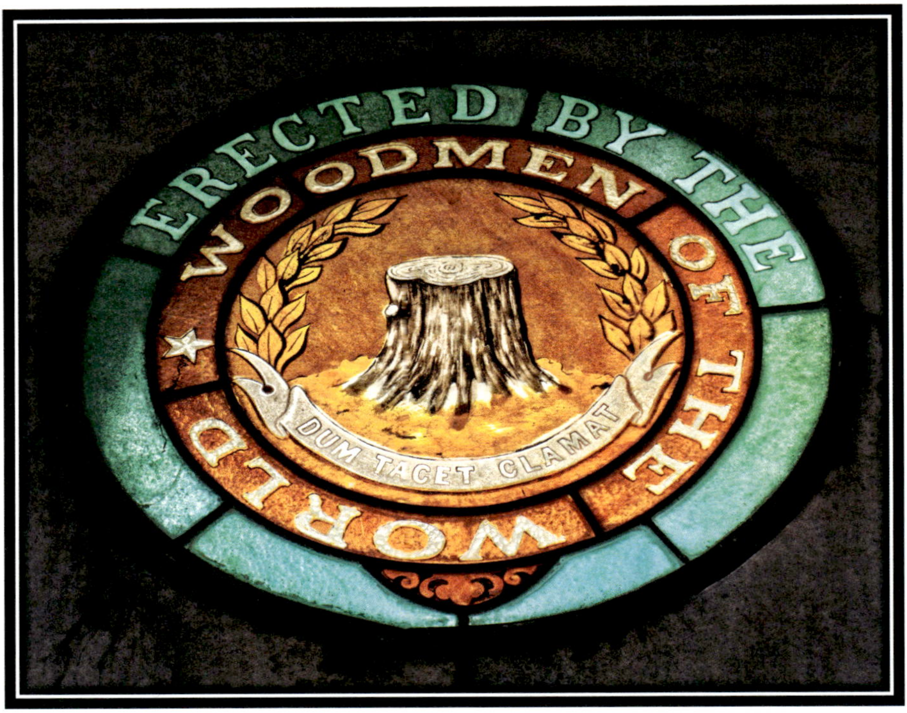

140. "Woodmen of the World" Mausoleum (1907)

Metairie Cemetery, Section D

---

141. "Dibert" Mausoleum (c.1912)►

Metairie Cemetery, Section 56
Charles Lawhon, architect
Albert Weiblen Marble and Granite Co., builders
Stained glass designed by Harry Eldredge Goodhue of Boston

Both *Metairie Cemetery: An Historical Memoir* and *New Orleans Architecture Volume III: The Cemeteries*, in conflicting accounts, report Jean Duffy as the architect of this mausoleum. I defer to the attribution given within the *Albert Weiblen Marble and Granite Company Office Records* of the Southeastern Architectural Archive at Tulane University.

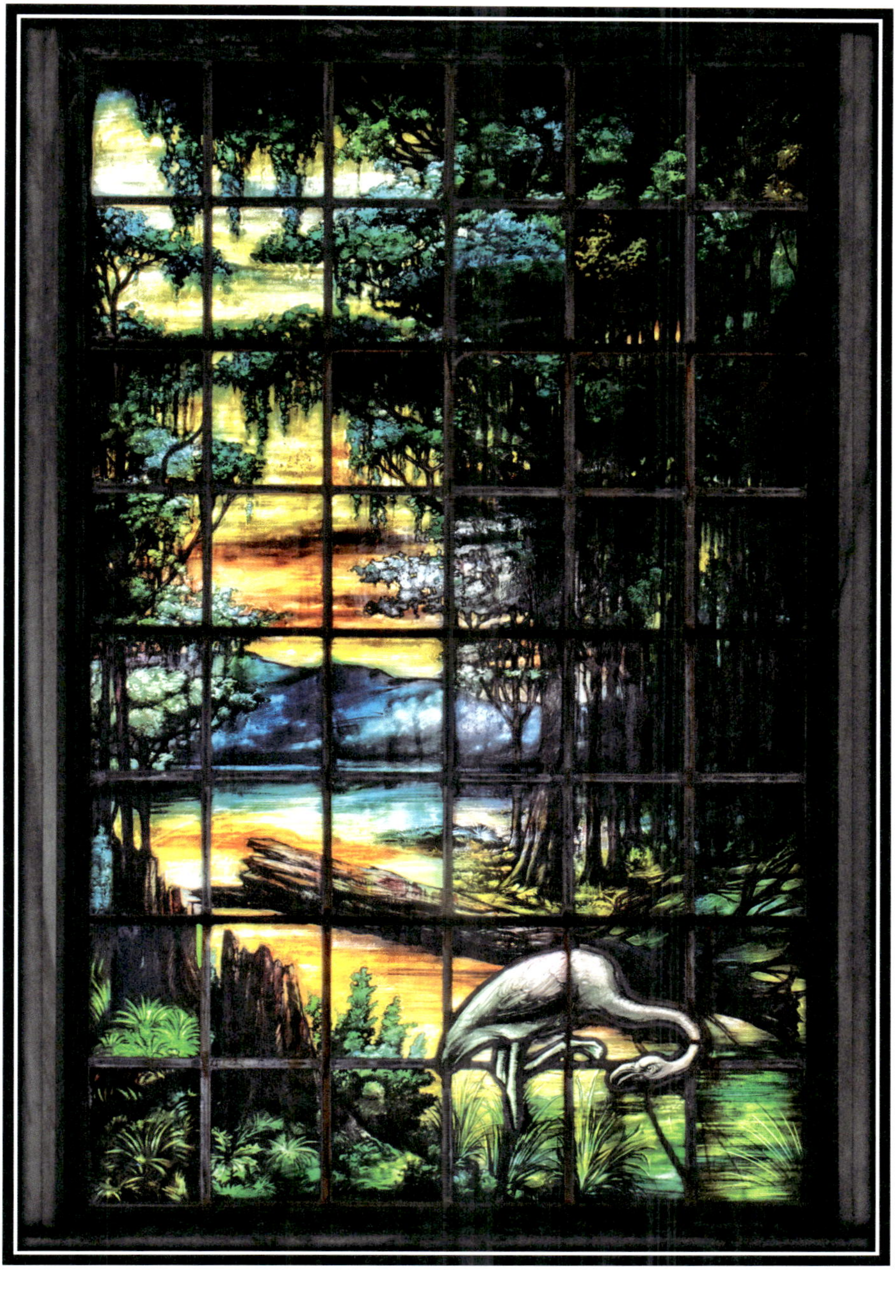

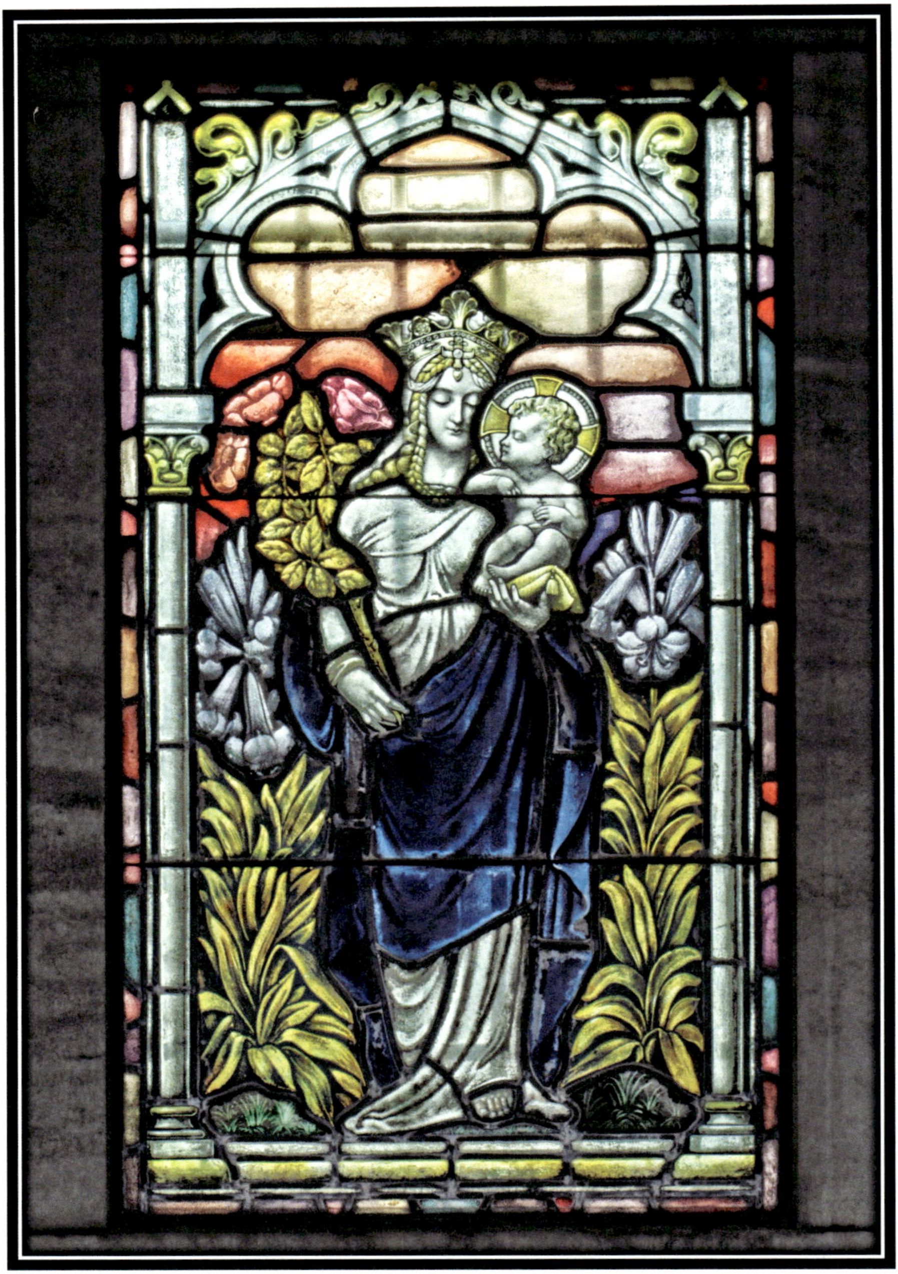

142. "Licalzi" Mausoleum (c.1913)
Metairie Cemetery, Section 7

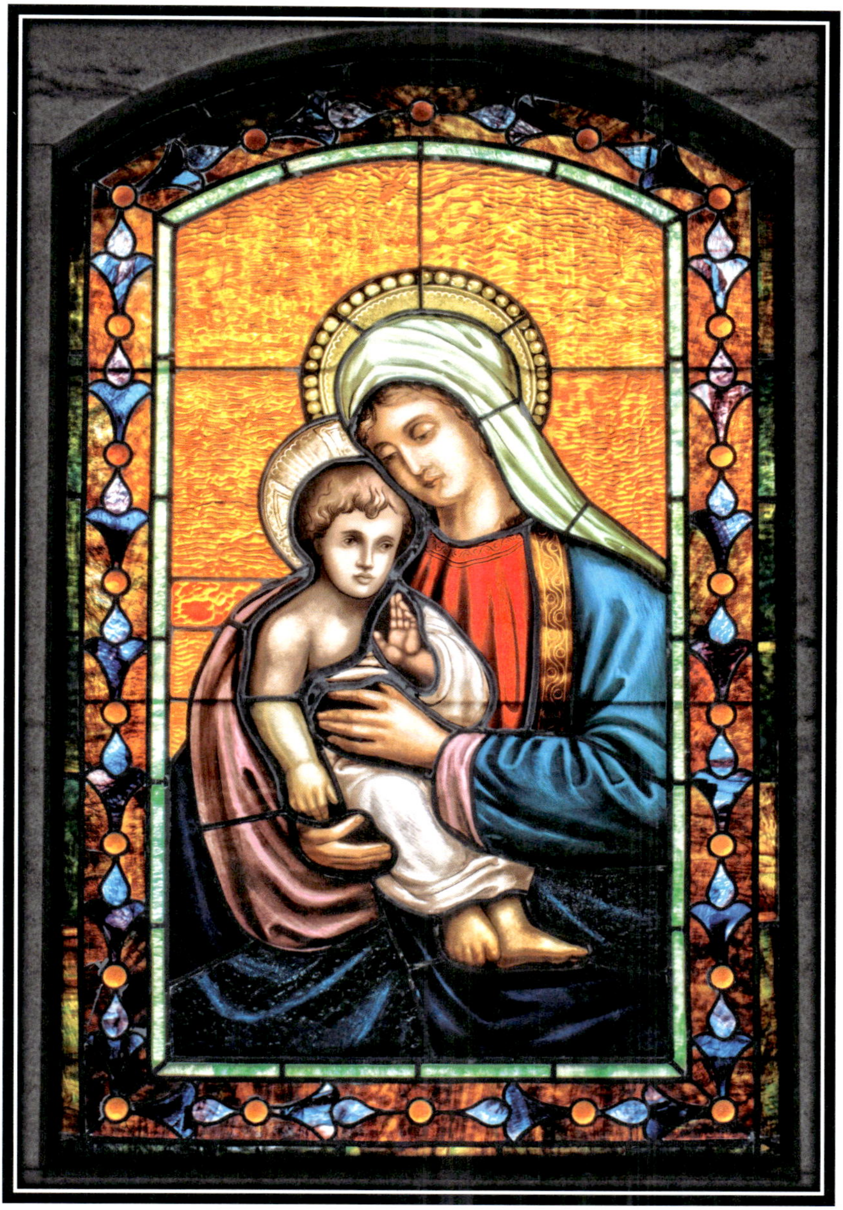

143. "Koen-Martinez" Mausoleum (c.1915)

Metairie Cemetery, Section 4
Charles L. Lawhon, architect
Albert Weiblen Marble and Granite Co., builders

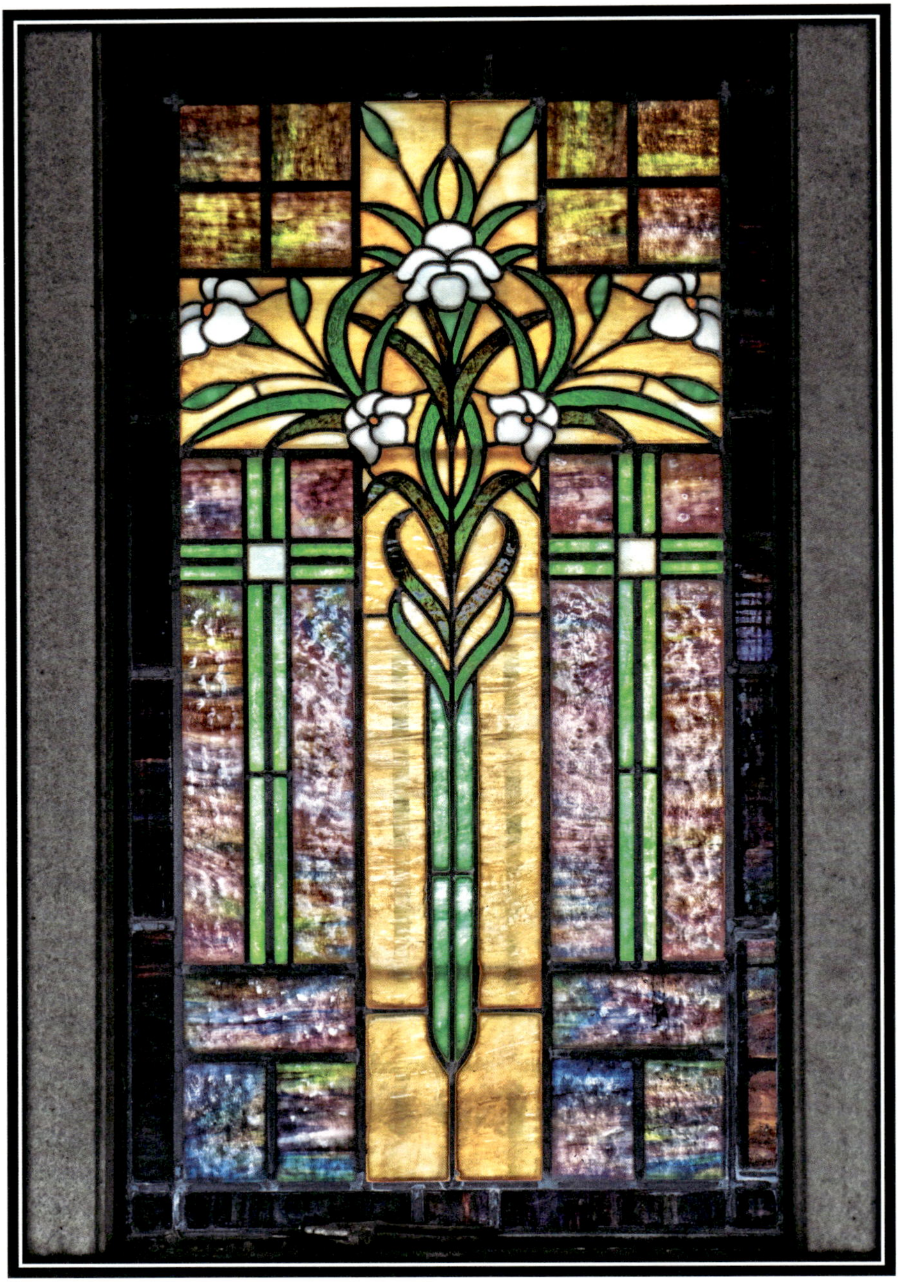

144. "Mauberret" Mausoleum (c.1918)
Metairie Cemetery, Section E

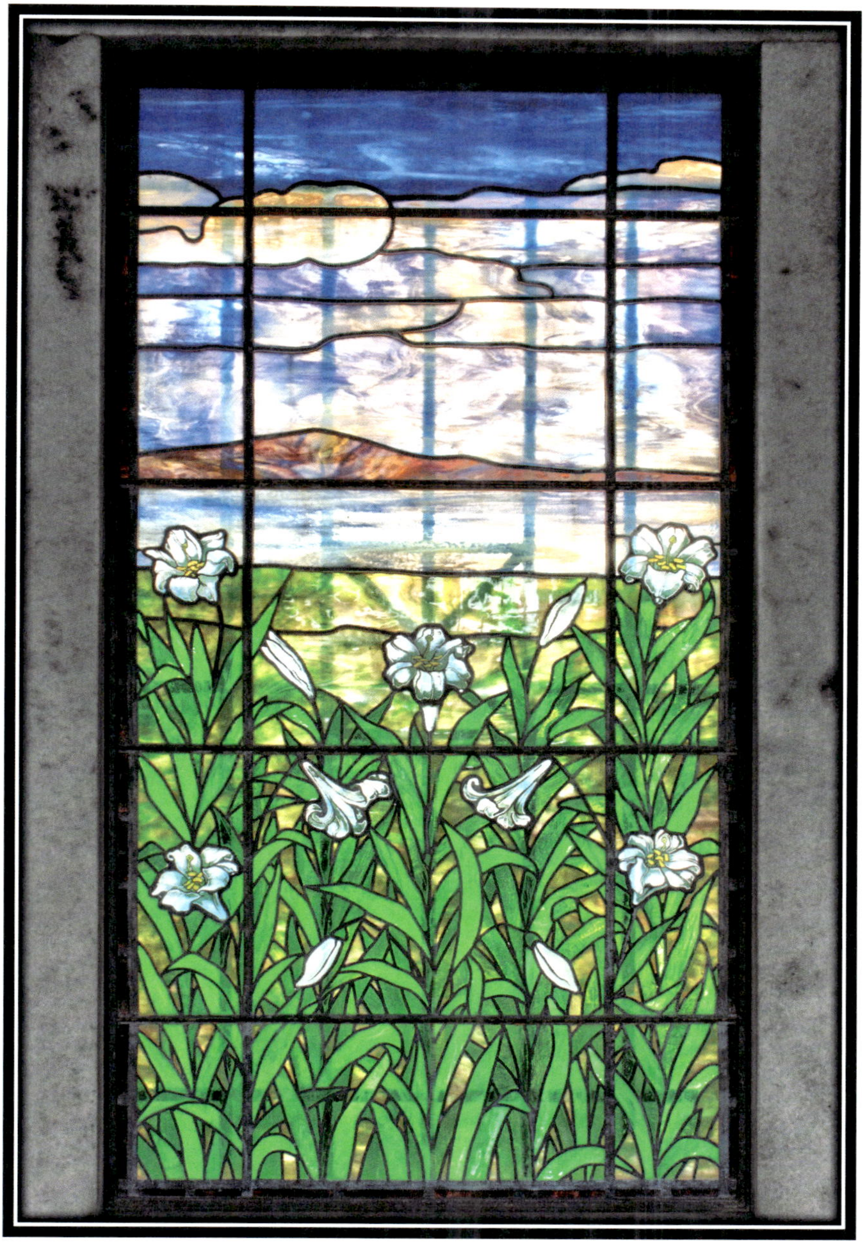

145. "Charles F. Buck" Mausoleum (1919)
Metairie Cemetery, Section 89
Emile Weil & Charles L. Lawhon, architects
Albert Weiblen Marble and Granite Co., builders

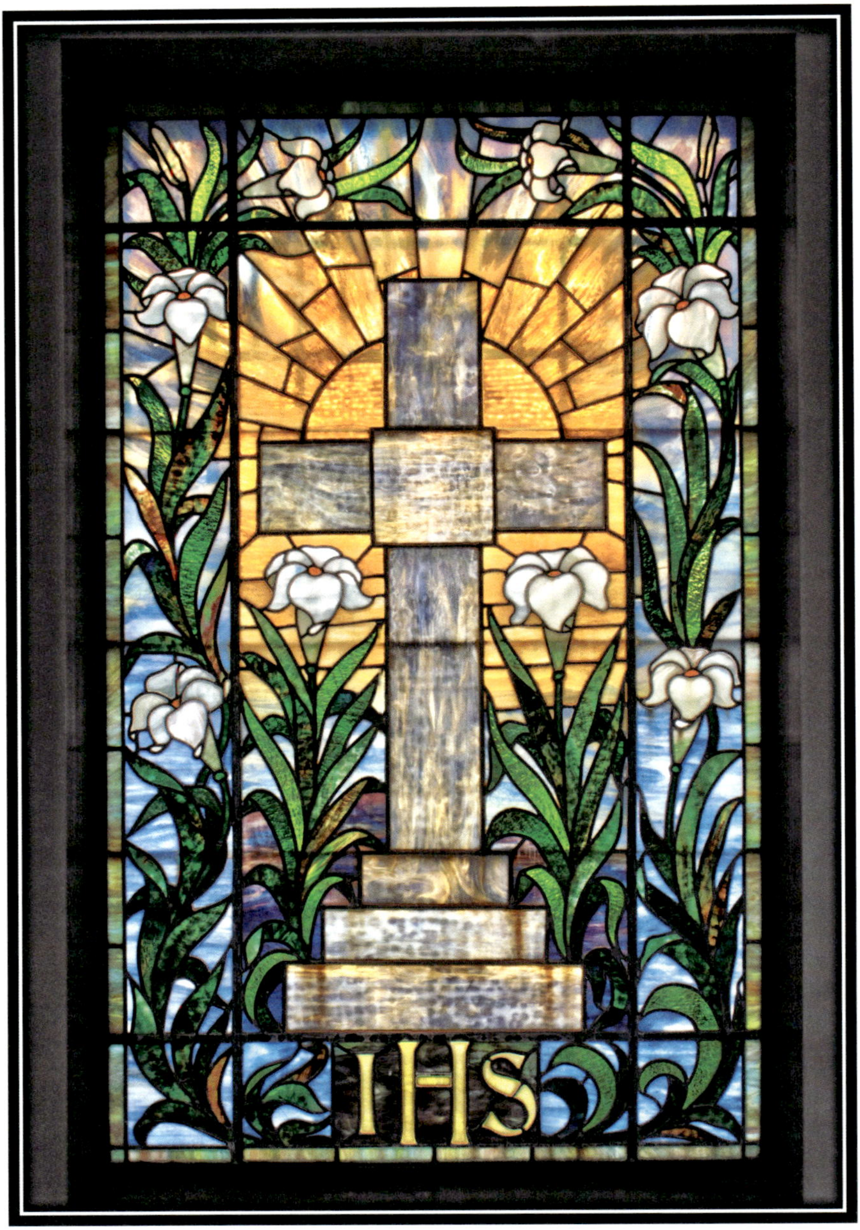

146. "Maumus" Mausoleum (1919)
Metairie Cemetery, Section 85
Charles L. Lawhon, architect
Albert Weiblen Marble and Granite Co., builders

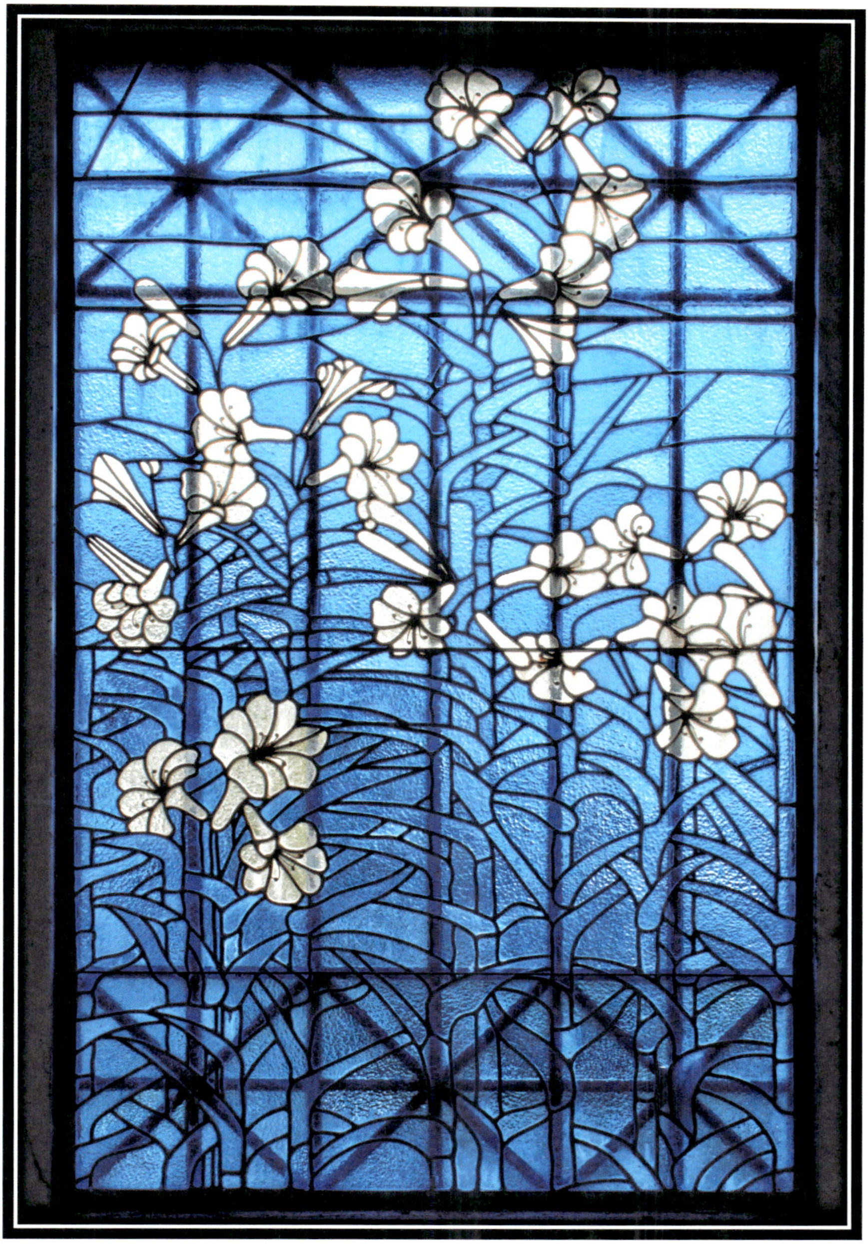

147. "Vatter" Mausoleum (c.1919)

Metairie Cemetery, Section 123
Victor Huber, builder

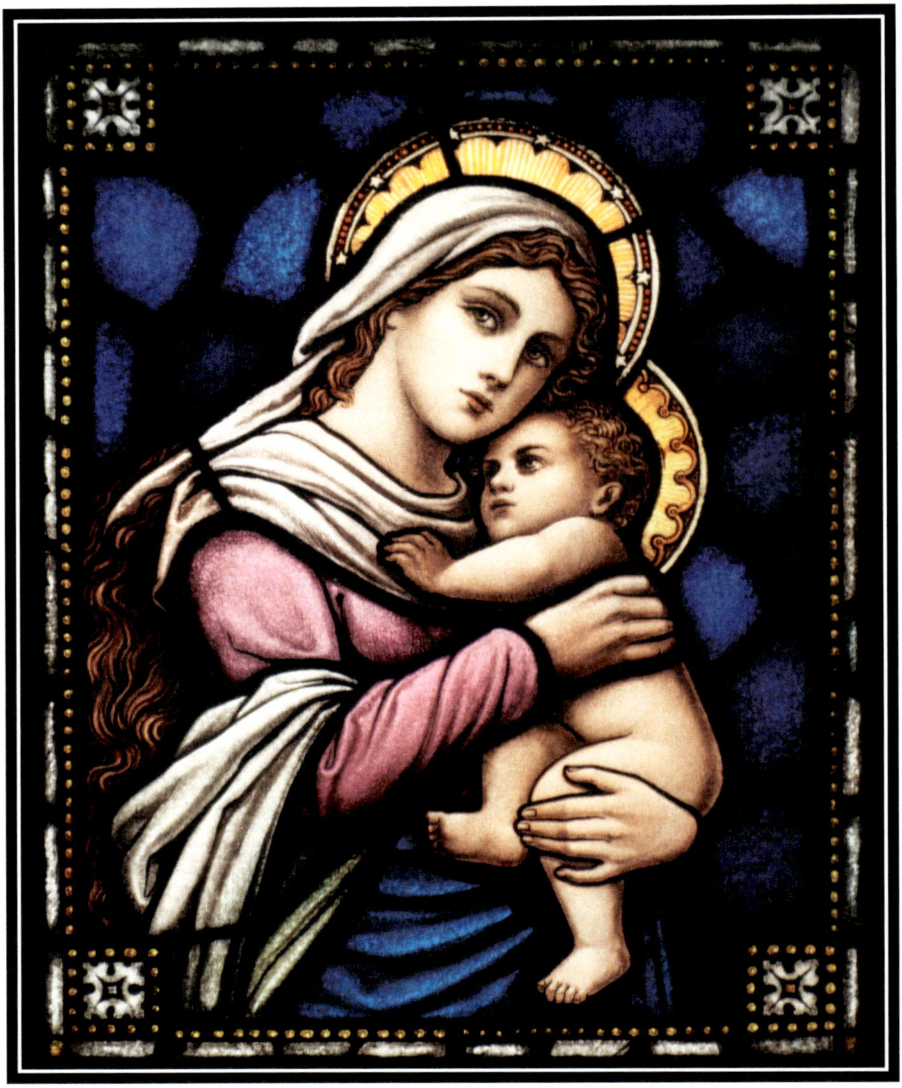

148. "Diassellis" Mausoleum (c.1930)

Metairie Cemetery, Section 49
Albert Weiblen Marble and Granite Co., builders

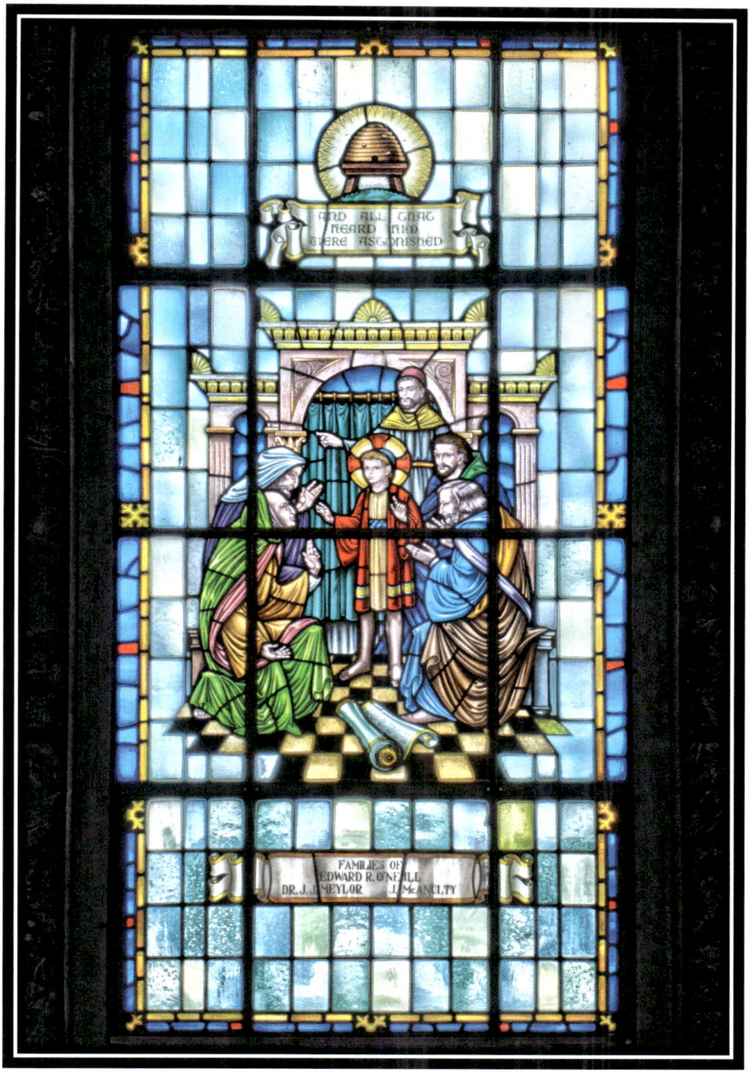

149. Lake Lawn Park Cemetery Community Mausoleum (1950-1951)

Jules K. de la Vergne and John M. Lachin, Jr., architects

Multiple windows at this site were designed by Willet Windows, a successor firm of Willet Studios of Philadelphia, and installed in the 1970s. A smaller group designed by J. Wippel & Co. of Great Britain [pictured] were installed in the late 1960s. Numerous replacement windows designed by Reinarts Studios of Winona, Minnesota were installed post-Katrina.

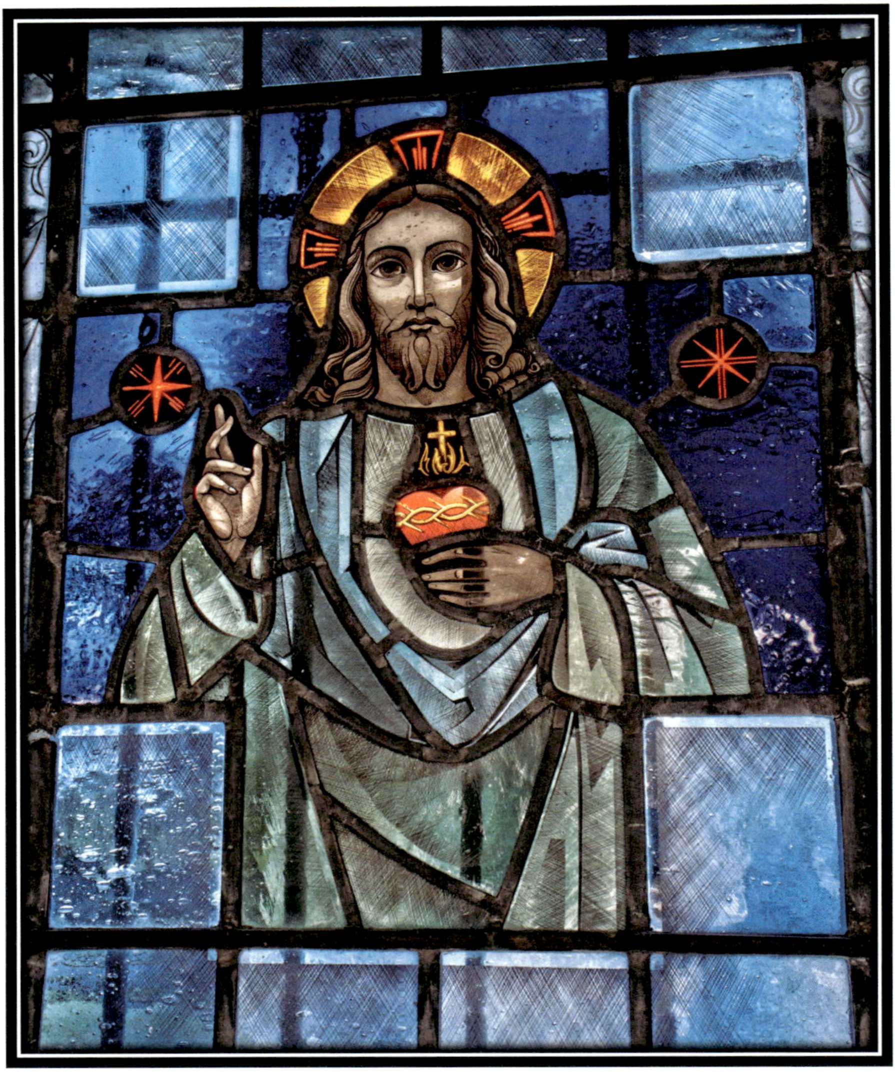

150. "Anthony J. Sciambra" Mausoleum (c.1959)
Metairie Cemetery, Section 52

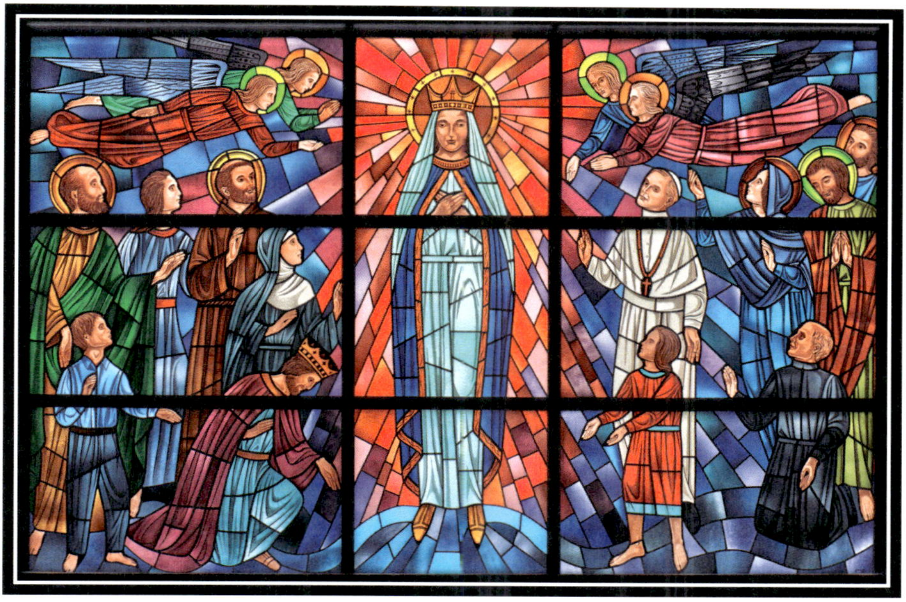

151. All Saints Community Mausoleum at Metairie Cemetery (1986)

Architect undetermined
Stained glass by Reinarts Studios of Winona, Minnesota.

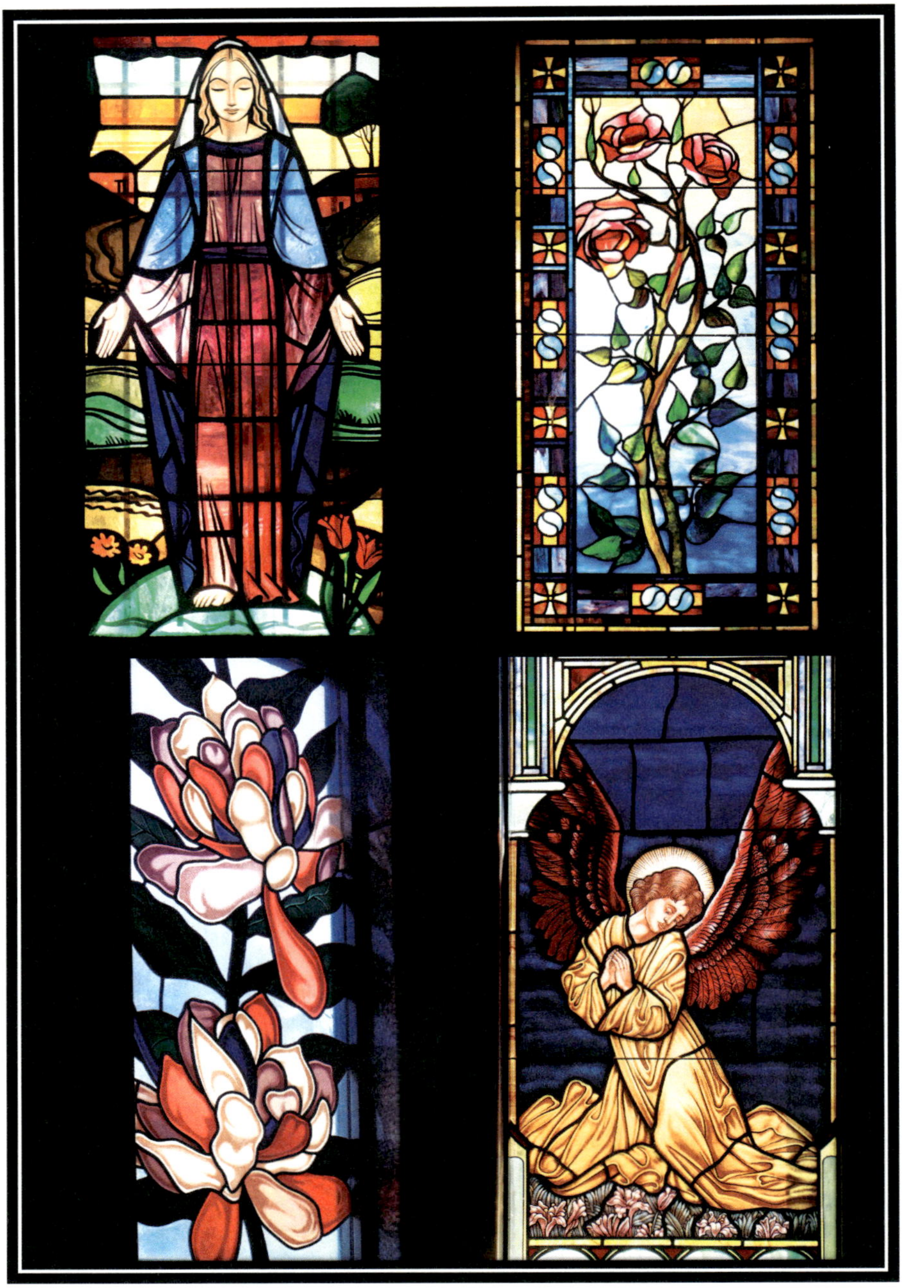

Aesthetic considerations of collage compel me to diverge at this point from the heretofore strictly chronological presentation of sites.

---

152. "Anthony L. Zuppardo" Mausoleum [top left]
Metairie Cemetery, Section 134
Built c.2001

153. "Torre" Mausoleum [top right]
Metairie Cemetery, Section 41
Built c.1927 by the Albert Weiblen Marble and Granite Co.

154. "Brown" Mausoleum [bottom left]
Metairie Cemetery, Section 129
Built c.1947 by the Albert Weiblen Marble and Granite Co.

155. "Bollinger-Cazes" Mausoleum [bottom right]
Metairie Cemetery, Section 129
Built c.1990s

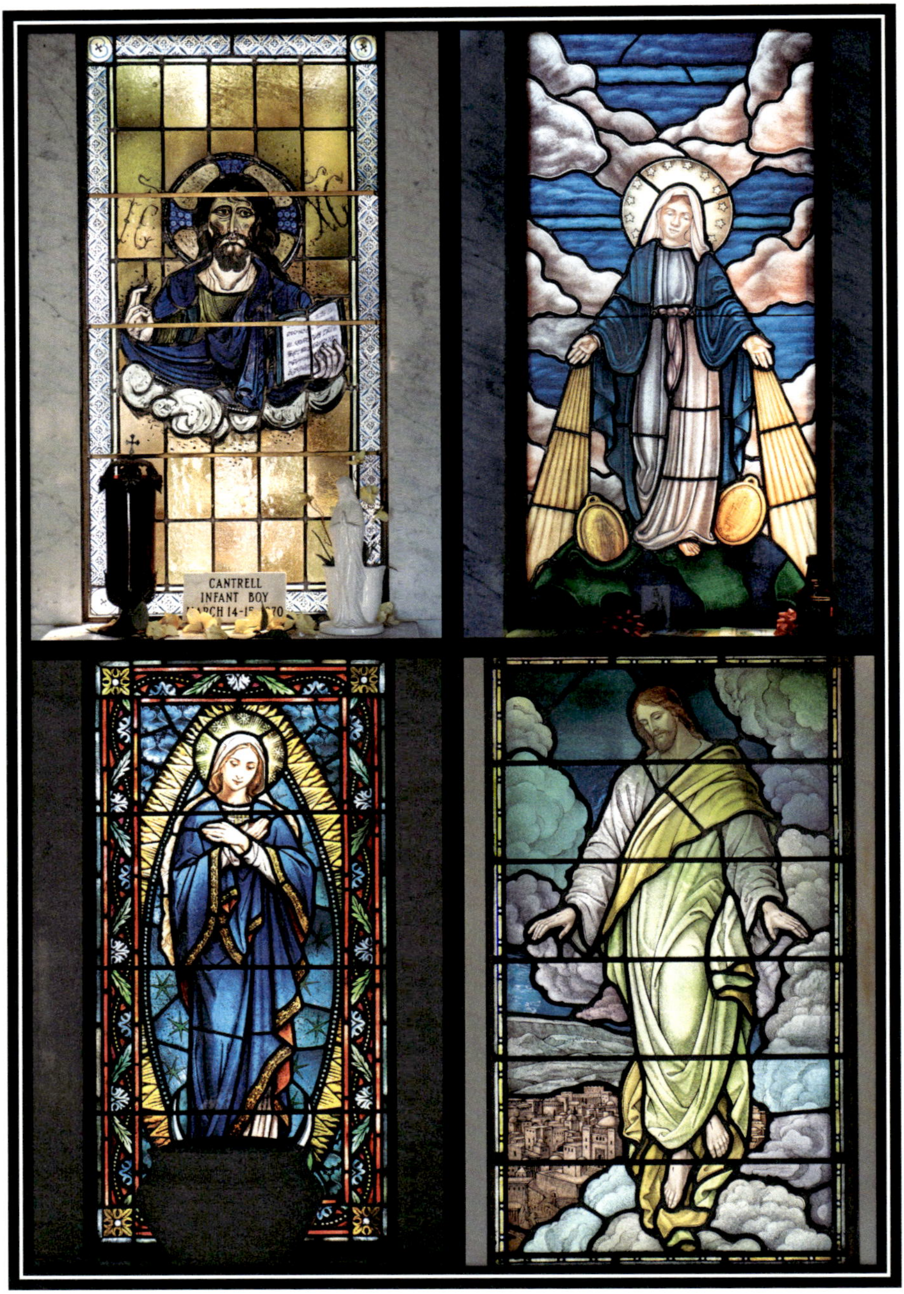
CANTRELL
INFANT BOY

156. "Antonino V. LaNasa" Mausoleum [top left]
Metairie Cemetery, Section 149
Built c.1970

157. "Steed" Mausoleum [top right]
Metairie Cemetery, Section 129A
Built c.2014

158. "Lawrence P. Smith" Mausoleum [bottom left]
Metairie Cemetery, Section 142
Built c.1975

159. "Harkey" Mausoleum [bottom right]
Metairie Cemetery, Section 157
Built c.1947 by the Alabama Marble Co.

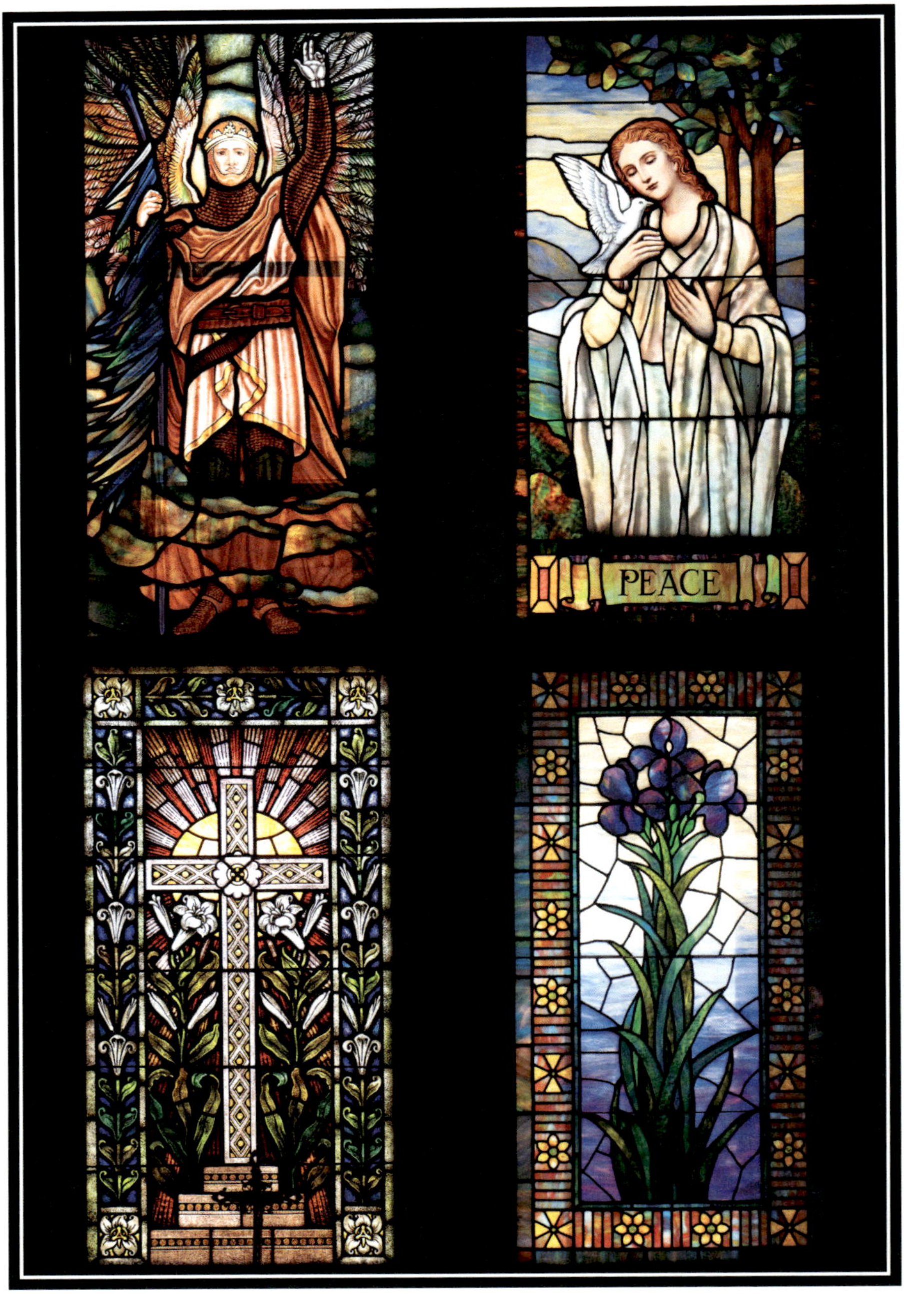
PEACE

160. "Khoury" Mausoleum [top left]

Metairie Cemetery, Section 129
Built c.1990s

161. "Bruning-McFadden" Mausoleum [top right]

Metairie Cemetery, Section 123
Built c.1925 by the Albert Weiblen Marble and Granite Co.
Albert Rieker, architect

162. "Lawrence Fabacher" Mausoleum [bottom left]

Metairie Cemetery, Section 9
Built c.1924 by the Albert Weiblen Marble and Granite Co.
Albert Rieker, architect

163. "Battistella" Mausoleum [bottom right]

Metairie Cemetery, Section 47
Built c.1924 by the Albert Weiblen Marble and Granite Co.
Albert Rieker, architect

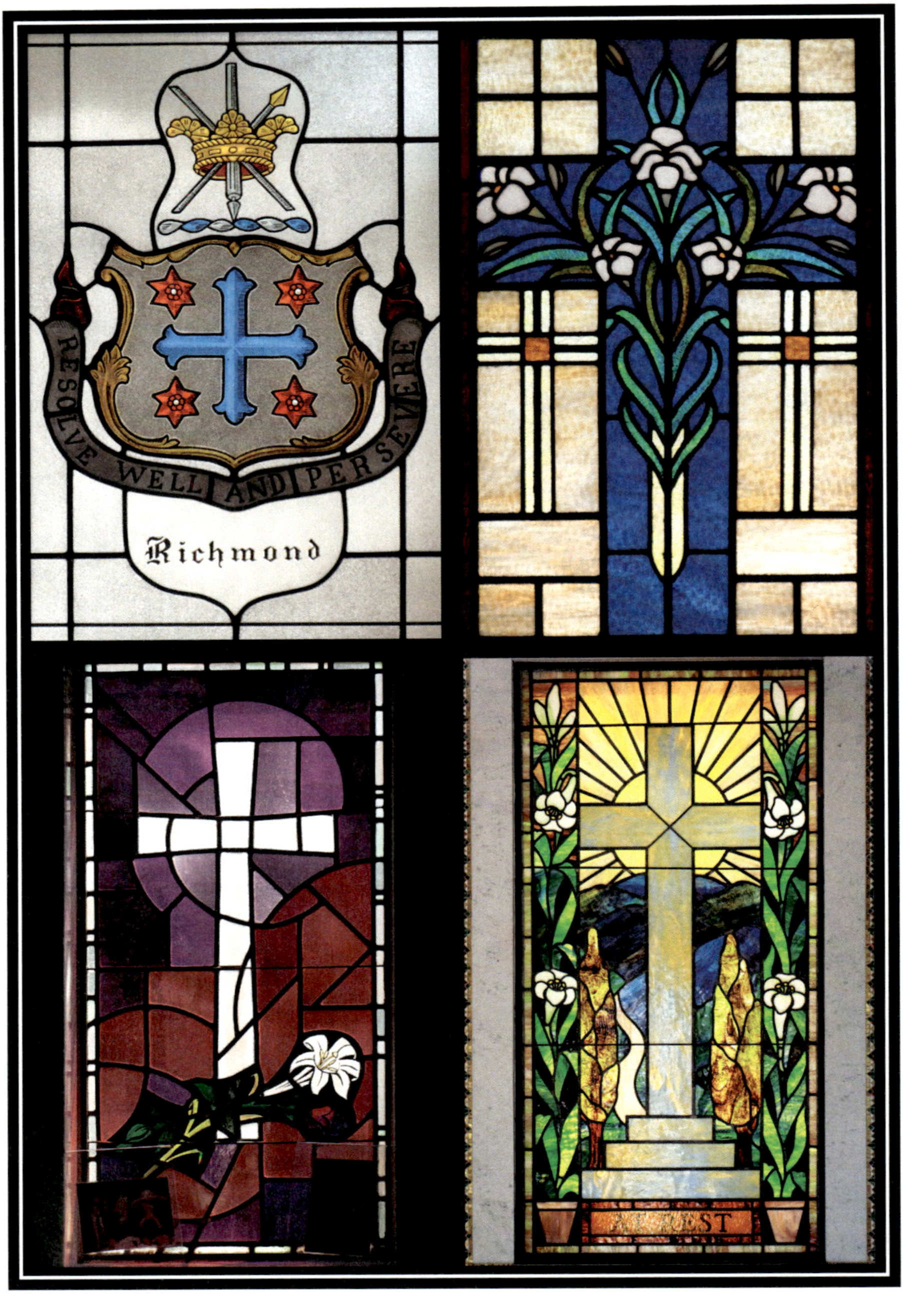
RESOLVE WELL AND PERSEVERE
Richmond

164. "Richmond" Mausoleum [top left]
Metairie Cemetery, Section 135
Built c.2018

165. "Montelepre" Mausoleum [top right]
Metairie Cemetery, Section 49
Built c.1941 by Victor Huber
Albert R. Huber, architect

166. "Family of Capt. William A. Bisso, Jr." Mausoleum [bottom left]
Metairie Cemetery, Section 133
Built c.1992

167. "S. D'Antoni" Mausoleum [bottom right]
Metairie Cemetery, Section 35
Built c.1923 by the Albert Weiblen Marble and Granite Co.
Among the *Albert Weiblen Marble and Granite Company Office Records* within the Southeastern Architectural Archive held at Tulane University are two conflicting attributions for the design of this mausoleum, one naming Stanley R. Poole the architect, another Albert Rieker.

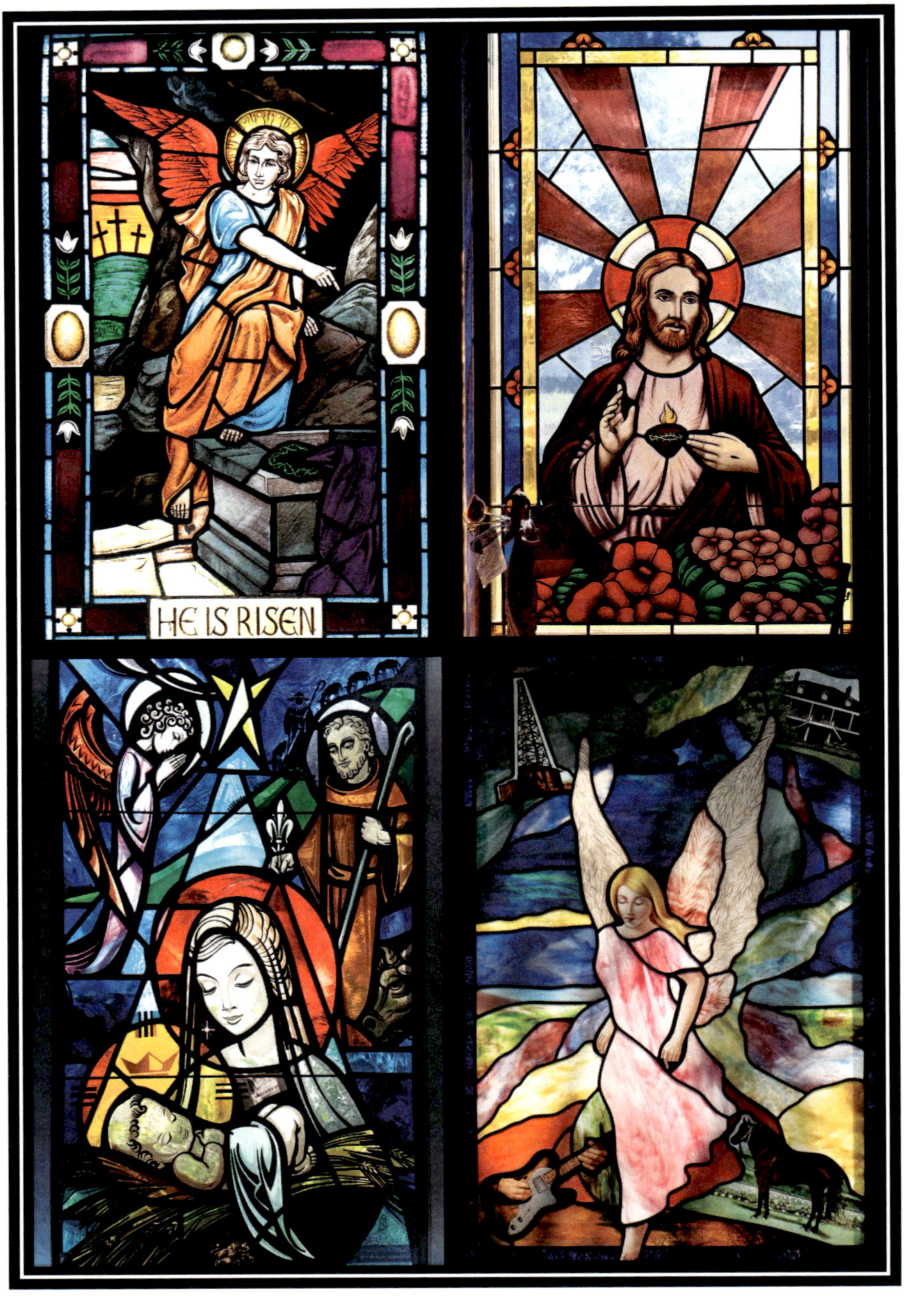
HE IS RISEN

168. "Robt. E. Smith" Mausoleum [top left]
Lake Lawn Park Cemetery
Built c.1962

169. "Comeaux" Mausoleum [top right]
Metairie Cemetery, Section 129A
Built c.2006

170. "A.H. Stall" Mausoleum [bottom left]
Metairie Cemetery, Section 134
Built c.1975
Stained glass by Conrad Pickel Studio
of New Berlin, WI

171. "Benoit" Mausoleum [bottom right]
Metairie Cemetery, Section 129A
Built c.2000s

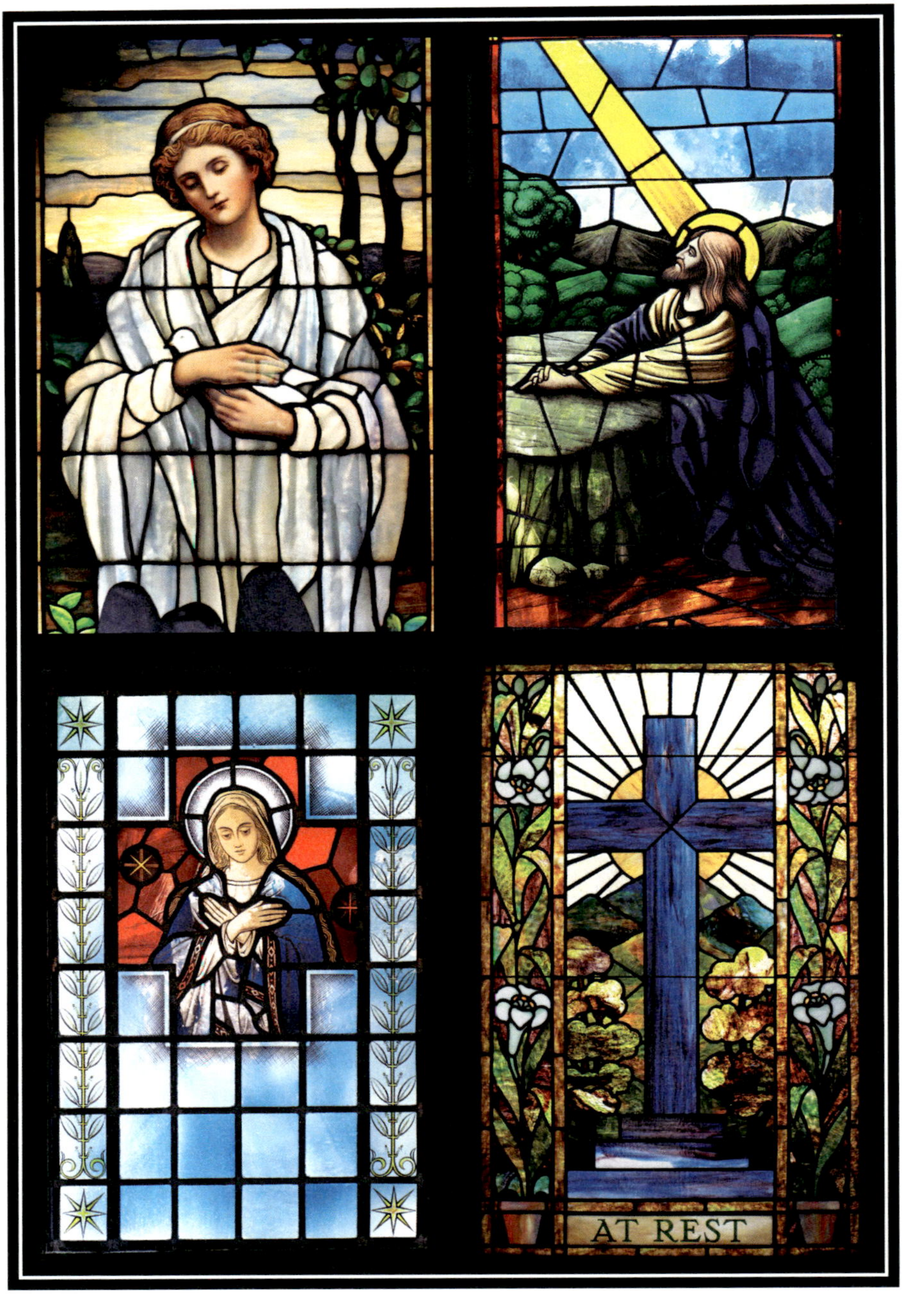
AT REST

172. "Luca Vaccaro" Mausoleum [top left]
Metairie Cemetery, Section 35
Built c.1924 by the Albert Weiblen Marble and Granite Co.
Albert Rieker, architect

173. Lake Lawn Park Cemetery Model Mausoleum
[top right]
Built c.2000s

174. "Marquer" Mausoleum [bottom left]
Metairie Cemetery, Section 52
Built c.1939

175. "Libby-Dufour" Mausoleum [bottom right]
Metairie Cemetery, Section 43
Built c.1928

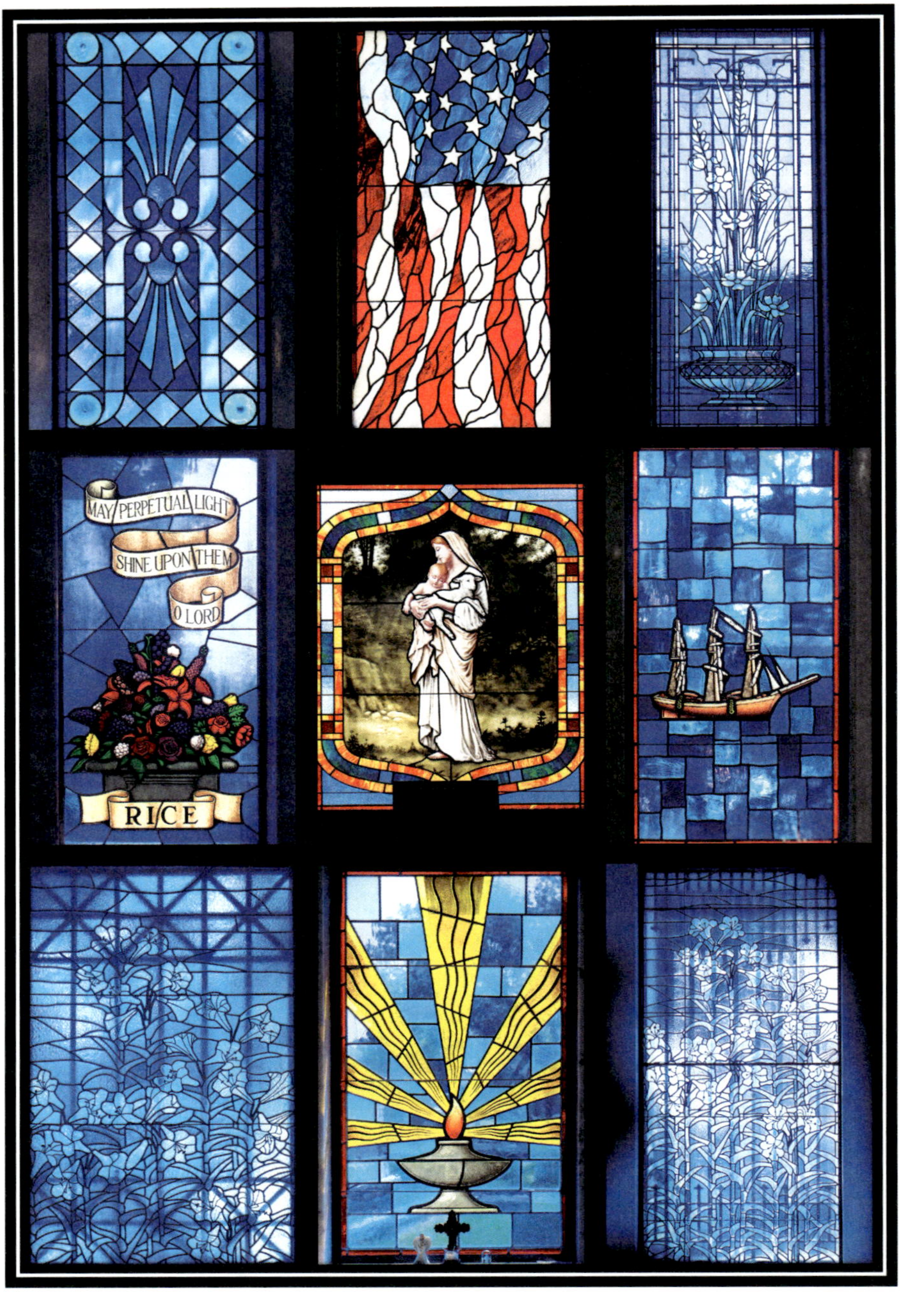
MAY PERPETUAL LIGHT
SHINE UPON THEM
O LORD
RICE

176. "Bull" Mausoleum [top left]
Metairie Cemetery, Section 163
Built c.1953
Ralph Phillippi, architect

177. "Laborde" Mausoleum [top center]
Metairie Cemetery, Section 135
Built c.2009
Stained glass by Attenhofer's Stained Glass Studio of Metairie

178. "W.H.D. Brook" Mausoleum [top right]
Metairie Cemetery, Section 87
Built c.1912

179. "Rice" Mausoleum [center left]
Metairie Cemetery, Section 129
Built c.2002

180. "B" (Thomas Milton Benson) Mausoleum [center]
Metairie Cemetery, Foot of Central Avenue
Built c.2018

181. "Paternostro-Carter" Mausoleum [center right]
Metairie Cemetery, Section 129B
Built c.1999

182. "Chapman H. Hyams" Mausoleum [bottom left]
Metairie Cemetery, Section B
Built c.1925 by the Albert Weiblen Marble and Granite Co.
Charles L. Lawhon, architect
Metairie Cemetery: An Historical Memoir, in a conflicting account, reports Favrot & Livaudais as the architects of this mausoleum.

183. "Copeland" Mausoleum [bottom center]
Metairie Cemetery, Section 129A
Built c.2004

184. "Downman" Mausoleum [bottom right]
Metairie Cemetery, Section 87
Built c.1928 by the Albert Weiblen Marble and Granite Co.
Charles L. Lawhon, architect

OTHER SITES

Find below a compilation of sites that are known to house stained glass but were pared from the roster of photographed commissions due to their inaccessibility.

185. St. Maurice Catholic Church (1857), 615 St Maurice Ave, Holy Cross, New Orleans. Fr. John Cambiaso, architect; E. St. Martin & E. Lacoste, builders. Deconsecrated post-Katrina; large, lower-level nave panes transplanted to Most Holy Trinity (*entry #131*) in Covington, Louisiana c.2016. Clerestory windows remain.

186. St. Elizabeth's Orphan Asylum ~ Prytania Street Addition Chapel (1880), 1314 Napoleon Ave, Uptown, New Orleans. Albert Diettel, architect. Converted to private residences. Former home of author Anne Rice. Second-floor windows are easily viewed from Prytania Street.

187. Howard Memorial Library Annex now known as Confederate Memorial Hall Museum (1889-1891; 1897), 929 Camp St, Central Business District, New Orleans. Thomas Sully of Sully & Toledano, architect; Thomas Sully of Sully, Burton & Stone, architect of 1897 portico and tower additions. A Great Seal of the Confederacy in stained glass, that appears to be original to the building, as well as a large pane dedicated in 1907 to the "Unknown Confederate Dead", grace the rear wall of this museum that recounts through an elaborate collection of artifacts an important era of New Orleans and United States history.

188. "Maginnis" Mausoleum (c.1889), Metairie Cemetery, New Orleans, Sec. 13.

189. The Round Table Club (1896), 6330 St Charles Ave, Audubon, New Orleans. Formerly a private residence, now home to a club that meets weekly on Thursday evenings. An impressive window is visible from the structure's parking lot.

190. Our Lady of Peace Catholic Church (1892-1902), 13281 LA-644, Vacherie. Harrod & Andry, architects.

191. Louise C. Thomas Hall Chapel (1911-1912) at Loyola University, 6363 St Charles Ave, Audubon, New Orleans. Rathbone DeBuys of DeBuys, Churchill & Labouisse, architect. Stained glass by John Morgan & Sons of New York City.

192. "Bobet" Mausoleum (c.1912), Metairie Cemetery, Sec. 44. Charles L. Lawhon, architect; built by the Albert Weiblen Marble and Granite Co.

193. "Walmsley" Mausoleum (c.1916), Metairie Cemetery, Sec. 5E. Charles L. Lawhon, architect; built by the Albert Weiblen Marble and Granite Co. *New Orleans Architecture Volume III: The Cemeteries*, in a conflicting account, reports Charles A. Orleans as this mausoleum's designer and builder and its years of construction as 1905-1906.

194. **"Joseph Vaccaro" Mausoleum (c.1920)**, Metairie Cemetery, Sec. 35. Albert Rieker, architect; built by the Albert Weiblen Marble and Granite Co.

195. **"B.G. Carbajal" Mausoleum (c.1921)**, Metairie Cemetery, Sec. B. Charles L. Lawhon, architect; built by the Albert Weiblen Marble and Granite Co.

196. **Napoleon Avenue Methodist Episcopal (1920-1922) now known as All Nations Fellowship**, 2524 Napoleon Ave, Freret, New Orleans. Architect undetermined.

197. **Shaw Hall Chapel & Library (1922-1923) at Notre Dame Catholic Seminary**, 2901 S. Carrollton Ave, Marlyville-Fontainebleau, New Orleans. Col. Allison Owen of Diboll & Owen, architect; Joseph Fromherz, builder. Stained glass windows by Rambusch Studios of New York City.

198. **St. Joan of Arc Catholic Church (1923)**, 8321 Burthe St, Leonidas, New Orleans. Architect undetermined.

199. **"Beer" Mausoleum (c.1923)**, Metairie Cemetery, Sec. 123. Albert Rieker, architect; built by the Albert Weiblen Marble and Granite Co.

200. **Sacred Heart of Jesus Catholic Church (1923-1924) now known as Greater Bibleway Church International**, 3200 Canal St, Mid-City, New Orleans. Emile Weil & Albert Bendernagel, architects; Lionel F. Favret, builder. Stained glass by Emil Frei Studios of St. Louis.

201. **"C.D. O'Connor" Mausoleum (c.1924)**, Metairie Cemetery, Sec. 35. Albert Rieker, architect; built by the Albert Weiblen Marble and Granite Co.

202. **Incarnate Word Catholic Church (1929)**, 8300 Apricot St, Leonidas, New Orleans. Andry & Feitel, architects. Primary stained glass by Emil Frei Studios of St. Louis. Now used as archdiocesan offices.

203. **St. John Bosco Chapel [Catholic] (1941) at Hope Haven**, 1111 Barataria Blvd, Marrero. Jack J.H. Kessels of Diboll-Kessels & Associates, architect. Primary stained glass windows created by Joep Nicholas depict the life of the chapel's namesake.

204. **St. Matthias Catholic Church (1941) now known as Blessed Trinity Catholic Church**, 4230 S. Broad Ave, Broadmoor, New Orleans. Herbert A. Benson & George H. Christy, architects; Chris Larsen Co., contractors.

205. **Gentilly Presbyterian Church (1950) now known as New Hope Community Church ~ East Campus**, 3700 Gentilly Ave, Gentilly Terrace, New Orleans. August Perez & Associates, architects; D.D. Pittman Contracting Co., builders.

206. **Old Holy Trinity Greek Orthodox Church (1951) now known as St. Luke's Episcopal Church**, 1222 N. Dorgenois St, Tremé-Lafitte, New Orleans. N.D. Calo of Vicksburg, Mississippi, architect; B.M. Dornblatt & Associates of New Orleans, engineers; Bartley & Binnings, builders.

207. **Mt. Zion Methodist Church (1952)**, 2722 Louisiana Ave, Central City, New Orleans. E.J. Hammond, architect; W. Larry Gremillion, builder.

208. Grace Episcopal Church (1953-1954), 3700 Canal St, Mid-City, New Orleans. August Perez & Associates + Lucien M. Haase, architects; D.D. Pittman Contracting Co., builders.

209. Second Baptist Church ~ Sixth District (1955), 4218 Laurel St, East Riverside, New Orleans. Schill Builders.

210. Saints Peter & Paul Catholic Church (1959), 66192 St Mary Dr, Pearl River. Architect undetermined.

211. "Schwegmann" Mausoleum (c.1980), Metairie Cemetery, Sec. 133.

212. "La Rocca" Mausoleum (c.1992), Metairie Cemetery, Sec. 132.

213. "Fertel-Duke" Mausoleum (c.1999), Metairie Cemetery, Sec. 129.

214. "W.K. Aucoin" Mausoleum (c.2001), Metairie Cemetery, Sec. 129B.

215. "Chalin O. Perez" Mausoleum (c.2003), Metairie Cemetery, Sec. 176.

216. "Canizaro" Mausoleum (c.2000s), Metairie Cemetery, Sec. 129.

BIBLIOGRAPHY

Ackel, Leslie. "Glass art a part of Covington revitalization" *Yada Yada Magazine*, Sept./Oct. 2007, pg. 29

Andrews, Patty. "St. Tammany Glass Art Treasures: Some Old, Some Made New" *Preservation In Print*, Oct. 2017, pg. 31

Andrews, Patty. "Uptown Glass with a German Accent" *Preservation In Print*, April 2018, pg. 37

Bornside, Bette B. and Rev. Teodoro Agudo. *St. Theresa of Avila Parish 1848-1998.* New Orleans: St. Theresa of Avila Parish, 1998.

Bozant, Kevin. *Port & Burgundy: A Pictorial History ~ St. Paul Lutheran Church New Orleans 1840-1990.* New Orleans: Kevin Bozant, 1990.

Bruno, R. Stephanie. "St. Rose de Lima Church, shuttered since Hurricane Katrina, comes back to life as Southern Rep Theatre" *Preservation In Print*, Sept. 2018, pg. 22-25

Caillouet, Bishop Louis Abel, *Our Lady of the Holy Rosary Church ~ New Orleans, Louisiana.* New Orleans: The Ladies Sodality of the Holy Rosary Church, unknown year.

Cangelosi, Glen and Patricia Ricci, *Confederate Memorial Hall: The Battle Abbey of the South ~ A Pictorial View.* New Orleans: De Simonin Publications, 2002.

Cangelosi, Jr., Robert J. *New Orleans Architecture Volume IX: Carrollton*. Baton Rouge, LA: Louisiana State University Press, 2020.

Christovich, Mary Louise, Leonard V. Huber and Peggy McDowell. *New Orleans Architecture Volume III: The Cemeteries.* Gretna, LA: Pelican Publishing Company, 2004.

Christovich, Mary Louise, Roulhac Toledano, Betsy Swanson, Pat Holden, Samuel Wilson, Jr. and Bernard Lemann. *New Orleans Architecture Volume II: The American Sector.* Gretna, LA: Pelican Publishing Company, 1998.

Christovich, Mary Louise, Sally Kittredge Evans and Roulhac Toledano. *New Orleans Architecture Volume V: The Esplanade Ridge.* Gretna, LA: Pelican Publishing Company, 2013.

Deane, Mark. "Three reasons to visit St. Michael Church in Convent" *WGNO-ABC: New Orleans' Very Own*, Dec. 9, 2016, https://wgno.com/news/three-reasons-to-visit-st-michael-church-in-convent/

DeBlieux, Robert B. *National Register of Historic Places nomination: Manresa House of Retreats; Jefferson College, Convent, LA.* Baton Rouge: National Register Staff, Division of Historic Preservation, State of Louisiana, 1985.

Florent, Katherine Joyce and Emma Royster Sampson. *Our Lady Star of the Sea 100 Year Anniversary ~ The Star of the City.* New Orleans: Our Lady Star of the Sea Parish, c.2011.

Friends of the Cabildo, The. *New Orleans Architecture Volume VIII: The University Section.* Gretna, LA: Pelican Publishing Company, 2011.

Friends of the Cabildo Associates of the Louisiana State Museum, The. *New Orleans Architecture Volume VII: Jefferson City.* Gretna, LA: Pelican Publishing Company, 2010.

Gandolfo, Henri A. *Metairie Cemetery: An Historical Memoir ~ Tales of its Soldiers, Statesman and Great Families.* New Orleans: Stewart Enterprises, 2004.

Gurtner, George. *Historic Churches of Old New Orleans.* New Orleans: Friends of St. Alphonsus, 1997.

Gurtner, George. *Our Lady of Prompt Succor: A Journey of Hope.* New Orleans: Ursuline Sisters of New Orleans, 2014.

Heck, Robert W. *Religious Architecture in Louisiana.* Baton Rouge, LA: Louisiana State University Press, 1995.

Luneau, Jean-François. *Félix Gaudin: Peintre-Verrier Et Mosaïste (1851-1930).* Clermont-Ferrand, France: Presses Universitaires Blaise-Pascal, 2006.

Mayer, Gabriel, Brian Clarke, Bernhard Graf, Martin Harrison and Gottfried Knapp. *Architecture | Glass | Art: Franz Mayer of Munich ~ Mayer'sche Hofkunstanstalt.* Munich, Germany: Hirmer Publishers, c.2014.

Mayer, Linda. "One-of-a-kind Tiffany stained glass windows at Tulane's Uptown campus" *Preservation Resource Center of New Orleans*, Nov. 16, 2018, https://prcno.org/one-kind-tiffany-stained-glass-windows-tulanes-uptown-campus/

Morris, Benjamin. "On the Trail of Emil Frei: New Orleans' Stained Glass" *Pelican Bomb*, March 26, 2015, http://pelicanbomb.com/art-review/2015/on-the-trail-of-emil-frei-new-orleans-stained-glass

Nolan, Charles E. *A History of the Archdiocese of New Orleans.* Strasbourg, France: Éditions du Signe, 2000.

Nolan, Charles E. *Cathedral-Basilica of St. Louis King of France ~ New Orleans, Louisiana.* Strasbourg, France: Éditions du Signe, 2009.

Nolan, Charles E. *The Old Ursuline Convent ~ New Orleans, Louisiana.* Strasbourg, France: Éditions du Signe, 2011.

Nolan, Charles E. *Splendors of Faith: New Orleans Catholic Churches, 1727-1930.* Baton Rouge, LA: Louisiana State University Press, 2010.

Paterson, Seale. "Nostalgia: Hope Haven" *myNewOrleans.com*, Nov. 30, 2018, https://www.myneworleans.com/nostalgia-hope-haven/

Patterson, Te'erika. "New Orleans church celebrating 175 years as a historical beacon" *The Philadelphia Tribune*, Sept. 6, 2019, https://www.phillytrib.com/news/new-orleans-church-celebrating-175-years-as-a-historical-beacon/article_b659173c-3015-5280-b0d2-630bff44d15a.html

Sebastien, James. "Attenhofer's Stained Glass Studio: Artisans Dedicated to Restoring New Orleans' Stained Glass Treasures" *Preservation In Print*, Oct. 2017, pg. 29-30

Southeastern Architectural Archive (SEAA), Special Collections Division, Tulane University Libraries

Sternberg, Mary Ann. *Along the River Road: Past and Present on Louisiana's Historic Byway*. Baton Rouge: Louisiana State University Press, 1996.

Tanner, Pame. "Stained glass tour heads to St. Louis Cathedral, St. Augustine and Our Lady of Guadalupe churches" *Preservation Resource Center of New Orleans*, Oct. 22, 2018, https://prcno.org/stained-glass-tour-heads-st-louis-cathedral-st-augustine-lady-guadalupe-churches/

Theis, James and Harriet Murrell. *The Stained Glass of Trinity Episcopal Church, New Orleans.* New Orleans: James Theis, 2017.

Toledano, Roulhac and Mary Louise Christovich. *New Orleans Architecture Volume VI: Faubourg Tremé and the Bayou Road.* Gretna, LA: Pelican Publishing Company, 2003.

Wilkinson, Claire and Daniel MacDonald. "Holiday Home Tour: Jackson Avenue Evangelical Congregational Church" *Preservation Resource Center of New Orleans*, Dec. 7, 2017, https://prcno.org/holiday-home-tour-jackson-avenue-evangelical-congregational-church/

Wilson, Samuel, Jr. *The Buildings of Christ Church.* New Orleans: The Louisiana Landmarks Society, 1997.

Wilson, Samuel, Jr. *The Church of St. Alphonsus.* New Orleans: Friends of St. Alphonsus, 1996.

Wilson, Samuel, Jr. *The First Presbyterian Church of New Orleans: Its Buildings and its Ministers.* New Orleans: The Louisiana Landmarks Society, 1998.

Wilson, Samuel, Jr., Bernard Lemann, Mary Louise Christovich, Roulhac Toledano and Betsy Swanson. *New Orleans Architecture Volume I: The Lower Garden District.* Gretna, LA: Pelican Publishing Company, 1998.

Wilson, Samuel, Jr., Roulhac Toledano, Sally Kittredge Evans and Mary Louise Christovich. *New Orleans Architecture Volume IV: The Creole Faubourgs.* Gretna, LA: Pelican Publishing Company, 2006.

PAMPHLETS and BROCHURES

(N.A. = "No Author Cited"; N.D. = "No Date";
All pamphlets and brochures are unpublished)

Christ Church Cathedral. [N.A.; N.D.]

A Cloud of Witnesses ~ A Guide to the Stained Glass Windows ~ St. Paul Lutheran Church In The Marigny. 2015. [N.A.]

History of Sacred Heart of Jesus Catholic Church (Lacombe, LA). Drena Hutchinson. c.2010

The History of St. Augustine Church. [N.A.; N.D.]

History of Saint Augustine Church in Historic Faubourg Tremé. [N.A.; N.D.]

Holy Ghost Catholic Church ~ Our New Church Building. c.2001. [N.A.]

Holy Ghost Church Hammond LA. [N.A.; N.D.]

Jackson Avenue Evangelical Congregation ~ New Orleans, Louisiana 1845-1995. c.1995. [N.A.]

The John Gayle Aiken III Memorial Window ~ First Floor Tower Room ~ Christ Church Cathedral ~ St. Charles Avenue, New Orleans 1948. William H. Forman, Jr. c. 2001.

Meditations: The Windows of Manresa. John R. May. [N.D.]

Most Holy Trinity Catholic Church (Covington, LA). [N.A.; N.D.]

National Votive Shrine of Our Lady of Prompt Succor. [N.A.; N.D.]

A Priceless Legacy: The History of Salem UCC (Evangelical & Reformed). [N.A.; N.D.]

Rayne Memorial United Methodist Church ~ We Welcome You ~ A Tour of the Historic Sanctuary. Fannie Rayne Ross and George Russ Ross. [N.D.]

St. Alphonsus Parish ~ Welcome to the Redemptorist Campus. Fr. Richard Thibodeau. [N.D.]

Saint Augustine Catholic Church Restoration Campaign. [N.A.; N.D.]

St. Francis of Assisi Roman Catholic Church and Emil Frei's Stained-Glass Windows ~ Uptown, New Orleans, Louisiana. David Doll, 2017.

St. John the Baptist Catholic Church ~ Established 1851 ~ A Brief History. [N.A.; N.D.]

St. Peter Catholic Church 1843-2018 ~ 175 Years: Peace, Love and Service (2018 Calendar). [N.A.]

Saint Stephen Catholic Church. [N.A.; N.D.]

Salem United Church of Christ ~ Memorial Windows. [N.A.; N.D.]

The Stained Glass Windows of St. Martin's Episcopal Church. Rev. William Gedge Gayle, Jr. [N.D.]

Trinity Episcopal Church Stained Glass Window Self-Guided Tour. Dr. Jim Theis. [N.D.]

Tulane University's Tiffany Windows. [N.A.; N.D.]

Venerable Henriette Delille. 2012. [N.A.]
Welcome to the Greek Orthodox Cathedral of the Holy Trinity. [N.A.; N.D.]
The Window Restoration Project ~ The Continuing Legacy of the Gordon Sisters. [N.A.; N.D.]
2019-2020 Directory: Presbyterian Women of Covington Presbyterian Church. 2020. [N.A.]

NEWSPAPER ARTICLES (1840-2018)

(All articles by staff writers and all papers based in New Orleans except where otherwise indicated.)

"St. Patrick's Church." Daily Picayune, Dec. 27, 1840, pg. 2
"The St. Louis Cathedral." Daily Picayune, Nov. 9, 1850, pg. 1
"The Cathedral of St. Louis." Daily Picayune, Jan. 15, 1851, pg. 2
"Paintings in the St. Louis Cathedral." Daily Picayune, Aug. 21, 1851, pg. 2
"Consecration of a Cathedral." Daily Picayune, Dec. 6, 1851, pg. 2
"Building Improvements. New Churches." Daily Picayune, Sept. 19, 1852, pg. 4
"Sabbath School Celebration." Daily Crescent, May 4, 1852, pg. 2
"Renting of Pews." Daily Picayune, Dec. 21, 1856, pg. 2
"St. Alphonsus's New Church Fair." Daily Picayune, Dec. 23, 1856, pg. 1
"The City." Evening Picayune, April 28, 1857, pg. 4
"Consecration of St. Alphonsus." Daily Picayune, July 28, 1857, pg. 1
"St. Alphonsus's Church Consecration." Daily Picayune, Aug. 1, 1857, pg. 2
"Church Corner-Stone Laying." Daily Picayune, April 24, 1858, pg. 1
"Local Intelligence." Daily Crescent, June 7, 1860, pg. 1
"Church of St. Vincent De Paul, Third District." Daily Picayune, Sept. 3, 1865, pg. 8
"The City. The Fair at the Opera House." Daily Picayune, Oct. 21, 1865, pg. 8
"A New Catholic Church." Daily Picayune, April 13, 1866, pg. 3
"Local Intelligence." Daily Crescent, Mar. 21, 1869, pg. 1
"St. Stephen's New Catholic Church." Daily Picayune, Nov. 21, 1871, pg. 10
"Church Dedication." Daily Picayune, Dec. 12, 1871, pg. 1
"The pews in the Roman Catholic Church…" Daily Picayune, Dec. 24, 1871, pg. 1
"Church Dedication." Daily Picayune, Jan. 9, 1872, pg. 1
"The lofty steeple of St. John…" Daily Picayune, May 9, 1872, pg. 1
"Building in New Orleans. Taxation Defied." Daily Picayune, June 16, 1872, pg. 2
"Fair for the Benefit of St. John the Baptist Church." Daily Picayune, Dec. 29, 1872, pg. 1
"City Improvements. New Stores, Factories and…" Daily Picayune, Sept. 19, 1875, pg. 2
"Church Dedication. New German Protestant Church…" Daily Picayune, April 3, 1876, pg. 2
"Larendon [Obituary]" Daily Picayune, July 5, 1884, pg. 1
"St. Stephen's Church." Daily Picayune, Dec. 13, 1886, pg. 8
"Christ Church. The Oldest Protestant…" Daily Picayune, April 10, 1887, pg. 10-11
"St. Stephen's Church." Daily Picayune, Dec. 5, 1887, pg. 8
"St. Stephen's Church." Daily Picayune, Jan. 2, 1888, pg. 2
"The Harris Memorial Chapel" Daily Picayune, June 4, 1889, pg. 4
"Memorial Minute." W.A. Snively; Daily Picayune, July 7, 1889, pg. 4
"Personal And General Notes." Daily Picayune, Sept. 14, 1889, pg. 4
"Death of Frederick W. Tilton." Daily Picayune, June 7, 1890, pg. 4
"Funeral Of F.W. Tilton." Daily Picayune, June 8, 1890, pg. 2

"Death of Charles Smith, of New Orleans, at Saratoga." Daily Picayune, Aug. 20, 1890, pg. 2
"Funeral Of Charles Smith." Daily Picayune, Aug. 26, 1890, pg. 4
"Death of Alphonse Bobet" Daily Picayune, Dec. 20, 1890, pg. 4
"A New Church." Daily Picayune, April 6, 1891, pg. 2
"Death Of Thomas Smith" Daily Picayune, Jan. 28, 1892, pg. 8
"Necrological. Funeral of Mr. Thomas Smith." City Item, Jan. 29, 1892, pg. 4
"St. Joseph's Church." Daily Picayune, Dec. 19, 1892, pg. 1, 8
"Capt. D.C. M'Can." Times-Democrat, July 28, 1893, pg. 9
"A Wealthy Orleanian." Daily Picayune, Aug. 7, 1893, pg. 9
"A Church Blessed And Dedicated." Daily Picayune, Jan. 22, 1894, pg. 3
"Personal And General Notes." Daily Picayune, Nov. 3, 1895, pg. 7
"A Chapel Dedication." Daily Picayune, Nov. 7, 1895, pg. 3
"A New Chapel" Daily Picayune, Nov. 12, 1895, pg. 12
"The Corner-Stone Of St. George Church" Daily Picayune, April 17, 1899, pg. 5
"St. George's Church, Which Opens To-Day" Daily Picayune, Feb. 4, 1900, pg. 20
"First Services In St. George Church." Daily Picayune, Feb. 5, 1900, pg. 3
"Fine Library On Tulane Campus." Daily Picayune, Mar. 21, 1900, pg. 3
"Tulane Adopts Library Plans." Daily Picayune, Nov. 13, 1900, pg. 7
"The News Here And Elsewhere" Item, April 2, 1901, pg. 7
"Corner Stone Laid." Item, June 9, 1901, pg. 6
"Tilton Memorial Library At Tulane" Daily Picayune, June 9, 1901, pg. 23
"William B. Schmidt's Long Life Ended." Daily Picayune, June 17, 1901, pg. 3
"Mr. Schmidt Rests In Lovely Metairie" Daily Picayune, June 18, 1901, pg. 11
"Mr. Ziegler's Condition." Daily Picayune, July 17, 1901, pg. 6
"Mr. Ziegler's Hurts Cause His Death" Daily Picayune, July 18, 1901, pg. 3
"Motormen Arraigned – For the Accident Which…" Daily Picayune, July 19, 1901, pg. 5
"Obsequies Of F.M. Ziegler" Daily Picayune, July 20, 1901, pg. 3
"The Consecration Of Vacherie's Fine Church." Daily Picayune, May 16, 1902, pg. 6
"A Catholic Church Built At Hammond." Daily Picayune, June 16, 1902, pg. 9
"News of the Architects." Detroit Free Press, Sept. 14, 1902, pg. 23
"Hammond Catholic Church Dedicated." Daily Picayune, Nov. 24, 1902, pg. 5
"Church Dedication." St. Tammany Farmer, May 2, 1903, pg. 5
"Cornerstone Of St. John's Church" Item, Oct. 5, 1903, pg. 5
"St. John Lutheran Church Dedicates New House" Daily Picayune, Mar. 21, 1904, pg. 11
"Carondelet Church To Be Masonic Cathedral" Daily Picayune, Feb. 23, 1905, pg. 14
"John H. Menge, The Prominent Citizen and…" Daily Picayune, April 4, 1905, pg. 2
"Captain Menge's Funeral." Daily Picayune, April 5, 1905, pg. 5
"New Church Site" Daily Picayune, April 5, 1905, pg. 8
"Evangelical Salems Church." Daily Picayune, Aug. 6, 1905, pg. 5
"Corner-Stone Laying." Daily Picayune, Aug. 7, 1905, pg. 3
"Mrs. R.M. Walmsley" Daily Picayune, Aug. 23, 1905, pg. 11
"Fine New Building To Replace Burned Church." Daily Picayune, Jan. 8, 1906, pg. 4
"Last Service In Old Carondelet Street Church" Daily Picayune, Jan. 15, 1906, pg. 7
"Carondelet Evangelical." Daily Picayune, Jan. 28, 1906, pg. 17
"Carondelet Church Corner-Stone Laid" Daily Picayune, Jan. 29, 1906, pg. 4
"New Church Lays Its Cornerstone" Item, Jan. 29, 1906, pg. 2
"Salem Evangelical. To Dedicate Its New Church…" Daily Picayune, Mar. 18, 1906, pg. 4
"Salem Evangelical New Church Is Dedicated" Daily Picayune, Mar. 26, 1906, pg. 16
"Corner-Stone Laying." Daily Picayune, Jan. 30, 1907, pg. 11
"New Church To Be Dedicated To-Day" Item, Jan. 30, 1907, pg. 8
"Corner Stone Laid." Item, Jan. 31, 1907, pg. 7
"Second Methodist Church To Be Handsome Edifice" Daily Picayune, Jan. 31, 1907, pg. 5

"Touro Synagogue Has Secured Avenue Site." Daily Picayune, May 18, 1907, pg. 4
"Rayne Methodist Invites Its New Jewish Neighbor" Daily Picayune, May 29, 1907, pg. 12
"Opening Of 2nd Methodist Church" Item, June 15, 1907, pg. 2
"Second Methodist Church" Daily Picayune, June 16, 1907, pg. 47
"Second Methodist Church Dedicated" Daily Picayune, June 17, 1907, pg. 5
"Woodmen Chiefs – Coming Sunday for the…" Daily Picayune, Oct. 30, 1907, pg. 4
"Woodmen Chiefs The City's Guests" Daily Picayune, Nov. 3, 1907, pg. 27
"Woodmen Unveil The Metairie Monument" Daily Picayune, Nov. 4, 1907, pg. 14
"Woodmen Unveil Tomb At Metairie" Item, Nov. 4, 1907, pg. 8
"Touro Synagogue Decides To Begin Building At Once." Daily Picayune, Feb. 5, 1908, pg. 4
"Corner Stone Of New Touro Laid." Daily Picayune, May 13, 1908, pg. 7
"Mater Dolorosa's New Church." Daily Picayune, Aug. 10, 1908, pg. 12
"Touro Synagogue Bids Farewell to Rayne Memorial." Daily Picayune, Dec. 26, 1908, pg. 5
"Touro Synagogue Dedication Night." Daily Picayune, Jan. 1, 1909, pg. 12
"New Touro Synagogue Dedicated With Much…" Daily Picayune, Jan. 2, 1909, pg. 5
"Dedicating The New Carrollton Church." Daily Picayune, Mar. 7, 1909, pg. 6
"New Mater Dolorosa Church Is Dedicated." Daily Picayune, Mar. 8, 1909, pg. 11
"Trinity Lutheran Lays Corner-Stone" Daily Picayune, Mar. 13, 1911, pg. 3
"Lutheran Notes." Herald, June 11, 1911, pg. 4
"Corner-Stone Of Thomas Hall Laid Yesterday At…" Daily Picayune, June 19, 1911, pg. 9
"Trinity Lutheran Rededicated, Old And New…" Daily Picayune, June 26, 1911, pg. 5-6
"Lutheran Notes." Herald, June 29, 1911, pg. 4
"Dr. Walmsley Dies From Operation" Item, Feb. 27, 1912, pg. 1
"Louise C. Thomas Hall At Loyola Dedicated To…" Daily Picayune, May 20, 1912, pg. 5
"J. Dibert, Banker And Leading Lumberman, Dead" Item, June 5, 1912, pg. 1, 6
"Captain John Dibert, Cypress Leader Dies At His…" Daily Picayune, June 6, 1912, pg. 7
"Body of W.H.D. Brook Laid Away Tuesday" Item, Aug. 6, 1912, pg. 9
"W.H.D. Brook" Daily Picayune, Aug. 6, 1912, pg. 6
"Mount Calvary Church" Daily Picayune, Nov. 23, 1912, pg. 4
"Lutheran Corner-Stone" Daily Picayune, Nov. 24. 1912, pg. 3
"Mount Calvary Lutheran Church Dedicated With…" Daily Picayune, Feb. 10, 1913, pg. 8
"Throngs At Dedication" Times-Democrat, Feb. 10, 1913, pg. 5
"Licalzi Dead" Daily Picayune, Nov. 4, 1913, pg. 13
"Tony Licalzi" Daily Picayune, Nov. 5, 1913, pg. 12
"Rebuild Church" Daily Picayune, Nov. 7, 1913, pg. 11
"New St. Francis De Assisi Church Planned At State…" Daily Picayune, Jan. 14, 1914 pg. 14
"New Church Lays Its Corner…" Times-Democrat & Daily Picayune, April 13, 1914, pg. 6
"Contract For Fine Church Edifice Let" Times-Picayune, June 19, 1914, pg. 6
"Cornerstone Laid Of St. Rose De Lima" Times-Picayune, Sept. 28, 1914, pg. 5
"Worship In New Church." Times-Picayune, Mar. 29. 1915, pg. 4
"Mrs. John Dibert, who will give $200,000…" Item, Mar. 19, 1916, pg. 14
"Death Of Mrs. J.H. Menge" Times-Picayune, Feb. 3, 1917, pg. 7
"Funeral Of Mrs. Menge On Saturday Afternoon" States, Feb. 3, 1917, pg. 3
"Negroes Buy Grace M.E. Church." Times-Picayune, Mar. 18, 1917, pg. 47
"Funeral Of Peter Torre Saturday" States, Nov. 3, 1917, pg. 2
"Peter Torre, Sr., Leader In N.O. Business, Dies" Item, Nov. 3, 1917, pg. 3
"P. Torre, Merchant And Banker, Dead" Times-Picayune, Nov. 4, 1917, pg. 23
"4 Sons Pallbearers At Torre Funeral" States, Nov. 4, 1917, pg. 20
"C.F. Buck, Sr., Noted Mason, Dead Here" States, Jan. 19, 1918, pg. 1, 3
"Charles F. Buck, Once Leader In Orleans, Dies" Item, Jan. 19, 1918, pg. 3
"Death Ends Career Of Charles F. Buck…" Times-Picayune, Jan. 20, 1918, pg. 1, 4
"Impressive Rites For Chas. F. Buck" States, Jan. 20, 1918, pg. 8

"Prepare For Dedication." Times-Picayune, Mar. 18, 1918, pg. 16
"Place Cornerstone At Lutheran Church" Times-Picayune, May 6, 1918, pg. 11
"Finishing Work On New Building" States, July 7, 1918, pg. 19
"Immanuel Church To Be Dedicated This Afternoon" States, Aug. 4, 1918, pg. 9
"Consecrate New Lutheran Church" States, Aug. 5, 1918, pg. 10
"New Building Dedicated." Times-Picayune, Aug. 5, 1918, pg. 5
"Mrs. Mauberret Dies At Canal Street Home" States, Sept. 12, 1918, pg. 6
"Victor Mauberret Bereaved By Death" Item, Sept. 12, 1918, pg. 1
"Mauberret Funeral At 4 P.M. Saturday" Item, Oct. 4, 1918, pg. 7
"Vic Mauberret Assessor Dead" States, Oct. 4, 1918, pg. 3
"Vic Mauberret, Long In Politics, Taken By Death" Times-Picayune, Oct. 4, 1918, pg. 4
"Leaders Of City And State Honor Vic Mauberret" States, Oct. 6, 1918, pg. 17
"St. Bernard Banker Dead." Times-Picayune, Nov. 1, 1918, pg. 10
"St. Bernard Loses One Of Her Most Substantial Men" States, Nov. 3, 1918, pg. 5
"Benjamin Moss Walmsley Dies." Times-Picayune, Nov. 6, 1918, pg. 6
"Interior of Beautiful New Catholic Temple" Item, Dec. 10. 1918, pg. 4
"Vatter" [Obituary] Times-Picayune, Jan. 11, 1919, pg. 2
"Prominent Arabi Woman Is Buried" States, Feb. 9, 1919, pg. 23
"Wine Merchant Dies." Times-Picayune, April 2, 1919, pg. 10
"R.M. Walmsley Clearing House Official, Dies' Item, Dec. 26, 1919, pg. 1, 6
"Clearing House President Dead" Times-Picayune, Dec. 27, 1919, pg. 1-2
"Walmsley To Be Buried Monday" States, Dec. 28, 1919, pg. 4
"Last Rites Held Monday for Robert M. Walmsley" Times-Picayune, Dec. 28, 1919, pg. 4
"Sons Conduct Mass for Bernardo G. Carbajal, Burial Friday..." Item, Mar. 12, 1920, pg. 9
"Two Priests Officiate at Funeral of Father" Times-Picayune, Mar. 13, 1920, pg. 21
"Stave Exporting Firm Head Dies" Times-Picayune, Mar. 29, 1920, pg. 4
"Edward Bobet Funeral To Be 4 P.M. Monday" Item, Mar. 29, 1920, pg. 6
"Edward J. Bobet Buried Monday" States, Mar. 29, 1920, pg. 5
"Funeral Services Held for Stave Manufacturer" Times-Picayune, Mar. 30, 1920, pg. 10
"Fire Destroys Church And Rectory At Paulina" States, June 27, 1920, pg. 4
"Orleans Honors Pearl Wight; Burial Monday" Item, July 5, 1920, pg. 1-2
"Pearl Wight, Big Figure In Orleans Public Life, Dies" Times-Picayune, July 5, 1920, pg. 1-2
"Pearl Wight's Funeral Held At 3 P.M. Monday" States, July 5, 1920, pg. 1
"Mrs. Wight Dies Seven Days After Husband" States, July 11, 1920, pg. 1
"John The Baptist Church In Edgar (sic), LA., Is Dedicated" States, Oct. 29, 1920, pg. 12
"Archbishop Shaw Blesses Laying Of Cornerstone" Times-Picayune, April 25, 1921, pg. 1-2
"Cornerstone Of New Church Laid" Item, April 25, 1921, pg. 4
"Cornerstone Laid In New Algiers Methodist Church" States, Oct. 17, 1921, pg. 10
"Catholic Church To Be Dedicated" Times-Picayune, Dec. 11, 1921, pg. 4
"Algiers M.E. Church South" Herald, Dec. 15, 1921, pg. 29-31
"3 Louisianians Are Ordained" Item, Dec. 19, 1921, pg. 7
"New Seminary Construction To Begin This Week" Times-Picayune, Jan. 30, 1922, pg. 3
"New Catholic Seminary" Item, Feb. 5, 1922, pg. 26
"Major Catholic Seminary Here Ready By Fall" Times-Picayune, Feb. 11, 1922, pg. 7
"Work Starts On College To Train Priests" Feb. 11, 1922, pg. 7
"Ursuline Nuns Given $100,000 For New Shrine" Times-Picayune, Mar. 17, 1922, pg. 1
"Bishop Christens Six Children In Algiers Church" Times-Picayune, Mar. 27, 1922, pg. 20
"Ku Klux Sends Money To Church" States, Mar. 27, 1922, pg. 14
"Algiers Pastor Accepts Klan Donation to Church And Lauds..." Item, Mar. 29, 1922, pg. 3
"Dedicate $50,000 Church May 14" Item, May 6, 1922, pg. 7
"57 Clergy at Laying Of Notre Dame Cornerstone" Item, May 8, 1922, pg. 38
"Hundreds See Cornerstone Of Seminary Laid" Times-Picayune, May 8, 1922, pg. 3

"Catholic Church To Be Dedicated" Times-Picayune, May 13, 1922, pg. 24
"To Dedicate New Church Of The Annunciation" States, May 13, 1922, pg. 3
"New Catholic Church Opened" Item, May 15, 1922, pg. 11
"New Church Is Dedicated Sunday" States, May 15, 1922, pg. 5
"$50,000 Catholic Church Is Opened" Times-Picayune, May 15, 1922, pg. 20
"Rare Windows As Memorials In St. Patrick's" Item, June 17, 1922, pg. 6
"Church Is To Lay Cornerstone As Tribute To Ideal" Times-Picayune, July 29, 1922, pg. 9
"Ground Is Broken For New Church" Times-Picayune, Aug. 5, 1922, pg. 9
"Work Commences On New Church Of St. Anthony" States, Aug. 5, 1922, pg. 2
"New Church Goes Up In Carrollton" States, Aug. 6, 1922, pg. 12
"Construction of Church Begins" Times-Picayune, Sept. 9, 1922, pg. 22
"St. Anthony of Padua Church" Item, Sept. 9, 1922, pg. 5
"Evangelical Congregation Building Church" Item, Sept. 23, 1922, pg. 5
"To Start Work On New $200,000 Catholic Church" States, Nov. 11, 1922, pg. 6
"Catholic Church To Be Fine Structure" Times-Picayune, Dec. 2, 1922, pg. 12
"Cornerstone for Church of Ursulines..." Times-Picayune, Dec. 10, 1922, sec. 4, pg. 1
"Formal Blessing Of Sorine (sic) Cornerstone" States, Dec. 10, 1922, pg. 17
"Cornerstone Set At Votive Shrine Of Ursuline Nuns" Times-Picayune, Dec. 11, 1922, pg. 11
"Impressive Rite At New Shrine" States, Dec. 11, 1922, pg. 14
"Ursulines Nuns Votive Shrine Is Dedicated" Item, Dec. 11, 1922, pg. 11
"$150,000 Church Site Is Prepared" Times-Picayune, Dec. 30, 1922, pg. 22
"Will Lay Cornerstone of St. Anthon's (sic) Feb. 4" Item, Jan. 27, 1923, pg. 7
"Cornerstone Laid For New Church" Times-Picayune, Feb. 5, 1923, pg. 3
"$53,000 Church To Be Dedicated On Sunday A.M." Item, Feb. 17, 1923, pg. 5
"New St. Matthew Church Dedicated" Times-Picayune, Feb. 19, 1923, pg. 3
"Priest Fulfills War Period Vow" Times-Picayune, Mar. 19, 1923, pg. 2
"C.H. Hyams Capitalist Dies Here In 85th Year" States, April 19, 1923, pg. 3, 10
"C.H. Hyams, 84, N.O. Capitalist Of Note, Dies" Item, April 19, 1923, pg. 1-2
"C.H. Hyams' Funeral Christ Church Today" Times-Picayune, April 20, 1923, pg. 1-2
"Hyams Funeral Largely Attended" States, April 20, 1923, pg. 18
"Last Rites Held For C.H. Hyams" Times-Picayune, April 21, 1923, pg. 5
"Locked In Ship Cabin He Defied Death" Meigs O. Frost; States, April 22, 1923, pg. 13-14
"The Notre Dame Seminary" Item, May 5, 1923, pg. 9
"Church Of Sacred Heart Dedicated" Times-Picayune, June 11, 1923, pg. 2
"Benefit Fair Planned." Times-Picayune, July 5, 1923, pg. 9
"Spend the Day at Abita Springs" [Advertisement] Times-Picayune, Aug. 12, 1923, pg. 53
"Death Of Mr. Lawrence Fabacher Wednesday" States, Aug. 15, 1923, pg. 1-2
"L. Fabacher Is Dead At 60 Of Pneumonia" Item, Aug. 15, 1923
"Fabacher, Noted Restaurant Man And Brewer, Dies" Times-Picayune, Aug. 16, 1923, pg. 3
"Many Attend Funeral Service For Fabacher" Item, Aug. 17, 1923, pg. 3
"Restaurateur's Funeral Is Held" Times-Picayune, Aug. 17, 1923, pg. 7
"B.K.A. Is Almost Flooded Out On Annual Outing" Times-Picayune, Aug. 20, 1923, pg. 1, 9
"B.K. of A. Outing At Abita Springs Marred by Rain" Item, Aug. 20, 1923, pg. 5
"Many Orphans At Fabacher Funeral" States, Aug. 26, 1923, pg. 4
"Notre Dame Seminary To Open Sept. 18" Item, Sept. 8, 1923, pg. 6
"Thousands Visit New Notre Dame Seminary In Day" Times-Picayune, Sept. 10, 1923, pg. 1
"St. Anthony's Church to Be Blessed Nov. 1" Item, Oct. 13, 1923, pg. 6
"Church Dedicated By Archbishop" States, Nov. 1, 1923, pg. 8
"Dedicate New Catholic Church" Times-Picayune, Nov. 2, 1923, pg. 21
"St. Anthony Of Padua Church Is Dedicated" Item, Nov. 2, 1923, pg. 13
"Seminary Of Priests In N.O. Is Dedicated" Item, Nov. 7, 1923, pg. 1
"Two Archbishops Dedicate Notre Dame Seminary" Times-Picayune, Nov. 8, 1923, pg. 1, 7

"Dedicate Votive Shrine Next Week" Times-Picayune, Dec. 29, 1923, pg. 22
"All Orleans Pays Tribute To Battle Day" Item, Jan. 8, 1924, pg. 11
"British Beaten By Jackson 109 Years Ago Today" Times-Picayune, Jan. 8, 1924, pg. 1-2
"Dedication Of New Ursuline Chapel Is Held" Item, Jan. 9, 1924, pg. 4
"Catholic Church Dedicated Sunday" Times-Picayune, Mar. 3, 1924, pg. 3
"New Sacred Heart Church Is Dedicated" Item, Mar. 3, 1924, pg. 17
"Beth Israel Lays Cornerstone For Its New Synagogue" Item, Mar. 17, 1924, pg. 9
"Cornerstone Of Temple Is Laid" States, Mar. 17, 1924, pg. 4
"New Church At Abita Nearing Completion" Item, Mar. 22, 1924, pg. 8
"The Church Of St. Jane De Chautel. (sic)" Item, Mar. 22, 1924, pg. 3
"Better Buildings Furnish Foundation For Greater…" Times-Picayune, April 6, 1924, pg. 30
"Chas. O'Connor City Leader Is Critically Ill" States, May 30, 1924, pg. 3
"N.O. Political Leader Is Near Death" Item, May 30, 1924, pg. 1
"C.D. O'Connor Is Dead After Long Illness" Item, May 31, 1924, pg. 11
"Mr. O'Connor, Leader Is Dead" States, May 31, 1924, pg. 1
"Chas. O'Connor's Funeral Sunday" States, June 1, 1924, pg. 10
"Death Ends Long Political Career" Times-Picayune, June 1, 1924, pg. 17
"Break Ground For Sunday School Home" Item, July 26, 1924, pg. 9
"Pastor To Start Work On School" Times-Picayune, July 26, 1924, pg. 20
"$60,000 Sunday School Assured" States, July 26, 1924, pg. 3
"Presbyterians To Start Work On New Building" Times-Picayune, July 27, 1924, pg. 4
"Ground Broken For New St. Charles Ave. Church Building" Item, July 28, 1924, pg. 2
"Pastor Breaks Ground For New Sunday School" Times-Picayune, July 28, 1924, pg. 7
"Westerners Pay $10,000,000 For 99 Years'…" Times-Picayune, Sept. 7, 1924, pg. 1, 19
"Skyscraper Will Replace Jesuits" States, Sept. 8, 1924, pg. 15
"Skyscraper, 16 Stories, For Baronne" Item, Sept. 8, 1924, pg. 2
"Archbishop Aids At Dedication" States, Sept. 14, 1924, pg. 14
"Come to the Dedication Today" [Advertisement] States, Sept. 14, 1924, pg. 31
"To Dedicate New Synagogue Here" States, Sept. 14, 1924, pg. 11
"Beth Israel In Imposing Temple" States, Sept. 15, 1924, pg. 10
"New Synagogue Is Dedicated" Times-Picayune, Sept. 15, 1924, pg. 22
"Presbyterian Church Opens New Building" Item, Mar. 2, 1925, pg. 3
"Sunday School Room Dedicated" States, Mar. 2, 1925, pg. 5
"Church Sunday School…" Henry H. Ahrens; Times-Picayune, Mar. 2, 1925, pg. 23
"New Presbyterian Sunday School Building" Item, Mar. 3, 1925, pg. 4
"Break Ground For Church" Times-Picayune, May 23, 1925, pg. 25
"New Church Stone Ceremony Sunday" Times-Picayune, June 20, 1925, pg. 9
"Work On 16-Story Building To Begin September…" Times-Picayune, July 15, 1925, pg. 1
"Another Scraper In Baronne Street" States, July 25, 1925, pg. 11
"$2,000,000 Skyscraper for Jesuit Site" Times-Picayune, July 25, 1925, pg. 1
"Jesuits' Bells Go To Grand Coteau" Meigs O. Frost; States, Aug. 30, 1925, pg. 12
"Aged Head of Koen Tobacco Company Dies" Item, Nov. 6, 1925, pg. 1
"Pioneer Cigar Importer, Bank Director, Dies" Times-Picayune, Nov. 7, 1925, pg. 1
"New St. Paul's" States, Nov. 15, 1925, pg. 26
"Church To Be Dedicated" Times-Picayune, Dec. 26, 1925, pg. 15
"Contracts" Times-Picayune, Jan. 14, 1926, pg. 21
"Dedicate St. Paul's Evangelical Church On Sunday, May 23" Item, May 1, 1926, pg. 3
"St. Paul's Church To Be Dedicated" Times-Picayune, May 1, 1926, pg. 6
"Dedication Of New St. Paul's Church Sunday" Item, May 22, 1926, pg. 5
"Dedication Today For New Church" Times-Picayune, May 22, 1926, pg. 22
"New St. Paul's Evangelical To Be Dedicated" States, May 22, 1926, pg. 16
"Algiers, Gretna News Happenings" Times-Picayune, July 4, 1926, pg. 9

"Dedicate Jesuit School Sunday" States, Sept. 26, 1926, pg. 4
"Jesuit Church Here Is Edifice Of Rare Beauty..." Item-Tribune, Nov. 28, 1926, pg. 17, 22
"Lutheran Church Remodeled" Times-Picayune, Dec. 4, 1926, pg. 29
"Church" Item-Tribune, May 22, 1927, pg. 32
"Contracts" Times-Picayune, Aug. 6, 1927, pg. 4
"Canal St. Presbyterian Church Contract Is Let" States, Aug. 7, 1927, pg. 43
"Jesuit School To Open Sept. 12" Alfred A. Theriot; Item-Tribune, Sept. 4, 1927, pg. 33, 38
"Work Will Start On Canal Church" Times-Picayune, Oct. 6, 1927, pg. 18
"Work Will Begin On New Church" Times-Picayune, Oct. 8, 1927, pg. 8
"Lay Cornerstone Of New Canal St. Church Sunday" Item, Oct. 8, 1927, pg. 1
"Presbyterians Lay Cornerstone" States, Oct. 8, 1927, pg. 8
"Cornerstone Of Sinai Is Laid" States, Nov. 14, 1927, pg. 13
"Exercises Mark Formal Building Of Temple Sinai" Times-Picayune, Nov. 14, 1927, pg. 2
"Canal Presbyterians To Hold First Service In New Church..." Item, Dec. 31, 1927, pg. 3
"$160,000 Church Gift Of Woman" States, Jan. 17, 1928, pg. 15
"Mrs. Bloomfield Gives $160,000 For New Church" Times-Picayune, Jan. 17, 1928, pg. 3
"Dedicate Canal Presbyterian On Sunday Morning" Item, April 28, 1928, pg. 3
"Building Finished By Presbyterians" Times-Picayune, April 28, 1928, pg. 23
"R.H. Downman Succumbs Here At Age Of 67" Times-Picayune, June 3, 1928, pg. 1, 19
"R.H. Downman, Lumberman, Dies At Home" Item-Tribune, June 3, 1928, pg. 1-2
"New Jesuit Church Arises On Old Site" Item, July 6, 1928, pg. 10
"New Temple Sinai Open For Inspection" Item-Tribune, July 15, 1928, pg. 7
"New Church To Be Started Soon" Item, July 20, 1928, pg. 3
"Break Ground For New Church" Item, July 28, 1928, pg. 3
"Break Ground For Church" Item-Tribune, July 29, 1928, pg. 6
"Break Ground For Church Sunday" States, July 29, 1928, pg. 39
"Breaking Ground Today For Newest Church On..." Times-Picayune, July 29, 1928, pg. 19
"Ground Is Broken For New Church" Times-Picayune, July 30, 1928, pg. 5
"Jesuit Church Bares Expert Building Plan" States, Sept. 2, 1928, pg. 25-26
"New Temple Sinai To Open On September 14..." Item-Tribune, Sept. 2, 1928, pg. 39
"Remarkable Foundation Bared By Jesuit Church Excavation" Item, Oct. 9, 1928, pg. 2
"Dufour Fatally Stricken On Trip To Atlantic City" Times-Picayune, Oct. 24, 1928, pg. 1-2
"Mr. Dufour's Death Shock To All City" States, Oct. 24, 1928, pg. 1, 7
"Services For Dufour Friday" New Orleans Item, Oct. 24, 1928, pg. 1, 3
"Crowd Pays Last Honor To Dufour, Noted Attorney" Times-Picayune, Oct. 27, 1928, pg. 3
"New Jesuit Church to Be Ready Next August" States, Oct. 28, 1928, pg. 26-27
"Start Work On Jesuit Church" Item-Tribune, Oct. 28, 1928, pg. 22
"Work Is Started On New Church" Times-Picayune, Oct. 31, 1928, pg. 14
"Services Friday To Start Opening Of Temple Sinai" Times-Picayune, Nov. 1, 1928, pg. 15
"Dedication Of Temple Sinai" States, Nov. 2, 1928, pg. 5
"New Temple Sinai Dedicated In Rite By..." Times-Picayune, Nov. 3, 1928, pg. 20
"All Invited To New Temple" Item-Tribune, Nov. 4, 1928, pg. 4
"Drive First Pile New Holy Name Of Mary Church" States, Dec. 11, 1928, pg. 10
"Shaw Will Bless New Church Here" Item-Tribune, Feb. 24, 1929, pg. 18
"Corner Stone Laid For New Church" Times-Picayune, Feb. 25, 1929, pg. 3
"The Church" Item, Mar. 6, 1929, pg. 10
"Algiers, Gretna News Happenings" Times-Picayune, April 19, 1929, pg. 29
"Clergy To Direct Laying Of Stone" Times-Picayune, April 20, 1929, pg. 12
"Incarnate Word Church Erected on Dante Street" Times-Picayune, May 19, 1929, pg. 30
"Funeral of Urban Koen, Tobacco Merchant, Age 78" States, May 30, 1929, pg. 8
"Urban Koen Dies At Age Of 78" Times-Picayune, May 30, 1929, pg. 3
"345 Millions Construction Work Projected For..." Item-Tribune, Aug. 25, 1929, pg. 39, 42

"All City Joins Appeal For Aid To Jesuit Church" Times-Picayune, Sept. 8, 1929, pg. 26
"Pastor To Finish Jesuit Church" Item-Tribune, Sept. 8, 1929, pg. 9
"Biever Lays Silver Brick" Item-Tribune, Sept. 22, 1929, pg. 6
"Funeral Rites For Henry Beer To Be Held Here" Times-Picayune, Oct. 14, 1929, pg. 2
"To Bury Henry Beer In Orleans" States, Oct. 14, 1929, pg. 6
"Algiers and Gretna News Notes" Item, Nov. 21, 1929, pg. 26
"Dedicate Newest Algiers Church" States, Nov. 25, 1929, pg. 7
"Impressive Rites Dedicate Algiers $200,000…' Times-Picayune, Nov. 25, 1929, pg. 29
"New Algiers Church Built With Religious…" Times-Picayune, Dec. 1, 1929, pg. 43
"Church On Avenue Dedicated Today By…" Times-Picayune, Feb. 2. 1930, pg. 20
"New Church Open To Public Sunday" States, Feb. 2, 1930, pg. 21
"To Dedicate Church Sunday" Item-Tribune, Feb. 2, 1930, pg. 16
"Simple Services Dedicate Church" States, Feb. 3, 1930, pg. 13
"School Built And Church In…" Joseph T. Armstrong; Item-Tribune, Feb. 16, 1930, pg. 43
"Lay St. Leo Church Cornerstone Sunday" Item. Feb. 22, 1930, pg. 2
"Corner Stone Laid For New Church" Times-Picayune, Feb. 24, 1930, pg. 4
"Cornerstone Of New Church Laid" States, Feb. 24, 1930, pg. 5
"Jesuit Church Is Dedicated" States, Mar. 3, 1930, pg. 3
"General Auto Head Is Dead" Item, June 4, 1930, pg. 2
"Services for Mayor's Father to Be Held at Prytania…" Times-Picayune, July 25, 1930, pg. 3
"Stately Church Building For St. Roch Avenue" Times-Picayune, Aug. 31, 1930, pg. 32-33
"Archbishop Will Dedicate New Catholic Church" Times-Picayune, Oct. 4, 1930, pg. 4
"Archbishop Presides at New Church Dedication" States, Oct. 6, 1930, pg. 6
"Shaw Blesses Church Of St. Leo The Great" Item, Oct. 6, 1930, pg. 34
"Corner Stone Laid For New Church To Cost…" Times-Picayune, Dec. 15, 1930, pg. 17
"Lay Corner Stone For New Church" States, Dec. 15, 1930, pg. 10
"Archbishop Shaw To Dedicate New Church Sunday" Item, Sept. 26, 1931, pg. 3
"Archbishop To Aid Dedication" Item-Tribune, Sept. 27, 1931, pg. 19
"To Dedicate New Church On Sunday" States, Sept. 27, 1931, pg. 9
"Church Dedicated By Archbishop" States, Sept. 28, 1931, pg. 16
"Dedication Held At New $150,000 Catholic…' Times-Picayune, Sept. 28, 1931, pg. 12
"Battistella" [Obituary] Item, Nov. 15, 1933, pg. 2
"Home Building Permits Close to Record Week" Times-Picayune, July 19, 1936, pg. 60
"Luca Vaccaro Rites Planned" Item, Nov. 30, 1936, pg. 1, 7
"Luca Vaccaro, Sr., 79, Dies Suddenly At His…" Times-Picayune, Nov. 30, 1936, pg. 1, 3
"Set Funeral For Luca Vaccaro, 79" States, Nov. 30, 1936, pg. 5
"Luca Vaccaro Funeral Held" Item, Dec. 1, 1936, pg. 1
"Vaccaro Services To Be Held Today" Times-Picayune, Dec. 1, 1936, pg. 5
"Final Services In First Church" States, April 12, 1938, pg. 5
"Work Started at Site for First Presbyterian…" Times-Picayune, April 12, 1938, pg. 1, 3
"Ground Is Broken For New Church" Times-Picayune, May 3, 1938, pg. 15
"Thousands Will See Masons Lay Cornerstone" States, July 9, 1938, pg. 3
"Cornerstone Is Laid For New Church" Item, July 11, 1938, pg. 10
"Masonic Groups Lay Cornerstone For New Church" Times-Picayune, July 11, 1938, pg. 19
"Mrs. Dibert Dies; Long Ill" Sunday Item-Tribune, Aug. 28, 1938, pg. 1
"Last Rites Held For Mrs. Dibert" Item, Aug. 29, 1938, pg. 3
"Mrs. John Dibert Deeply Mourned" States, Aug. 29, 1938, pg. 10
"Building of Presbyterian Church Progresses" Times-Picayune, Nov. 16, 1938, pg. 15
"New Presbyterian Church Nears Completion" Item, Dec. 5, 1938, pg. 6
"New Church To Be Dedicated" States, April 5, 1939, pg. 17
"Presbyterians Plan Programs For Dedication" Times-Picayune, April 8, 1939, pg. 6
"Great Doors To Swing Open On A New Era For…" Item-Tribune, April 9, 1939, pg. 19

"Dedicate New Church Edifice" States, April 10, 1939, pg. 11
"Easter Throngs Fill New Church For Dedication" Times-Picayune, April 10, 1939, pg. 6
"Torre" [Obituary] Times-Picayune, June 30, 1939, pg. 2
"Marquer" [Obituary] States, Dec. 12, 1939, pg. 4
"Cornerstone To Chapel Laid" Item, Nov. 4, 1940, pg. 5
"Rites Conducted At Cornerstone For New Chapel" Times-Picayune, Nov. 4, 1940, pg. 8
"2 Archbishops To Officiate" Item, April 17, 1941, pg. 36
"Hope Haven to Dedicate New Church" Times-Picayune, April 20, 1941, pg. 36
"Dedicate Chapel In Colorful Ceremonies At Hope Haven" April 21, 1941, pg. 18
"Ceremonies To Mark Cornerstone Laying Of New..." Item-Tribune, May 25, 1941, pg. 21
"Son, 9, Of Assistant Coroner Succumbs" Times-Picayune, July 26, 1941, pg. 2
"Priest Dies, But Dream Comes True" Item, Dec. 23, 1941, pg. 21
"New Structure, Altar Blessed By Archbishop" Times-Picayune, Dec. 24, 1941, pg. 27
"Mrs. Anne Downman Dies at 74" Item, Aug. 20, 1942, pg. 2
"Mrs. Downman Dies At Hotel Dieu" States, Aug. 20, 1942, pg. 1
"Last Tribute To Mrs. R.H. Downman" States, Aug. 21, 1942, pg. 22
"Mrs. J.W. Libby, Expires At Home" Times-Picayune, Aug. 14, 1943, pg. 3
"Obsequies For Mrs. Libby" Item, Aug. 14, 1943, pg. 3
"Final Services Held For Joseph Vaccaro" Item, May 1, 1945, pg. 20
"Joseph Vaccaro Dies At 89 Years" Times-Picayune, May 1, 1945, pg. 1
"Joseph Vaccaro Funeral Today" States, May 1, 1945, pg. 3
"Gloria Dei Votes For New Church" Item, June 14, 1947, pg. 2
"Metairie Baptist Church Bids Let" Item, July 9, 1949, pg. 3
"Ground-Breaking Ceremonies Set" Times-Picayune, July 10, 1949, pg. 13
"Break Ground For Baptist Auditorium" Item, July 11, 1949, pg. 12
"Church Building Project Slated" Times-Picayune, Aug. 7, 1949, pg. 18
"$240,000 Building Planned By Church" Item, Aug. 8, 1949, pg. 15
"Automobile, Phone Indispensable To Pastor" Robert Ireland; Item, Nov. 5, 1949, pg. 14
"Metairie Growing Up Fast! 50,000 Seen in 5 Years" States, Dec. 8, 1949, pg. 5
"Construction Begins on 2nd Unit of Presbyterian..." Times-Picayune, Dec. 17, 1949, pg. 14
"Educational Unit Addition Rounds Out 9-Year Plan" States, Dec. 17, 1949, pg. 6
"Old Dream Comes True For Church" Item, Dec. 17, 1949, pg. 3
"Ground Broken For New Church" Item, Jan. 9, 1950, pg. 4
"Ground Is Broken for New Church" Times-Picayune, Jan. 9, 1950, pg. 11
"Work Is Near Completion On New Sanctuary" States, Feb. 25, 1950, pg. 16
"Big Mausoleum Planned Here" States, Mar. 8, 1950, pg. 5
"Lake Lawn Park Plans Revealed" Times-Picayune, Mar. 8, 1950, pg. 42
"$1 Million Mausoleum Slated For City" Item, Mar. 8, 1950, pg. 6
"Cornerstone Of New Gentilly Presbyterian..." Times-Picayune, April 11, 1950, pg. 15
"Expansion Fund Drive To Open Monday" Item, April 16, 1950, pg. 6
"Redeemer Cornerstone Ceremonies Tomorrow" States, April 22, 1950, pg. 6
"Service Is Held For New Church" Times-Picayune, April 24, 1950, pg. 24
"New Greek Orthodox Church Planned" Item, May 24, 1950, pg. 33
"New Sanctuary to Be Dedicated" Times-Picayune, May 27, 1950, pg. 16
"Construction to Begin on First Evangelical Church" Times-Picayune, July 23, 1950, pg. 84
"Bruning" [Obituary] Item, Sept. 1, 1950, pg. 4
"Lake Lawn Park, Inc., to Build $1 Million..." Times-Picayune & States, Oct. 8, 1950, pg. 93
"Break Ground Tomorrow for New Church" States, Oct. 21, 1950, pg. 6
"Ceremonies To Mark Site For Church" Item, Oct. 21, 1950, pg. 5
"Church Building To Be Dedicated" Times-Picayune, Nov. 4, 1950, pg. 7
"Church Will Dedicate New Education Building" Item, Nov. 4, 1950, pg. 4
"Bishop To Dedicate Cornerstone" Item, Nov. 18, 1950, pg. 4

"Lutherans To Dedicate New Church" Item, Nov. 25, 1950, pg. 4
"New Church Dedication Sunday" States, Nov. 25, 1950, pg. 6
"Services to Open, Dedicate Redeemer Church…" Times-Picayune, Nov. 25, 1950, pg. 13
"Dedication Held In Two Services" Times-Picayune, Nov. 27, 1950, pg. 18
"Plan Church Building On Canal Street" Item, June 14, 1951, pg. 6
"Church Won't Stay Down; Will Rise for Third Time" States, June 23, 1951, pg. 5
"U.S. Okays Construction Of Church" Item, July 1, 1951, pg. 25
"Architects Set For New Church" Times-Picayune, July 7, 1951, pg. 7
"Church to Transfer Fading Records in Cornerstone…" Times-Picayune, July 7, 1951, pg. 7
"Evangelical Church Lays Cornerstone" Item, July 8, 1951, pg. 25
"Greek Orthodox Church Dedication Is Set for Sunday" Times-Picayune, July 14, 1951, pg. 7
"Baptist Group Elects Officers" Times-Picayune, July 21, 1951, pg. 7
"Still Going Strong at 80, With 58 Years in Ministry" States, July 21, 1951, pg. 5
"Creosote Pilings Used in New Church Construction" Times-Picayune, July 22, 1951, pg. 42
"New Church Plans Made" Item, July 22, 1951, pg. 23
"Decisions Listed In Zoning Cases" Times-Picayune, July 24, 1951, pg. 20
"Work Is Progressing…" States, Aug. 18, 1951, pg. 5
"Break Ground Monday For Gentilly Church" States, Aug. 25, 1951, pg. 5
"Begin Construction Of New Catholic Church" States, Aug. 28, 1951, pg. 15
"New Church's Dedication Scheduled for Sunday" Times-Picayune, Dec. 1, 1951, pg. 12
"Oldest Member, 94, to Open Doors Of Church's Fifth…" States, Dec. 1, 1951, pg. 5, 12
"Evangelical Church Will Be Dedicated" Item, Dec. 2, 1951, pg. 24
"Mrs. Edith Dufour Last Rites Today" States, Dec. 10, 1951, pg. 3
"Rites Arranged For Mrs. Dufour" Times-Picayune, Dec. 10, 1951, pg. 2
"Ceremony Is Set At Site Of Church" Times-Picayune, Dec. 22, 1951, pg. 14
"Ground Breaking For New Church Set" States, Dec. 22, 1951, pg. 5
"Grace Church's Petition Heard" Times-Picayune, Jan. 25, 1952, pg. 20
"Church Plan Disclosed" Item, Jan. 28, 1952, pg. 10
"Battistella Funeral Set Saturday" Item, Mar. 21, 1952, pg. 6
"New St. Rita's Church Work Set" Times-Picayune, Mar. 22, 1952, pg. 10
"St. Rita Church Contract Let" Item, Mar. 23, 1952, pg. 6
"Up and Down the Street" Times-Picayune, April 30, 1952, pg. 22
"$685,000 St. Rita's Church Groundbreaking Rites Set" States, May 24, 1952, pg. 5, 10
"Opening Services Held In New Church" Times-Picayune, July 28, 1952, pg. 43
"Beautiful New Churches Rise Throughout City" Item, Sept. 9, 1952, pg. 7
"Archbishop At St. Rita Ceremony" Item, Oct. 15, 1952, pg. 38
"Church Dedication Slated" States, Nov. 1, 1952, pg. 10
"Bishop Will Head Service" Item, Nov. 2, 1952, pg. 58
"Church Receiving New Furnishings" Times-Picayune, Nov. 5, 1952, pg. 13
"St. Anna's Dedicated" States, Nov. 8, 1952, pg. 11
"Bishop Dedicated St. Anna's" Item, Nov. 9, 1952, pg. 44
"St. James Major Dedication Held" Times-Picayune, Dec. 19, 1952, pg. 16
"New Buildings, Better Facilities…" Times-Picayune & States, Jan. 25, 1953, sec. 11. pg. 10
"New St. Rita's Church Rises…" Times-Picayune, Jan. 25, 1953, pg. 184
"Church Dedication Set at Mandeville" Times-Picayune, Feb. 7, 1953, pg. 11
"Archbishop Will Dedicate Church" Times-Picayune, Feb. 14, 1953, pg. 7
"Ceremony Set At Mandeville" Item, Feb. 15, 1953, pg. 21
"Start Of Grace Church Planned" Times-Picayune, Mar. 21, 1953, pg. 10
"Grace Church Ceremony Set" Item, Mar. 22, 1953, pg. 51
"New Structure Will Be Erected" Times-Picayune, Mar. 23, 1953, pg. 16
"Lutheran Church to Hold Cornerstone Rites Sunday" Times-Picayune, Mar. 28, 1953, pg. 13
"New Lutheran Church to Lay Cornerstone" States, Mar. 28, 1953, pg. 7

"Ceremony Set At Gloria Dei" Item, Mar. 29, 1953, pg. 28
"Sculpture Work Is Ready for New St. Rita's Church" Times-Picayune, July 18, 1953, pg. 7
"Bishop Noland to Conduct Three Orleans Services" Times-Picayune, Oct. 10, 1953, pg. 16
"Episcopal Church To Lay Stone" Item, Oct. 11, 1953, pg. 49
"Dedicate St. Rita Church Sunday" States, Oct. 17, 1953, pg. 6
"Dedication of St. Rita's Church, Rectory Sunday" Item, Oct. 18, 1953, pg. 6
"Blessing Given To New Church" Times-Picayune, Oct. 19, 1953, pg. 5
"Gloria Dei Lutheran Church to Be Dedicated…" Times-Picayune, Dec. 12, 1953, pg. 14
"New Lutheran Church Dedication Is Tomorrow" States, Dec. 12, 1953, pg. 7
"Lutherans To Dedicate New Church" Item, Dec. 13, 1953, pg. 19
"Church Pastor Heard At Rites" Times-Picayune, Dec. 14, 1953, pg. 46
"Lutherans Dedicate New Gloria Dei Church" States, Dec. 14, 1953, pg. 6
"Church Spring Drive Planned" Times-Picayune, April 24, 1954, pg. 22
"Final Services Set Sunday at St. Andrew's Episcopal" Times-Picayune, Aug. 28, 1954, pg. 8
"New Grace Episcopal Church to Be Dedicated…" Times-Picayune, Sept. 11, 1954, pg. 7
"New Grace Church Being Dedicated" Item, Sept. 12, 1954, pg. 23
"Prelates Bless New Structure" Times-Picayune, Sept. 13, 1954, pg. 14
"Break Ground Sunday for New Episcopal Church" States, Oct. 16, 1954, pg. 6
"St. Andrew's Episcopal Sets Ground Breaking" Item, Oct. 17, 1954, pg. 9
"Church Scheduled" Times-Picayune, Jan. 2, 1955, sec. 6, pg. 21
"New Church Planned as Edifice" Times-Picayune, Jan. 2, 1955, sec. 9, pg. 9
"50 Years of Growth" [Advertisement] Times-Picayune & States, Jan. 2, 1955, sec. 6, pg. 6-7
"Relocation Of St. Paul's Is Planned" Item, Jan. 23, 1955, pg. 9
"Start Slated Sunday on New $516,000 Church at…" Times-Picayune, Feb. 12, 1955, pg. 8
"Architect's Sketch of new Church…" Item, Feb. 13, 1955, pg. 11
"Lay Cornerstone of New Episcopal Church On Sunday" States, Mar. 12, 1955, pg. 6
"Bishop Speaks For Dedication" Times-Picayune, Mar. 14, 1955, pg. 55
"Orleans Negro Church Notes" States, June 18, 1955, pg. 7
"$80,000 Church Will Be Dedicated Sunday" Item, June 19, 1955, pg. 9
"Episcopal Church to Be Dedicated" Times-Picayune, Oct. 1, 1955. pg. 10
"New Episcopal Church Dedication Set Sunday" States, Oct. 1, 1955, pg. 5
"St. Andrew's To Dedicate New Building In Ceremony" Item, Oct. 2, 1955, pg. 26
"Dean Speaker At Dedication" Times-Picayune, Oct. 3, 1955, pg. 30
"2 Bishops Bless New Church Here" States, Oct. 3, 1955, pg. 29
"Blessing of New Church Cornerstone to Be Oct. 20" Times-Picayune, Oct. 12, 1955, pg. 20
"Fraternity Sets Services Sunday" Times-Picayune, Nov. 12, 1955, pg. 45
"Catholic Church to Be Dedicated" Times-Picayune, Nov. 26, 1955, pg. 13
"Work Starts Soon On New Church" States, Dec. 20, 1955, pg. 15
"Church Pilings To Be Driven" Item, Jan. 1, 1956, pg. 6
"New Church Ceremony" States, Jan. 9, 1956, pg. 13
"Hold Groundbreaking" States, Jan. 14, 1956, pg. 27
"Dedication of New Church Building Is Planned…" Times-Picayune, April 22, 1956, pg. 106
"Contract for New Church is Signed" States, April 24, 1956, pg. 19
"St. Paul's Slates Ground-Breaking Rites Tuesday" States, May 5, 1956, pg. 4
"St. Paul's Church To Break Ground" Item, May 6, 1956, pg. 17
"New Church at Westwego Will Be Dedicated…" Times-Picayune, May 26, 1956, pg. 18
"Salvador D'Antoni Dies Here" Item, Jan. 3, 1957, pg. 1, 6
"Salvador D'Antoni, Fruit Firm Cofounder, Is Dead" States, Jan. 3, 1957, pg. 1, 4
"Salvador D'Antoni Final Rites Held" States, Jan. 4, 1957, pg. 2
"Cornerstone Laid For New Church" States, Feb. 11, 1957, pg. 32
"St. Paul Church Ceremony Held" Times-Picayune, Feb. 11, 1957, pg. 18
"New Metairie Church to Be Blessed Mar. 3" States, Feb. 23, 1957, pg. 4

"Archbishop To Dedicate Church" Item, Feb. 24, 1957, pg. 2
"Church Notes – New Metairie Church to Be Blessed Mar. 3" States, Feb. 23, 1957, pg. 4
"New Building of St. Agnes Church…" Item, Mar. 24, 1957, pg. 10
"Church Ceremonies" States, June 1, 1957, pg. 5
"St. Agnes Church Dedication Today" Item, June 16, 1957, pg. 35
"Blesses New Church" States, July 29, 1957, pg. 3
"Leading The Dedication…" Times-Picayune, July 29, 1957, pg. 7
"Here's New St. Christopher's Church…" Item, Sept. 15, 1957, pg. 44
"New Episcopal Church to Open" States, Sept. 28, 1957, pg. 4
"Episcopal Church to Be Consecrated by Bishop" States, Nov. 9, 1957, pg. 4
"St. Paul's to Consecrate Church at Rites Sunday" Times-Picayune, Nov. 9, 1957, pg. 24
"$204,156 Church Project Is Ok'd" Times-Picayune, Jan. 25, 1958, pg. 10
"St. Martin's Plans OK'd" Item, Jan. 26, 1958, pg. 19
"Church Cornerstone to Be Blessed Sunday" Times-Picayune, Feb. 8, 1958, pg. 10
"Lay Cornerstone Of Church Sun." States, Feb. 8, 1958, pg. 4
"New St. Martin's Episcopal Church to Start Soon" Times-Picayune, Feb. 23, 1958, pg. 88
"Libby Leaves Tulane Million" Times-Picayune, April 30, 1958, pg. 1
"Church Will Open New Building Bids" Times-Picayune, June 28, 1958, pg. 18
"Ground Breaking Set by Church" Times-Picayune, June 28, 1958, pg. 18
"Church Ground Will Be Broken" Times-Picayune, July 12, 1958, pg. 14
"Groundbreaking Rites Sunday" States, July 12. 1958, pg. 4
"St. Martin's Rite At 4 P.M." Item, July 13, 1958, pg. 6
"Ground Was Broken…" Item, July 15, 1958, pg. 22
"New Church Site Will Be Blessed" Times-Picayune, July 17, 1958, pg. 73
"New Church at Chalmette To Be Ready by…" Times-Picayune, Nov. 22, 1958, pg. 14
"Religious Structures Built…" Wesley Jackson. Times-Picayune, Jan. 25, 1959, sec. 8, pg. 17
"Ground-Breaking Sunday" Times-Picayune, Mar. 14, 1959, pg. 18
"Cornerstone Is Laid For Church" Times-Picayune, Mar. 16, 1959, pg. 42
"Ground Was Broken…" Times-Picayune, Mar. 16, 1959, pg. 22
"Church, Rectory to Cost $1,170,766" Times-Picayune, May 9, 1959, pg. 30
"Episcopal Church To Be Dedicated" Times-Picayune, Aug. 8, 1959, pg. 19
"Bishop Jones to Conduct Dedicatory Rites Sunday" Times-Picayune, Aug. 22, 1959, pg. 8
"N.O. Contractor Taken by Death" Times-Picayune, Oct. 4, 1959, pg. 30
"Bishop Martin To Participate" Times-Picayune, Oct. 24, 1959, pg. 14
"Plans to Dedicate New…" Mercedes S. Munster; Times-Picayune, Dec. 3, 1959, pg. 66
"Dr. Montelepre Services Today" Times-Picayune, Dec. 15, 1959, pg. 1
"Dedication Set For January 8" Times-Picayune, Jan. 2, 1960, pg. 14
"Area Church Progress Was Impressive in 1959" Times-Picayune, Feb. 1, 1960, pg. 19
"Already A Landmark…" States-Item, Aug. 27, 1960, pg. 4
"$1,750,000 First Methodist Center Ready to Open" Times-Picayune, Oct. 29, 1960, pg. 17
"9 Former Pastors to Take Part in New Church Rites" States-Item, Oct. 29, 1960, pg. 4
"New Catholic Buildings to Be Dedicated, Blessed" Times-Picayune, Dec. 31, 1960, pg. 10
"Church, School Dedication Set In…" Gary Hymel; States-Item, Jan. 7, 1961, pg. 13
"New Church Work Keeps High…" Wesley Jackson; Times-Picayune, Jan. 29, 1961, pg. 117
"Harkey" [Obituary] Times-Picayune, April 21, 1961, pg. 2
"Dedication Set For St. Dominic" States-Item, May 27, 1961, pg. 4
"New St. Dominic Church's Dedication Is Set for…" Times-Picayune, May 27, 1961, pg. 28
"Blessing Given To New Church" Times-Picayune, May 31, 1961, pg. 48
"Rites Mark Opening of New Church" States-Item, May 31, 1961, pg. 11
"Funeral Slated For Developer Robert Smith" States-Item, Mar. 12, 1962, pg. 7
"Services Today For James Bull" Times-Picayune, Nov. 11, 1963, pg. 1
"Proposed St. Edward the Confessor Complex" Times-Picayune, Sept. 11, 1964, pg. 7

"Work Will Begin Shortly On St. Edward Facilities" States-Item, Sept. 12, 1964, pg. 4
"Mass Celebrated at St. Edward" Times-Picayune, Dec. 6, 1964, pg. 132
"A Contract is signed…" States-Item, Dec. 26, 1964, pg. 5
"N.O. Area Is Completing New…" Wes Jackson; Times-Picayune, Jan. 24, 1965, pg. 154
"Church Buildings Spring Up" Wesley Jackson; Times-Picayune, Jan. 30, 1966, pg. 155
"Services Held for Mrs. Bull" Times-Picayune, July 26, 1966, pg. 19
"Nativity Programs Are Planned" Times-Picayune, Dec. 21, 1968, pg. 26
"The Hannah Chapel…" States-Item, Dec. 21, 1968, pg. 5
"Hannah Chapel Dedication Held" Times-Picayune, Dec. 23, 1968, pg. 35
"Methodists Dedicate New Chapel" States-Item, Dec. 23, 1968, pg. 24
"La Nasa Rites Will Be Today" Times-Picayune, Jan. 20, 1970, pg. 13
"Rice" [Obituary] Times-Picayune, Aug. 8, 1972, pg. 16
"LaNasa" [Obituary] States-Item, Oct. 3, 1972, pg. 4
"Harkey Private Rites Saturday" Times-Picayune, Dec. 22, 1972, pg. 1, 11
"Smith" [Obituary] Times-Picayune, Dec. 18, 1973, pg. 24
"Ground-Break Ceremonies Set" Times-Picayune, May 18, 1974, pg. 32
"Now Under Construction…" Times-Picayune, July 27, 1974, pg. 37
"Chapel Ground-Breaking Is Friday" Times-Picayune, May 15, 1975, pg. 95
"Tulane Plans Ceremonies" Times-Picayune, May 15, 1975, pg. 21
"Aurora Church Plans Consecration Sunday" Times-Picayune, May 17, 1975, pg. 76
"Digging In Friday…" Times-Picayune, May 17, 1975, pg. 15
"Sanctuary consecration set" States-Item, May 17, 1975, pg. 4
"Stall Rites Are Monday" Times-Picayune, June 1, 1975, pg. 17
"Albert Stall services are held" States-Item, June 2, 1975, pg. 11
"Gates of Prayer Synagogue Dedication Sept. 5-7" Times-Picayune, Aug. 10, 1975, pg. 35
"Congregation to Move by Motorcade" Times-Picayune, Aug. 30, 1975, pg. 22
"Brown" [Obituary] States-Item, Sept. 2, 1975, pg. 8
"Dedication rites mark first Metairie synagogue" States-Item, Sept. 5, 1975, pg. 10
"L.P. Smith, Builder, Dies" Times-Picayune, Oct. 30, 1975, pg. 28
"The Chapel Comes…" Frank L. Schneider, Times-Picayune, Nov. 9, 1975, pg. 115
"Dedication of Chapel Set May 14" Times-Picayune, May 4, 1976, pg. 16
"Two Students Admire…" Times-Picayune, May 15, 1976, pg. 62
"Church in Slidell to Be Dedicated" Times-Picayune, Jan. 23, 1977, pg. 32
"Many Archdiocese Projects" Times-Picayune, Jan. 30, 1977, pg. 20
"This Young Man…" Times-Picayune, Mar. 6, 1978, pg. 8
"Mrs. Stall Rites Today" Times-Picayune, Dec. 21, 1978, pg. 28
"Archdiocese Makes 1978 Constructive" Times-Picayune, Jan. 28, 1979, pg. 163
"St. Philip Neri Parish to Dedicate New Edifice" Times-Picayune, June 2, 1979, pg. 22
"Groundbreaking Today for St. Clement Church" Times-Picayune, July 21, 1979, pg. 61
"Steeple Set In Place" Times-Picayune, Dec. 6, 1980, pg. 19
"Mrs. Harkey Services Set" Times-Picayune, Mar. 6, 1980, pg. 26
"Jeff church to be…" Angela M. Carll; Times-Picayune/States-Item, May 21, 1983, pg. 77
"Dazzling designs…" Roger Green; Times-Picayune/States-Item, Dec. 17, 1983, pg. 101
"Kenner church sanctuary designed by…" Times-Picayune/States-Item, Dec. 24, 1983, pg. 63
"Church's ground breaking Sunday" Times-Picayune, May 27, 1984, pg. 382
"Faith, hard work…" Wesley Jackson; Times-Picayune/States-Item, July 20, 1985, pg. 28
"Greeks celebrate opening…" Joan Kent; Times-Picayune/States-Item, Dec. 8, 1985, pg. 40
"Greek Orthodox cathedral opened" Associated Press; Times-Picayune, Dec. 9, 1985, pg. 21
"Cathedral on the…" Liz Scott; Times-Picayune, Jan. 12, 1986, 'Dixie' section, pg. 18-19
"Open Invitation" [Advertisement] Times-Picayune, Oct. 30, 1986, pg. 169
"Catholics schedule cemetery services" Times-Picayune, Oct. 31, 1986, pg. 28
"Bethany Lutheran basks in new glow" Times-Picayune, Nov. 27, 1988, pg. 312

"Bethany Lutheran sets dedication ceremony" Times-Picayune, Dec. 4, 1988, pg. 364
"Churches" Times-Picayune, Dec. 18, 1988, pg. 355
"Capt. William Bisso" [Obituary] Times-Picayune, Jan. 23, 1992, pg. 35
"S. Henry LaRocca" [Obituary] Times-Picayune, Sept. 28, 1992, pg. 15
"D'Antoni" [Obituary] Times-Picayune, Nov. 21, 1992, pg. 45
"Pioneer Lakeview developer Hedwig Helen Smith…" Times-Picayune, Jan. 30, 1993, pg. 29
"Tulane starts art center" Times-Picayune & States, Feb. 16, 1995, pg. 70
"Grocery pioneer dies at 83" Times-Picayune, Mar. 7, 1995, pg. 1, 8
"John G. Schwegmann" States, Mar. 7, 1995, pg. 14
"Active art month at local…" David Rivé; Times-Picayune & States, April 16, 1995, pg. 183
"From the top" Times-Picayune, Aug. 27, 1995, pg. 263
"Church rises from ashes with…" Shalmali Pal; Times-Picayune, April 27, 1996, pg. 67
"Lillian 'Lili' Johnson Bisso" [Obituary] Times-Picayune & States, June 9, 1996, pg. 44
"Glass a…" Gwendolyn Thompkins; Times-Picayune & States, July 30, 1996, pg. 13-14
"Art center to be dedicated today" Times-Picayune & States, Oct. 9, 1996, pg. 24
"Church marks anniversary" Pat Thevenot; Times-Picayune, Jan. 26, 1997, pg. 161
"Crown, Glory" Times-Picayune, Oct. 3, 1997, pg. 39
"Sanctuary to be opened" Pat Thevenot; Times-Picayune, Oct. 19, 1997, pg. 184
"Clockmaker dedicates…" Natalie Pompilio; Times-Picayune, Oct. 25, 1997, pg. 41-42
"Dream come true" Times-Picayune, Oct. 30, 1997, pg. 219
"Fathers, daughters dance, dine at…" Baton Rouge Advocate, Mar. 4, 2001, pg. 4H
"LaPlace parish gets a new…" Angel Thompson; Times-Picayune, June 3, 2001, pg. 438-439
"Aucoin" [Obituary] Times-Picayune, June 17, 2001, pg. 48
"Frances Zuppardo, supermarket founder" Times-Picayune, Aug. 10, 2001, pg. 34
"Steakhouse Giant Dies" Times-Picayune, April 17, 2002, pg. 1, 10
"Award-winning poet, painter Stan…" Susan Larson; Times-Picayune, Dec. 10, 2002, pg. 9
"Political lion Chalin Perez dies" Steve Cannizaro; Times-Picayune, July 11, 2003, pg. 1, 6
"Parish paid dearly for colorful…" James O'Byrne; Times-Picayune, July 12, 2003, pg. 63
"William Copeland, Popeyes executive" Times-Picayune, Sept. 18, 2004, pg. 24
"Stained Glass" Hammond Daily Star, Nov. 9, 2005, pg. 8A
"Testimonial in glass" Lake Charles Press, April 2, 2006, pg. E1, E3
"Canizaro" [Obituary] Times-Picayune, April 16, 2006, pg. 49
"Sterling Comeaux, furniture retailer" Times-Picayune, July 31, 2006, pg. 28
"Anthony Zuppardo, 93…" Michelle Hunter; Times-Picayune, April 6, 2007, pg. 49
"Mandeville church…" St. Tammany bureau; Times-Picayune, May 10, 2007, pg. 381-382
"MQP Gets Started On…" Elizabeth Moore; Times-Picayune, June 7, 2007, pg. 458, 461
"Monumental Tour" Judy Walker; Times-Picayune, July 26, 2007, pg. 145-146
"first & grace unity" Bruce Nolan; Times-Picayune, Feb. 17, 2008, pg. A-1, A-12, A-13
"New Church" Times-Picayune, April 24, 2008, pg. 11E
"Mary, Queen of…" Margaret Schonberg; Times-Picayune, Aug. 24, 2008, pg. 394-395
"MQP Parishioners Give…" Elizabeth Moore; Times-Picayune, Nov. 16, 2008, pg. 421, 423
"Laborde" [Obituary] Times-Picayune, April 24, 2009, pg. 27
"Brown" [Obituary] Times-Picayune, Dec. 5, 2009, pg. 34
"Old Metairie church dedication Sunday" Times-Picayune, Jan. 28, 2010, pg. 1E-2E
"Groundbreaking ceremony for…" Phil White; Times-Picayune, Sept. 26, 2010, pg. 221, 224
"Slidell church to rise again…" Christine Harvey; Times-Picayune, Oct. 3, 2010, pg. 23-24
"St. Genevieve's Groundbreaking" New Orleans Times-Picayune, Oct. 7, 2010, pg. 247
"Sacred Ties" Times-Picayune, May 8, 2011, pg. 203
"St. Genevieve to celebrate…" Tara McLellan; Times-Picayune, Jan. 1, 2012, pg. 144-145
"Steed" [Obituary] Times-Picayune, June 30, 2014, pg. 26
"Tom Benson, Tycoon Who…" Richard Goldstein; New York Times, Mar. 16, 2018, pg. 2

[For all indices, numbers without brackets indicate page numbers; numbers within brackets indicate position within the book's list of sites.]

INDEX of SITES

[Mausoleums are reported as the names appear upon their façades, no last names first.]

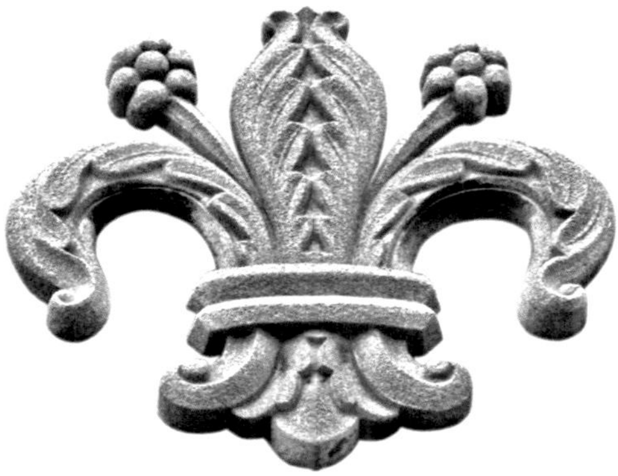

INDEX of PEOPLE and ORGANIZATIONS

GEOGRAPHICAL INDEX

NEW ORLEANS NEIGHBORHOODS

SUBURBS & OUTER LOUISIANA

ABOUT the AUTHOR

Author, photographer and architectural historian Dale A. Carlson was born and raised along the northeastern shores of Lake Michigan where, as an adolescent, he developed a fascination with the city of Detroit. Throughout the 1990s Mr. Carlson studied art, journalism and graphic design at four Michigan colleges including Michigan State University, while simultaneously migrating closer and closer to the Motor City. In 2004 he made southeast Oakland County his permanent home, and in 2019 he earned an associate degree in photographic technology from Oakland Community College. He serves on the City of Berkley, Michigan's Historical Committee and has authored two volumes regarding Detroit's architectural history, *Corrado Parducci: A Field Guide to Detroit's Architectural Sculptor* and *Kahn's Detroit: A Field Guide to Albert Kahn Designs of the Metro Area*. He calls the city of New Orleans his second home and credits his late wife, Carolin Venegas Jones, whom he married in 2014, for inspiring his ventures into publishing and photography.

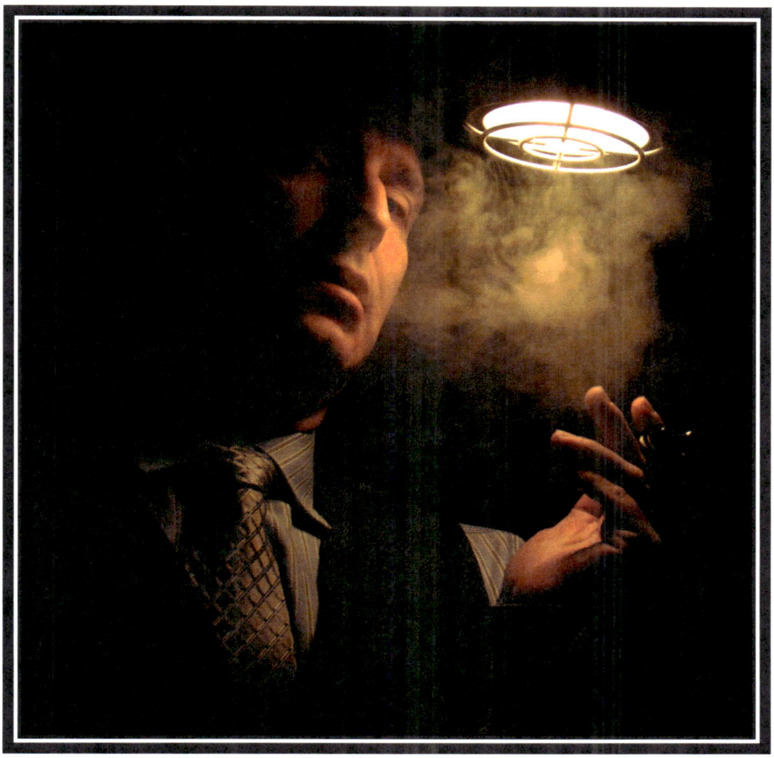